Conflict of Laws

BY HERMA HILL KAY
University of California, Berkeley

Eighteenth Edition

D1594922

THE **barbri** GROUP

THOMSON
★
BAR/BRI

EDITORIAL OFFICES: 111 W. Jackson Blvd., 7th Floor, Chicago, IL 60604
REGIONAL OFFICES: Chicago, Dallas, Los Angeles, New York, Washington, D.C.

SERIES EDITOR
Elizabeth L. Snyder, B.A., J.D.
Attorney At Law

QUALITY CONTROL EDITOR
Sanetta M. Hister

Summary of Contents

Text Correlation Chart

Gilbert Law Summary CONFLICT OF LAWS	Brilmayer, Goldsmith *Conflict of Laws* 2002 (5th ed.)	Currie, Kay, Kramer *Conflict of Laws* 2001 (6th ed.)	Weintraub, Borchers *Conflict of Laws* 2000 (11th ed.)
I. DOMICILE			
A. General Considerations	Page 40-57, 214, 303-309	Page 30-38, 414, 541-587, 739-794, 797-799	Page 7-34, 52-54
B. Domicile Determined by Law of Forum	40	43-47, 67-68, 353-363	7-34, 443-449, 497-502, 761-765, 776-778
II. JURISDICTION OF COURTS			
A. Introduction	445-446	366-375, 411-416, 433-446	35-52, 128-157
B. Types of Jurisdiction	486-564, 815-839	416-433, 494-496	120-140
C. General Bases for Jurisdiction	446-564, 642-656	16, 367-449, 482-483, 607-650, 734, 739	35-172, 442-443, 905-910, 984-989
D. Competent Court	655	479-486, 623-650	140-143
E. Notice and Opportunity to Be Heard—"Procedural Due Process"	341-349, 354-394	369, 403, 435-446	144-157
F. Continuance of Jurisdiction		479-486, 572-580	118-119
G. Limitations on Exercise of Jurisdiction	400-402, 446-451, 462, 487, 532, 582, 588, 589-618, 619-625, 625-637	342-345, 348-353, 372-375, 394-404, 724	158-205, 994-996
III. CHOICE OF LAW—GENERAL CONSIDERATIONS AND PERVASIVE PROBLEMS			
A. General Considerations			172-190, 392-402, 722-753
B. Pervasive Problems			
1. Introduction		2-17, 89-97, 727-828	
2. Renvoi	119-129, 309-315	17-25, 60-69, 244-252, 786	443-449, 498, 500-505, 784-787
3. Depeçage	119	239-244	541
4. Characterization	114-119	38-47, 90-91	377-381, 443-445, 488-497, 508-509, 701-704, 781-786
5. Proof of Foreign Law	173-179	82-88	392-403
IV. APPROACHES TO CHOICE-OF-LAW PROBLEMS			
A. Introduction		38-60, 239-244, 304-363	337-449, 494-502, 541
B. Selecting the Appropriate Law			
1. Statutory Directives	312-315, 322-325, 333-340, 577-582	68-69, 89-95	419-443, 448, 542-543
2. Choice-of-Law Theories	114-129, 240-252, 309-315, 333-338	2-13, 38-59, 115-225, 234	326-370, 403-509, 514-528
3. Application of Choice-of-Law Theories in Practice	182-183, 215-236	1-6	4-5
V. CHOICE OF LAW IN SPECIFIC SUBSTANTIVE AREAS			
A. Torts	1-23, 114-119, 141-146, 188-200, 228-252, 252-279, 304-309, 342-349, 533, 562-563	13-17, 38-55, 69-73, 82-85, 92, 119-150, 155-168, 195-202, 206-222, 225-233, 244-256, 277-288, 353-363, 404-405, 502-503, 516, 665-668	403-412, 419-443, 455-464, 497-502, 514-527, 548-549, 553-561, 562-577, 606-637, 644-649

Gilbert Law Summary CONFLICT OF LAWS	Brilmayer, Goldsmith *Conflict of Laws* 2002 (5th ed.)	Currie, Kay, Kramer *Conflict of Laws* 2001 (6th ed.)	Weintraub, Borchers *Conflict of Laws* 2000 (11th ed.)
B. Contracts	10, 23-40, 219-228, 262-303	17-25, 38-40, 43-47, 59-60, 74-75, 90-92, 98-109, 115-117, 168-172, 199-200, 203-206, 402-405, 793-796	158-170, 456-486, 511-514, 535-549, 577-581, 595-606
C. Property	72-81, 96-119	25-32, 60-63, 90-92, 109-114, 486-497, 794-795	484-494, 508-509, 542-543, 784-816, 916-973
D. Corporations	81-96	38, 173-174	916-973
E. Workers' Compensation	349-354, 662-676	38, 150-155, 311-320	984-1016
F. Family Law	57-72, 700-722	36-37	336-344, 454, 820-935
VI. TRADITIONAL DEFENSES AGAINST APPLICATION OF FOREIGN LAW			
A. Local Public Policy, Penal Laws, and Revenue Laws	7, 65-72, 166-173, 661-662	68-82	15-16, 297-302, 378-392, 505-507, 701-705
B. "Substance" vs. "Procedure"	146-158, 223, 304-309, 315-318, 383-394	48-60, 92-95, 177-179, 341, 374-405	403-448, 497-502, 505-507
VII. CONSTITUTIONAL LIMITATIONS AND OVERRIDING FEDERAL LAW			
A. Influence of the United States Constitution	305-307, 341-344, 437-479, 564, 691-692	304-363	318-376
B. Conflict Between Federal and State Law	131-137, 565-625, 810	623-726	635-722
VIII. RECOGNITION AND ENFORCEMENT OF FOREIGN JUDGMENTS			
A. Underlying Policies	639-656, 810	27-28, 311-342, 453-540, 817-828	216-222, 243-254
B. Requirements for Recognition of Foreign Judgments	700-721	450-462, 466-467, 497-503, 558-559, 587-591, 817-828	279-297, 889-916
C. Effect to Be Given to Foreign Judgments	612-618, 632-689	450-497, 502-503, 578, 589-591	199-203, 227-279, 312-317, 829-830
D. Defenses to Recognition or Enforcement of Foreign Judgments	642-700, 810	454-492, 817-828	279-317
E. Family Law Judgments	660-661, 700-721	488-492, 495-496, 541-587	838-904

Capsule Summary

I. DOMICILE

A. GENERAL CONSIDERATIONS

1. Definition   §1
Domicile is a legal fiction connecting a person to a specific locality for a particular purpose. Domicile is significant for **both** jurisdictional and choice-of-law purposes.

2. "Domicile" vs. "Residence"   §5
Domicile requires **physical presence** within the state **and** the **intent to remain** there indefinitely; residence merely requires physical presence.

3. Three Types of Domicile

    a. Domicile of origin   §7
    At birth, an infant is assigned the domicile of the parents.

    b. Domicile of choice   §8
    Acquisition of a domicile of choice requires (i) **physical presence** and (ii) an **unconditional intent to remain** there indefinitely. Until both elements are present, the previous domicile controls.

        (1) Multiple dwelling places   §17
        If a person has more than one home, traditionally his principal home is his domicile; if not determinable, the home first acquired determines domicile. However, under the modern view, which examines one's contacts with the jurisdictions, a person may simultaneously be domiciled in different states for different purposes.

        (2) Continuity of domicile   §23
        A present domicile remains **until a new domicile is acquired**. An involuntary absence (*e.g.*, imprisonment) does not forfeit one's domicile.

    c. Domicile by operation of law   §27
    Traditionally, certain persons were deemed incapable of acquiring a domicile of choice and were assigned one by law.

        (1) Wives   §28
        At common law, a wife acquired the domicile of her husband.

Today, there is a **rebuttable presumption** that a wife's domicile is that of her husband.

(2) Minors
If born to married parents, a minor acquires the domicile of the father; if the minor is a nonmarital child, he takes the domicile of the mother.

(3) Incompetent persons
Very little mental capacity is required to choose a domicile. If unable to choose a domicile, an incompetent person retains that of his parents.

B. DOMICILE DETERMINED BY LAW OF FORUM
In resolving the issue of domicile, the governing law is that of the forum.

II. JURISDICTION OF COURTS

A. INTRODUCTION

1. Definition
Jurisdiction refers to the courts' power to affect parties' personal status, personal interests, or property rights.

2. Essential Requirements for Proper Jurisdiction

a. Constitutional basis
There must be **sufficient contacts** between the state and the person or thing.

b. Competent court
The court must have the **statutory** authority to hear the case.

c. Procedural due process
All parties must be given **reasonable notice and an opportunity to be heard**.

3. Constitutional Principles

a. Historical view—"presence power"
Under this view, a state could exercise jurisdiction over persons or property **physically present** within the state.

b. Present view—"minimum contacts"
If the defendant is not physically present within the state, due process requires minimum contacts among the defendant, the forum, and the litigation so as to not offend **"traditional notions of fair play and substantial justice."**

B. TYPES OF JURISDICTION

1. In Personam Jurisdiction
A court with in personam jurisdiction has authority to determine the parties' rights and duties and to **bind them personally**. The court's judgments can be enforced **directly** against the person or property of the parties.

is a sufficient basis, but many statutes that require residence are interpreted to require domicile.

c. Appearance or consent §92
A nonresident's voluntary appearance in an action is a sufficient basis for jurisdiction. There is, however, an **exception for a "special appearance"** to challenge **only the court's jurisdiction,** which must be filed **before** other pleadings.

(1) Express consent §98
A party's express consent given **before or after** suit is filed supports in personam jurisdiction. Although consent to jurisdiction is **strictly construed**, forum selection clauses (cognovits) are enforceable **if reasonable**.

(2) Implied consent §105
The nonresident motorist statutes, which were precursors to the long arm statutes, relied on a fictional implied consent as a jurisdictional basis, by providing that the nonresident motorist had consented to suit by using the state's highways. Modern courts uphold such statutes under the **minimum contacts** basis of jurisdiction (see below).

d. Minimum contacts §111
There must be certain "minimum contacts" with the forum such that maintenance of the suit does not offend **"traditional notions of fair play and substantial justice."**

(1) "Presence" within forum state—general jurisdiction §120
There is a sufficient basis for jurisdiction where there are such **continuous and systematic dealings** between the defendant and the forum that it is fair and reasonable to subject the defendant to jurisdiction (i.e., that the nonresident is "doing business" locally). Jurisdiction is **unlimited** in scope.

(2) Liability producing act—limited jurisdiction §125
The **purposeful** commission of an act within the state is also a sufficient basis to exercise jurisdiction over the defendant but only as to **claims arising out of that act**. The basic test is whether it is **fair to expect the defendant to appear and defend** in the forum.

e. "Long arm" statutes §142
The minimum contacts doctrine has been implemented through state "long arm" statutes that grant courts power to assert jurisdiction over a defendant on the basis of **forum-related activities**. Long arm statutes may enumerate specific acts that give rise to jurisdiction, and/or may allow jurisdiction on **any basis** allowable **under the Constitution**.

(1) Common statutory provisions §149
The following "specific acts" are typical:

(a) **Transaction of any business** within the state;

forum. However, the agreement is ineffective if contrary to the forum's fundamental policy.

(1) Consumer transactions §299
In consumer cases, the transaction must bear a **reasonable relationship** to the chosen law and cannot deprive the consumer protection of the laws of her resident state.

(2) Impact §300
Note that only two states have adopted this new U.C.C. section so far.

2. Choice-of-Law Theories §301
Absent a statutory directive, the forum court will apply the theory followed in the jurisdiction to resolve choice-of-law problems. The various theories are:

a. Traditional "vested rights" approach (First Restatement) §302
The law of the state in which the rights of the parties **"vest"** (*i.e.,* where the particular act occurred or the particular relationship was created) governs **all substantive issues** in the case.

(1) Methodology §303
The traditional approach uses a two-step analysis:

(a) **The forum must characterize** the lawsuit into a basic legal category (*e.g.,* contracts, torts, etc.); and

(b) **The connecting factor** (the significant event or thing) must be **localized** to a particular jurisdiction, and the law of that state applies to all issues of the case.

(2) Escape devices §307
Since mechanical application of this approach may lead to harsh and unjust results, escape devices exist allowing the court to reach the "equitable" result (*e.g.,* substantive-procedure distinction, alternative legal characterizations, renvoi, local public policy, etc.).

b. "Most significant relationship" approach (Second Restatement) §313
The law of the state with the **most significant relationship** to the **particular issue** should govern that issue. Note that each issue is analyzed separately.

(1) Methodology §314
The court analyzes **specific contacts** (which vary with the subject matter) in connection with general choice-of-law principles including:

(a) **The needs of interstate and international systems**;

(b) **The forum's relevant policies**;

(c) **The policies of other states involved**;

(d) **The protection of justified expectations**;

dismiss if forum non conveniens is available, or apply the law of one of the interested states.

Where neither the forum nor another state has an interest, the forum should apply its own law unless it decides to apply the law it prefers on the merits.

Because of the difficulty in identifying the underlying policies and the unpredictability of the governmental interest approach, alternative approaches have been suggested.

This approach basically follows the governmental interest approach except in a true conflicts case, where Von Mehren and Trautman require the court to *identify the "predominantly" concerned state,* and apply its law, or if there is no such state, to *weigh the status* of the conflicting laws (effectiveness and current trends in the law) and apply the strongest one. Weintraub requires analysis of similar factors combined with choice-of-law principles specific to the subject matter involved (*e.g.,* torts, contracts, etc.). These principles then reach a *"rational solution."*

The "proper law" is determined by existing *"true choice-of-law rules"* (statutory or common law). If no true rules, then forum law should be applied—if forum is "proper" (*i.e.,* has sufficient contacts and thus application is reasonable).

"Principles" applicable to general fact patterns should be developed with a view toward accommodating conflicting laws and affording fair treatment to the parties; the principles then determine the "preferred law" (*e.g.,* in torts, usually the preferred law is that of the state of injury; in contracts, the preferred law is that which validates the contract, etc.).

This approach *rejects all "rules" and "formulas"* and focuses on five basic choice-influencing considerations: predictability of results; maintenance of interstate and international order; simplification of the judicial task; advancement of forum's interests; and application of the better rule of law.

Today, the majority of courts have adopted an analysis common to many of the modern approaches—focusing on the policies behind the various laws and the policies underlying the substantive area in general—in determining which state is interested in having its law applied. Although the methodologies of the states differ, the results are generally the same, and thus it has been suggested that a *"common law" of conflicts* is gradually emerging.

V. CHOICE OF LAW IN SPECIFIC SUBSTANTIVE AREAS

A. TORTS

1. General Approaches

2. Analysis of Specific Torts Problems

a. Wrongful death cases

injury. Under the modern approaches, the court considers whether it was reasonably foreseeable that that state's law will apply.

---

of *performance*. *Problem:* Questions of validity and performance may overlap.

3. Choice of Law §582

Generally, the forum applies *its own law*; this is constitutional as long as the forum has a *"legitimate interest"* in regulating the employment relationship (*e.g.,* forum is the place of injury, hiring, etc.).

4. Multiple Awards §583

Injured workers may file claims and recover awards under several states' statutes as long as all such states have a *legitimate interest* in the employment relationship. If multiple recoveries are awarded, a prior award is *credited against subsequent ones* so that the worker receives the *largest award* allowed by the statutes of the various states in which claim was made.

a. Independent tort actions §585

The limitation against multiple recoveries does *not* apply to independent tort actions against the employer or third parties if such actions are permitted under forum law.

F. FAMILY LAW

1. Marriage

a. Choice of law regarding validity of marriage §587

The validity of a marriage is determined by whichever law *upholds* the marriage (*i.e.,* place of celebration or parties' domicile), at least where not grossly offensive to the forum's public policy or mores. The validity of *common law marriages* is governed by the law where the relationship was entered into.

b. Validity of remarriage after divorce §596

Where either or both spouses violate a prohibition against remarriage within a certain period after divorce in another state, the validity of the second marriage depends on whether the remarriage was *before final decree* (usually void) or *after final decree* (split of authority—majority upholds second marriage; minority holds second marriage void). In deciding whether to uphold the second marriage, the court considers:

(1) Law of *spouses' domicile* after remarriage;

(2) *Type of proceeding* in which raised;

(3) *Where suit is brought*;

(4) *Length of marriage*.

c. Statutes §606

Under the federal Defense of Marriage Act, states can refuse to recognize same sex marriages valid where performed.

2. Change in Status of Children

a. Status at birth §610

A child at birth is characterized as a marital child if born during his parent's lawful marriage, although many states' statutes provide that children of void or voidable marriages are marital children.

credit" to the **"public acts, records** and **judicial proceedings"** of every other state. "Public acts" include statutory and case law. "Judicial proceedings" include judgments of state court and quasi-judicial tribunals.

a. Effect on choice of law §690

The application of other states' laws is not required in every conflicts case (it would be impossible where there are multistate contacts). Rather, the forum is free to apply its own law, wherever it has a **legitimate interest** in doing so (*i.e.*, the "reasonable relationship" test).

b. Limitation on forum's power to exclude foreign claims §695

Full faith and credit does limit the use of local public policy as a **defense** to the application of foreign law. *Example:* In a wrongful death action, the state must provide a forum for its residents who die elsewhere, but the forum may apply its own law.

3. Privileges and Immunities Clause §697

The Privileges and Immunities Clause entitles citizens of each state to the privileges and immunities of "citizens of the several states." Only **"essential" activities** and **"basic" rights** are protected by the Clause, but the Court may be moving toward a more pragmatic approach (*e.g.*, state must have a **substantial reason** for the **difference in treatment of nonresidents** apart from the mere fact of lack of state citizenship).

B. CONFLICT BETWEEN FEDERAL AND STATE LAW

1. Problem §701

Where there is **concurrent** federal and state court jurisdiction, two questions arise: (i) if an action is filed in **state court**, to what extent must **federal law** be applied; and conversely, (ii) if it is filed in **federal court**, to what extent must **state law** be applied? The nature of the particular issue determines the answer.

2. Where Federal Right Involved §702

If the claim or defense involves a "federal right" (*i.e.*, one arising under the United States Constitution, statutes, or treaties), **federal law alone** governs that issue, regardless where suit is filed.

a. "Federal law" §704

This is defined as the United States Constitution and all statutes, administrative orders or regulations, and federal court decisions that interpret and implement the same.

b. State "procedural" rules §705

If the suit is brought in state court, that state's procedural rules apply—unless a novel procedural rule would defeat a federal right.

3. Where No Federal Right Involved—*Erie* Doctrine §706

With respect to nonfederal questions, **state substantive law** always governs. *Rationale:* This eliminates "forum shopping" between state and federal courts. However, if suit is brought in federal court, **federal procedural rules** apply.

court judgments in state courts, but a federal implementing statute provides that a federal court judgment will be recognized and enforced by state and other federal courts, and state court judgments will be recognized in federal courts.

or where Congress has provided that all states have **concurrent juris-diction**.

D. DEFENSES TO RECOGNITION OR ENFORCEMENT OF FOREIGN JUDGMENTS §802
In certain cases the res judicata policies behind the Full Faith and Credit Clause and the comity principle may be outweighed by other factors, and the forum may decide to *relitigate* an issue.

1. State Court Judgments

a. Lack of jurisdiction in F1 §803
Where the defendant *did not appear* in the F1 proceeding, F2 is free to determine the sufficiency of F1's jurisdiction according to due process and *F1's* own standards (*i.e.,* F1's findings as to its own jurisdiction need not be given full faith and credit). *But note:* Where the defendant *appeared*, F1's findings as to its jurisdiction *cannot* be collaterally attacked (this is the *"bootstrap doctrine"*).

b. F1 judgment not "last in time" §811
The judgment "last in time" *supersedes* any earlier, inconsistent judgment between the same parties relating to the same cause of action.

c. Fraud in procurement of F1 judgment §813
The early view was that fraud was not recognized as a defense, but the injured party could seek to enjoin enforcement of the judgment. The *modern view* is that if the judgment is subject to the equitable defense of fraud in F1, the defense will be recognized and applied in F2.

d. Nature of original cause of action

(1) Contrary to F2's public policy §815
This defense is *very limited*. Ordinarily, the F2 court cannot go behind the F1 judgment and refuse to enforce it simply because F2 would not recognize such a cause of action.

(a) Exception §816
The federal Defense of Marriage Act (*supra*) creates an exception to the Full Faith and Credit Clause as applied to the recognition of same-sex marriages. The Act has not yet been judicially interpreted, and it is unclear whether it applies to judgments or only to statutes.

(2) Claim barred by F2's statute of limitations §817
F2 may *not* refuse to enforce an F1 judgment because F2's statute of limitations would have barred such a suit.

(3) Claim based on tax or penal liabilities §818
While the forum need not apply another state's tax or penal laws, the Supreme Court has held that the forum must enforce another state's *tax judgments* and has indicated the same rule may apply to *penal judgments*. However, the general rule remains that F2 will not enforce F1's penal judgments.

b. Basis for jurisdiction §900

The early view was that the domicile of the child was the only sufficient basis. Today, more than half the states have adopted the *UCCJEA*, which accords primary jurisdiction over custody issues to the *home state* (*i.e.*, the state where the child lived with a parent (or person acting as a parent) for at least six consecutive months immediately before the child custody proceeding). Similarly, the Parental Kidnapping Prevention Act (*supra*) gives priority to the home state, *i.e.*, that state having a significant connection with the custody dispute.

c. Procedural due process requirements §904

Regardless of the basis of jurisdiction, the natural parent must be afforded *notice and a hearing* in any custody proceeding.

4. Paternity Actions §907

The usual purpose of such proceedings is to subject the alleged father to a support obligation; thus, the action is treated as an in personam action, requiring jurisdiction over the father.

Approach to Exams

While some exam questions on a Conflict of Laws exam may home in on one specific issue (*e.g.,* "under the Second Restatement view, how would the court rule?"), often a question calls for a broad analysis of jurisdictional issues, choice of law, and enforcement of judgments. For these types of questions, the following basic approach will be helpful:

I. JURISDICTION

Does the court have power to hear and determine the matter before it?

A. ESSENTIAL REQUIREMENTS

Proper jurisdiction has three elements: (i) an *adequate constitutional basis* for jurisdiction; (ii) a *competent court*; and (iii) *procedural due process.*

1. Constitutional Basis

To determine what basis for jurisdiction is required, classify the action according to the type of relief sought: "in personam," "in rem," or "quasi in rem." (Remember that certain actions may be partly "in personam" and partly "in rem"—*e.g.,* a divorce action where spousal support is sought.)

a. "In personam" actions

These require personal jurisdiction over the defendant—*i.e.,* a *constitutionally sufficient "minimum contact"* between the forum state and the person or entity over whom jurisdiction is sought.

(1) *Traditionally recognized bases* for "in personam" jurisdiction include personal service within the state, local domicile, appearance, and consent.

(2) Recall that *"long arm" statutes* may extend the personal jurisdiction of local courts over those "doing business" or "committing tortious acts" within the state. If your question mentions a statute, test it as follows:

(a) *Does it apply* to the parties or transactions before the court (*i.e.,* a statutory interpretation problem)?

(b) If so, is the *application constitutional* (*i.e.,* are there sufficient "contacts" for due process)?

b. "In rem" and "quasi in rem" actions

These require jurisdiction over property. Remember that the basis for in rem and quasi in rem jurisdiction is now the same as for in personam actions—*i.e., "minimum contacts"* among the defendant, the forum state, and the subject of the litigation sufficient to satisfy "traditional notions of fair play and substantial justice."

2. Competent Court
Besides having jurisdiction over the parties or property, the particular court hearing the action must be competent according to its own standards; *i.e.,* it must have been empowered by the state to hear and determine the *particular type of case* (*e.g.,* proper monetary jurisdiction).

3. Procedural Due Process
Finally, the defendant must be given *reasonable notice* of the proceedings and an *opportunity to be heard* therein.

B. DEFENSES TO JURISDICTION
If you find all three requirements for jurisdiction, stop and consider any reasons why the court might *decline to exercise jurisdiction* in the situation before it—*e.g.,* forum non conveniens, inability to grant effective relief, fraud, force, or privilege, etc.

II. CHOICE OF LAW
Assuming the court has jurisdiction, you next need to think about *which state's laws* should apply where the case involves contact with several different states.

A. METHODOLOGY
Consider whether the forum should apply foreign law.

1. Traditional "Vested Rights" Approach
Under the "vested rights" approach, the forum applies the law of the place in which the rights of the parties *"vest."* This is usually the place *where cause of action "arose."*

a. Characterization
The forum court and you must first determine the nature of the case involved—*e.g.,* "torts," "contracts," "property." This characterization is made by the forum in accordance with its *own* definitions and standards and without reference to any foreign law.

b. Choice-of-law rules
The forum court then applies whichever choice-of-law "rules" govern the problem as characterized (*e.g.,* all "torts" problems are governed by the law of the "place of wrong").

2. Modern "Local Law" Approach
Under the "local law" approach, the forum applies its own rules of law but may make reference to "appropriate" foreign rules in certain types of cases.

a. Identify precise issue involved

Rather than attempting to characterize the case as a whole (*e.g.,* a "torts" problem), modern approaches focus on the ***particular issues*** to be resolved; *i.e.,* is the issue one of damages, privilege, standard of conduct, etc.? Therefore, you should separate the issues in your question.

b. Various theoretical approaches applied

Then, the court generally will adopt the rule of law—forum or foreign—that bears most significantly on that particular issue. While a number of theories have been advanced, courts tend to make their choice based on one of the three theories below (or some combination thereof). If your question tells you which theory the forum uses, discuss that theory, but if you don't know which theory is favored by that court, discuss all three.

(1) "Most significant relationship" approach

Isolate the ***nature and number of contacts*** in each of the states involved, and make reference to the law of the state having the most significant relationship to the particular issue(s) involved;

(2) "Governmental interest analysis" approach

Determine the ***policies and interests*** behind the conflicting rules of each state involved, and apply the law of the place that has an interest in resolving that particular issue (remember though that the forum will apply its own law unless it has no legitimate interest in doing so); *or*

(3) "Better law" approach

Choose between ***laws***, rather than jurisdictions, using various considerations to focus on the rule of law that is most appropriate to the issue at hand.

B. HOW MUCH FOREIGN LAW SHOULD BE APPLIED?

1. "Substance" vs. "Procedure"

You also need to determine whether the foreign law should be applied to all issues and aspects of the case, or only to those that are "outcome determinative." Generally, the law of the ***forum will apply to all procedural matters***.

2. "Renvoi"

Decide if the forum should look to the law that the foreign state would apply to purely internal litigation there, or to the law that it would apply to a problem involving multistate contacts (*i.e.,* the foreign state's "whole law").

C. LIMITATIONS

Consider whether there are *any defenses or constitutional limits* on the choice of law to be applied.

III. JUDGMENTS

If a judgment has already been rendered, you should ask what effect it should be given in proceedings in another state or country.

A. REQUIREMENTS FOR RECOGNITION

1. Sister-State Judgments

Full faith and credit *must* be given if the judgment is *final* and *"on the merits,"* and if the court rendering judgment had *sufficient jurisdiction* (above).

2. Foreign Judgments

For foreign judgments, recognition would be based on doctrines of *comity* and *res judicata*, but the requirements are basically the same as for sister-state judgments.

B. SCOPE OF RECOGNITION

Be sure to consider what *issues* are concluded by the former judgment (doctrine of res judicata) and what *persons* are bound by it (rules as to parties and privies).

C. DEFENSES TO RECOGNITION

Remember that a foreign judgment is *always* subject to attack for *lack of jurisdiction*, except where the parties are estopped to challenge it. Otherwise, only limited defenses (fraud, public policy in certain cases) are available.

Chapter One: Domicile

CONTENTS

Chapter Approach

Domicile is a means of connecting a person to a place for a particular purpose. Domicile is likely to show up on your conflicts exam in one of two ways:

1. It may appear as an issue in a question about *jurisdiction*—e.g., is the defendant domiciled in the forum state for purposes of *exercising jurisdiction over his person?*

2. Or domicile may be an issue in a question about *choice of law*—e.g., is the plaintiff or defendant domiciled in the forum so that the forum has a *reasonable basis for applying the forum law?*

Regardless of which type of domicile issue you find, your analysis of the domicile issue will be the same. You must decide which of the *three types of domicile*—domicile of origin, domicile of choice, or domicile by operation of law—is applicable, and which of the three types is supported by the facts given in your question.

A. General Considerations

1. **Definition [§1]**
    Domicile is the "legal tool" employed to attach a person to a particular locality for some particular purpose; *i.e.,* it is a statement of the legal conclusion that there is a sufficient "contact" or relationship between the person and the particular state or country so that its laws may be applied to the person's affairs or so that its courts may hold the person subject to its jurisdiction. Typically, a person is considered domiciled at his home—*i.e.,* the "place" where the person has been *physically present and intends to remain* indefinitely.

2. **Significance [§2]**
    Domicile is significant for *both* jurisdictional and choice-of-law purposes.

    a. **Jurisdictional basis [§3]**
        Domicile is an accepted basis for in personam jurisdiction over an individual (*see infra*, §85) and is also the principal basis for jurisdiction in matters concerning personal status—*e.g.,* divorce (*see infra*, §835).

    b. **Choice-of-law problems [§4]**
        Where the issue is which state's law is to be applied to a particular transaction

that has "contacts" with various states, the party's domicile may be deemed the most important "contact." For example, if a person is domiciled in State X, its laws will normally govern the inheritance of his chattels even though his death occurs in State Y and the chattels are located at all times in State Z; this is true whether the matter is litigated in X, Y, Z, or some other state altogether (*see infra*, §532).

3. "Domicile" vs. "Residence" [§5]

The term "domicile" signifies more than mere physical presence; it is an individual's "legal home." "Residence," on the other hand, is defined as mere physical presence within the state.

a. Note

Despite this distinction, the terms "residence" and "domicile" are often used interchangeably. Most statutes use the word "residence" but are interpreted in terms of domicile (*see infra*, §90), although the interpretation of a statute may vary with the type of legislation being construed and the legal problem raised thereunder.

EXAM TIP   **gilbert**

Be sure you know the difference between *domicile* (physical presence with the *intent to remain there indefinitely*) and *residence* (mere physical presence). However, if in an exam question you see a statute requiring "residence," recall that such statutes are often interpreted as requiring domicile. Therefore, you must consider both the purpose of the statute and the effect of construction.

---

b. Distinguish

Some statutes require residence for a specific duration in addition to domicile; *e.g.*, divorce statutes often contain a residency requirement. Such requirements have been challenged on the grounds that they impair the constitutional right to travel freely from state to state. [*Compare* **Dunn v. Blumstein**, 405 U.S. 330 (1972)—striking down state's voting registration statute which imposed a two-month residency requirement, *with* **Sosna v. Iowa**, 419 U.S. 393 (1975)—upholding a one-year waiting period for divorce]

4. Three Types of Domicile [§6]

There are three basic types of domicile:

(i) *Domicile of origin:* An infant at the time of birth acquires the domicile of his parents.

(ii) *Domicile of choice:* This is the most important type of domicile, involving a person's intentional selection of a "legal home."

gilbert

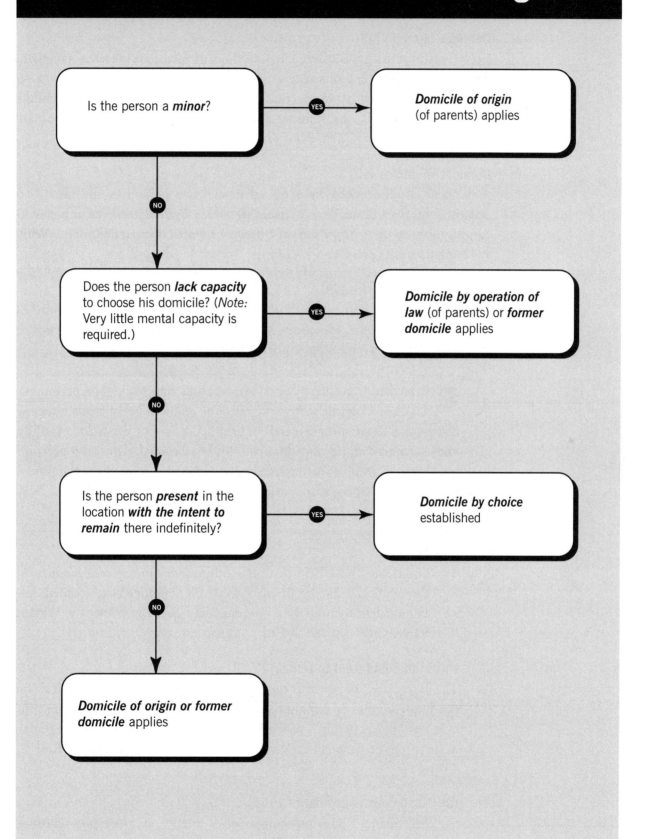

Is the person a *minor*?

YES → *Domicile of origin* (of parents) applies

NO ↓

Does the person *lack capacity* to choose his domicile? (*Note:* Very little mental capacity is required.)

YES → *Domicile by operation of law* (of parents) or *former domicile* applies

NO ↓

Is the person *present* in the location *with the intent to remain* there indefinitely?

YES → *Domicile by choice* established

NO ↓

Domicile of origin or former domicile applies

(iii) *Domicile by operation of law:* Certain domiciles arise irrespective of intention by operation of law (*e.g.*, in parent-child relationships; *see infra*, §§27 *et seq.*).

a. Domicile of origin [§7]

Every person must have a domicile and thus, at birth, an infant is assigned a domicile of origin. The domicile of origin is the domicile of the parents—of the father if the child is born to married parents, of the mother if the child is nonmarital. (Basically, the domicile of origin is a domicile by operation of law; *see infra*, §§30-33.)

b. Domicile of choice [§8]

A domicile of choice may be acquired wherever a person legally capable of obtaining his own domicile establishes (i) some *physical presence* in a new location, (ii) with the *unconditional intent to remain* there indefinitely. [**White v. Tennant**, 8 S.E. 596 (W. Va. 1888)]

(1) Physical presence [§9]

There must be some *actual, physical presence* in the new location to establish a domicile. However, a protracted period of residence is *not* required. Presence for a mere instant will suffice.

---

e.g. **Example:** Immediately upon arrival at the new location, a person may acquire a domicile there—provided the requisite intent element (below) is present. [Restatement (Second) of Conflict of Laws ("Rest. 2d") §16] But until such arrival, no new domicile can be obtained. Thus, if a person is killed on the way to the intended new home, the domicile at the time of death is still the person's former residence. [*In re* **Jones' Estate**, 182 N.W. 227 (Iowa 1921)]

(a) Note

Some cases have held that physical presence in the *near vicinity*, although not in the precise place to which the move was intended, may be sufficient to establish a new domicile. [*See, e.g.*, **Winans v. Winans**, 91 N.E. 394 (Mass. 1910)]

(2) Unconditional intent to remain [§10]

The individual's presence at the new location must be coupled with an unconditional intent to remain there *indefinitely*. This does not mean "forever" or "permanently"; it is sufficient that the person intends to remain at least for the time being (something more than temporarily). [Rest. 2d §18]

(a) Distinguish—residence [§11]

"Residence" has no requirement of intent; *i.e.*, *mere physical presence* is sufficient to establish residence.

(b) Motive for change immaterial [§12]

As long as a person moves with the requisite intent to remain indefinitely, he will acquire a new domicile regardless of the reasons for the change.

---

e.g. **Example:** Plaintiff moved from West Virginia to Virginia for the express purpose of being able to sue in the federal courts on the basis of diversity of citizenship. Because there was sufficient evidence that Plaintiff intended to remain in Virginia indefinitely, she was held to have established a domicile there. [**Williamson v. Osenton,** 232 U.S. 619 (1914)]

(c) Mental capacity [§13]

To change domicile, a person need only exhibit sufficient understanding to voluntarily choose a new residence. Thus, even a person adjudicated an incompetent (*i.e.*, who has no capacity to contract or make a will) may be capable of changing domicile. [*In re* **Phillips' Estate,** 269 Cal. App. 2d 656 (1969)]

(d) Determining intent [§14]

Whether a person has the requisite intent to remain indefinitely at the place he resides is determined by his words and conduct—*i.e.*, whether he has manifested the intent to make *this* place his "principal home."

1) Conduct may be determinative [§15]

In this regard, "actions often speak louder than words." If a person by his *conduct* indicates the intent to remain indefinitely at his residence in a state, he may be held to be domiciled there notwithstanding frequent oral or written statements of an intent to be domiciled elsewhere. [*In re* **Dorrance's Estate,** 163 A. 303 (Pa. 1932)—decedent frequently expressed intent to be domiciled in New Jersey, which has lower tax rates, but court found that his domicile was in Pennsylvania, where he spent most of his time]

2) Effect of mistake [§16]

If a person evidences his intent to remain indefinitely where he resides, he will be held domiciled there even if it turns out that he was mistaken about where he lived.

---

e.g. **Example:** The Murphy family owned the State Line Hotel, in which they made their home. They believed the hotel to be mostly in New York based on a boundary marker. They considered themselves to be New York citizens, and licenses for the hotel were issued by that state. However, when the states

---

remarked their boundary, it was discovered that the marker had been in the wrong place and that the principal rooms of the hotel were actually in Massachusetts. The court held that the Murphys were domiciled in Massachusetts. The "reasonableness" of the error was deemed immaterial. [**Blaine v. Murphy,** 265 F. 324 (D. Mass. 1920)]

3) Effect of multiple dwelling places [§17]

If a person has more than one dwelling place, his "principal home" is his domicile. If it is impossible to determine which is his "principal" home, domicile will be whichever of the homes was first acquired, since there is no reason to conclude that this initial domicile was superseded. [Rest. 2d §20]

(e) Absence of intent to remain [§18]

If a person does not indicate any intent to remain indefinitely where he resides, his domicile of origin remains. [**Edmundson v. Miley Trailer Co.,** 211 N.W.2d 269 (Iowa 1973)—itinerant horse trainer held domiciled in state he had left as a youth throughout nomadic career which took him everywhere that horses were shown]

(3) "Unitary" concept of domicile [§19]

Traditionally, domicile was seen as a unitary concept—*i.e.,* one that did not change, regardless of the particular issue involved—and the tests above for acquisition of a domicile of choice were strictly adhered to in all cases.

(a) Rationale

The concept of domicile was considered a useful legal tool in establishing a connection between a person and state since it ensured predictability of results and simplified judicial tasks. It was felt that such functions might be defeated if a person could have more than one domicile.

(b) Modern view [§20]

Today, the rigidity with which the tests for acquisition of domicile of choice are applied depends upon the particular issue involved; *i.e.,* the amount of "contact" with a state that must be shown to establish one's domicile may vary in different types of litigation.

Example: In the *Dorrance* cases, *supra,* §15, the analysis by the Pennsylvania court as to whether the decedent had acquired a new domicile in New Jersey was very rigid, because if he had, his old domicile (Pennsylvania) would have lost substantial inheritance taxes. However, if decedent's domicile had been important only to determine which state's intestate succession laws applied, a different result might have been reached.

---

1) Distinguish—"contact" required in other situations [§21]

Similarly, the amount of "contact" required to establish domicile as a basis for in personam jurisdiction (*see infra*, §85) or to institute a divorce action (*see infra*, §§838-844) may be entirely different from that required in a probate proceeding.

2) Effect—multiple domiciles possible [§22]

Under the modern approach, a person may very well be considered domiciled in different states for different purposes at the same time! [*See, e.g.,* **Hershkoff v. Board of Registrars,** 321 N.E.2d 656 (Mass. 1974)—student attending college away from home can establish domicile for voting purposes, even though his parent's home remains his domicile for other purposes]

(4) Continuity of domicile [§23]

Under the long-standing view, a present domicile *remains until a new domicile is acquired*—i.e., until both the intent and physical presence requirements are satisfied. For this reason, a person can have only one domicile at a time, and it is impossible to be without a domicile. [Rest. 2d §19; *In re* **Jones' Estate,** *supra*, §9]

(a) Involuntary absence does not forfeit domicile [§24]

Persons imprisoned or committed to an institution in another state are still held domiciled at their homes. Likewise, persons entering military service retain their last civilian domicile, no matter how long they are away, unless there is clear and convincing proof of adoption of a new domicile in the interim. [**Wilson v. Wilson,** 189 S.W.2d 212 (Tex. 1945)]

1) Military service [§25]

When a person is in military service, establishing an intent to remain "indefinitely" at a new residence is usually quite difficult. [*See, e.g.,* **Estate of O'Neill,** 176 S.E.2d 527 (S.C. 1970)—deceased sailor held domiciled at place he had lived when he enlisted in the Navy 50 years ago] This may operate quite unfairly in divorce cases, in that it prevents service personnel stationed away from their domicile from securing a divorce (because divorce actions must be brought in the state of one's domicile). For this reason, several states have enacted statutes providing that service personnel who have been stationed locally for a certain period of time (usually one year) are "conclusively presumed" to be local domiciliaries for purposes of instituting divorce actions.

2) Distinguish—residence [§26]

This continuity of domicile is another distinction between "residence" and "domicile" since a person does lose his "residence" when he moves out of the state. [**Cohen v. Daniels,** 25 Iowa 88 (1868)]

EXAM TIP   **gilbert**

While the general rule is that a person can have **only one domicile**, there are instances where a person **can have multiple domiciles** (e.g., a student away from home may use his college home as his domicile for voting purposes while still using his parents' home as his domicile for other purposes). Therefore, in an exam situation, look to see what **type of issue/cause of action** is involved because how stringent your analysis is often depends on the issue involved. Then look to see **which approach**—traditional or modern—is appropriate. If it is unclear, discuss the traditional view, and then mention the modern view allowing for multiple domiciles.

---

c. Domicile by operation of law [§27]

Certain individuals, such as *married women, minors, and incompetent persons,* traditionally have lacked the capacity to acquire a domicile of choice during the period of their incapacity. In such cases, the law determines the individual's domicile.

(1) Domicile of a wife

(a) Common law [§28]

At common law, a wife automatically acquired her husband's domicile and retained it until she separated from him and established her own domicile of choice.

1) Comment

This rule often operated unfairly, in that a wife was denied the right to choose which law should govern her affairs and estate, although her husband could make that choice. Moreover, where a husband deserted his wife and kept changing his (and hence her) domicile, it would be impossible for the wife to maintain a divorce action (since such actions must be brought in the domicile).

2) Note

England still follows the common law rule, although divorce actions are now permitted by statute when one spouse has left the country.

(b) Modern view [§29]

Today, many courts retain a *presumption* that a wife's domicile is that of her husband, but the presumption is *rebuttable*. Thus, a wife can establish a domicile separate from that of her husband, even while happily married to him, and thereby choose the laws that will apply to her affairs. [**Williamson v. Osenton,** *supra,* §12] The Restatement (Second) of Conflict of Laws provides that a married woman chooses her domicile. In most cases, she and her husband will choose the same domicile while they are living together.

(2) Domicile of a minor [§30]

Generally, the domicile of a minor, like domicile of origin, is that of the father, if the minor is born to married parents. Where the father is dead or the minor is a nonmarital child, the child takes the domicile of the mother. [*In re* **Henning's Estate,** 128 Cal. 214 (1900)]

(a) Separated parents [§31]

If the parents separate, a minor's domicile is with the parent having custody. [Rest. 2d §22]

(b) Deceased parents [§32]

If both parents die, a minor generally will be held domiciled with the relatives or guardian with whom the child lives. [*In re* **Huck,** 257 A.2d 522 (Pa. 1969)]

(c) Emancipated minor [§33]

A minor cannot establish a domicile of choice unless he becomes emancipated (*i.e.,* released from parental care by marriage or economic independence).

(3) Domicile of incompetent persons [§34]

As indicated above, relatively little mental capacity is required to establish a domicile by choice. A person who lacks even this minimal competency to choose a home will retain the domicile of his parents. [Rest. 2d §23]

(a) Time of incompetency [§35]

An individual who chooses a domicile and then becomes incompetent will retain his domicile of choice.

(b) Institutionalized incompetent [§36]

An insane or incompetent person who is kept in an asylum or institution generally does not acquire a domicile of choice there, but retains his prior domicile. [96 A.L.R. 1236]

B. Domicile Determined by Law of the Forum

1. Basic Rule [§37]

In resolving the issue of domicile for choice-of-law purposes, the governing law is that of the forum (*i.e.,* the state in which the suit is brought). [**Torlonia v. Torlonia,** 142 A. 843 (Conn. 1928)] This is true even where the domicile is in another state or country. [*In re* **Annesley,** [1926] Ch. 692]

---

e.g. **Example:** Monique is born in New York, but goes to France at an early age and remains there her whole life. After her death intestate, litigation is commenced in New York to determine which of Monique's relatives should inherit certain personal property she left in New York. The New York court decides that the distribution of personal property should be governed by the law of the decedent's domicile. In deciding where Monique was domiciled, the New York court applies its own tests and standards, and if it decides that she was domiciled in France, it is immaterial whether a French court would agree.

---

a. Rationale

This is the doctrine of "characterization," under which the forum applies its own laws as to *definition of terms* because (i) the local tribunal is better able to handle a problem if it can apply its own concepts and definitions, and (ii) this doctrine helps avoid renvoi problems (*see infra,* §257).

2. Effect—Conflicting Determinations of Domicile [§38]

The effect of the characterization doctrine often has been to negate any attempt to achieve uniform results in multistate controversies. In the famous *Dorrance's Estate* cases (*see supra,* §15), for example, the highest courts of two states (New Jersey and Pennsylvania) examined the decedent's domicile to determine whether their respective states could impose inheritance taxes on the decedent's estate. Each court defined domicile in its own terms and, by its own standards, found that the decedent was domiciled in its state, and imposed inheritance taxes accordingly so that inheritance taxes had to be paid to both states!

a. Constitutional considerations [§39]

There was apparently no violation of constitutional rights in the *Dorrance* cases because the state courts were merely determining the decedent's domicile, and it was entirely proper for each to apply its own concepts and tests of domicile, regardless of determinations by any other state court. [Rest. 2d §7]

(1) But note

The Supreme Court has indicated that the imposition of multiple state death taxes would violate due process if such taxes were to exceed the value of the estate. [**Massachusetts v. Missouri,** 308 U.S. 1 (1939)]

(2) And note

The Court will entertain a case brought under its original jurisdiction between two states, each claiming to be the decedent's domicile, where the Eleventh Amendment prevents resort to federal statutory interpleader to resolve the controversy [**Cory v. White,** 457 U.S. 85 (1982)] and where the combined total of taxes due under state and federal law is alleged to deplete the estate [**California v. Texas,** 457 U.S. 164 (1982)].

3. Constitutional Limitation [§40]

There are also constitutional due process limits on characterizations that operate arbitrarily or prejudicially against nonresidents. For example, it might violate the Fourteenth Amendment Due Process Clause for a forum to adopt some unique concept of "domicile" to justify application of its laws to nonresidents. [*See* Rest. 2d §7, comment e]

Chapter Two:
Jurisdiction of Courts

CONTENTS

Chapter Approach

Chapter Approach

Conflicts examinations often have questions that concern jurisdiction. Keep in mind that there are three essential elements of jurisdiction:

1. *A constitutional basis for asserting jurisdiction over the person or property* involved ("minimum contacts");

2. *A competent court* to hear the type of case (according to statute); and

3. *Procedural due process* (notice and opportunity to be heard).

In most jurisdiction questions, the court is competent to hear the type of case involved; thus, that element is met. The issue for you to resolve generally deals with the constitutional basis: Does the forum court have constitutional power to bind the parties before it by its judgment? Most often the specific question is *jurisdiction over the defendant*, because plaintiff has submitted to the forum's jurisdiction by filing suit. Your analysis then will have to determine whether the defendant has *sufficient minimum contacts* with the forum such that its assertion of jurisdiction does not violate due process. After that, you may also need to consider the procedural due process requirements: Did defendant have *proper notice* of the proceedings against him?

A. Introduction

1. Definition of Jurisdiction [§41]

"Jurisdiction" generally refers to the power of a state, normally exercised through its courts, to establish or alter legal relationships between individuals in a dispute affecting their personal status, their personal interests, or their interests in property that will be binding within that state. (*See* general discussion in Civil Procedure Summary.)

2. Essential Requirements for Proper Jurisdiction [§42]

In every case, the proper exercise of jurisdiction depends on the existence of three essential elements:

a. Constitutional basis [§43]

First, constitutional due process requires that the forum state have an adequate basis for jurisdiction over the person or property involved; *i.e.*, there must be *sufficient "contacts"* between the state and that person or thing. (*See infra*, §49.)

b.   Competent court [§44]

Second, the court in which the action is pending must have authority *under its own local statutes* to entertain the action in question (*e.g.*, proper monetary limits, correct venue, equity jurisdiction). Note that this is *not* a constitutional requirement, but one of statutory power. (*See infra*, §§197-204.)

c.   Procedural due process [§45]

Finally, constitutional due process requires that all parties to an action be afforded *reasonable notice and opportunity to be heard*. (*See infra*, §§205 et seq.)

3.   Relationship Between Jurisdiction and Choice of Law—"Minimum Contacts" [§46]

As will be discussed *infra*, jurisdiction and choice-of-law decisions are interrelated: The Due Process Clause limits the state's authority to assert jurisdiction over an interstate transaction or nonresident defendants, just as due process considerations limit the forum's power to apply its own substantive law to resolve the case at bar. For the forum court to apply its own law—or for that matter, exercise jurisdiction over an interstate case—the forum must have *"minimum contacts"* with the parties, property, or underlying events such that the application of its law would be *"fair"* (*see infra*, §126). Therefore, a determination of proper jurisdiction may also justify the court's application of its own law.

a.   But note

While jurisdiction and choice-of-law decisions are interrelated, different considerations may also arise in the two areas. For example, there may be situations in which a state has sufficient contacts with the controversy to justify applying its own law, but it is unable to subject a defendant to suit there. Conversely, the state may have jurisdiction over the defendant but lack sufficient interest in the suit to apply its law.

4.   Relationship Between Jurisdiction and Enforcement of Judgments [§47]

A judgment rendered by a court without proper jurisdiction is considered void and cannot constitutionally be recognized in other states. But if the court's exercise of jurisdiction was proper, its judgment is entitled to such recognition under the Full Faith and Credit Clause (provided the other requirements of the Clause are met). (Enforcement of judgments is discussed in detail *infra*, §§729 et seq.)

5.   Constitutional Principles

a.   Historical view—"presence power" [§48]

Until fairly recently, the "presence power" theory established in **Pennoyer v. Neff,** 95 U.S. 714 (1877), constituted the exclusive basis for American law on jurisdiction. Under this theory, a state had to have *physical power* over the parties or property in order to exercise judicial jurisdiction. Accordingly, a state could exercise jurisdiction over persons or property *present* within the state, even though the state had no connection with the underlying transaction.

> **Example:** Under the "presence power" approach, even temporary physical presence is sufficient for jurisdiction. Thus, a court can exercise jurisdiction over a nonresident defendant who may have been passing through the state when served with process (*see infra*, §72).

b. Present view—"minimum contacts" [§49]

The present view, however, is that in actions relating to interests in or the status of property, if the defendant is not present in the state, "minimum contacts" are necessary to provide a basis for jurisdiction. The Due Process Clause has been interpreted to require the establishment of *"minimum contacts"* among the defendant, the forum state, and the litigation, so that the forum's exercise of jurisdiction will not offend *"traditional notions of fair play and substantial justice."* [**Shaffer v. Heitner**, 443 U.S. 186 (1977)]

> **Example:** In *Shaffer, supra*, the plaintiff brought a shareholder's derivative suit in Delaware against nonresident officers of a Delaware corporation. Because personal jurisdiction could not be obtained over the defendants, the plaintiff obtained a levy on their shares in the corporation under a Delaware statute that provided that the shares were deemed to be present at the corporation's headquarters. The Supreme Court held that the mere statutory "presence" of the defendants' stock in Delaware was not a sufficient "contact" with that state to justify its exercise of jurisdiction, because the action was unrelated to their stock and involved conduct outside the state by nonresidents.

(1) Comment

Given its broadest reading, *Shaffer* would have overruled **Pennoyer v. Neff**, *supra*, and raised serious doubts about traditional "single contact" bases for acquiring jurisdiction over nonresident defendants (*e.g.*, mere physical presence). However, three members of the Supreme Court have refused to read *Shaffer* this broadly. They pointed out that *Shaffer*, like **International Shoe Co. v. Washington** (*infra*, §116), involved the assertion of jurisdiction over an absent defendant, not one who was served personally in the state. Consequently, they argued, *Shaffer* "stands for nothing more than the proposition that when the 'minimum contact' that is a substitute for physical presence consists of property ownership it must, like other minimum contacts, be related to the litigation." [**Burnham v. Superior Court**, 495 U.S. 604 (1990)] (Other implications of *Shaffer* and *Burnham* are discussed *infra*, §§64, 75, 173 *et seq.*)

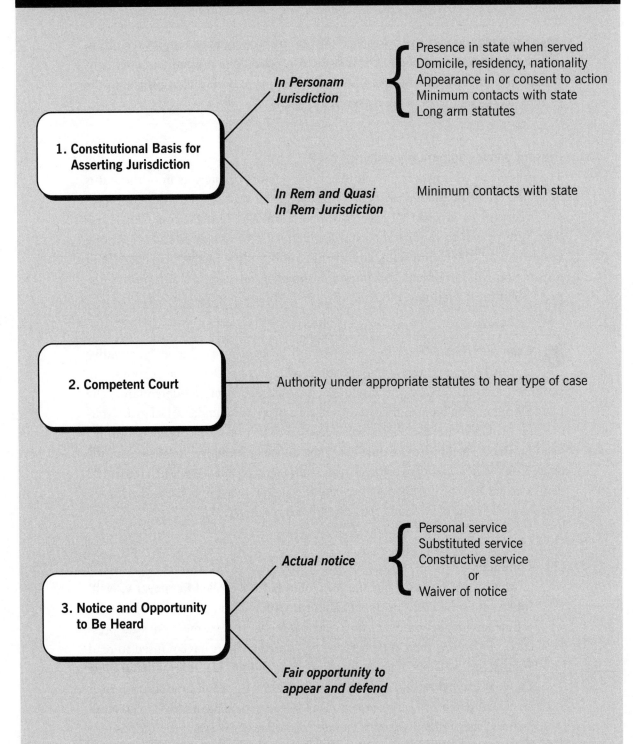

1. Constitutional Basis for Asserting Jurisdiction

In Personam Jurisdiction

{ Presence in state when served
Domicile, residency, nationality
Appearance in or consent to action
Minimum contacts with state
Long arm statutes

In Rem and Quasi In Rem Jurisdiction

Minimum contacts with state

2. Competent Court

Authority under appropriate statutes to hear type of case

3. Notice and Opportunity to Be Heard

Actual notice

{ Personal service
Substituted service
Constructive service
or
Waiver of notice

Fair opportunity to appear and defend

B. Types of Jurisdiction

1. In General [§50]

Traditionally, three types of judicial jurisdiction have been recognized. The extent to which these three classifications have survived **Shaffer v. Heitner,** *supra,* is uncertain, but it is helpful to understand them.

2. In Personam Jurisdiction [§51]

A court with in personam jurisdiction has the authority to determine the rights and duties of the parties and the power *to bind the parties personally.* Courts usually have acquired such power by service within the state or some other constitutionally sufficient "contact" with the party (*see infra,* §§70 *et seq.*).

a. Enforcement [§52]

In personam decrees or judgments can be enforced directly against the person or property of the parties before the court.

(1) Injunctions [§53]

Injunctions—decrees commanding a party to perform or refrain from performing a particular act—are enforceable by contempt processes (*i.e.,* imprisonment for nonperformance). (*See* Remedies Summary.)

(2) Money judgments [§54]

Most money judgments are enforceable only by execution against the property of the judgment debtor. However, certain money judgments—such as spousal or child support decrees—can be enforced by contempt as well as by execution.

3. In Rem Jurisdiction [§55]

Where the subject of an action is some item of property (a "res") located in the state, the court may exercise in rem jurisdiction *as to that property*. This enables the court to determine the *rights of the entire world in that specific property*, and no personal jurisdiction is required.

Examples: There are very few types of actions in which courts exercise purely in rem jurisdiction. The most common examples are eminent domain proceedings (in which the state takes property for a public use and the taking terminates the interests of all persons therein), statutory forfeiture proceedings (*e.g.,* cars used for unlawful transportation of narcotics), and probate proceedings involving local property.

a. Enforcement [§56]

Where a court exercises in rem jurisdiction, its decree alone is effective to alter the status of title or otherwise determine the rights of everyone in the world in the subject property.

4. Quasi In Rem Jurisdiction [§57]

A court having quasi in rem jurisdiction may determine the *rights of particular persons in specific property* within the court's control. Quasi in rem jurisdiction differs from in personam jurisdiction in that the court *cannot impose a personal obligation* upon the parties, and it differs from in rem jurisdiction because the court *cannot determine the rights of all persons* in the thing before the court.

a. Types of quasi in rem jurisdiction [§58]

There are two types of quasi in rem jurisdiction, one similar to in rem jurisdiction, and the other more similar to in personam jurisdiction.

(1) Jurisdiction to affect title of particular claimants [§59]

The first type of quasi in rem proceeding involves a determination of the title or interest of *particular persons* (as opposed to determining the rights of the entire world) in the property before the court. The state's power over the "res" gives the court power to alter or affect the rights of particular persons in such property even without personal jurisdiction over them.

Examples: Most actions to establish or extinguish an interest in property (*e.g.*, quiet title actions or mortgage foreclosure actions) are of this type.

(a) Enforcement [§60]

As in the case of in rem jurisdiction, the court's power over the "res" makes its decree effective by itself to alter or affect the interests in the property of those persons who are parties to the action. For example, a decree foreclosing a mortgage itself establishes title in the lender (mortgagee) and extinguishes the debtor's (mortgagor's) interest.

(b) Procedural due process required [§61]

All persons whose interests are to be affected by the exercise of quasi in rem jurisdiction must be named as parties defendant and must be afforded adequate notice and opportunity to appear (*see infra*, §205).

(c) Limitation—no personal obligations [§62]

A court exercising quasi in rem jurisdiction is empowered to affect only interests in the "res"; *i.e.*, it cannot impose personal obligations unless it has personal jurisdiction over the defendant. Thus, for example, the court in a mortgage foreclosure action could properly extinguish the interest of the debtor (mortgagor) in the mortgaged property, but it could *not* enter a deficiency judgment against the debtor for the balance of the mortgage debt without personal jurisdiction.

(2) Quasi in rem jurisdiction to enforce in personam claim [§63]

The second type of quasi in rem proceeding involves a technique for converting a purely in personam claim into a proceeding "sounding" in rem, which could be employed where personal jurisdiction over the defendant could not be obtained. If, at the commencement of what would otherwise have been an in personam action, the plaintiff brought local assets of the absent defendant before the court (by writ of attachment, sequestration, garnishment, etc.), the court could assume jurisdiction over the assets and thereafter treat the action as in rem to the extent of the assets before it; *i.e.,* even though the claim sued upon was totally *unrelated* to those assets, the court could use the assets as a springboard to jurisdiction so that if defendant were held liable, *those assets* could be used to satisfy the liability. Since the proceeding was "quasi in rem," personal jurisdiction over defendant was not required—although without it, the court's power would of course be limited to the assets before it.

e.g. **Example:** Paolo sues Donna, who is a nonresident, for $5,000 damages on a personal injury claim. Even though Paolo cannot obtain personal jurisdiction over Donna, he can still attach whatever property Donna has in the state. If the court holds Donna liable, its judgment will be enforceable against this property, but the judgment will not be enforced against Donna's other assets because there would be no personal jurisdiction over her.

(a) Impact of *Shaffer* [§64]

The Supreme Court in **Shaffer v. Heitner,** *supra,* §49, further subdivided this second type of quasi in rem jurisdiction into two parts and imposed rules and requirements for the exercise of such jurisdiction (*see infra,* §§174-176). The two parts are:

1) Cases in which the *plaintiff's claim is related to the presence of the defendant's property* in the forum state (*e.g.,* where the plaintiff is injured on property owned by the defendant and located in the forum)—here exercise of jurisdiction is generally *valid*; and

2) Cases in which the *plaintiff's claim is unrelated to the specific property* attached or seized as the basis for quasi in rem jurisdiction—here exercise of jurisdiction is generally *invalid*.

It is important for you to be able to distinguish between the three types of jurisdiction. Remember:

(i) *In personam jurisdiction* allows the court to bind a party *personally*;

(ii) *In rem jurisdiction* allows the court to determine the rights of the *entire world* as to an item of *property*, but the *parties are not personally bound*; and

(iii) *Quasi in rem jurisdiction* allows the court to determine the rights of *particular persons in specific property* but the court *cannot bind the parties personally or determine the rights of the entire world*.

5. In Personam Actions vs. In Rem Actions [§65]

Whether personal jurisdiction over the defendant is required in a particular proceeding turns on whether the action is in rem or in personam.

a. Determinative factor—type of relief sought [§66]

Classification of an action as in rem or in personam depends on the *type of relief* sought by the plaintiff. If the plaintiff seeks to assert or acquire rights in a *specific piece of property* (real or personal), the action is in rem or quasi in rem. If the plaintiff is asserting *only a general claim* against the defendant, the action is in personam.

Examples—in rem actions: Typical *quasi in rem* proceedings are suits to foreclose a lien, to effect a partition, to quiet title, for ejectment and for specific recovery of chattels. Common *in rem* actions are probate, admiralty, and escheat proceedings.

Examples—in personam actions: Suits for injunctions, damages, or other monetary claims are examples of in personam actions. *Note:* A suit for trespass or injury to land is in personam rather than in rem. Even though the subject of the action is a particular piece of realty, the relief sought is *monetary damages*.

b. "Local" vs. "transitory" actions [§67]

In rem and quasi in rem actions are "local"; *i.e.*, they may be brought *only at the situs of the property* involved. However, most in personam actions are "transitory" and may be maintained against the defendant *in any forum where personal jurisdiction can be established* (subject to the willingness of that forum to hear the action; *see infra*, §§225 et seq.).

(1) Exception [§68]

Actions for *trespass to land* are an exception to the rule above. As a relic from common law days, most courts hold that such actions are "local" (albeit in personam) and thus maintainable only at the situs of the land. [**Livingston v. Jefferson,** 15 F. Cas. 660 (D. Va. 1811)] This exception has been criticized vigorously by many modern authorities [*see, e.g.,* 40 Minn. L. Rev. 191 (1955)] and has been rejected in a few states (*e.g.,* New York).

EXAM TIP   **gilbert**

Remember, in determining whether an action is in personam or in rem (or quasi in rem), ask yourself if the plaintiff is seeking damages or some other type of relief against the defendant himself, or is the plaintiff seeking to establish rights in some specific real or personal property? If the action seeks relief *against the defendant*, the action is *in personam*, and may be brought against the defendant anywhere where personal jurisdiction is appropriate (subject to the willingness of that forum). If the action revolves around *property rights*, the action is *in rem or quasi in rem* and may only be brought where the property is situated.

C. General Bases for Jurisdiction

1. Bases for In Personam Jurisdiction [§69]

As noted previously, the first requirement for jurisdiction is that there be a constitutionally sufficient basis for jurisdiction over the persons or property involved. The bases for in personam jurisdiction are discussed below.

a. Personal service on defendant physically present in state

(1) Traditional rule [§70]

Under the traditional rule, personal service of a locally issued summons or other legal process on a defendant while he is *physically present* in a state will subject him to the personal jurisdiction of the local courts. [Rest. 2d §28] Under the older cases, this was the only way in which personal jurisdiction could be obtained. [*See* **Pennoyer v. Neff,** *supra,* §49] Modern cases, however, recognize other methods for obtaining in personam jurisdiction (*see* below).

(2) What constitutes "personal service" [§71]

The summons or other court process must be handed to the defendant or otherwise served upon him in a form and manner prescribed by the law of the forum state. (*See* Civil Procedure Summary.)

(3) What constitutes "physical presence" in state

(a) Traditional rule—"transient" presence sufficient [§72]

Historically, temporary physical presence in the state when served has been sufficient for personal jurisdiction. Therefore, the defendant could be a transient, rather than a resident or domiciliary of the state. [**Darrah v. Watson,** 36 Iowa 116 (1872)]

1) Presence in airplane [§73]

Following this view, personal service has been held to confer jurisdiction even when the defendant was only fleetingly present—*e.g.*, on an airplane flying over the state. [**Grace v. MacArthur,** 170 F. Supp. 442 (E.D. Ark. 1959)]

2) Presence in representative capacity [§74]

However, if the defendant is served in some representative capacity (*e.g.*, as the executor of an estate), he must be present in the forum state in that representative capacity. Thus, if the individual is merely there on a vacation trip or the like, personal service would not confer jurisdiction.

(b) Reaffirmation of transient jurisdiction [§75]

After **Shaffer v. Heitner** (*see supra*, §49), the constitutionality of "transient jurisdiction" was open to question. *Shaffer* rejected the sufficiency of a "single contact"—*i.e.*, defendant's ownership of property unrelated to the cause of action—as a basis for in personam jurisdiction. The opinion stressed that "all" assertions of jurisdiction must satisfy the *International Shoe* "minimum contacts" standard (*see infra*, §116). Thus, other "single contact" tests, such as transient jurisdiction, needed reexamination. **Burnham v. Superior Court** provided the opportunity to reexamine the transient jurisdiction rule in light of *Shaffer*.

1) Burnham v. Superior Court [§76]

A New Jersey husband was personally served with process in his wife's California divorce action while he was temporarily present in California on business and had stopped by her home to visit his children. The Court unanimously agreed that California's assertion of jurisdiction over the nonresident defendant personally served in the state did not violate the Due Process Clause. [**Burnham v. Superior Court,** *supra*, §49]

a) Rationales

The Court's reasoning in *Burnham* was sharply divided. *Justice Scalia and two other Justices* reasoned that the transient jurisdiction rule itself constituted one of the ancient and continuing "traditional notions of fair play and substantial justice" that lie at the core of the due process standard. Therefore, it need not be tested against more modern elaborations of that standard, such as those embodied in *Shaffer* or *International Shoe*. **Justice Brennan and three other Justices** believed that the transient jurisdiction rule must be tested under the fairness standard developed in those more recent cases, but concluded that the rule normally met that standard. A transient defendant actually avails himself of significant benefits by visiting the forum state: "His health and safety are guaranteed by the State's police, fire, and emergency medical services; he is free to travel on the State's roads and waterways; he likely enjoys the fruits of the State's economy as well." **Justice White** was unwilling to disturb the transient jurisdiction rule, at least where the defendant's presence in the forum state was intentional; **Justice Stevens** concurred in the judgment for the reasons given in all three separate opinions, concluding that together they demonstrated that *Burnham* was "a very easy case."

b)   Comment

The result in *Burnham* seems clearer than its rationale. It appears safe to assume, however, that no further constitutional questions will be raised about the much-criticized rule of transient jurisdiction, at least where the nonresident defendant intentionally entered the territory of the forum state. While physically present there, he subjects himself to the possibility of personal service that will sustain in personam jurisdiction over him on matters unrelated to the purpose of his visit.

(c) Traditional exceptions [§77]

Even before the Court's decision in *Shaffer*, certain exceptions to the principle of transient jurisdiction were recognized:

1)   Fraud or force [§78]

Where the plaintiff defrauded the defendant into entering the jurisdiction where he was served, or where the defendant was seized and dragged into the state, personal service has been held insufficient to establish in personam jurisdiction. [**Blandin v. Ostrander,** 239 F. 700 (2d Cir. 1917)]

a)   Constitutional vs. discretionary limitation [§79]

While the Supreme Court has never ruled on the point, many authorities argue that if a person was deceived or dragged into a state, the "minimum contacts" required by due process for exercise of jurisdiction are lacking (*see* above). The Restatement takes the position that the court has jurisdiction in such cases but simply refuses to exercise it as a matter of judicial discretion. [*See* Rest. 2d §83]

2) Immunity from service [§80]

A similar result occurs where the defendant is served locally but is exempt from service of process (*e.g.*, a member of Congress on investigative mission is exempt from service).

a) Persons involved in litigation [§81]

Persons coming into a state for purposes of litigation in its courts are commonly exempted from service of process while so engaged. [**Lamb v. Schmitt,** 285 U.S. 222 (1932)] This applies most strongly to *witnesses*, in view of public policy encouraging their attendance and testimony, but many states grant the exemption to litigants and attorneys as well.

1/ Exception [§82]

A number of cases have denied immunity to nonresidents entering the state to defend a *criminal* charge—at least with respect to service in connection with a civil suit growing out of the same event involved in the criminal prosecution. [51 Com. L.Q. 411 (1966)]

2/ And note—other basis for jurisdiction [§83]

Where the forum has some *other adequate basis for jurisdiction* over the defendant, the fact that he was served with process while immune does not affect the court's power over him. For example, "long arm" statutes (*see infra*, §142) frequently authorize courts to assert personal jurisdiction against persons doing business within the state. Where such statutes are in effect, jurisdiction may be upheld even if service on such a person was made when he entered the state as a witness in completely unrelated litigation. [**Severn v. Adidas,** 33 Cal. App. 3d 754 (1973)]

3/ Termination of immunity [§84]

In any event, immunity from service ends within a reasonable time after the judicial proceeding has been concluded.

When faced with an exam question dealing with whether service is proper on a defendant who was "incidentally" present in the state or merely "passing through" (*e.g.,* on a business trip, testifying in a trial, visiting relatives, etc.), you should first discuss that although the transient jurisdiction rule was questioned in case law, the Supreme Court ultimately *reaffirmed its constitutionality*. Next, you should address the possibility of applying one of the *traditional exceptions* (*i.e.,* fraud, use of force, or immunity from service). However, keep in mind that despite these exceptions, there may be *other adequate bases for jurisdiction*, including the use of long arm statutes as well as other policy-based rationales. Simply put, courts have still found all sorts of reasons, rationales, and loopholes to continue allowing service, even sometimes circumventing a situation where a person would otherwise be immune from service. These decisions often turn on the public policy of encouraging people to be good citizens and help the justice system by coming into the state to testify when needed, and the public policy of not advocating fraud. Consequently, one policy sometimes outweighs another.

b. Domicile, residence, or nationality

(1) Domicile [§85]

Domicile alone has been held to be a constitutionally sufficient basis for in personam jurisdiction. The forum state may empower its courts to exercise personal jurisdiction over local domiciliaries *even while they are outside the state*. [**Milliken v. Meyer,** 311 U.S. 457 (1940)]

(a) Rationale

Domicile is a constitutionally sufficient "contact" (relationship) between the state and the person over whom jurisdiction is sought. Persons domiciled within a state receive many privileges and rights, and as a corollary may be subjected to suit within the state as an "incident of domicile."

1) Note

There are also *practical considerations* for this rule. The defendant will likely anticipate being sued at home—even on actions arising elsewhere—and it is convenient to have at least one forum in which jurisdiction is free from question. (On the other hand, domicile may be extremely attenuated or even fictional, thereby lessening the likelihood that defendant would reasonably anticipate being sued there.)

2) Constitutional issue

It should be noted that domicile, when used as a basis for personal jurisdiction over an absent defendant, is a "single contact" test that serves as a substitute for personal service within the state. As such, it may be subject to reexamination in light of **Shaffer v. Heitner,** even after **Burnham v. Superior Court.**

(b) Necessity of statute [§86]

The "contact" that justifies jurisdiction is between the forum state and the defendant. It must appear that the state has, by statute, conferred its power upon local courts. In the absence of a statute, local courts have no authority over domiciliaries outside the state.

(c) Time of domicile [§87]

Most courts require that an absent defendant be shown to be domiciled in the forum state *at the time the suit is brought*. [Rest. 2d §29]

1) Statutory modification [§88]

Occasionally, statutes approve jurisdiction where the defendant was domiciled locally at the time the *cause of action arose* (*e.g.*, the defendant was domiciled in forum state at time of wrong, but moved to another state before action was filed). The United States Supreme Court has not ruled on the constitutionality of such statutes, but they have been upheld on the state level. [*See, e.g.*, **Owens v. Superior Court,** 52 Cal. 2d 822 (1959); **Cooke v. Yarrington,** 229 A.2d 400 (N.J. 1973)]

(d) Procedural due process requirements [§89]

In every case, the absent domiciliary must be given *adequate notice and opportunity to be heard*—*i.e.*, "substituted service" (personal service outside the state) if his whereabouts are known, or "constructive service" (by publication) if his whereabouts are unknown. (*See infra,* §§208 *et seq.*)

(2) Residence [§90]

Residence alone is a constitutionally sufficient basis for in personam jurisdiction.

(a) Rationale

It has been argued that if residence is substantial enough to make the exercise of jurisdiction "reasonable"—*e.g.*, a person in military service permanently stationed within the forum state although technically domiciled elsewhere—it should also be a sufficient basis for personal jurisdiction. [Rest. 2d §30]

(b) But note

There is remarkably little authority on this point. One reason is that many statutes that ostensibly authorize courts to exercise personal jurisdiction over local "residents" are interpreted as requiring domicile. [*See, e.g.*, **Owens v. Superior Court,** *supra*]

(3) Nationality (citizenship) [§91]

Just as domicile has been considered a sufficient "contact" between the person and the state to confer in personam jurisdiction even while the person is absent from the state, nationality is deemed a sufficient "contact" to justify assertion of personal jurisdiction over a United States citizen by federal courts when he is outside the country. [Rest. 2d §31]

---

e.g. **Example:** The Supreme Court has upheld the constitutionality of a federal statute requiring United States citizens abroad to return home when subpoenaed as witnesses in federal criminal proceedings. The statute provided for adequate notice to the citizen through service of the subpoena by the United States consul in the foreign country. [**Blackmer v. United States,** 284 U.S. 421 (1932)]

(a) Necessity of statute?

It is generally assumed that Congress must authorize the federal courts to exercise personal jurisdiction over citizens outside the country—*i.e.*, that federal courts have no inherent jurisdiction over citizens abroad. [Rest. 2d §31, comment d]

1) Comment

While the Supreme Court has not passed on the point, it can be argued that federal courts have such power independent of statute on the theory that the Constitution confers the "judicial power" on the federal courts and that jurisdiction over citizens, wherever they are, is inherent in the federal judicial power.

EXAM TIP | **gilbert**

Don't forget the general principles of domicile that were covered in the first chapter of this Summary: There are three different types of domicile (*i.e.*, origin, choice, operation of law), and domicile and residence are not the same. Unlike domicile, residence can be established by *mere physical presence*; no intent is required.

---

c. Appearance or consent

(1) Appearance [§92]

A party's voluntary appearance in an action is sufficient in itself for the assertion of personal jurisdiction over the party in that action. [Rest. 2d §33]

(a) Rationale

The appearance constitutes a sufficient "contact" between the forum state and the individual with respect to the litigation. There is no due process violation because the defendant always has the alternative of not appearing in the action, letting judgment go against her by default, and collaterally attacking the judgment on the basis of lack of jurisdiction (*see infra*, §§803-810).

(b) What constitutes an "appearance" [§93]

Any sort of appearance by the party (*e.g.*, in person or through an authorized attorney) is sufficient, if the forum state chooses to assert it as the basis for jurisdiction. [**York v. Texas,** 137 U.S. 15 (1890)]

1) Exception—appearance to challenge court's jurisdiction [§94]

All states now permit a defendant to appear in some form for the purpose of objecting to jurisdiction of the forum without subjecting herself to jurisdiction based on that appearance.

a) Challenge to jurisdiction must come first [§95]

In some states, this appearance must be labeled a "special" appearance, and the defendant may challenge *only* the court's exercise of personal jurisdiction—*i.e.*, if other pleadings or motions are included with the "special" appearance and challenge to jurisdiction, the appearance will be deemed a general appearance and will subject the defendant to the court's jurisdiction. In other states, the "special" appearance rule has been *somewhat* eliminated, in that a "special" appearance is no longer required, and it is sometimes even allowable to file other motions with the motion contesting the court's jurisdiction. However, even in those states, the challenge to jurisdiction still *must come first*. Otherwise, the defendant will be deemed to have waived the personal jurisdiction issue.

(c) Extent of jurisdiction conferred

1) Appearance by defendant [§96]

By appearing, a defendant submits to jurisdiction of the forum state only with respect to the action in which she appears and only as to the causes of action pleaded in the complaint at the time of her appearance.

a) Effect

If the plaintiff thereafter amends the complaint to set up new causes of action, he must obtain jurisdiction over the defendant as to those new causes of action. [*Ex parte* **Indiana Transportation Co.,** 244 U.S. 456 (1917)]

b) But note

If the amendments do not constitute a "new" cause of action, the defendant is bound by the original appearance—

apparently even where the amendment raises the amount of plaintiff's demand. [**Everitt v. Everitt,** 4 N.Y.2d 13 (1958)—amendment filed after defendant's appearance sought 10 times the amount claimed in the original pleading]

2) Plaintiff's institution of suit [§97]

A nonresident plaintiff who files suit in the forum state submits himself to the personal jurisdiction of the forum—not only as to matters pleaded in the complaint, but also with respect to any cause of action that the defendant asserts against him by way of counterclaim or cross-action. [Rest. 2d §34]

a) Rationale

If a plaintiff wishes to avail himself of local judicial process, he should also be amenable to suit in local courts on causes of action related to and growing out of his suit. [**Adam v. Saenger,** 303 U.S. 59 (1938)]

b) Distinguish

In all other cases, nonresident litigants coming into the state are *exempt* from service of process while engaged in the litigation (*see supra,* §§81 *et seq.*).

(2) Express consent [§98]

A party's express consent to the jurisdiction of local courts, whether given *before* or *after* suit is commenced, will serve as a sufficient basis for in personam jurisdiction in that action, and it may also constitute a waiver of procedural due process (*see infra*). [**National Equipment Rental Ltd. v. Szukhent,** 375 U.S. 311 (1964)]

(a) Analysis [§99]

Consent represents a different concept in personal jurisdiction. Every other basis for in personam jurisdiction involves some "contact" or relationship between the forum state and the individual who is sought to be bound. Where consent is the basis, however, there need be *no* *"contact"* at all.

(b) What constitutes effective "consent" [§100]

Consent may grow out of contract or it may be purely gratuitous. However, unless supported by consideration, the consent may be revoked at any time prior to suit.

(c) Illustration—"cognovits" [§101]

The most common form of consent to jurisdiction is the so-called cognovit—a clause in a contract that provides that in the event of breach, the breaching party agrees to submit herself to the jurisdiction of the courts of a named state in any action to enforce the contract.

Such an agreement effectively confers personal jurisdiction over the consenting party even if she has never been in the state and has had no dealings or "contacts" whatsoever with that jurisdiction. [**Egley v. T.B. Bennett & Co.**, 145 N.E. 830 (Ind. 1924)]

1) Scope of cognovits

Cognovits may (and usually do) go further and provide for a waiver of process, service by mail, or even a confession of judgment against the breaching party. (The validity of such provisions is discussed *infra*, §216.)

2) Limitations [§102]

There is no effective consent (and hence no jurisdiction) if the party lacked capacity to consent, or if the consent was obtained by fraud or as part of an adhesion contract (*i.e.,* where one party occupies a substantially inferior bargaining position. *See* Contracts Summary).

(d) Strict interpretation of consent [§103]

Typically, consent to jurisdiction is strictly construed; jurisdiction will be denied if it is not exactly within the terms of the consent given. [**Grover & Baker Sewing Machine Co. v. Radcliffe**, 137 U.S. 287 (1890)—contract authorized confession of judgment "by an attorney"; judgment entered by notary held void]

---

e.g. **Example:** An agreement that "rights under this contract shall be determined by the laws of State X" (*i.e.,* a choice-of-law provision) does not, without more, confer personal jurisdiction over the contracting parties.

---

cf. **Compare:** But an agreement that "any dispute arising under this contract shall be settled by arbitration in accordance with the statutes of State X" has been held to be an agreement to submit to the jurisdiction of an arbitration board in State X and to the courts in State X, if necessary, for enforcement of the arbitrator's award. [**Gilbert v. Burnstine**, 255 N.Y. 348 (1931)]

EXAM TIP	gilbert

Note the difference between a choice-of-law provision and a consent clause. Generally, the **choice-of-law provision** merely states something along the lines of "the law of State X will determine the rights under this action," and this statement alone does **not amount to consent**. On the other hand, a **consent clause** contains additional teeth, such as a statement that "any dispute arising under this contract shall be resolved through arbitration conducted in accordance with the laws and statutes of State X," and may constitute sufficient consent to confer jurisdiction.

1) Enforceable if reasonable [§104]

If contract terms relating to jurisdiction are *unambiguous* and *reasonable*, the agreement usually will be upheld.

---

e.g. **Example:** An American company contracted with a German company to tow its drilling rig from Louisiana to a point off the coast of Italy. The contract provided that any dispute arising from the contract must be decided in the London Court of Justice. This clause was held prima facie valid because the contract's terms were fully negotiated by parties of equal bargaining power and there was no evidence of fraud or "serious" inconvenience. [**The Bremen v. Zapata Off-Shore Co.,** 407 U.S. 1 (1972)]

---

(3) Implied consent [§105]

The first "long arm" statutes (*see infra*, §§142 *et seq.*) relied on the fiction of implied consent as the basis for jurisdiction over nonresidents who would otherwise not be subject to personal jurisdiction of the forum state. A party who engaged in certain acts or conduct within the state was *deemed to have consented* to the jurisdiction of local courts, even where she explicitly stated that she did *not* consent. [**Washington v. Superior Court,** 289 U.S. 361 (1933)]

(a) Illustration—nonresident motorist statutes [§106]

State statutes typically provide that a nonresident motorist who drives into the state thereby appoints a designated local official (*e.g.,* the local secretary of state) as her agent for accepting service of process in any action arising out of her use of local highways.

1) Constitutionality [§107]

Nonresident motorist statutes have been upheld on the "implied consent" theory. [**Hess v. Pawloski,** 274 U.S. 352 (1927)]

2) Scope of jurisdiction conferred [§108]

The extent of jurisdiction conferred under such a statute depends on its wording, but the statutes tend to be broadly phrased and interpreted.

a) Such statutes usually are interpreted to permit suit *by nonresident* as well as resident plaintiffs—as where the plaintiff and defendant are both merely passing through the state when involved in an accident.

    b)   Suit may also be permitted with respect to accidents on **private property**, rather than public, if the statute is broad enough.

    c)   Some of these statutes purport to subject a **nonresident's executor or administrator** to local jurisdiction in the event of the motorist's death. The Supreme Court has not passed on the validity of such extensions, and lower courts are split thereon.

        1/   Some courts have held such extensions unconstitutional on the ground that no act by an individual can subject her executor to the jurisdiction of a foreign court, or have held that the "appointment" of the local secretary of state terminates upon the nonresident's death. [*See* **Hendrix v. Jenkins,** 120 F. Supp. 879 (M.D. Ga. 1954); 64 Harv. L. Rev. 98 (1950)]

        2/   However, a number of other decisions are contrary, holding that the nonresident's "consent" (albeit fictional) is binding on a personal representative as well. The rationale is that a tortfeasor's death should not affect the power of the forum to grant relief. [**Leighton v. Roper,** 300 N.Y. 434 (1950)]

(b) Requirement of procedural due process [§109]

It is essential that nonresidents being subjected to jurisdiction on an "implied consent" theory be given **reasonable notice** of the proceedings, so that they have an opportunity to appear and defend (*see infra*, §205).

1) Note

In dealing with nonresident motorist statutes, the Supreme Court has held that the **statute itself** must require such notice. Unless it does, there is no jurisdiction even though adequate notice may in fact have been given. [**Wuchter v. Pizzuti,** 276 U.S. 13 (1928)—invalidating nonresident motorist statute that required only service on an official in forum state, even though notice of action in this particular case was served personally on defendant outside state]

(c) Present day analysis—minimum contacts [§110]

Modern courts almost universally discard the "implied consent" fiction and uphold nonresident motorist statutes and similar provisions as a valid exercise of state power **under the "minimum contacts" basis** of jurisdiction (*see* below).

TYPES OF CONSENT		**gilbert**
TYPE	**EXAMPLE**	**SCOPE OF JURISDICTION**
EXPRESS	Contract term (*e.g.,* cognovit)	Limited to terms of consent— strictly construed
IMPLIED	Nonresident motorist statute	Depends on wording of statute—tends to be broadly construed but must be notice and opportunity to appear

d. Minimum contacts with forum ("doing business") [§111]

It is recognized today that a forum state may exercise personal jurisdiction over any nonresident with whom it has such "minimum contacts" that jurisdiction does not offend basic concepts of due process.

(1) Background—problems of jurisdiction over foreign corporations [§112]

Historically, a corporation was subject to personal jurisdiction only in the state in which it was incorporated, because that was the only place in which it was "present." [**Bank of Augusta v. Earle,** 38 U.S. 519 (1839)] As a result, foreign corporations simply were not accountable in other states for wrongs committed there. As might be expected, various legal fictions consequently were developed to justify personal jurisdiction over out-of-state corporations.

(a) Presence of officer [§113]

A few courts held that *service on any officer* of the corporation who was *physically present* in the state was equivalent to service on the corporation, even though the officer may have been merely passing through the state.

(b) Implied consent [§114]

Later, the "implied consent" theory (above) was adopted; *i.e.,* if local statutes conditioned the right of a foreign corporation to do business within the state on its agreeing to submit to jurisdiction of the local courts, any foreign corporation so engaged was deemed to have "impliedly consented" to local jurisdiction. [**Washington v. Superior Court,** *supra,* §105]

(c) Regular business operations [§115]

Still later, courts held that a foreign corporation that maintained *regular business operations* in the state should be deemed "present," and thus subject to personal jurisdiction in that forum. [**Doherty & Co. v. Goodman,** 294 U.S. 623 (1935)]

(2) Modern rule [§116]

The modern view stems from **International Shoe Co. v. Washington,** 326 U.S. 310 (1945), in which the Supreme Court rejected the legal fictions above and held that the only requirement for in personam jurisdiction over a foreign corporation was "certain *minimum contacts*" with the forum state such that maintenance of the suit does not offend *"traditional notions of fair play and substantial justice."*

(a) Impact [§117]

Under *International Shoe*, jurisdiction is no longer measured by fictional "presence" or "consent" of a foreign corporation. Rather, a forum can assert its power as far as permitted by "due process of law."

(b) Extension to partnerships and individuals [§118]

Although the "minimum contacts" doctrine originally evolved with respect to jurisdiction over foreign corporations, the language and rationale of *International Shoe* subsequently has been applied to nonresident *individuals and partnerships* as well (*see supra*, §49).

1) But note

The fact that "minimum contacts" exist between the forum state and a nonresident *partnership* is not by itself enough to justify the forum's asserting jurisdiction over the nonresident partners *individually*. Thus, if a partnership in State A does sufficient business in State B to justify B's exercise of jurisdiction over the partnership, any judgment rendered in B would be enforceable only against assets of the partnership itself and not against the individual (nonpartnership) assets of nonresident partners who were not otherwise subject to jurisdiction in B. [**Lewis Manufacturing Co. v. Superior Court,** 140 Cal. App. 2d 245 (1956)]

(c) Extension to jurisdiction over sister states [§119]

It has also been held that other *states* whose activities within the forum amount to sufficient "minimum contacts" are subject to jurisdiction of forum courts with respect to those activities. And the forum is *not* required to recognize any claim of sovereign immunity from the other state, at least where the injured party is a resident of the forum state. [**Nevada v. Hall,** 440 U.S. 410 (1979)—Nevada held subject to jurisdiction of California courts in suit for injuries caused in California by a Nevada state employee driving a state car on state business]

(3) "Presence" within forum state—general jurisdiction [§120]

"Minimum contacts" clearly exist whenever there are such *continuous and systematic dealings* between the nonresident and the forum state as to justify the conclusion that the nonresident is *"doing business"* locally—in effect, a showing of its *presence* within the state.

(a) Test [§121]

Under this approach, courts are concerned primarily with the *quantity* of "contacts" with the nonresident—*i.e.*, whether it maintained a local office, personnel, assets, bank accounts, warehousing, advertising, telephone listings, etc. Also, whether the nonresident's activities are *continuous* and *systematic*, as opposed to merely sporadic or isolated transactions, is especially important.

(b) Application [§122]

A nonresident who regularly maintains a local business office, or local sales or service representatives, is clearly subject to personal jurisdiction in the forum state. But the "minimum contacts" doctrine extends to other situations as well.

Example: A foreign corporation that maintains no local office or personnel, but has a local independent distributor who performs the functions of a local office (*e.g.*, directing sales, advertising, storing goods) has been held to be "doing business" locally. [**Cosper v. Smith & Wesson Arms Co.,** 53 Cal. 2d 77 (1959)] The fact that the foreign corporation requires all orders to be accepted at its home office is not determinative. [**International Shoe Co. v. Washington,** *supra*]

Example: A foreign corporation operating a television station outside the state but directing its signal to local residents, soliciting business and advertisements from such residents, has been held to be "doing business" locally. [**WASZ, Inc. v. Lyons,** 254 F.2d 242 (6th Cir. 1958)]

(c) Unlimited scope of jurisdiction [§123]

A nonresident defendant whose activities and contacts with the forum state will support the conclusion that she is "doing business" locally is subject to the *general* jurisdiction of the forum state; she can be sued on *any and all transitory causes of action, whether or not related to her local activities*. Like a resident of the forum, she may be held liable for her acts *anywhere*, regardless of the lack of relationship to her local activities. [**Perkins v. Benguet Consolidated Mining Co.,** 342 U.S. 437 (1952); Rest. 2d §47(2)]

Example: A resident of California was permitted to bring an action in California against a nonresident airline company for injuries sustained in a plane crash in England, although the crash was in no way caused by or related to the company's activities (ticket and purchasing offices) in California. [**KLM v. Superior Court,** 107 Cal. App. 2d 495 (1951)]

1) Caution

However, where the cause of action is *not* related to the nonresident's local activities, the courts generally require much *more substantial* "contacts" within the forum state. [**Fisher Governor Co. v. Superior Court,** 53 Cal. 2d 222 (1959)]

(d) Personal jurisdiction as sanction for failure to comply with discovery orders [§124]

Since establishing "minimum contacts" is often a matter of proving facts peculiarly within the knowledge of the defendant, the Supreme Court has held that a defendant who failed to comply with a federal court order to produce documents that might enable plaintiff to prove such contacts would be *deemed to have minimum contacts* for purposes of asserting personal jurisdiction. [**Insurance Corp. of Ireland v. Compagnie Des Bauxites,** 456 U.S. 694 (1982)]

1) Rationale

The Court distinguished subject matter jurisdiction and personal jurisdiction, noting that personal jurisdiction may be waived or conferred by consent (unlike subject matter jurisdiction). Also, a defendant may be estopped from raising an objection to personal jurisdiction.

2) Concurrence

Justice Powell's concurrence stated that plaintiff had made a prima facie showing of minimum contacts necessary to establish personal jurisdiction, and defendant's failure to comply with the discovery order in the face of that showing could be seen as a tacit concession that jurisdiction existed.

(4) "Liability producing act"—limited jurisdiction [§125]

The "minimum contacts" doctrine is not limited to cases in which the nonresident defendant is "present" in the forum state. A state may also assert personal jurisdiction over a nonresident who is not "present" locally if the nonresident has *purposefully* initiated some *liability producing activity* within the forum state. In this case, however, jurisdiction is *limited to suits arising out of such activity*. [**McGee v. International Life Insurance Co.,** 355 U.S. 220 (1957)]

(a) Test [§126]

The basic test is whether, given the nature of defendant's activities, it is *fair to expect her to appear and defend* in the forum state. [**Hanson v. Denckla,** 357 U.S. 235 (1958)] Two elements must be established:

1) Purposeful forum-related activity [§127]

The nonresident defendant must be shown to have purposefully engaged in some activity by which she obtained real benefits from the forum state or otherwise relied on the privileges or protection of its laws.

a) *The quality and nature* of defendant's acts, rather than their number, is the important factor. The question is whether the defendant has intentionally availed herself of benefits, privileges, or protection within the forum state. [**Buckeye Boiler Co. v. Superior Court,** 71 Cal. 2d 893 (1969)]

2) Reasonableness of suit in forum [§128]

Second, it must appear that the forum state is a *fair and reasonable place for trial*. In this regard, the courts consider the same basic factors involved in forum non conveniens (*see infra*, §227):

a) *Hardships to the nonresident defendant* in having to appear and defend herself locally;

b) *Hardships to plaintiff* in having to litigate elsewhere;

c) *Interest of the forum state* in the litigation or in regulating the activities involved. [**McGee v. International Life Insurance Co.,** *supra*]

(b) Application [§129]

Under the above standard, jurisdiction over nonresident defendants may be upheld where the only "contact" with the forum state is the *single, isolated transaction on which the lawsuit is based*.

1) Soliciting insurance outside of state [§130]

A Texas insurance company was held subject to jurisdiction in California because it had sold a policy to (and collected premiums from) a California resident, even though the company was not regularly "doing business" in California and had no "contacts" with that state except for its dealings by mail with the single policyholder who instigated litigation. [**McGee v. International Life Insurance Co.,** *supra*]

a) Rationale

It is sufficient for purposes of due process that a suit is based on a contract that had substantial connection with the forum state. Defendant's use of the mails to send the policy into California and collect the premiums from a resident of that state is a sufficiently purposeful act to avail itself of benefits within the state. [**McGee v. International Life Insurance Co.**, *supra*]

2) Distributing magazines outside of state [§131]

A publisher who distributes magazines in a distant state may be held accountable in that state for damages resulting there from an allegedly defamatory story. [**Keeton v. Hustler Magazine, Inc.**, 465 U.S. 770 (1984)] Similarly, the editor of a magazine and the reporter who wrote an allegedly defamatory story may be held accountable in a state where the magazine's distribution caused damage to the plaintiff. [**Calder v. Jones**, 465 U.S. 783 (1984)]

3) Product liability cases [§132]

Manufacturers of defective products that cause injury may be subject to personal jurisdiction wherever they send their products, even though the defendant manufacturers have no other "contacts" whatever with that forum. [**Duple Motor Bodies, Ltd. v. Hollingsworth**, 417 F.2d 231 (9th Cir. 1969)—English manufacturer sold product knowing it was destined for use in Hawaii; held subject to jurisdiction there for injuries caused by product]

a) Rationale

It is not offensive to "fair play and substantial justice" that manufacturers defend the safety of their products wherever they have placed them, directly or indirectly. [**Duple Motor Bodies, Ltd. v. Hollingsworth**, *supra*]

b) Potential jurisdiction in any state where use foreseeable [§133]

Under this approach, manufacturers may be subject to personal jurisdiction in *any state* in which it is *reasonably foreseeable* that their products will be sold, used, or consumed. It follows that if manufacturers have reason to foresee *nationwide* use of the products, they would be subject to jurisdiction *in every state*. [8 Will. L.J. 54 (1972)]

1/ Exception—liability of retailer or distributor [§134]

The Supreme Court has held that the state in which a plaintiff was injured in an automobile accident could not assert jurisdiction over the nonresident *retailer* who sold the car to plaintiff outside the forum or the nonresident *regional distributor* whose sales were also outside the forum. (Jurisdiction over the manufacturer and importer of the car was not in question.) [**World-Wide Volkswagen Corp. v. Woodson,** 444 U.S. 286 (1980)] The Court stressed that neither the retailer nor the distributor had entered the automobile market in the forum state since neither did any business there, shipped or sold any products there, had any agents for service of process, or advertised in any media calculated to reach customers in that state.

a/ "Foreseeability" not enough [§135]

The majority of the Court in *World-Wide Volkswagen* held that the foreseeability of plaintiff's driving into the forum state was not enough to justify personal jurisdiction under the *International Shoe-Shaffer* standard of due process. The Court noted that the only connection between defendants' conduct and the forum state (Oklahoma) was "the fortuitous circumstance that a single Audi automobile, sold in New York to New York residents, happened to suffer an accident while passing through Oklahoma."

b/ Dissent

Four justices dissented from the majority opinion in *World-Wide Volkswagen* on the basis of defendants' purposeful action in choosing to become part of a nationwide (even global) network for marketing and servicing automobiles and relying on the unique mobility of the automobile as a product.

4) Servicing out-of-state trust beneficiaries [§136]

A Delaware trustee was held not subject to the jurisdiction of a Florida court simply because the creator of the trust had moved his domicile to Florida and the trustee thereafter had mailed distributions to him there. *Rationale:* The defendant trustee had not purposefully initiated a relationship with Florida or done anything to avail itself of the benefits, privileges, or protections of Florida law. It had merely continued to serve a client who had previously lived elsewhere. [**Hanson v. Denckla,** *supra,* §126]

5) Long-distance purchases [§137]

Similarly, where a California seller sought out a New York buyer for its goods, and the buyer had no "contact" with California other than replying by mail and telephone to the seller, the New York buyer was held not subject to jurisdiction in California. *Rationale:* The buyer had not purposefully initiated the transaction in California and would have been unfairly disadvantaged if forced to defend the case far from home. [**Interdyne Co. v. SYS Computer Corp.**, 31 Cal. App. 3d 508 (1973)]

a) Distinguish

The result is unclear where the out-of-state buyer *does* initiate the transaction. Some authorities suggest that an isolated purchase order by mail or telephone to a local seller is still not enough "minimum contact" to satisfy due process, at least where the buyer was located at a great distance and the amount involved was comparatively small so that it might offend "fair play and substantial justice" to require the buyer to appear and defend the suit locally. [**Hamilton Brothers, Inc. v. Peterson**, 445 F.2d 1334 (5th Cir. 1971); *but see* **Parke-Bernet Galleries, Inc. v. Franklyn**, 26 N.Y.2d 13 (1970)—where state court upheld jurisdiction over out-of-state buyer who responded to national advertisement]

6) Noncommercial actions [§138]

A New York father was held not subject to California jurisdiction in a child support case, where the parents' marital domicile was in New York but the wife moved to California with their child after their separation. The Court noted that the father's activities arose from his "personal, domestic" relations rather than from commercial actions and concluded that he had *not received sufficient benefits* from his child's presence in California to make him susceptible to suit in that forum. [**Kulko v. Superior Court**, 436 U.S. 84 (1978)]

7) Limited scope of jurisdiction [§139]

Recall that in every instance, jurisdiction based upon a defendant's liability producing acts is limited to *causes of action arising out of such acts*—i.e., the defendant cannot be sued on other, unrelated causes of action. [**McGee v. International Life Insurance Co.**, *supra*, §125]

 Example: A foreign corporation did not have sufficient contacts with Texas to support in personam jurisdiction over a cause of action (wrongful death) unrelated to those contacts where its only contacts consisted of sending its chief executive officer to Texas for a contract negotiating session, accepting checks in New York drawn on a Texas bank, purchasing goods and services from a Texas corporation, and sending its employees to Texas for training. [**Helicopteros Nacionales de Colombia, S.A. v. Hall,** 466 U.S. 408 (1984)]

a) Distinguish—"presence" within forum [§140]

Where the nonresident defendant's activities are such that he is found to be "present" or "doing business" locally, he can be sued on any and all transitory causes of action, even though unrelated to his activities in the forum state (*see supra*, §120).

b) Act and injury occurring elsewhere [§141]

Where a continuous presence is not shown, jurisdiction is usually limited to causes of action arising out of defendant's act within the forum state. Normally, this means that both defendant's act and the injury to plaintiff must have occurred within the forum state. But some cases have upheld jurisdiction even where the accident and injury occurred outside the state—as long as a *"substantial nexus" to the defendant's forum related activities* was shown. [**Cornelison v. Chaney,** 16 Cal. 3d 143 (1976)]

> **Example:** In *Cornelison, supra,* a California court was held to have jurisdiction over a nonresident trucker in an action stemming from a traffic accident in Nevada while the truck was en route to California. The defendant trucker's occasional runs to and from California were not sufficient to constitute "doing business" in the state (so there was no jurisdiction as to unrelated causes of action). However, such runs were held to be a "purposeful, forum-related activity" supporting jurisdiction as to any cause of action which bore a "substantial nexus" to the activity. The court found this "nexus" in the fact that, although the accident occurred in Nevada, the defendant was en route to California at the time, and driving a truck into the state was the forum-related activity upon which jurisdiction was founded.

e. "Long arm" statutes [§142]

The "minimum contacts" doctrine recognizes that each state has the power to

"MINIMUM CONTACTS" SUFFICIENT FOR JURISDICTION

BASES OF "MINIMUM CONTACTS"

"PRESENCE" (DOING BUSINESS) IN FORUM

Test: *Quantity of contacts* + *Nature of contacts*

such as: Must be *continuous and*
- Office in forum   *systematic,* not sporadic or
- Personnel in forum   isolated
- Other assets in
  forum
- Bank accounts in
  forum
- Advertising
  directed to forum

Result: *General Jurisdiction*—court has personal jurisdiction over defendant for *any and all causes of action*

LIABILITY PRODUCING ACTIVITY IN FORUM

Test: *Purposeful forum-* + *Forum fair & reasonable place*
related activity   *for trial*

Quality and nature of   Consider:
contacts important, not   - Hardship to nonresident to
number (single contact   appear and defend
may be sufficient)
           - Hardship to plaintiff to litigate
Defendant must have   elsewhere
intentionally availed
herself of benefits,   - Interest of forum in litigation or
privileges, or protection   activities
of forum

Result: *Limited Jurisdiction*—personal jurisdiction limited to suits *arising out of liability producing activity* in forum

assert personal jurisdiction over nonresidents in suits *arising out of their forum-related activities*, as long as maintenance of the suit does not offend "traditional standards of fair play and substantial justice." On the state level, this doctrine has been implemented by the enactment of "long arm" statutes which permit the state to exercise jurisdiction over nonresidents.

(1) Statute necessary [§143]

A state court has no inherent power over residents of other states. Thus, unless a long arm statute of some type has been enacted by the legislature, local courts cannot exercise personal jurisdiction over a nonresident regardless of the activities or "contacts" that may be present.

(2) "Specific acts" long arm statute [§144]

The original Illinois long arm statute, enacted in 1956, is the most common form of long arm statute. This type of statute enumerates various *specific acts* or criteria which, if committed in the state, will submit the actor to state jurisdiction with respect to any cause of action arising from the act. [*See* former Ill. Rev. Stat. ch. 110, ¶2-209]

(a) Distinguish—California-type statute [§145]

The 1970 California long arm statute does not enumerate specific acts, but authorizes courts of that state to exercise jurisdiction *on any basis permitted under the Constitution*—so that the Due Process Clause is the only limitation (*see supra*, §§70 *et seq.*).

(b) Distinguish—current Illinois statute [§146]

The current Illinois long arm statute combines both types of statutes. It enumerates specific acts or criteria and provides a final "catch-all" clause that authorizes jurisdiction in any other case as long as it is constitutional under federal or state law. [*See* 735 ILCS 5/2-209]

(3) Analysis [§147]

Where a "specific acts" statute is in effect, a two-step analysis is required:

(i) *Does the statute apply?* First, it must appear that the statute—by its terms or by reasonable construction—was meant to confer jurisdiction on local courts with respect to the kind of transaction involved in the present litigation. (This is a problem of statutory interpretation.)

(ii) *Is it constitutional?* Assuming that the statute applies, one must then determine whether such application is consistent with the "minimum contacts" doctrine; *i.e.*, would maintenance of the suit be consistent with "traditional standards of fair play and substantial justice"?

APPROACH TO LONG ARM STATUTES

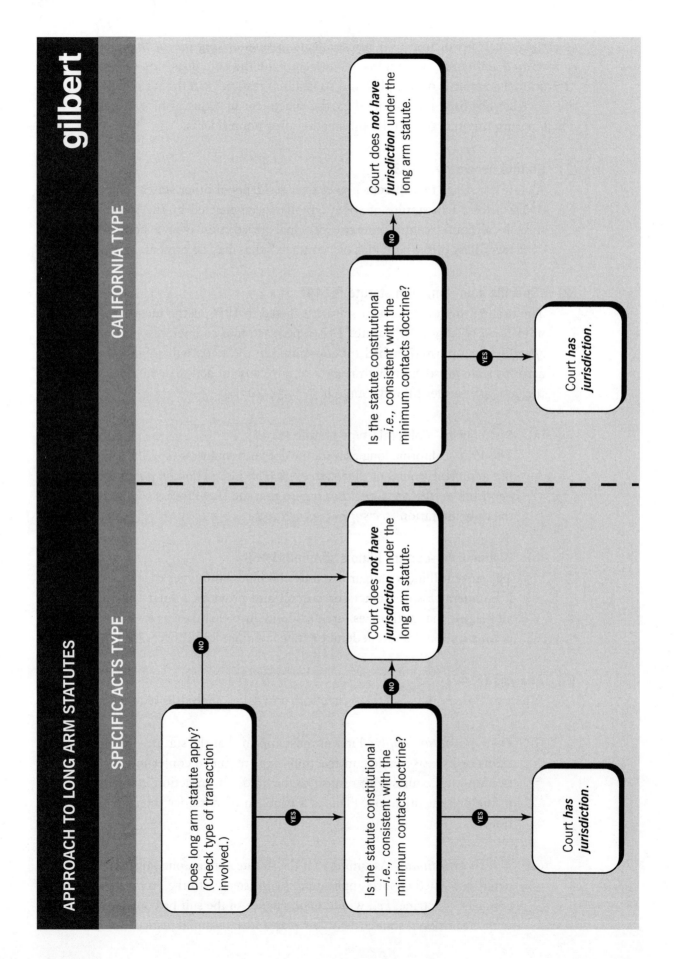

SPECIFIC ACTS TYPE

Does long arm statute apply? (Check type of transaction involved.)

→ **YES** → Is the statute constitutional —*i.e.*, consistent with the minimum contacts doctrine?

→ **NO** → Court does *not have jurisdiction* under the long arm statute.

→ **NO** → Court does *not have jurisdiction* under the long arm statute.

→ **YES** → Court *has jurisdiction.*

CALIFORNIA TYPE

Is the statute constitutional —*i.e.*, consistent with the minimum contacts doctrine?

→ **NO** → Court does *not have jurisdiction* under the long arm statute.

→ **YES** → Court *has jurisdiction.*

(a) **Distinguish—analysis under California-type statute [§148]**

The California-type statute merges these two questions. By conferring jurisdiction upon its courts that is as broad as the Due Process Clause, the statute presents only the constitutional "minimum contacts" issue.

(4) **Common statutory provisions [§149]**

While "specific acts" long arm statutes vary as to the acts upon which personal jurisdiction may be asserted, the provisions discussed below are typically included in such statutes. (The Supreme Court has not yet imposed any constitutional standard beyond the "purposeful, forum-related activity" requirement in **Hanson v. Denckla,** *supra,* §126.)

(a) **Transaction of any business within the state [§150]**

Several state long arm statutes authorize local courts to exercise personal jurisdiction over a nonresident (individual, partnership, or corporation) who *"transacts any business* within this state." [*See* N.Y. Civ. Prac. Law §302(a)(1); 735 ILCS 5/2-209(a)(1)]

1) **"Transaction of any business" [§151]**

It seems to be generally agreed that the phrase "transaction of any business" is intended to be broader than the old "doing business" terminology (*supra,* §§120–123). Thus, for example, jurisdiction can be asserted against a nonresident on the basis of a *single transaction* rather than requiring continuing business activities (or "presence") in the forum state. [**United States v. Montreal Trust Co.,** 358 F.2d 239 (2d Cir. 1966)]

2) **"Within forum state"**

a) **Restrictive view [§152]**

Some courts have taken a restrictive view of what constitutes the transaction of business "within" the forum state, requiring that the nonresident defendant or his agents perform some business act while physically present within the state. [**Gobark v. Addo Machine Co.,** 158 N.E.2d 73 (Ill. 1959)—sale of machine by New York defendant to Illinois plaintiff held not to be transaction of business "within" Illinois because sale concluded entirely by mail]

b) **Broad view [§153]**

Reflecting an awareness of the full reach of due process under the *Hanson* and *McGee* decisions, other courts have adopted a broader view as to what constitutes business done "within" the state. For example, a California resident was held subject to the personal jurisdiction of a

New York court where he had submitted a telephone bid (from California) on paintings being sold at an art auction in New York City. This was considered a sufficient "purposeful activity" in New York under the "transaction of any business" section of the New York long arm statute. [**Parke-Bernet Galleries, Inc. v. Franklyn**, *supra*, §137]

(b) "Commission of a tortious act within the state" [§154]

A number of statutes subject a nonresident (individual or corporation) to the personal jurisdiction of local courts with respect to suits arising out of the "*commission of any tortious act* within the state." Such jurisdiction is grounded in the state's police power to control tortious conduct within its borders. [*See, e.g.,* 735 ILCS 5/2-209(a)(2); N.Y. Civ. Prac. Law §302(a)(2); 24 A.L.R.3d 532] Statutes of this type are little more than extensions of nonresident motorist statutes (*see supra*, §§106-110), without the fiction of "implied consent."

1) "Tortious act" [§155]

To establish jurisdiction under these statutes, it is enough that the defendant is *alleged* (not proved) to have committed a tortious act within the state. Otherwise, the defendant's liability would have to be litigated twice—first on the jurisdictional issue and again later on the merits. [**Nelson v. Miller**, 143 N.E.2d 673 (Ill. 1957)]

2) "Within the state" [§156]

The phrase "within the state" can create problems of statutory construction. Since a "tortious act" requires both an act by the defendant and injury to the plaintiff, does the statute apply where the defendant's act takes place outside the state but causes injury to the plaintiff within the state?

a) "Physical presence" theory [§157]

Some courts have interpreted the statute as requiring *both* the defendant's act and the plaintiff's injury to take place within the state. Under this construction, there would be no long arm jurisdiction where the defendant commits a tortious act outside the state causing injury to a plaintiff within the state—as when a nonresident manufacturer ships negligently produced goods into the state, where they cause injury to the plaintiff. [**Erlanger Mills, Inc. v. Cohaes Fibre Mills, Inc.**, 239 F.2d 502 (4th Cir. 1956); **Feathers v. McLucas**, 15 N.Y.2d 443 (1965)]

1/ And note

Under this view, long arm jurisdiction would also be lacking where the defendant acted within the state but the injury took place outside the forum state. [*See* 19 A.L.R.3d 65]

b) "Place of effect" theory [§158]

Other courts faced with this situation have adopted a "place of effect" theory—*i.e.*, that a tortfeasor must be *deemed "present"* wherever the act causes injury. This permits jurisdiction over nonresidents who never physically enter the state but whose acts or products cause injuries therein. [**Gray v. American Radiator & Standard Sanitary Corp.,** 176 N.E.2d 761 (Ill. 1961)—Ohio corporation that manufactured safety valve attached to heater in Pennsylvania was held subject to jurisdiction in Illinois where the heater exploded, injuring plaintiff]

1/ Rationale

The manufacturer of a product puts it in the "stream of commerce"; thus, it is reasonably foreseeable that the product will be used (and may cause harm) elsewhere. Thus, the manufacturer can be held liable anywhere in the "stream." [**Metal-Matic Inc. v. Eighth Judicial District Court,** 415 P.2d 617 (Nev. 1966)]

Example: Following this approach, a nonresident who sends fraudulent statements into the forum state by mail or telephone may be held liable for damages resulting from a recipient's reliance within the state on the statements. [**Murphy v. Erwin-Wasey Inc.,** 460 F.2d 661 (1st Cir. 1972)]

c) Criticism [§159]

Neither the "physical presence" nor the "place of effect" theory is entirely satisfactory. Requiring "presence" has the obvious shortcoming of not reaching an actor who purposefully causes injury in the forum state but remains at all times outside the state. And requiring injury within the state ("place of effect") allows an actor to escape jurisdiction in the state where he acted, if the injury occurred elsewhere.

1/ Note

Because of these shortcomings, some "long arm" statutes have been amended to extend jurisdiction if *either* the act or the injury takes place in the forum state. For example, section 302(a)(3) of the New York Civil Practice Law & Rules authorizes New York courts to exercise personal jurisdiction if the defendant had caused an injury within the state resulting entirely from his acts outside the state, at least where the defendant is regularly engaged in interstate commerce.

d) Broader interpretation constitutionally permissible [§160]
Nothing in the Constitution requires the narrow interpretation that some courts have given to the above statutory provisions; *i.e.*, due process is satisfied as long as the exercise of jurisdiction does not offend "traditional notions of fair play and substantial justice." This probably allows jurisdiction where a nonresident purposefully acted to cause the injuries involved *or* where he intended or should have foreseen that his acts would cause injury (*see supra*, §§133-134).

1/ Application
Among other things, this interpretation would reach the manufacturer who sends a defective product into the forum state as part of a nationwide distribution—even if the actual injury resulted from use of the product outside the state as where, *e.g.*, Plaintiff buys Manufacturer's product in forum state, but uses it while on vacation trip elsewhere.

e) First Amendment limitation on jurisdictional analysis rejected [§161]
First Amendment concerns do not receive special considerations in cases involving jurisdiction over nonresident journalists or editors in a libel action. The First Amendment protections are present in the constitutional limitations on the substantive (libel) law applicable in such suits (*i.e.*, the requirement of proof of actual malice [*see* **New York Times, Inc. v. Sullivan,** 376 U.S. 254 (1964)]), and need not be taken into account in the "already imprecise inquiry" about jurisdiction [**Calder v. Jones,** *supra,* §131].

(c) "Ownership of property situated within the state" [§162]
Mere ownership of local property is *not* a sufficient basis to subject a nonresident to personal jurisdiction in matters **unrelated to that property.** [*See* **Shaffer v. Heitner,** *supra,* §64] However, a state may confer jurisdiction over nonresidents as to *causes of action arising*

from the "ownership, use, or possession of property within the state." [*See, e.g.*, Mass. Gen. Laws ch. 223A, §3(e)]

1) Application [§163]

Such statutes have been upheld in the case of injuries to local residents arising out of the improper operation or maintenance of local property by nonresident owners. [*See* **Dubin v. City of Philadelphia**, 34 Pa. D. & C. 61 (1938)]

a) And note

Some courts have approved jurisdiction over a nonresident property owner sued for breach of a contract relating to use or development of the property. [**deLeo v. Childs**, 304 F. Supp. 593 (D. Mass. 1969)—architect entitled to maintain suit locally against nonresident owner for breach of contract regarding design and construction of improvements on local property]

(d) "Matrimonial domicile in the state" (regarding domestic relations actions) [§164]

Several states have laws authorizing personal jurisdiction based on *"maintenance of a matrimonial domicile"* in the state if the action is for divorce or separate maintenance. [*See, e.g.*, 735 ILCS 5/2-209(a)(5)]

1) Purpose [§165]

Under such provisions, an abandoned spouse can obtain personal jurisdiction over the other spouse where they last lived together—instead of having to resort to tracking down the absent spouse and bringing suit where that spouse is ultimately located. This is vitally important because personal jurisdiction over the absent spouse is usually required for spousal support, property, and child custody awards (*see infra*, §§874-880).

(e) "Breach of contract" [§166]

A statute that purports to subject nonresidents to personal jurisdiction in local courts on causes of action arising from contracts "entered into or to be performed within the state" *might be too broad.*

1) Limitation [§167]

The validity of such statutes depends upon constitutionally *sufficient "minimum contacts"* within the forum state. A contract may be technically "made" or "entered into" where the offeree mails acceptance. However, if the offeree was merely passing through the state at the time, this is probably not a constitutionally sufficient "contact" for personal jurisdiction in actions arising under the contract; *i.e.*, it would suffer from the same infirmities as the transient rule (*see supra*, §75).

2) Note

Perhaps for this reason, most states subsume "breach of contract" actions under the general "transaction of business" category for long arm jurisdiction (*see supra*, §150).

3) Application—specific statute upheld as long as minimum contacts

A Florida corporation entered into a franchise agreement with two Michigan residents who allegedly breached the agreement by failing to make required payments in Florida. The Court held that there was jurisdiction over the Michigan defendants under the Florida long arm statute, which conferred jurisdiction over any person who "breaches a contract in this state by failing to perform acts required by the contract to be performed in this state" if the cause of action arose from the alleged breach. The Court stressed however that the contract alone would not have been sufficient to confer jurisdiction. The accompanying negotiations that led to the contract, the parties' contemplated future dealings resulting from the contract, the existence of a choice-of-law clause in the contract specifying the application of Florida law to govern the agreement, and the parties' actual course of conduct, taken together, were the factors that made up the minimum contacts necessary to afford due process to the defendants. [**Burger King Corp. v. Rudzewicz,** 471 U.S. 462 (1985)]

(f) "Liability producing act" [§168]

A few statutes have simply granted local courts personal jurisdiction over nonresidents who *cause injury to occur* within the state.

EXAMPLES OF COMMON "SPECIFIC ACTS" PROVISIONS IN LONG ARM STATUTES — gilbert

THE FOLLOWING SPECIFIC ACTS ARE OFTEN BASES FOR CONFERRING PERSONAL JURISDICTION UNDER A STATE'S LONG ARM STATUTE:

☑ *Transaction of business* within state (*Note:* This is broader than "doing business within state" basis)

☑ *Commission of tortious act* within state

☑ *Ownership of property* situated within state for actions involving *ownership, use, or possession of property*

☑ In actions for divorce or separate maintenance, *having a matrimonial domicile* in state

☑ *Breach of contract* if sufficient minimum contacts with state

☑ *Causing liability-producing injury* in the state

(g) "Due process" as only limitation [§169]

As noted previously, the California long arm statute authorizes jurisdiction "on any basis not inconsistent with the Constitution of this state or of the United States." [Cal. Civ. Proc. Code §410.10] The statute makes no distinction among types of in personam actions, or among actions in personam, in rem, or quasi in rem.

Example: A Nebraska trucker has been held subject to personal jurisdiction in California in an action arising out of a traffic accident in Nevada. Since the trucker made occasional trips to and from California (purposeful forum-related activities) and was en route to California at the time the accident occurred, jurisdiction was held to be consistent with due process. [**Cornelison v. Chaney,** *supra*, §141]

---

1) Possible adverse effects [§170]

While the broad constitutional standard in the California statute avoids the interpretative problems of more specific statutes in the "specific acts" mold, it also creates considerable uncertainty as to the scope of jurisdiction conferred. Guidelines must be worked out on a case-by-case basis, and the statute may validate grounds for jurisdiction not presently conceived or contemplated. [79 Harv. L. Rev. 1121 (1965)]

EXAM TIP	gilbert

When addressing issues of personal jurisdiction, it is safe to follow the rationale that courts will find personal jurisdiction wherever they can as long as the defendant has the *requisite contacts* to make such a finding reasonable and as long as the constitutional requirements of *notice and opportunity to be heard* are met.

2. Bases for Jurisdiction In Rem and Quasi In Rem [§171]

As was discussed *supra*, §§55-64, in rem and quasi in rem jurisdiction concern a court's power to affect title or rights in specific property within the state where personal jurisdiction over the owner is *not* obtained.

a. Former rule [§172]

Until recently, the only thing required for the exercise of jurisdiction in rem and quasi in rem was power over the "res." As long as the property in question was located within the forum state, the court could adjudicate all claims with respect thereto, and personal jurisdiction over the nonresident claimants was not required (*see supra*, §55).

(1) Rationale

The state was deemed to provide protection (police, fire, etc.) for all property within its borders and thus had the reciprocal sovereign power to control the ownership of such property. Whether the owner was subject to the court's personal jurisdiction, or even whether the action was related to the local property, was immaterial.

b. Modern rule—"minimum contacts" required [§173]

Under the present Supreme Court rule, however, the same basis for jurisdiction is required for in rem, quasi in rem, and in personam actions—*i.e.*, the *International Shoe* standard of minimum contacts. [**Shaffer v. Heitner,** *supra,* §49]

(1) Rationale

Regardless of its label ("in rem" or "quasi in rem"), a proceeding involving property is really a proceeding against persons—since an adverse judgment affects the owner of the property by divesting her of rights therein. Therefore, to justify its exercise of jurisdiction, the court must have a basis for asserting power over the interests of persons in that property. [**Shaffer v. Heitner,** *supra*]

(2) Actions unrelated to local res [§174]

It follows that the mere presence of a res within the forum state, absent other contacts, is *not a sufficient basis* for exercising jurisdiction in actions *unrelated* to the property. Accordingly, the former concept of quasi in rem jurisdiction based on the seizure of a nonresident's local property to adjudicate some unrelated personal claim is no longer viable. [**Shaffer v. Heitner,** *supra*—majority applied minimum contacts standard and found insufficient nexus between corporate officers and directors, their ownership of corporate shares, and the fictional situs of those shares in Delaware to justify the Delaware court's assertion of jurisdiction over derivative suit brought by plaintiff]

(a) Note

The majority in *Shaffer* expressly reserved for future consideration those cases in which no other forum is available to the plaintiff.

(b) Exception—maritime attachment cases [§175]

Shaffer did not affect traditional quasi in rem jurisdiction in admiralty cases. The rationale is that quasi in rem jurisdiction is particularly important here, since disputes often involve persons absent from their homes for long periods of time with assets located away from home. [**Grand Bahama Petroleum Co. v. Canadian Transportation Agencies, Ltd.,** 450 F. Supp. 447 (W.D. Wash. 1978); **Amoco Overseas Oil Co. v. Compagnie Nationale,** 459 F. Supp. 1242 (S.D.N.Y. 1978)]

(3) Actions related to local res [§176]

On the other hand, where the action in question *relates to the local property,* mere presence of the res within the state should generally satisfy the "minimum contacts" standard, and *permit* in rem or quasi in rem jurisdiction. In most disputes involving title to or possession of some local res, local courts can probably adjudicate the issues without personal jurisdiction over nonresident owners or claimants. (Actions to affect title of particular claimants (*supra*, §§58-61) and actions arising from the ownership or use of property (*supra*, §§62-63) are both categorized as "actions related to the local res.")

(a) Rationale

The benefits and protections furnished by the state to property within its borders justify local court jurisdiction in disputes involving title or possession to such property. Among other things, this operates to assure marketable title to local property and is an effective procedure to resolve disputes in a forum where important records and witnesses are likely to be located. [**Shaffer v. Heitner**, *supra*]

(b) Procedural safeguards required [§177]

Even though the court need not have personal jurisdiction over the nonresident defendants in such cases, each defendant must still be given *adequate notice and opportunity to be heard* (see *infra*, §206).

1) Hearing before seizure? [§178]

The Supreme Court has intimated that "proper procedures" must be complied with *before* any seizure of property can serve as the basis for in rem or quasi in rem jurisdiction. Exactly what procedures are constitutionally required is still an open question, but *some notice* of the proceedings prior to seizure, plus a *judicial hearing* in which the claimant establishes at least a probability of eventual recovery, would appear to be required. [*See* **Shaffer v. Heitner**, *supra*, §49—citing cases that invoke such safeguards in seizure of a debtor's assets such as **Sniadach v. Family Finance Corp.**, 395 U.S. 337 (1969)]

(4) Attachment of local assets to secure potential judgment elsewhere [§179]

While a nonresident's ownership of local assets is not enough to confer jurisdiction to adjudicate claims against her unrelated to those assets, local courts apparently can still order attachment of those assets *as security* for a judgment being sought in a forum where she *is* subject to personal jurisdiction.

(a) Rationale

If this were not the case, a wrongdoer who had all assets in one state but was not subject to personal jurisdiction there could frustrate attempts to collect any judgment against her.

(b) Result

In such cases, therefore, courts of the state in which the property is located can assume jurisdiction for the limited purpose of issuing an attachment pending the outcome of litigation in the other state. [**Carolina Power & Light Co. v. Uranex,** 451 F. Supp. 1044 (N.D. Cal. 1977)]

EXAM TIP   **gilbert**

If faced with a question involving the issue of jurisdiction over a nonresident defendant in an in rem or quasi in rem action, look first at whether the *action is related to the property located in the forum state*. If the action is related to the property, then the minimum contacts standard is satisfied, and personal jurisdiction over the defendant *probably* is not required. But if the action is unrelated to the property, then the court needs *personal* jurisdiction over the defendant. However, don't forget that even if a court doesn't have personal jurisdiction over the defendant, the court can still order attachment of that unrelated property *to serve as security* for a judgment obtained in the forum that *did* have personal jurisdiction over the defendant.

---

c. Special problems with intangible property [§180]

There is often a problem in determining the "situs" of intangible rights or property for purposes of in rem or quasi in rem jurisdiction. It must be shown that the claim in question is sufficiently grounded within the forum state so that jurisdiction is proper.

(1) Intangible rights attached to document [§181]

Where intangible rights are connected with a document or other tangible asset, the situs of the document or asset may determine the situs of the intangibles.

(a) Document embodying intangible rights [§182]

Where a document embodies all intangible rights or claims connected therewith as a matter of law, a court having jurisdiction over the document traditionally has had power over all such intangible rights as well.

---

e.g. **Example—negotiable instruments:** Negotiable instruments are the best example. As a matter of law, all rights and claims are merged in the instrument (*see* Commercial Paper & Payment Law Summary). Thus, a court having jurisdiction over a negotiable promissory note or check has been able to determine all rights therein even if the instrument is made payable in another state and all parties to the instrument are nonresidents. [Rest. 2d §363]

---

e.g. **Example—stock certificates:** Stock certificates are another example. Under the law of most states, ownership of a stock certificate is equivalent to ownership of the shares represented thereby.

Hence, if the certificate is before the court, the court can adjudicate any dispute relative to the shares even though the corporation and all parties to the dispute are nonresidents not subject to personal jurisdiction locally. [**Cities Service Co. v. McGrath,** 342 U.S. 330 (1952)]

1) Impact of *Shaffer* [§183]
Note that the results above may be different today as a result of the decision in **Shaffer v. Heitner,** *supra*.

(b) Intangibles not embodied in document [§184]
Where the document or tangible chattel does not embody all intangible rights connected therewith, mere jurisdiction over the chattel is not necessarily a sufficient basis for jurisdiction over the intangible rights associated with it; *i.e.*, other "contacts" with the forum state would have to be shown.

Example—passbook: A savings account passbook does not embody ownership of the account. Thus, the mere fact that a court has jurisdiction over the passbook would not in itself give the court power to determine ownership of a bank account located in another state in an action involving nonresident claimants.

(2) Purely intangible rights [§185]
Jurisdiction over purely intangible interests (*e.g.*, unsecured debt, contract claim) has been the subject of considerable controversy. The issue is whether jurisdiction over the debtor is enough by itself to give a court jurisdiction over the debt—particularly where conflicting claims are being made by nonresident claimants.

Example: Suppose Debtor owes Creditor $5,000. Debtor lives in California and Creditor lives in New York. Creditor assigns the debt to Stranger as security for some separate obligation. A dispute later arises between Creditor and Stranger, and the question is to whom Debtor must pay the $5,000. Creditor goes to California (Debtor's residence) and has a writ of garnishment served on Debtor. Can the California court decide whether Creditor or Stranger is entitled to the money without personal jurisdiction over Stranger—*i.e.*, can it exercise quasi in rem jurisdiction?

(a) Earlier rule [§186]
A number of earlier decisions held that the "situs of the debt follows the debtor," so that as long as the debtor was served with process locally (writ of garnishment or sequestration), the local court

would have in rem jurisdiction as to the debt. The court could then examine *all* rights and liabilities related to the debt and decide who owed what to whom—without personal jurisdiction over the creditor or other claimants. [*See* **Harris v. Balk,** 198 U.S. 215 (1905)]

(b) Modern rule [§187]

However, this can no longer be the law, since it would violate "traditional standards of fair play and substantial justice" for a court to cut off or affect the rights of nonresident claimants over whom it has no personal jurisdiction (*i.e.,* who have no other contact with the forum state). Jurisdiction over the debtor, *without more*, cannot be regarded as sufficient for due process purposes. [*See* **Shaffer v. Heitner,** *supra*, §49]

1) Distinguish—sufficient contacts [§188]

But this does not mean that personal jurisdiction over all claimants is required in such matters; *other "contacts" may be sufficient*. For example, a local musicians' union was engaged in a contract dispute with the national union over control of pension funds paid by local employers. A California court held that garnishment of those funds was a sufficient basis for jurisdiction to adjudicate the conflicting claims, even though the national union was not subject to personal jurisdiction in California. In light of the "totality of contacts" (the contract, the employees, the services rendered), maintenance of suit locally was held to be consistent with "traditional standards of fair play and substantial justice." [**Atkinson v. Superior Court,** 49 Cal. 2d 338 (1957)]

(c) Debtor protected against double liability [§189]

As long as the court has an adequate basis for quasi in rem jurisdiction, its decree is effective by itself to establish title to the debt and extinguish all conflicting claims. Once the debtor pays the debt in accordance with the decree, she is thus protected against further liability. If she is sued later by one of the claimants in another state, the judgment is a good defense. [Rest. 2d §68, comment d]

(3) Liability insurance policy as basis for jurisdiction—New York rule [§190]

For many years, New York courts, largely alone, allowed local plaintiffs to sue nonresident defendants if the nonresident's liability insurance carrier was doing business in New York. The theory was that the insurance carrier's contractual duty to defend the nonresident was a "debt" owing to the nonresident, which was sufficient property for exercise of quasi in rem jurisdiction. [**Seider v. Roth,** 17 N.Y.2d 111 (1966)]

> **Example:** While traveling in Vermont, Paulie, a resident of New York, is involved in an auto accident with Danielle, a Canadian citizen. Danielle is insured by XYZ Insurance Co., which has its principal office in Connecticut but is also "doing business" in New York. Paulie can file a personal injury action against Danielle in New York. Even if he cannot get personal jurisdiction over Danielle, he can attach XYZ's contractual obligation to defend Danielle.

(a) Limitations [§191]

Without real explanation, the New York courts held that only local plaintiffs could invoke this rule; *i.e.*, nonresidents could not sue. Also, any judgment obtained was limited to the face amount of the defendant's insurance; he was not personally liable for any excess. [**Minichiello v. Rosenberg**, 410 F.2d 106 (2d Cir. 1969); **Farrell v. Piedmont Aviation, Inc.**, 411 F.2d 812 (2d Cir. 1969)]

(b) Criticism [§192]

The New York rule was sharply criticized on the ground that the insurer's obligation to defend under the policy was at most a *contingent* liability (*i.e.*, **if** the defendant is served and sued **and if** he is held liable, the insurer must pay the judgment). As such, it is illogical to claim that this liability (debt) arose prior to the time suit was filed, or that it had a "situs" in every state where the insurer was doing business.

(c) Unconstitutionality [§193]

In **Rush v. Savchuk**, 444 U.S. 320 (1980), the United States Supreme Court held that a state could not obtain jurisdiction over a nonresident defendant based on the presence within the state of his insurer.

1) Impact of *Shaffer* [§194]

The Court in *Rush* reasoned that since *Shaffer* overruled **Harris v. Balk**, *supra*, §186, it undercut the foundation for *Seider* and the New York rule. Moreover, the court insisted that the *insured*, not the insurer, was the true defendant in *Seider* cases. Hence, the contacts between the insured and the forum state must be examined. In *Rush* and in most *Seider*-type cases, there were no contacts between the insured and the forum state except for the presence of the insurer. That sole contact was held insufficient to meet the *International Shoe* test.

2) Direct action rationale [§195]

The court in *Rush* also rejected the rationale for *Seider* advanced in *Minichiello*, *supra*—*i.e.*, that it was a direct action suit against the insurer, bypassing the necessity for a prior judgment against the insured. The Court reasoned that jurisdiction over the out-of-state insured was a prerequisite to suing the insurer.

(d) Necessity of contacts with defendant [§196]

The Court pointed out that the *Seider* cases stressed the forum's interest in hearing the case of its resident plaintiff (*see supra*, §190). But under *International Shoe*, it is the contacts between defendant and the forum that are critical. If those contacts are absent, due process is violated.

D. Competent Court

1. In General [§197]

The second essential requirement for judicial jurisdiction (besides a sufficient basis for jurisdiction) is that the court in which the action is brought be **competent**; *i.e.*, it must have authority under the appropriate statutes of the forum state to exercise jurisdiction in the particular kind of case. While an adequate basis for jurisdiction (*supra*) and procedural due process (*infra*) are constitutional in nature, competency is primarily a question of **statutory law**—*i.e.*, whether the sovereign that created the court has empowered it to hear and determine this dispute.

2. Jurisdiction Over Parties and Subject Matter [§198]

The state must have conferred on the particular court the **authority to enter a judgment** binding the **parties** who are before it with respect to the **kind of action** sued upon (subject matter of the suit).

a. Parties [§199]

There is rarely a problem of competence where the parties are local residents or have been served in the state. Where nonresidents are involved, however, it must be shown that the state has conferred jurisdiction on its courts to render a personal judgment against the nonresident—*e.g.*, through a long arm statute (*see supra*, §142).

b. Subject matter [§200]

Judicial power usually is distributed among various courts or classes of courts in the state. Thus, municipal or inferior courts may have power only to hear cases involving certain monetary amounts, *e.g.*, up to $5,000, or matters involving title to land may have to be litigated in chancery or probate courts.

(1) Federal courts [§201]

Federal courts are empowered to exercise either "federal question" jurisdiction or, provided the amount in controversy exceeds $75,000, "diversity of citizenship" jurisdiction. (*See* Federal Courts or Civil Procedure Summary.)

c. **Venue [§202]**

In certain instances, venue may affect the competence of the court. Where the action involves real property, venue generally is proper only in the county in which the land is located. If the action were filed in any other county of the state, the court would be incompetent to hear the action (and in this situation venue is said to be "jurisdictional"). (*See* Civil Procedure Summary.)

3. **Standards for Determining Competence [§203]**

The competency of a court is judged strictly by the standards in effect in the forum state. If competent under such standards (and the other two jurisdictional requirements of jurisdiction over the subject matter and over the parties are met), its judgment will be entitled to full faith and credit in other states—regardless of its competency under the standards of any other state.

Example: If F1 statutes authorize its justice courts to enter judgments up to $5,000, an F1 justice court judgment in that amount cannot be attacked in F2 on the grounds that justice courts in F2 are not competent to render judgments of that size.

a. **Effect of findings regarding competence [§204]**

However, F1's findings of fact as to its own competency are not conclusive. Its competency can always be challenged on collateral attack in F2 by showing that the F1 court in reality was not a competent court *according to F1's* own standards.

Example: In **Thompson v. Whitman**, 85 U.S. 457 (1873), the F1 court made a finding of fact that a certain ship was located in F1's territorial waters and accordingly held that there was proper jurisdiction. Collateral attack in F2 was allowed to show that the ship was actually in different waters and that the F1 court was not competent under its own standards.

(1) **Limitation**

Note that collateral attack in F2 on F1's findings of jurisdictional facts is allowed *only where the defendant did not appear* in the F1 proceedings. Otherwise, F1's findings may be res judicata—whether the jurisdiction issue was raised or not (*see infra*, §§804-805).

E. Notice and Opportunity to Be Heard—"Procedural Due Process"

1. **In General [§205]**

In addition to a sufficient basis for jurisdiction and a competent court, due process of law requires that reasonable steps be taken in each case to give the defendant *actual notice* of the proceedings and a *fair opportunity to appear* and defend.

2. Service of Process [§206]

Various types of service may be available for giving notice to the defendant. The problem is to decide which type of service is constitutionally sufficient in a given case:

(i) *Personal service*—pleadings delivered to the defendant personally;

(ii) *Substituted service*—in accordance with a statute or court rule, pleadings mailed to the defendant at her home (usually requiring some return receipt) or delivered to her home and left with a person of suitable age; or

(iii) *Constructive service*—notice of the proceedings published in a local newspaper or posted in the community.

The Supreme Court has enunciated the broad guidelines that service must be of a type "reasonably calculated" to give defendant the requisite *notice and opportunity to appear.* [**Mullane v. Central Hanover Bank & Trust Co.,** 339 U.S. 306 (1950)]

3. Defendants Within the State [§207]

Where the defendant is physically present in the state, and her whereabouts are known, *personal service* is normally required, but other methods reasonably calculated to give notice may be allowed under certain circumstances if authorized by statute or court rule.

a. Note

Merely leaving a copy of the summons at the defendant's home or place of business is generally not enough since this runs the risk that the defendant may never see it. [**Womble v. Commercial Credit Corp.,** 203 S.E.2d 204 (Ga. 1974)] And where there was testimony that children in a public housing project occasionally tore down notices of forcible entry and detainer actions posted on the doors of apartments, failure to use additional means of notice, such as the mails, was held to violate due process. [**Greene v. Lindsey,** 456 U.S. 444 (1982)]

b. But note

However, such methods are permissible where it is shown that defendant has been concealing herself or evading service.

4. Nonresident Defendants [§208]

Where the defendant is not present within the state, the type of service required depends upon practical considerations—*i.e.,* what method is most likely to bring the matter to the defendant's attention so that she would have notice and an opportunity to appear and defend.

a. Whereabouts or identities unknown [§209]

As to defendants whose whereabouts or identities are unknown, *constructive service* (*i.e.*, by publication) may be sufficient because under the circumstances it is the best method available.

b. Whereabouts known [§210]

But where the defendant's location is known, due process requires more—not necessarily the best method possible, but at least a method *"reasonably calculated"* to give the defendant *actual notice* of the proceedings. In this regard, the Supreme Court has emphasized that substituted service by mail is a method "reasonably calculated" to give such notice, while personal service outside the state would be even better. [**Mullane v. Central Hanover Bank & Trust Co.**, *supra*]

c. What constitutes "reasonable" notice [§211]

Regardless of whether the action is in rem or in personam, the requirement that notice be *reasonable* applies. What is "reasonable" depends on the particular circumstances involved. Historically, service by publication alone was deemed adequate for in rem and quasi in rem actions, while something more was required for in personam actions. However, recent cases have held that published notice without more will not suffice in *any* action where the defendant's identity and whereabouts are known. [**Schroeder v. City of New York**, 371 U.S. 208 (1962); **Walker v. City of Hutchinson**, 352 U.S. 112 (1956)]

(1) Rationale

A proceeding involving property is actually a proceeding *against persons*, in that their interests in property are affected by such judgments.

(2) Statute itself must require reasonable notice [§212]

Moreover, it is probably *not* enough that a nonresident defendant is shown to have received actual notice of the proceedings. Rather, the authorizing statute itself must require such notice, and the notice must be given in the manner provided by statute. [**Wuchter v. Pizzuti**, *supra*, §109]

(a) Application

Most long arm statutes require that the pleadings be delivered to the nonresident defendant personally where she resides. Some permit service by registered mail with return receipt requested. (*See* Civil Procedure Summary.)

(b) Note

The method to be followed is determined strictly by the law of the forum, although some states also permit service in accordance with the law of the place where defendant was served. [Cal. Civ. Proc. Code §417.20(c)]

(3) More stringent forms of service may be required [§213]

With courts increasingly being empowered to assert personal jurisdiction over nonresidents under long arm statutes, the more limited the "contacts" with nonresidents the more stringent the notice requirements will have to be in order to assure due process (*i.e.,* that the defendant in fact had the opportunity to appear and defend). As yet, the United States Supreme Court has not specified precisely what form of service is required in such actions.

5. Waiver or Other Agreements Between the Parties [§214]

There is a growing trend among contracting parties to attempt to control which courts may hear any litigation arising out of their agreements (*see supra*, §101). To accomplish this, contracts frequently contain "cognovit" provisions by which one or both parties purport to "waive" service of process in any such litigation, to accept service by mail, or to appoint an agent to receive and accept service on behalf of the party.

a. Agent to accept service [§215]

A contractual provision by which a nonresident appoints a local agent to accept service of process in any action arising under the contract is valid as long as it is negotiated in good faith and is not part of an adhesion contract (*i.e.,* where one party occupies a substantially inferior bargaining position; *see* Contracts Summary). [Restatement of Judgments §18]

(1) Note

The validity of such provisions may be challenged if the agent appointed is a mere "straw person" (*i.e.,* someone whom the nonresident defendant does not even know) *and who fails to notify* the nonresident defendant.

 Compare: In **National Equipment Rental Ltd. v. Szukhent** (*supra*, §98), the Supreme Court upheld service on an unknown appointee (who turned out to be the plaintiff's wife) where it appeared that the appointed agent had in fact properly notified the nonresident defendant of the proceedings. Since the defendant had received actual notice, the Court found no violation of due process.

---

b. Cognovits [§216]

Even a provision completely *waiving* service of process and authorizing a confession of judgment in any action arising out of the contract may be upheld under the proper circumstances. Due process rights to notice and hearing prior to the entry of a civil judgment may be waived, provided the waiver is *"voluntary, knowing and intelligently made"* between parties of *substantially equal bargaining power*. [**Overmyer Co. v. Frick Co.**, 405 U.S. 174 (1972)]

Example: In *Overmyer*, the Court affirmed a cognovit judgment where the debtor defendant was a large corporation that had executed the cognovit with full awareness of its legal consequences. *And note:* Another important factor in the *Overmyer* case was that local statutes provided an effective postjudgment procedure to remedy inadvertent defaults (*e.g.*, a discretionary reopening of the judgment if a valid defense can be shown). Absent such a remedy, the Court indicated that the cognovit also might be unenforceable.

cf. **Compare:** The Court indicated, however, that the result would be different in the case of an adhesion contract (*see supra*), and lower courts have in fact refused full faith and credit to cognovit judgments arising out of such contracts. [*See, e.g.*, **Atlas Credit Corp. v. Ezrine,** 25 N.Y.2d 219 (1969)]

EXAM TIP   **gilbert**

When deciding whether service on a defendant is proper, remember that *personal service is the most desirable method*, followed by *substituted service*, because these are the methods most likely to actually reach your defendant. *Constructive service* should only be used where the *defendant's whereabouts truly are not known and cannot be ascertained*. This is true for nonresident defendants as well as for resident defendants. Where the parties have a previous agreement waiving service (cognovits), look at the identity of these parties. Where both parties are individuals or both parties are corporations, courts will be more likely to uphold such an arrangement. However, if one party is a corporation and the other party is an individual, or there is an otherwise *"unequal bargaining position,"* there is a possibility that the court will look at this as an adhesion contract and strike the agreement.

F. Continuance of Jurisdiction

1. **Subject Matter Jurisdiction [§217]**

    Once jurisdiction has been obtained by the court in a particular action, it continues until the final winding up of the action. No matter how many appeals, retrials of the action, or the like may be involved, jurisdiction of the court remains. This is especially important in probate, child custody, and domestic relations cases where the litigation may continue or be renewed over a period of many years. [**Berlin v. Berlin,** 210 A.2d 380 (Md. 1965)]

2. **Personal Jurisdiction [§218]**

    Accordingly, once a court obtains personal jurisdiction over a party, the party remains subject to that jurisdiction even though she subsequently leaves the state. [**Michigan Trust Co. v. Ferry,** 228 U.S. 346 (1916)]

3. **Notice [§219]**

    Although jurisdiction is retained, it may be necessary to give the defendant notice and an opportunity to be heard in any subsequent proceedings that could modify the rights and obligations in an earlier order (*e.g.*, a proceeding for modification of alimony or child support following a divorce).

G. Limitations on Exercise of Jurisdiction

1. In General [§220]

Even where the three essential requirements for proper jurisdiction (sufficient basis, competent court, and compliance with procedural due process) exist, the forum court may refuse or be unable to entertain an action for the following reasons:

2. Agreement by Parties to Litigate in Another State ("Prorogation Agreements") [§221]

Contracting parties often agree that "any litigation arising from or connected with the contract shall be had in the courts of State X and in no other state." If one of the parties then brings an action on the contract in State Y, the question becomes what effect should State Y give to the agreement?

a. Former rule [§222]

Traditionally, such agreements were not effective. It was held to be against public policy for private parties to oust a court from jurisdiction since "jurisdiction springs from the law." [**Nashua River Paper Co. v. Hammermill Paper Co.**, 111 N.E. 678 (Mass. 1916)]

b. Modern rule [§223]

Under the modern view, however, such an agreement *is effective* provided it is *reasonable and fair*. Basically, this requires that the agreement specify a jurisdiction with which the parties have had some contact so that litigation in the selected jurisdiction would not be oppressive or unfair to either party. (*Note:* Courts in other states will refuse to exercise jurisdiction as a matter of *discretion*.) [**The Bremen v. Zapata Off-Shore Co.**, *supra*, §104; Rest. 2d §80]

(1) "Reasonable and fair" [§224]

Mere inconvenience or expense to a party in having to litigate in the designated forum is not enough to render the agreement "oppressive" or "unfair," because such inconvenience and expense were foreseeable when the agreement was entered into. [**Smith, Valentino & Smith, Inc. v. Superior Court**, 17 Cal. 3d 491 (1976)]

3. Fraud, Force, and Privilege [§225]

As discussed earlier (*supra*, §§77 *et seq.*), a person served with process while in the state under fraud, force, duress, or some recognized privilege (congressional investigators, etc.) ordinarily is not subject to jurisdiction. Some authorities assert that the court has no jurisdiction under these circumstances, but most agree that the court *has* jurisdiction over the party but simply *refuses to exercise* it as a matter of *discretion*. [Rest. 2d §§82, 83]

a. In rem and quasi in rem jurisdiction [§226]

The same principle applies where in rem or quasi in rem jurisdiction is obtained through fraud, etc.—as where the defendant's property is brought into the forum through trickery. [**Commercial Air Charters, Inc. v. Sundorph Aero Corp.,** 57 F.R.D. 84 (D. Conn. 1972)—court declined to exercise quasi in rem jurisdiction where P's friend "rented" D's airplane, after misrepresenting where he intended to fly it, and flew it into forum state to allow P to levy attachment]

4. Doctrine of Forum Non Conveniens [§227]

A court in its discretion may also refuse to exercise its jurisdiction—*i.e.,* stay or dismiss an action—if it determines that the forum is an ***unfair or seriously inconvenient place*** for trial as to any party and that a more convenient place is available. [Rest. 2d §84; **Beach v. Youngblood,** 247 N.W. 545 (Iowa 1933)]

a. Source of doctrine [§228]

Forum non conveniens is part of the court's inherent supervisory power over its own jurisdiction. It is available in all federal courts [**Gulf Oil Corp. v. Gilbert,** 330 U.S. 501 (1947)] and in most state courts [**Missouri *ex rel*. Southern Railway v. Mayfield,** 340 U.S. 1 (1950)]—even where a federal claim is sued upon. A few states have even embodied the doctrine in a statute. [*See* Cal. Civ. Proc. Code §410.30]

b. How raised [§229]

Typically, forum non conveniens is raised by a motion to dismiss or abate the action. Such a motion is usually treated as a general appearance by the defendant—so that by making the motion she waives any defect in personal jurisdiction.

(1) Note

A few states, however, allow a defendant to raise the objection without waiving an objection to personal jurisdiction. [Cal. Civ. Proc. Code §418.10]

c. Disposition [§230]

If the court finds that the local forum is a "seriously inconvenient" place for trial, it may either ***stay or dismiss*** the action. If it dismisses, it loses jurisdiction; if it merely stays the action, however, the court may resume proceedings if the foreign action is unreasonably delayed.

d. Determinative factors [§231]

In deciding whether the local forum is an "unfair" or "seriously inconvenient" place for trial, the court usually weighs the following factors:

(1) *Plaintiff's preference* as to forum—This is to be given great weight, and unless the balance of convenience is strongly in favor of some other forum, the plaintiff's choice of forum will be respected. [Rest. 2d §84, comment c(1)]

    (a) ***But when the plaintiff represents foreign parties litigating a foreign cause*** of action and when the suit has been filed in the United

States rather than the foreign country where the injury occurred, the plaintiff may not defend against a motion to dismiss based on forum non conveniens simply because the law applicable in the foreign forum is less favorable. [**Piper Aircraft Co. v. Reyno,** 454 U.S. 235 (1981)] *Note:* Plaintiff's choice of a more favorable law is simply one factor—not even a particularly weighty one—to be considered in determining whether the forum is "unfair" or "seriously inconvenient."

(2) *Residence of the parties*—An action is rarely dismissed on grounds of forum non conveniens where the plaintiff is a bona fide resident of the forum state. That state is deemed to have an interest in protecting its citizens from the inconvenience and expense of having to litigate their claims elsewhere.

   (a) *And some states hold that a suit brought by a local plaintiff* (except perhaps a plaintiff who is merely a nominal representative of foreign beneficiaries or creditors) cannot be dismissed on the basis of forum non conveniens. At most, the court may stay the action pending proceedings in the forum alleged to be more convenient. [**Archibald v. Cinerama Hotels,** 15 Cal. 3d 853 (1976)]

      1) Some courts apply the same rule if the plaintiff chooses to file suit at the *defendant's residence* in effect holding that the doctrine of forum non conveniens can be invoked only when all parties are nonresidents.

      2) But not all courts agree. Some hold that the local residence of either party does *not* prevent dismissal under forum non conveniens if there is otherwise "no real connection" of the cause of action to the forum state.

(3) *Residence of witnesses and availability of process* for compelling their attendance.

(4) *Ease of access to sources of proof.*

(5) *Costs to defendant of bringing willing witnesses and parties to the forum.*

(6) *Plaintiff's motives for bringing suit in the local forum* (*e.g.,* forum shopping? harassment of the defendant?).

(7) *Availability of an alternative forum* in which relief may be obtained. This is essential, since the statute of limitations may have run in the other forum or the defendant may not be subject to jurisdiction there.

(8) *Likelihood of forum's judgment being enforceable.*

(9) *Interests of forum state* in the matter (*e.g.*, clearing local court calendars, cost of trial).

FORUM NON CONVENIENS—FACTORS TO CONSIDER **gilbert**

TO DETERMINE WHETHER THE FORUM IS "UNFAIR" OR "SERIOUSLY INCONVENIENT," THE COURT WILL CONSIDER:

☑ *Plaintiff's preferred forum*—this factor is given great weight, although the court will consider *plaintiff's motives for choosing forum* (e.g., forum shopping or harassment would cut against this factor)

☑ *Residence of parties*—if plaintiff is a bona fide resident of forum, forum usually hears case

☑ *Residence of witnesses and availability of process* for compelling their attendance

☑ *Ease of access to sources of proof* and *costs* to defendant for bringing willing witnesses

☑ *Availability of alternate forum* in which relief may be obtained

☑ *Likelihood of forum's judgment being enforceable*

☑ *Interests of forum state in matter*

---

e. **Impermissible factors [§232]**

A state may not decline to exercise jurisdiction (under the guise of "forum non conveniens" or otherwise) solely because the cause of action sued upon arises under the laws of another state. Such refusal would violate the Full Faith and Credit Clause. [*See* **Hughes v. Fetter,** 341 U.S. 609 (1951), *and see infra,* §695]

f. **Federal statute regarding transfer of cases [§233]**

A statutory extension of forum non conveniens is found in 28 U.S.C. section 1404(a), which provides that a federal court that determines that it is not a "fair and appropriate" place for trial of an action may *transfer* the action to another appropriate federal district, *if the action could have been filed there* originally. [**Norwood v. Kirkpatrick,** 349 U.S. 29 (1955)]

(1) **Broader than forum non conveniens [§234]**

A change of venue in federal courts under section 1404(a) (or similar state rules) may be ordered upon a lesser showing of inconvenience than is required to invoke forum non conveniens. Change of venue merely involves a transfer, rather than the dismissal required under forum non conveniens.

(2) Effect of transfer [§235]

A transfer under section 1404(a) has no effect on jurisdiction or choice of law. The court to which the action is transferred inherits whatever jurisdiction over the parties the transferring court had; and it will apply the choice-of-law rules in effect in the state in which the transferring court was located. [**Van Dusen v. Barrack,** 376 U.S. 612 (1964)]

g. Increasing importance of forum non conveniens [§236]

Forum non conveniens (and federal court transfer rules) has become increasingly important. Under the "minimum contacts" doctrine and state long arm statutes (discussed previously), a plaintiff may acquire jurisdiction over defendant in some state far from defendant's home where it would be seriously inconvenient to defend. Forum non conveniens allows the court to regulate such abuses by refusing to exercise jurisdiction where, although constitutionally permissible, it would be unfair to proceed. [16 Wayne L. Rev. 1162 (1970)]

5. Unreasonable Burden on Interstate Commerce [§237]

Where maintenance of an action in local courts would impose an "unreasonable burden" on interstate commerce, the courts cannot exercise jurisdiction. Dismissal here is *mandatory*, not merely a matter of discretion.

Example: In **Davis v. Farmers Cooperative Equity Co.,** 262 U.S. 312 (1923), a Minnesota statute authorized local courts to exercise in personam jurisdiction over railroads "doing business" in the state; the statute was construed to apply even where the only "business" done by an out-of-state railroad was the maintenance of a local ticket agent who solicited traffic for the railroad's lines in other states. The Supreme Court assumed that the statute conferred an adequate basis for jurisdiction over the out-of-state railroad, but held that it imposed an intolerable burden on interstate commerce because every railroad having a ticket agent in Minnesota would be forced to defend in that state against actions completely unrelated to its activities in Minnesota. (In *Davis,* the plaintiff was suing for damage allegedly caused by the defendant railroad in Kansas.)

---

a. Caution [§238]

The holding in *Davis* should not be carried too far, because almost every transitory cause of action against a foreign corporation imposes some "burden" on interstate commerce. The burden must be shown to be clearly "unreasonable" before the Commerce Clause limits jurisdiction. [*See* **Scanapico v. Richmond, Fredricksburg & Potomac Railroad,** 439 F.2d 17 (2d Cir. 1970)]

6. Inability to Grant Relief Sought [§239]

The local court can provide relief only within the framework of its own system. Where the relief sought is outside the framework (a relatively rare occurrence), the court *must* dismiss the suit.

Example: In **Slater v. Mexican National Railroad**, 194 U.S. 120 (1904), it was held that a Texas court should have dismissed a suit for wrongful death where the plaintiff was suing under a Mexican statute (the death having occurred in Mexico) and seeking a type of relief provided under Mexican law (a revisable judgment for damages, similar to a pension) which Texas courts were unable to grant.

7. Statutory Attempts to "Localize" Jurisdiction [§240]

Occasionally, states have enacted statutes that purport to reserve "exclusive jurisdiction" in local courts for certain causes of action arising in the state—*e.g.*, wrongful death actions arising from deaths within the state or claims for workers' compensation benefits from injuries within the state. Typically, such statutes provide that any such claim must be litigated in local courts and "cannot be prosecuted elsewhere." If the claimant files the action in another state's court, what is the effect of such restrictions?

a. One state cannot oust other states of jurisdiction [§241]

Each sovereign state determines the competency (subject matter jurisdiction) of its own courts. Such jurisdiction is therefore not affected by statutes in another state that attempt to "localize" a transitory cause of action—even where the cause of action sued upon was created by the statute that seeks to limit jurisdiction to courts of the enacting state. [Rest. 2d §91]

Example: An Alabama statute created a cause of action for industrial injuries and required that suits for such injuries "be brought in a court of competent jurisdiction in the state of Alabama, and not elsewhere." Claimant brought suit in Georgia, and the Supreme Court held that the Georgia courts had valid jurisdiction notwithstanding the limitation in the Alabama statute. [**Tennessee Coal, Iron & Railroad v. George**, 233 U.S. 354 (1914)]

Example: A workers' compensation award in F1 (the place of employee's residence and injury) which imposed liability under a workers' compensation act in effect in F2 (employer's place of business) has also been upheld even where the F2 Act purported to create "an exclusive remedy" which could be afforded "only" by the administrative agency in F2. The Supreme Court held that F1—having jurisdiction over the parties and a legitimate interest in the matter in dispute—was free to adopt and apply the F2 Act. The "exclusive remedy limitation" in the F2 Act was not entitled to full faith and credit outside F2, since it could be used to subvert F1's free choice of law. [**Crider v. Zurich Insurance Co.**, 380 U.S. 39 (1965)]

b. Comment—forum not compelled to hear such cases [§242]

It should be emphasized that a forum is not *compelled* to accept jurisdiction of a cause of action created under the laws of a sister state. The above cases merely hold that *if* the forum accepts jurisdiction of the case, it is not bound by any limitations on jurisdiction imposed by the law of another state.

8. **Statutes Closing Local Courts to "Unqualified" Foreign Corporations [§243]**

All states have statutes that require foreign corporations to "qualify" to do business within the state. ("Qualification" usually means that the foreign corporation must pay state taxes and appoint a local agent to accept service of process in any litigation arising out of business done locally.) Under many such statutes, corporations that fail to "qualify" are denied access to local courts; *i.e.*, they cannot sue or defend themselves in local litigation.

a. **Constitutional limitation [§244]**

Such statutes violate the Commerce Clause if applied to foreign corporations that do not operate regularly within the state and whose intrastate activities are merely "fleeting events" in what are otherwise interstate business transactions. [**Allenberg Cotton Co. v. Pittman**, 419 U.S. 20 (1974)]

Example: In the *Allenberg Cotton* case, *supra*, a Mississippi farmer reneged on a contract to sell his cotton crop to a Tennessee corporation. When the buyer sued for damages, the court denied relief on the ground that the Tennessee corporation had never "qualified" to do business locally. The Supreme Court held that the buyer was protected by the Commerce Clause from having to comply with the statute, since the buyer had no regular business activities in Mississippi and its crop contract with the farmer was but an "integral step in a vast stream of interstate commerce affecting cotton."

---

(1) **Distinguish—"minimum contacts" standard [§245]**

Even such limited intrastate activities would probably be sufficient "minimum contacts" to serve as a basis for personal jurisdiction in an action against the foreign corporation growing out of such activities. [*See* **McGee v. International Life Insurance Co.**, *supra*, §125]

EXAM TIP	gilbert

Whenever you encounter an exam situation involving an "unorthodox" agreement as to jurisdiction (*e.g.*, a set of facts that fall outside the three essential requirements for jurisdiction—*i.e.*, sufficient constitutional basis, competent court, and compliance with due process), always ask yourself "*is this fair*—do all parties have an opportunity to present their cases, and is there a level playing field?" If not, then it is likely that the forum will strike down the agreement as void, and refuse to give deference to the parties' choice of law provisions and instead apply its own.

Chapter Three: Choice of Law—General Considerations and Pervasive Problems

---

CONTENTS

Chapter Approach

A few general considerations and problems pervade the choice-of-law process. The most important of the problem areas are renvoi, depeçage, and characterization. These problems tend to be associated with particular approaches to choice of law (discussed in the next chapter). Thus, when you see an exam question raising the issue of *characterization* (whether the problem is one of contract or tort, substance or procedure), you will probably discuss the traditional approach of the First Restatement or the most significant relationship approach of the Second Restatement. On the other hand, a question raising the issue of *depeçage* is more likely to call for discussion of a modern approach. Finally, questions raising the issue of *renvoi* may require analysis of either the traditional or modern approaches, since renvoi is discussed in connection with both.

A. General Considerations

1. **Nature of Choice-of-Law Problems [§246]**

   If transactions or events occur entirely within a single state and involve only residents of that state, there is no choice-of-law problem. Should a dispute arise, the parties ordinarily will litigate in the state in which all the events occurred, and that state will consult its own law to provide the rule of decision. However, when one or more of the events giving rise to the litigation has occurred *outside the state* or country in which the suit is brought, or when one or more of the parties is a *nonresident*, a choice-of-law problem may arise. In this case, the forum court may look to the law of one or more other states or countries, in addition to its own, to select the appropriate rule for decision.

2. **Scope of Choice-of-Law Problems [§247]**

   Choice of law relates to whether, or to what extent, the forum will recognize and apply *foreign law* (another state or country's law) to resolve a case that has "contacts" with more than one jurisdiction. The subject is broad enough to cover both interstate and international cases. Because most American decisions concern the interstate situation, this Summary will address itself primarily to choice-of-law problems involving interstate transactions. However, international cases are worth a brief mention here.

   a. **International choice-of-law problems [§248]**

      While international cases are generally considered in the same framework as interstate cases (*see infra*, §§277 *et seq.*), the following additional considerations that must be taken into account:

      (1) **Diplomacy [§249]**

         Since foreign interests are involved, "diplomacy"—*i.e.*, the necessity of maintaining international order and goodwill—may require a more delicate approach than when only sister states are involved. [Leflar, American Conflicts Law §6]

(a) Note
Results may differ depending on the particular nation involved—considering the similarities and dissimilarities between the procedural and substantive laws of the other nation and those of the forum.

(2) Proof of law [§250]
If the law to be applied by the American forum is that of a foreign nation whose legal system is not drawn from English sources and whose language is other than English, discovering the content of that law may prove to be a difficult task (*see infra,* §269). As a result, the forum court may be inclined to reject the foreign law and apply its own law instead.

(3) Forum non conveniens [§251]
Application of forum non conveniens (*see supra,* §227) is less likely where dismissal of the action would remit the law suit to a foreign court rather than the court of a sister state. Because dismissal is unlikely, one scholar has suggested that choice of the foreign rule "may be required in order to avoid unfair application of the forum rule." [Ehrenzweig, Private International Law 21 (1967)]

(4) Foreign treaties [§252]
Finally, the United States Constitution recognizes foreign treaties as "the law of the land," and thus treaties govern fact situations covered by them. To date, however, few private lawsuits have arisen under such treaties.

(5) Note—Full Faith and Credit Clause does not apply [§253]
The Full Faith and Credit Clause of the United States Constitution (Article IV, section 1) requires that each state give "full faith and credit" to the "public acts, records, and judicial proceedings of every other state." The Clause does not apply to foreign acts, records, or judgments.

b. Comment [§254]
It has been suggested that the framework established for choice-of-law cases within the federal system (*see infra,* §§276 *et seq.*) is inadequate to treat international cases, due to the different considerations involved. [Ehrenzweig, Private International Law 21 (1967)]

3. Source of Choice-of-Law Problems [§255]
With modern means of communication and transportation, and the concomitant increase in disputes overlapping state (and national) boundaries, choice-of-law problems have become an increasingly important part of the legal process.

B. Pervasive Problems

1. Introduction [§256]

In addition to the general considerations above, there are concepts unique to choice of law which are often referred to as the "pervasive problems" of the subject.

2. Renvoi [§257]

A forum's choice-of-law rules may refer a matter to a foreign law for decision. The question then becomes is the reference to the *whole body* of the foreign law (including its choice-of-law rules) or to the purely *internal* rules of the foreign system (*i.e.,* those rules that would apply to local litigation with no outside contacts)? If the forum decides to apply the *whole law* of the other state, the choice-of-law rules of that state may differ from those of the forum—perhaps referring the forum court back to its own law or to that of a third jurisdiction ("renvoi"). If the forum decides to apply *only the local law* of the other state, renvoi does not arise.

Example: Decendent, a State B domiciliary, dies leaving stock certificates located in State A. The corporation in which the stock is held is located in State C. In inheritance litigation brought in State A (the forum), the court decides that this particular type of problem should be determined according to the law of decedent's domicile (State B). But to which law of State B should reference be made: (i) that which State B would apply if the litigation were purely local in nature; or (ii) State B's own choice-of-law rule as to this particular type of problem, which might, for example, refer the matter or decision to the law of the place where the certificates are located (State A) or to the law of the place where the corporation is located (State C)?

---

a. Conflict in choice-of-law rules [§258]

Renvoi, then, is a "conflict in choice-of-law rules." There is a *"remission"* where the other state's choice-of-law rules *refer the forum back to its own law* (*i.e.,* State A's choice-of-law rule looks to the law of State B and State B's choice-of-law rule looks back at State A's law). Alternatively, there is a *"transmission"* where choice-of-law rules in the other state *refer the forum to the law of a third state* (*i.e.,* State A's choice-of-law rule looks to the law of State B and State B's choice-of-law rule looks to the law of State C).

b. Basic positions on renvoi problem

(1) Reject renvoi (majority view) [§259]

The simplest method of handling the renvoi problem, and the majority views is that the forum (State A) should reject the "renvoi" and look only to the *internal* law of State B (and not to B's choice-of-law rules). [*In re Tallmadge*, 109 Misc. 696 (1919)]

(a) Restatement view [§260]

This is the position taken by both the First and Second Restatements, subject to certain exceptions adopting "whole renvoi" position (*see* below). The "policy-oriented" approaches to choice of law (*see infra*, §§319 *et seq.*) also reject the renvoi.

(2) Partial renvoi [§261]

Under minority view, the forum should accept the "renvoi" or reference back from the foreign conflict-of-laws rule, but *only to local internal law*.

---

e.g. **Example:** Following its local choice-of-law rule, the State A forum looks to State B's "whole law" (including B's choice-of-law rules). State B courts would decide the problem by reference to State A's law (or the law of some third state). State A will hold that B's reference to State A's law (or to the third state's law) is to A's *internal* law only, rather than to its choice-of-law rule (which would bounce the issue back to State B, etc.).

---

(3) Whole renvoi [§262]

Under a third view, the forum would approach a choice-of-law problem as the foreign court would. If the foreign court refers back to the forum law—including its choice-of-law rules, which would then refer it back to the foreign court—the forum should accept this "final bounce back" but only to the extent of the foreign state's internal law. [*In re* **Annesley**, *supra*, §37]

(a) Result [§263]

The local court usually ends up applying the foreign jurisdiction's internal law—the same result as if it had *rejected* the renvoi.

1) But note

There may be exceptional cases where the two positions differ, and the local court following the whole renvoi approach may end up applying its own local law. [*See, e.g., In re* **Schneider's Estate**, 198 Misc. 1017 (1950)—New York court, attempting to decide case as Swiss court would, determined that Swiss court would apply New York internal law only (*i.e.*, would not look to New York's "whole law"); thus, New York court applied its own law]

(b) Criticism [§264]

The "whole renvoi" position is commonly attacked on the "international lawn tennis" argument—*i.e.*, that each court might continuously look to the other's conflicts rule, bouncing the reference back and forth ad infinitum! But this has never happened in practice; one court has always accepted the reference back in partial

gilbert

RENVOI POSITIONS—AN EXAMPLE

		PARTIAL RENVOI	WHOLE RENVOI
SITUATION:	Forum law holds that **State B law** should apply to matter. State B's law holds that **Forum law** should apply to matter.		
PROBLEM:	If the Forum applies its choice-of-law rules, it will look to State B's choice-of-law rules, which will refer it back to the Forum's choice-of-law rules, and so on, bouncing the matter back and forth forever!		
SOLUTIONS:	**REJECT RENVOI** (Majority view)	**PARTIAL RENVOI**	**WHOLE RENVOI**
APPLICATION	Forum doesn't play "renvoi." Forum looks only to **internal** law of State B (not B's choice-of-law rules).	Forum bounces to State B's **whole** law (includes choice-of-law rules). State B law bounces back to Forum. Forum accepts but applies only its **internal** law.	Forum bounces to State B's **whole** law (includes choice-of-law rules). State B law bounces back to Forum. Forum accepts, but following its choice-of-law rules, applies only State B's **internal** law.
RESULT	State B's internal law applied.	Forum's internal law applied.	State B's internal law applied.

renvoi (as applying to its internal law only), thereby ending the "tennis match."

(c) Federal Tort Claims Act [§265]

The Federal Tort Claims Act specifies that in a tort case against the government, the government's liability shall be determined by "the law of the place where the act or omission occurred." [28 U.S.C. §1346(b)] This provision has been held to require a reference to the whole law of the place of act or omission, including its conflicts rules. [**Richards v. United States,** 369 U.S. 1 (1962)]

(d) Comment [§266]

The "whole renvoi" position may be the most logical and fair approach to choice-of-law issues since the primary goal in deciding these problems is uniformity of decision. When a local court tries to decide the matter as the foreign court would, this does the most to assure uniformity, regardless of the specter of "international lawn tennis."

1) Note

For this very reason, the Second Restatement—which generally rejects renvoi (*see* above)—adopts the whole renvoi approach as to issues involving title to land or testate and intestate succession to movables. [Rest. 2d §§223, 260, 263]

3. Depeçage [§267]

In determining which law to apply in a conflicts case, the traditional "vested rights" approach to choice of law (*see infra*, §§302-312) directs the forum to analyze cases as a whole and apply the law of a single state to all the issues presented. Conversely, all the modern approaches direct the forum to focus *on each specific issue separately*. Under the modern approaches, therefore, the laws of *different states* may govern the resolution of the different issues presented in the case. This is known as "depeçage" (*see infra*, §290).

4. Characterization [§268]

For purposes of analysis, characterization is the process whereby factual situations are classified to fit *established legal categories* (*e.g.,* contracts, torts, property). As discussed *infra* (§§285, 304), characterization is an integral part of the choice-of-law process, but its significance varies with the different choice-of-law approaches (*see infra*, §§276 et seq.).

5. Proof of Foreign Law [§269]

Traditionally, the content of foreign law—even that of a sister state—was considered to be a question of fact. If a party asserted a claim or defense under foreign law, he was thus required to *plead and prove* that law as if it were a fact (*i.e.,* by bringing in an expert witness to testify).

a. **Modern practice [§270]**

In modern practice, however, American courts are empowered by statute to take *judicial notice* of the law of sister states or of the United States.

(1) **Laws of other nations [§271]**

When considering the laws of a foreign nation, some states still require pleading and proof of the foreign law as if it were a factual issue. Other states have adopted the Interstate and International Procedure Act, which permits courts to determine the foreign law as a matter of law.

(2) **Consequences of failure to prove foreign law [§272]**

The law of the forum determines the consequences stemming from failure to prove foreign law. In an international case, the forum may therefore take one of three actions if the foreign law has not been proved:

(a) **Dismiss the suit [§273]**

If the foreign law is not proved, the forum may dismiss the case. For example, in **Walton v. Arabian American Oil Co.**, 233 F.2d 541 (2d Cir. 1956), plaintiff sued on a tort committed by defendant's agents in Saudi Arabia. Plaintiff failed to plead or prove the law of Saudi Arabia and attempted instead to rely on the law of the forum (New York). The court directed a verdict for defendant, on the ground that plaintiff had not made out an essential element of his case— namely, the law of the place of wrong.

(b) **Apply presumptions [§274]**

Rather than dismiss the suit, the forum may resort to a presumption that the law of the other state is *similar to its own* and then apply its own law. This presumption has been extended to include "rudimentary principles of justice" in non-common-law states.

(c) **Apply law of forum [§275]**

Finally, a few courts and commentators advocate application of the forum's own law where no other law has been established in its place, on the theory that the parties either acquiesced in that law or waived the right to rely on the foreign law by failing to prove it.

Chapter Four:
Approaches to
Choice-of-Law Problems

CONTENTS

Chapter Approach

Chapter Approach

When you see a choice-of-law question on your conflicts exam (as you undoubtedly will), you should write your answer in terms of the choice-of-law approach the forum court follows. But what approach is that?

1. *If your question tells you which approach is to be used,* for example, "assume that the forum follows the approach to choice of law suggested by the Restatement (Second) of Conflicts," then obviously you should answer the question in terms of that approach (Second Restatement's "most significant relationship").

2. *But if no approach is specified* in the question, you should analyze the question in terms of several different approaches. The following four approaches, or a combination of them, are used by most American courts today and should be discussed in your answer:

    a. *Traditional "vested rights" approach of the First Restatement*—under this approach, the law of the state in which the parties' rights "vested" (*i.e.,* were created) applies;

    b. *"Most significant relationship" approach of the Second Restatement*—under this approach, the law of the state having the most significant relationship to the parties and the transaction in light of the particular issue applies to that issue;

    c. *Currie's "governmental interest analysis" approach*—under this approach, the court considers the underlying policies of the laws of the states involved and the interest of the states in furthering those policies to decide which law should be applied to the particular issue; and

    d. *Leflar's "better law" approach*—this approach rejects "rules" and "formulas," and based on particular considerations, selects the better law.

This chapter also discusses the "functional analysis" approaches (von Mehren and Trautman, Weintraub), "lex fori" (Ehrenzweig) approach, and "principles of preference" (Cavers) approach. Whether you need to discuss these theories on your exam will depend upon the emphasis of your professor and conflicts course.

A. Introduction

1. In General [§276]

Choice-of-law rules are primarily judge-made; very few statutes have been enacted in this area (*see infra,* §§292-300), and the Constitution has only a limited impact (*see infra,* §680). As a result, understanding the various choice-of-law positions adopted requires some consideration of the underlying policies and theories.

2. Should the Forum Apply Foreign Law? [§277]

The mere fact that a transaction involves out-of-state "contacts" does not mean that foreign law automatically should apply. There may be valid reasons for the forum to apply its own laws without reference to the laws of any other state involved.

a. Does forum law control? [§278]

As a first step, the forum court must determine whether *any valid statute or rule in its own jurisdiction* (lex fori) purports to govern the out-of-state transaction. If so, the forum court is bound to apply its own rules of law (subject only to possible constitutional objections if there are insufficient "contacts" with the forum state).

---

e.g. **Example:** A statute in the forum state declares that "minor domiciliaries lack capacity to enter into contracts anywhere." Preteen, a minor domiciled in the forum state, enters into a contract in another state where she would have capacity. She is then sued in the forum. The forum will clearly apply its own law, because it expressly covers contracts entered into "anywhere" by minor domiciliaries.

---

(1) Note

As a practical matter, however, most laws of the forum will not expressly or impliedly govern out-of-state transactions. The forum court must therefore decide whether such locally oriented rules should be construed to apply to the out-of-state transaction as well.

b. Is forum constitutionally required to apply foreign law? [§279]

As long as the forum has a *legitimate relationship* ("contact") with the parties or transaction involved in the litigation, neither the Full Faith and Credit Clause nor the Fourteenth Amendment Due Process Clause requires it to adopt or apply the laws of any other state. As a result, the forum court is generally free to apply its own law as a constitutional matter.

c. Are there reasons not to apply local law? [§280]

Since there is generally no constitutional compulsion to apply foreign law, one might assume that the forum court should merely apply its own law in every case. However, there are two reasons why this may not be desirable:

(1) "Forum shopping" [§281]

If each state applied only its own rules, this could encourage plaintiffs to "forum shop"—*i.e.,* to find a state whose law was most favorable to the plaintiff's case and sue there (assuming the plaintiff could obtain jurisdiction).

(2) Interests of justice [§282]

More generally, application of the forum's own rules may not be consistent with the interests of justice in many cases. This would certainly seem to be true where the forum has no real interest in the litigation beyond the fact that it is the forum (*i.e.,* all of the substantive "contacts" are with another state). Indeed, this is one of the rare cases where the Constitution may prohibit the forum from applying its own law. [*See* **Home Insurance Co. v. Dick,** 281 U.S. 397 (1930); *and see infra,* §683]

CHECKLIST FOR WHEN FORUM LAW SHOULD APPLY **gilbert**

A FORUM SHOULD APPLY ITS OWN LAW IF:

☑ A valid forum statute or rule governs;

☑ Forum has a legitimate relationship (sufficient contacts) with the parties or transaction; *and*

☑ Considering forum shopping and interests of justice, there is no reason *not* to apply forum law

---

3. Which Law Should Apply? [§283]

Assuming that the forum court is willing to consider application of foreign rules of law in a case involving both local and out-of-state "contacts," the question becomes *which law* should it apply?

a. Characterization [§284]

Under the concept of characterization (*see supra,* §268), the forum court always defines words or terms according to its own standards. For example, whether a party is a "minor," whether a particular business entity is a "corporation," or where a person maintains her "domicile" are all issues to be settled according to the forum's own definitions of these terms. It is immaterial that the question arises in a case involving significant "contacts" with another state; the forum is not concerned with how those terms would have been defined under foreign law.

(1) Traditional role of characterization in choice of law [§285]

Historically, the doctrine of characterization was very important in the analysis and resolution of choice-of-law problems. A two-step process was generally applied in each case: (i) first determining whether the issue was substantive or procedural; and (ii) if substantive, determining which substantive area of law (*e.g.,* torts, contract, etc.) was in issue.

(a) "Substance" vs. "procedure" [§286]

If the particular issue involved could *affect the outcome* of the case, it would be characterized as *"substantive,"* and reference to the laws of some other state might then be justified. But if the issue was *not* outcome determinative, it was *"procedural"* and governed by the forum's own rules—regardless of the out-of-state nature of the litigation. (*See infra,* §§638 *et seq.*)

Examples: Rules governing pleading, joinder of parties, service of process, remedies, order of liability, etc., usually were regarded as procedural matters. However, rules governing evidence, burden of proof, Statute of Frauds, and statute of limitations presented more complex problems. (*See infra,* §§638 *et seq.*)

(b) Characterization as to type of problem involved [§287]

Once an issue was classed as "substantive" (*i.e.,* outcome determinative), the forum court would then characterize the kind of problem involved (*i.e.,* "tort," "contract," "property," etc.) and apply the appropriate choice-of-law rule (*e.g.,* the law of the place of injury would govern a "torts" problem).

(2) Criticisms [§288]

The characterization process often served to conceal or distort a court's reasoning in choice-of-law decisions. For example, the process was often used to justify a conclusion that the court had reached for other reasons. Courts would usually first decide which state's laws they felt should apply and then "characterize" the problem so as to reach this result.

(a) And note

Numerous problems simply could not be classified in one rigid category or another; *e.g.,* a suit for breach of duty of care founded on a contractual obligation involves elements of both "torts" and "contracts." To force such problems into one particular category could therefore undermine interests that should have been protected.

b. Modern de-emphasis of characterization [§289]

Recognizing these shortcomings, modern authorities de-emphasize the role of characterization in the choice-of-law process, omitting it entirely where it would complicate analysis of the case.

(1) Reliance on "depeçage" [§290]

Rather than employing the broad characterization process, modern courts tend to focus on the particular issue involved (*see supra,* §267).

(2) Impact [§291]

Under this "depeçage" approach, issues in the same case may be governed by the laws of different states. [88 Harv. L. Rev. 347 (1974)] For instance, in a torts case, the forum court might apply the law of the state of injury to determine whether the defendant's conduct was "negligent," but then apply the law of the forum (if the forum was the common domicile of the plaintiff and defendant) to determine the degree of defendant's liability.

(a) Note

In some cases, use of the depeçage technique may mean that a defendant who would not be liable under the *whole* law of either state could be held liable where the laws of both states are applied on different issues.

B. Selecting the Appropriate Law

1. Statutory Directives [§292]

For the most part, choice-of-law rules are contained in case law rather than in statutes. If the forum does have a statutory rule, however, the court must follow that directive, assuming it is constitutional. Some of the few such statutes are the following:

a. Federal Tort Claims Act [§293]

The Tort Claims Act [28 U.S.C. §§1346, 2671 *et seq.*] subjects the United States to tort liability "under circumstances where the United States, as a private person, would be liable to the claimant in accordance with the law of the place where the act or omission occurred." The Act has been interpreted to require application of the *whole* law (including conflicts law) of the place where the defendant's acts or omissions occurred. [**Richards v. United States,** *supra,* §265] Thus, federal courts hearing claims under the Act must look to the choice-of-law theory adopted by the state where the tortious event took place.

(1) Diversity cases [§294]

The *Richards* decision (*supra*) achieves a result similar to that in **Klaxon Co. v. Stentor Electric Manufacturing Co.,** 313 U.S. 487 (1941), which directed federal courts hearing diversity cases to apply the conflict-of-law rules of the state in which the federal court sits (*see infra,* §723).

b. "Borrowing" statutes [§295]

Many states have enacted special statutes of limitation that "borrow" the limitations period of the place where the cause of action arose or where the defendant resided. These statutes were designed to prevent "forum shopping": Adherence to the general rule that the forum should apply its own statute of limitations might encourage plaintiffs to seek out the forum with the most advantageous limitations period.

(1) Alternative approach—judicial construction [§296]

Some courts have reached similar results without a borrowing statute, by interpreting their statutes of limitation as inapplicable to cases where the real parties in interest are nonresidents or the cause of action arose elsewhere. [*See* **Heavner v. Uniroyal, Inc.**, 305 A.2d 412 (N.J. 1973)]

c. Foreign execution of wills [§297]

Statutes in a number of states likewise provide that a will executed in another state pursuant to the formalities required by the state of execution or the state of the testator's domicile will be recognized by the forum even though formalities under its own law may not have been met. [*See, e.g.,* Cal. Prob. Code §26] Such statutes can be viewed as a statutory choice-of-law rule referring the forum to the law of the place of execution or of the decedent's domicile. The Uniform Probate Code also adopts this approach.

d. Uniform Commercial Code [§298]

U.C.C. section 1-301, which in 2001 replaced former section 1-105 relating to choice-of-law, permits parties in *business-to-business* transactions to agree contractually that the law of a particular state or country will govern their rights and duties, and the agreement will be recognized "whether or not the transaction bears a relation" to the designated state in domestic transactions or to the designated state or country in international transactions. This change eliminates the requirement of former section 1-105 that the transaction bear "a reasonable relation to this state and also to another state or nation." The scope of section 1-301 is not unlimited, however. The agreement is not effective if it is contrary to a "fundamental policy" of the state or country whose law would govern in the absence of party agreement.

(1) Exception for consumer transactions [§299]

Section 1-301 does not apply, however, if one of the parties to the transaction is a *consumer*. In those cases, the transaction must *bear a "reasonable relation" to the state* or country designated, and application of the chosen law may not deprive the consumer of the protection of any rule of law of the state or country where the consumer resides, if that law both protects consumers and may not be varied by agreement. If the transaction is a sale of goods that takes place outside the consumer's state or country of residence, the chosen law may not deprive the consumer of the protection of any rule of law of the state or country where the consumer *both* makes the contract and takes delivery of the goods, if that law both protects consumers and may not be varied by agreement.

(2) Impact [§300]

Virtually all the states have adopted the U.C.C., and so the chief impact of former section 1-105 was to permit each state to apply its local variation of the Code where differences existed. New section 1-301 will greatly expand party autonomy in business-to-business transactions. To date, however, only two states have adopted section 1-301.

	TRADITIONAL "VESTED RIGHTS"	"MOST SIGNIFICANT RELATIONSHIP"	"GOVERNMENTAL INTEREST"
ANALYTICAL STEPS	1. Characterize the area of substantive law (*e.g.,* contracts or torts). 2. Localize the significant event or thing (the "connecting factor") in a particular state. 3. Apply the law of that state.	1. Consider the connecting facts: the specific contacts with each state. 2. Consider the policy-oriented principles: (i) Needs of interstate systems; (ii) Relevant policies of forum; (iii) Policies and interests of other involved states; (iv) Expectations of parties; (v) Basic policies underlying the substantive area of law; (vi) Predictability and uniformity of result; and (vii) Ease of determination of foreign law.	1. Assume the forum will apply its own law, unless requested to apply another. 2. If it is requested to apply another state's law, check for false conflict (forum or other state has no interest). 3. If false conflict, apply the law of interested state. 4. If true conflict, the forum reconsiders its policies. If the conflict cannot be avoided, forum applies its own law. 5. If the forum has no interest in applying its own law but two other states have a true conflict, it should dismiss the case if forum non conveniens is available; if not, it may apply law of the state that most closely resembles its own law. (Case of disinterested forum.) 6. If no interested state, most courts apply law of forum.
DOES APPROACH DIFFER ACCORDING TO SUBSTANTIVE AREA OF LAW?	Yes (*See* Chapter V for chart for specific areas)	Yes	No

2. Choice-of-Law Theories [§301]

Absent a constitutional mandate (*see infra*, §§680-700) or statutory directive, a forum court will apply the law of another state when the forum's choice-of-law theory so directs. A number of choice-of-law theories have been advanced by scholars and courts, but none of them has yet been accepted as fully satisfactory by all courts in all situations. Thus, you must become familiar with the theory and methodology of the basic approaches adopted to date.

a. Traditional "vested rights" approach [§302]

The "vested rights" approach to choice of law—espoused by the First Restatement (1934), Beale and Holmes—directs the forum in every case to apply the *law of the state in which the rights of the parties vest*. Rights are deemed to "vest" in the place where they are "created"—*i.e.,* in the state in which the particular act occurred or the particular relationship was created. The law of that state then governs *all substantive issues* in the case, no matter where suit is brought. In a tort action, for example, the rights and liabilities of the parties "vest" in the jurisdiction where the plaintiff's injury occurred, and the law of that state would be applied by all other jurisdictions.

(1) Methodology [§303]

The "vested rights" approach involves a two-step analysis:

(a) Characterization [§304]

The forum court must first "characterize" the lawsuit into a "basic" legal category—*e.g.,* torts, contracts, property.

(b) Localizing the connecting factor [§305]

The "vested rights" approach then directs the forum court to *localize the significant event or thing (the connecting factor)* in a particular jurisdiction and apply the law of that state. For instance, the choice-of-law rule for torts provides that the law of the place of wrong governs; the "place of wrong" in turn is defined to be the place where the "last act necessary to create liability" occurred. That place thus becomes the connecting factor between the tort characterization and the jurisdiction whose law will be applied. (The various choice-of-law rules for specific subject areas are discussed *infra*, §§384 *et seq.*)

(2) Application of relevant law [§306]

After following the above methodology, the forum "mechanically" applies the law of the jurisdiction in which the significant event or thing occurred, without regard to its substantive content. The traditional approach rests on the theory that choice-of-law rules "simple in form and capable of easy administration should promote uniformity of result, enhance predictability, and discourage forum shopping." However, strict application of the traditional choice-of-law rules in this approach can lead to serious hardships and unjust results.

Example: Defendant, a Connecticut automobile leasing company, leased a car to Driver. Plaintiff, the passenger in the car, was injured in Massachusetts. A Connecticut statute subjected Defendant to liability for any injuries arising out of the use and operation of its leased vehicles. Massachusetts, on the other hand, had no such statute. Under the traditional approach, the tort choice-of-law rule provides that the law of the place of injury (Massachusetts) governs all issues. Therefore, under Massachusetts law, Plaintiff could not maintain an action against Defendant, even though the Connecticut statute was designed to regulate leasing companies. (*Note:* The Connecticut court was not happy with this result, and characterized the case differently; *see infra,* §309.) [**Levy v. Daniels' U-Drive Auto Renting Co.,** 143 A. 163 (Conn. 1928)]

(a) Escape devices [§307]

As indicated in the example above, to avoid harsh and unjust results, courts operating under the traditional approach often reach decisions based on the "equities" presented and justify the result through various "escape" devices.

1) "Substance-procedure" distinction [§308]

Since the forum is required to apply only the *substantive law* of the jurisdiction chosen, it is free to apply its own procedural law. Thus, if the law otherwise applicable involves a statute of limitations, Statute of Frauds, burden of proof, or evidentiary issue, the forum may choose to regard the issue as "procedural" to escape applying another jurisdiction's law. (The substance-procedure distinction is further discussed *infra,* §§638 *et seq.*)

2) Alternative characterizations [§309]

Where alternative characterizations are available, courts often characterize the facts so as to ensure just results. In **Levy v. Daniels' U-Drive Auto Renting Co.,** *supra,* the court characterized the matter as a contract rather than a tort dispute and applied the contract choice-of-law rule (*i.e.,* the law of the place of contracting). Under this characterization, Connecticut law governed and Plaintiff was afforded a remedy.

3) Renvoi [§310]

Where renvoi might ultimately lead the forum to apply its own internal law, it could be used as a means of avoiding the application of foreign law. The First Restatement, however, authorizes reference to a jurisdiction's "whole" law only in cases dealing with title to land or with divorce. (*See supra,* §§257-266.)

4) Local public policy [§311]

Finally, the traditional approach does not require the forum to apply a law that *violates its own public policy*. If the other state's law is against such public policy, the forum is free to ignore it and *apply its own law*. Typically, this "escape" has been used to avoid recognition of marriages that are valid where performed but invalid (*e.g.,* polygamous or incestuous) under local law.

EXAM TIP   **gilbert**

When an exam question requires you to use the traditional "vested rights" approach, and you have characterized the action and applied the relevant law according to this approach, you may find that the result will be unjust to one of the parties. If so, remember to look to the *escape devices* to see if you can secure a more equitable result. Especially useful is trying to recharacterize the matter as another area of law—often in an exam question a contract case can be recharacterized as a tort and vice versa.

CHECKLIST OF TRADITIONAL APPROACH "ESCAPE DEVICES"   **gilbert**

IF A RESULT UNDER THE TRADITIONAL APPROACH SEEMS UNJUST, BE SURE TO SEE WHETHER A BETTER RESULT CAN BE REACHED BY USING ONE OF THE FOLLOWING DEVICES:

☑ *Regarding the issue as procedural,* which allows the forum to apply its own law;

☑ *Characterizing the facts as a different area of law* (e.g., as a contract rather than tort);

☑ *Using renvoi* to apply the forum's internal law;

☑ *Avoiding recognition* of the other state's law *as violative of the forum's public policy*.

---

(3) Decline in use of traditional approach [§312]

The notion that a right is "created" by the law of some particular jurisdiction implies that there is some overriding body of law that delineates which jurisdiction can "create" specific rights and duties and compels the courts of every other state to recognize rights so "created." But there is no such superlaw and courts increasingly have come to realize that their reference to foreign law is a matter of their own choice and discretion. Thus, while a few jurisdictions in the United States still adhere to the traditional approach, *most courts have abandoned* it in favor of one of the other approaches discussed below.

Although the traditional approach has fallen out of favor, that doesn't mean that you don't have to know it for your exam. Many exams contain a choice-of-law question that does **not specify which approach** the forum uses. If no approach is specified in a question, your answer must analyze the problem using **at least** the "big three" approaches: the traditional approach, the most significant relationship approach, and the governmental interest approach, and maybe the better law approach as well (*see infra*).

b. **"Most significant relationship" approach [§313]**

The Second Restatement (1971) and its Chief Reporter, Professor Willis Reese adopt a compromise between relatively specific choice-of-law rules, such as the traditional approach (*supra*), and a more freewheeling policy analysis that relies heavily on the "governmental interest" approach (*see infra*, §319). This approach rejects the traditional notion that all substantive issues in a case must be governed by the law of a single state and directs the forum to *focus separately on the specific issues* raised. The Second Restatement also recognizes that events often have significant connections with more than one state. Therefore, it abandons the rigid "single contact" view of the vested rights approach in favor of applying the law of the state that has the *"most significant relationship"* to the parties and the transaction in light of the particular issue involved. At the same time, however, the Second Restatement retains the objectives of the First Restatement—*i.e.*, to promote uniformity of result, enhance predictability, and discourage forum shopping (*see supra*, §306).

When answering a question requiring analysis under the "most significant relationship" approach, remember that you analyze **each issue** and **decide for that particular issue** which state's law should be applied. So, for example, if a case has two issues to be determined, it is possible that one issue will be decided using the forum's law and one issue decided using the law of another state. It all depends on the contacts involved and the policy-oriented principles.

(1) **Methodology [§314]**

As noted, the Second Restatement focuses on identifying the state with the most significant relationship to the particular issue involved on the basis of seven general choice-of-law principles.

(a) **Choice-of-law principles [§315]**

Section 6 of the Second Restatement lists the following choice-of-law principles:

1) *Needs of interstate and international systems*—It is desirable to harmonize relations and commercial intercourse between states and nations.

2) **Relevant policies of forum**—The forum should evaluate the purpose of its own law to determine whether that purpose would be furthered by applying that law in the instant case.

3) **Policies of other states involved and respective interests in having their policies applied**—The forum should also analyze the purposes behind the laws of other interested states to ascertain whether those purposes would be furthered by the application of their laws.

4) **Protection of justified expectations**—In the case of **contracts** and other such transactions, the forum should examine the parties' expectations as to what law would govern their affairs. (*Note:* This factor is **not** considered in tort cases.)

5) **Basic policies underlying the particular field of law**—A choice-of-law decision should also reflect the basic policies underlying the particular field of law involved. For example, one basic policy of contract law is to validate contracts wherever possible.

6) **Certainty, predictability, and uniformity of result**—These objectives are preferred over negative factors such as forum shopping.

7) **Ease in determination and application of law to be applied**—This is purely a matter of convenience and should not outweigh the goal of attaining a desirable result. In a particular case, however, it may discourage application of esoteric law (especially that of foreign nations).

(b) Specific contacts for each kind of problem [§316]

The Second Restatement also establishes **specific contacts**—which vary according to the substantive area of law involved—to be used in applying the general principles (above) to identify the state with the most significant relationship to the issue in question.

Example: In deciding whether the defendant's **conduct** was negligent in a personal injury case, the most significant relationship may be with the place where the defendant acted. But with respect to the **measure of damages**, the most significant relationship may be with the place where the injured party was domiciled and where his financial losses were sustained. [*See* **Woodward v. Steward,** 243 A.2d 917 (R.I. 1968)]

(2) Criticism [§317]

The basic criticism of the Second Restatement approach is that a choice-of-law analysis based on the relative "significance" of contacts is of little help since courts will generally look to choice-of-law rules to determine the significance of the contact. Moreover, different courts may reach different conclusions as to what is "significant" and what is not.

(3) Second Restatement approach in practice [§318]

As a practical matter, courts adopting the Second Restatement generally identify the state with the most significant relationship not in terms of "specific contacts" but with reference to a "governmental interest" approach (below). [*See, e.g.,* **Gutierrez v. Collins**, 583 S.W.2d 312 (Tex. 1979)]

c. "Governmental interest analysis" (Currie) approach [§319]

Governmental interest analysis rests on the theory that choice-of-law problems should be considered in light of the underlying *policies* (*i.e.,* purposes or functions) of the laws of the involved states and the respective *interests* of those states in furthering such policies.

(1) Developed as reaction to traditional approach [§320]

The governmental interest approach developed largely as a reaction to the traditional approach, which required a forum to apply a particular state's law without regard to whether its underlying policy would be furthered thereby. Under the traditional approach, the forum was often placed in the irrational position of denying its own legitimate governmental interests in applying its local law to a particular case while at the same time not advancing the governmental interests of the state whose law was applied. Recognizing this anomaly, Professor Brainerd Currie suggested that the forum court, as an instrument of state policy, should *apply its own law wherever it has a legitimate interest in doing so.* If the forum has no legitimate interest in applying its own law, it should then apply the law of a state that does have a legitimate interest in such application.

(2) Methodology [§321]

Under the governmental interest approach, the forum, upon the request of a party, examines the substance of the relevant laws—its own and those of the other states involved—to *ascertain their underlying policies.* Once such policies are defined, the forum will determine which state has an interest in having its law applied to the specific issue. As noted above, the *law of the forum will not be displaced* by that of another state if the court determines that the forum's interests would be advanced by applying its own law.

Example: Suppose the law of the forum prohibits married women from making contracts guaranteeing their husbands' credit. A married woman domiciled in the forum enters into a contract in State X guaranteeing her husband's credit. He fails to pay and the creditor, who resides in State X, sues her in the forum state. The policy behind the forum's law is to protect married women against improper influence by their husbands and was enacted to protect residents of the forum state. Since the married woman is a resident of the forum state, the forum court should recognize a governmental interest in applying its law to protect her. On the other hand, State X's policy is to uphold freedom of contract and encourage commerce. Since the creditor is a resident of State X, these policies were intended for his benefit. Despite the competing interests here, the forum court would apply its own law, since the forum has an interest in such application. If the creditor had succeeded in obtaining jurisdiction over the married woman in State X, that state might have decided to further its own interest by applying X law. [*Based on* **Milliken v. Pratt,** 125 Mass. 374 (1878)]

(3) Applications

(a) "False conflicts"—where only one state has a legitimate interest [§322]

Where the forum finds that *only one* of two or more states with ostensibly conflicting laws has a legitimate interest in the application of its law, the forum will apply the law of the interested state. This situation is known as the "false problem" or "false conflict" case.

Example: Host and Guest, both domiciled in the forum, were driving in State X when Host negligently drove into a stone wall, injuring the plaintiff Guest. The forum does not have a host-guest statute, but permits recovery based on ordinary negligence. The forum has an interest in the application of its policy of allowing recovery from negligent hosts, since both Host and Guest are residents of the forum. The fact that State X has a contrary policy limiting the host's liability to protect her against an ungrateful guest (or perhaps to prevent collusive suits against the host's insurance company) is a "false conflict" in this case because State X has no contrary interest in the assertion of its policy; *i.e.,* neither Host nor her insurance company are residents of or doing business in State X. The forum should thus apply its own law as that of the only interested state. [**Babcock v. Jackson,** 12 N.Y.2d 473 (1963)]

Compare: If the suit above had been brought in State X, the State X court should follow the same analysis to reach the same result: it should apply the law of the common domicile of Host and Guest because it has no real interest in protecting a nonresident.

(b) **"True conflict"—where both states have legitimate interests in the case [§323]**

A "true" conflicts case exists where *more than one state* has a legitimate interest in having its law applied to the issue, and the laws of the interested states conflict.

1) **"Preference for law of forum" [§324]**

In a true conflicts case, Currie suggests that the court should recognize the interests of the forum by applying its own law—even though this would defeat the interests of the other states involved.

a) **Possibility of differing results [§325]**

Because of the conflicting interests between states, true conflicts cases will result in different outcomes depending on where the suit is brought. Each interested state, as a forum, would apply its own law.

b) **Reconsideration of interests [§326]**

Currie therefore advises that when the forum is faced with an "ostensible true conflict," it should *reconsider its interests and those of the other state*. It may be that a more "restrained and moderate" interpretation of the conflicting interests will allow the forum to avoid the conflict by applying a common policy of both states. However, if the forum still finds that a conflict between legitimate interests is unavoidable, it should apply its own law.

c) **Illustration [§327]**

Suppose the forum has a law placing spendthrifts under guardianship and permitting the guardian to avoid the spendthrift's contracts. Spendthrift, his family, and his guardian are all residents of the forum. Without the knowledge or consent of his guardian, Spendthrift goes to State X and enters into a contract with a State X creditor. Spendthrift fails to repay monies advanced to him under the contract and his guardian avoids the contract. The creditor then files suit in the forum state.

1/ **Policy**

The policy of the forum law is to protect the families and estates of spendthrifts against improvidence, and the forum has an interest in applying its law because Spendthrift and his family are forum residents. On the other hand, State X has a policy of upholding freedom of contract and promoting interstate commerce. It, too, has an interest in applying its policy to benefit a resident creditor, particularly since Spendthrift came to State X to seek out the creditor. Assume also that the creditor had made a reasonable investigation without learning of Spendthrift's disability.

2/ Result

The forum court probably could not avoid this true conflict by a more moderate or restrained interpretation of its own interests or those of State X, and hence would apply its own law. Presumably State X would likewise apply its law if the suit had been brought there. [*See* **Lilienthal v. Kaufman,** 395 P.2d 543 (Or. 1964)]

2) "Comparative impairment" approach [§328]

Another approach to resolution of "true" conflicts cases, suggested by Professor William F. Baxter, is that of "comparative impairment," in which a federal court would assume jurisdiction in cases of true conflict and would apply the law of the state whose underlying policies would be ***most impaired*** if its laws were not applied to resolve the case. Baxter believed that neither of the two conflicting states could resolve the conflict, but if an impartial federal court could do so, Currie's solution of having each state apply its own law could be avoided. Baxter recognized that his approach would require that **Klaxon Co. v. Stentor Electric Manufacturing Co.** (*supra*, §294; *and see infra*, §723) be overruled.

Example: Nevada tavernkeeper (defendant) served liquor to an obviously intoxicated Californian, who later drove into California and injured the plaintiff, a California resident. California law imposes civil liability on tavernkeepers for injuries inflicted by their patrons, but Nevada law does not. Each state had a legitimate interest in protecting its citizens: California had an interest in protecting citizens injured in California by intoxicated drivers, while Nevada had an interest in protecting its resident tavernkeepers from civil liability. The California court disregarded Baxter's analysis insofar as it called for a federal court to decide true conflicts and undertook to incorporate his comparative impairment analysis as a matter of state law. It proceeded to evaluate which state's interest would be the more impaired if its law were not applied, concluding that California's interest in discouraging tavernkeepers from selling liquor to intoxicated patrons would be seriously undermined if out-of-state tavernkeepers could not be held liable whereas Nevada's interest in protecting resident tavernkeepers should not protect those who, like the defendant, regularly sell to and solicit California patrons. The court therefore applied its own (California) law. [**Bernhard v. Harrah's Club,** 16 Cal. 3d 313 (1976)]

Example: A key employee of the plaintiff California corporation was injured on the defendant corporation's premises in Louisiana. Louisiana did not permit corporations to recover damages arising from the loss of a key employee's services. California had a statute that might have permitted such suits, and the California court assumed that the statute would be so interpreted. The court then found a *true conflict* arising from California's interest in protecting its corporation from economic harm and Louisiana's conflicting interest in shielding its corporate tortfeasors from undue financial burdens. The court resolved this conflict by holding that California's law was unusual and outmoded, while that of Louisiana was modern and progressive. California's interest in having its own law applied was therefore less strong than that of Louisiana. (*But note:* The California court failed to examine the domestic policy of its own statute before deciding the choice-of-law questions. Had it done so, it might have found that the California statute did not create a cause of action for "key employee" suits, and there would have been no conflict with Louisiana law. *Also note:* The court imported factors into the comparative impairment analysis, such as the relative value of the conflicting laws, that are not part of Baxter's concept.) [**Offshore Rental Co. v. Continental Oil Co.,** 22 Cal. 3d 157 (1978)]

---

(4) Problems with interest analysis [§329]

When the forum has *no interest in applying its own law—i.e.,* it is a "disinterested third state"—the Currie approach may present problems where more than one other state has an interest or where no other state has an interest.

(a) False conflicts in disinterested forum [§330]

If the ostensible conflict between the other two states is "false" (*i.e., only one* of them has an interest in having its law applied), the forum will simply apply the law of the only interested state. This type of case does not present any real difficulties.

Example: An automobile collision occurs in State X, in which Defendant, a State Y resident, is responsible for the death of Plaintiff's husband, a resident of State Z. Plaintiff files a wrongful death action against Defendant in State Y. The laws of both Y and Z permit unlimited liability for wrongful death actions. However, State X limits liability for wrongful death to $25,000. This limitation is to protect defendants against excessive liability in cases where Plaintiff is recovering for the death of another. However, State X has no interest in applying its law to protect Defendant, who is a resident of State Y. Likewise, since State Y permits unlimited liability, it has no interest in giving Defendant a windfall by applying X law on his behalf. At the same time, State Y has no real interest in applying its own law, because Plaintiff does not reside there. State Z, on the other hand, is interested in providing full recovery to its residents. *Result:* State Y is a disinterested third state with respect to damages, and thus would apply the law of State Z, the only interested state. [*See* **Reich v. Purcell,** 67 Cal. 2d 551 (1967)]

(b) True conflicts in disinterested forum [§331]

If the forum determines that the other states involved have legitimate interests in applying their competing policies, a true conflict is presented.

1) Dismissal [§332]

If the doctrine of forum non conveniens (*see supra,* §227) is available, the forum should dismiss the case in this situation.

2) Choice between the laws of the interested states [§333]

Where forum non conveniens is not available, the forum must apply the law of one of the interested states. (In such a case, application of forum law may be unconstitutional.)

a) Note

In choosing the competing laws, the forum may either (i) act like a legislature and make a value judgment as to which law it thinks is better or sounder, or (ii) apply the law which most resembles its own (on the theory that the forum legislature has already determined that law to be better or sounder).

Example: If Defendant in **Reich v. Purcell** (*supra,* §330) were a resident of State X and Plaintiff moved to State Y after the decedent's death, forum non conveniens would not be available (*see supra,* §231). Assuming a conflict could not be avoided by a more moderate or restrained interpretation, the forum might apply the law of that state more similar to its own—*i.e.,* the unlimited liability law of State X.

(c) "Unprovided for case" [§334]

This situation arises where *neither the forum nor the other states* involved have an interest in application of their respective laws.

e.g. **Example:** Plaintiff, a resident of State X, is injured while riding as a guest in a car garaged in State Y but driven in State X by Defendant, a resident of State Y. Plaintiff brought suit in State Y. State X has a guest statute that would prevent liability if applied to the case. State Y has no guest statute. But since State X has no interest in applying its guest statute to protect State Y defendants, and State Y has no interest in providing compensation for State X residents injured in State X, neither state has an interest in having its law applied. [*See* **Labree v. Major,** 306 A.2d 808 (R.I. 1973)]

1) Currie's proposed solutions [§335]

Currie advanced four possible solutions for the forum court to the problem of the "unprovided for case":

(i) Apply the law of that state that provides "*a better solution* to the underlying social and economic problem";

(ii) Selfishly *protect the local driver* against the claims of foreign plaintiffs;

(iii) Reach the same result as in (ii) by applying a more sophisticated rule that would *treat foreign plaintiffs as they would be treated in their home states*; or

(iv) Apply the *law of the forum*, since application of another state's law is not justified.

Currie preferred the fourth alternative, rejecting the first approach as giving courts greater discretion in conflicts cases than in domestic cases and rejecting the second and third suggestions as presenting constitutional difficulties.

(5) Criticisms of governmental interest analysis [§336]

The two primary criticisms of the governmental analysis approach involve the difficulty in identifying the policies behind the laws applied to determine the interests of the different states and the unpredictability of this approach.

(a) Difficulty in identifying underlying policies [§337]

The primary criticism launched against the governmental interest approach is the difficulty involved in ascertaining the policies behind the various laws in order to identify interested states. Not only are policy considerations often unarticulated, but also most law has developed without reference to multistate events—so that the underlying policies would not necessarily reflect an "interest" with respect to interstate cases. [*See* Leflar, American Conflicts of Law §92; Brilmayer, 78 Mich. L. Rev. 392 (1980); Korn, 83 Colum. L. Rev. 772 (1983)]

(b) Unpredictability of approach [§338]

Other critics argue that the more moderate and restrained interpretation of policies required in a true conflicts case obliges the court to perform a legislative task, and that a weighing of conflicting policies serves to negate uniformity of result. Consequently, parties never know in advance which state's interests will be deemed paramount.

EXAM TIP   **gilbert**

Because the governmental interest approach requires you to *identify the competing policies* behind laws and *consider the states' interests* in applying their laws to an issue, answering a question using this approach will be a little harder for you than just applying the hard-and-fast rules of the traditional approach. In your answer *you must show how* you came to your decision as to the proper law to apply. Start with the position that *forum law will be applied* if the forum's interests will be advanced. But don't stop there. Analyze the policies of any other state and determine whether the other state would be interested in applying its law. If it appears so, discuss whether there is a *false conflict* (only one state really is interested—that's easy, apply the law of that state), a *true conflict* (more than one state really are interested—a little harder and may result in the forum applying its law just to end the matter), or *no interested state* at all (again forum law would probably be applied).

---

d. Alternative modern approaches to choice of law [§339]

In recent years, legal scholars have formulated various alternative approaches to choice-of-law issues.

EXAM TIP   **gilbert**

Like the governmental interest approach, the following approaches all *analyze policies and interests*. How thoroughly you need to know the details of these modern approaches depends on your professor and course materials.

---

(1) "Functional analysis" approaches [§340]

Two approaches, one espoused by Professors Arthur von Mehren and Donald Trautman and the other by Professor Russell Weintraub, adopt a "functional analysis" for choice-of-law problems. Both essentially follow the governmental interest approach, but offer different solutions to "true conflicts" situations (*supra*, §§323-328).

(a) von Mehren and Trautman approach [§341]

Under this approach, the term "concerned jurisdiction" is substituted for "interested state" under the governmental interest approach (*supra*). Basically, the forum is directed to locate concerned jurisdictions, identify the *"predominantly concerned jurisdiction,"* and apply the law of that state to the particular issue in question. (Under the governmental interest approach, the "moderate and restrained" interpretation achieves this result.) In the absence of a predominantly concerned jurisdiction (*i.e.*, in a "true conflicts" case), this approach, unlike the governmental interest approach, requires the forum to "weigh" the status of the conflicting laws, considering the policies behind the laws in terms of both their effectiveness and current trends in the law.

1) Methodology [§342]

As noted above, the von Mehren and Trautman approach initially follows the governmental interest analysis approach. The forum is required to examine the laws of the various states involved and determine which states have shown "concern"— expressly or impliedly—that their laws be applied. If the respective laws are the same or if the policies of the various states are not in conflict (a *"false conflicts"* case), the results are the same as those reached under governmental interest analysis. However, if both the laws and the policy considerations conflict (a *"true conflicts"* case), the court would apply the following analysis:

a) Identify and apply law of predominantly concerned jurisdiction [§343]

A jurisdiction may be found to be "predominantly" concerned because its concern *outweighs* that of another jurisdiction (due to its relationship to the multistate aspects of the case) or because its *aggregate concerns* are greater than any individual concern of another jurisdiction.

b) Where no predominantly concerned jurisdiction—weigh "status" of various laws [§344]

If the forum court is unable to identify the predominantly concerned jurisdiction in a "true conflicts" case, it must weigh the status of the respective laws and underlying policies, with a view toward reaching a functionally sound and just result. The court should consider the following factors:

1/ *How forceful is the policy*—is it waning, or does it represent an emerging trend in the law?

2/ Does the jurisdiction *actively assert the policy*?

3/ Does the particular rule *effectively assert the policy*, and is it an *appropriate* way to assert such policy?

4/ What is the *relative significance* to the concerned jurisdictions of *vindicating* their policies?

c) "Last resort" solution [§345]

Finally, if the weighing process likewise fails to resolve the conflict, von Mehren and Trautman offer two additional techniques:

1/ Apply the law of jurisdiction having *"effective control"* (*e.g.*, the law of the situs of immovables); or

2/ If no jurisdiction has effective control, apply the law of the forum—*provided that the forum is a concerned jurisdiction*. If the forum is "neutral" (or "disinterested" under the governmental interest analysis approach), it should dismiss the suit or render an "impartial solution" (*i.e.*, apply the law that in its view represents the better policy or which most resembles its own law).

(b) Weintraub approach [§346]

Like the von Mehren and Trautman analysis, the Weintraub approach follows governmental interest analysis up to the point of a "true conflict." At that point, Weintraub proposes a *"rational solution"* based on the underlying policies of the interested states and general trends in the law.

1) Methodology [§347]

Weintraub's approach involves an examination of factors similar to those considered under the von Mehren and Trautman approach (*see supra,* §344) but which vary with the substantive area of law concerned. Weintraub then combines these factors into general choice-of-law rules representing to some extent a synthesis of the traditional approach (*see supra,* §§302-306) and governmental interest analysis (*see supra,* §§319-321).

a) Torts [§348]

In torts cases, four factors are identified for consideration and combined into a single choice-of-law rule.

1/ Factors [§349]

The court is concerned with:

a/ *Advancement of discernible trends* in the law (*e.g.*, loss distribution through liability insurance);

b/ *Prevention of unfair surprise* to defendants (not applicable to insurance company defendants);

c/ *Suppression of "anachronistic" laws* (*e.g.*, a state's failure to provide for survival of causes of action against the estate of a deceased tortfeasor, or creation of causes of action for alienation of affections); and

d/ *Scope of policies* underlying domestic laws of the involved states, as reflected in their choice-of-law rules.

2/ Rule [§350]

An actor is liable for conduct if she is liable under the law of any state whose interests would be significantly advanced by imposing liability, unless imposition of liability would unfairly surprise the actor.

b) Contracts [§351]

In contract actions, six factors are identified and combined into a choice-of-law rule focusing upon the validity of contracts.

1/ Factors [§352]

The court is concerned with:

a/ Recognition of the *rebuttable presumption that a contract is valid*;

b/ *Suppression of anachronistic laws* (*e.g.*, limitations on contractual capacity of married women) which serve to invalidate contracts;

c/ Whether the difference between validating and invalidating rules is one of *detail or basic policy*;

d/ *Prevention of unfair surprise* to party who expected to benefit from the contract;

   e/   Whether the contract is *"commercial" or "non-commercial"*; and

   f/   *Scope of underlying policies* in the domestic laws of states involved (as reflected in their choice-of-law rules).

2/ Rule [§353]

A contract is valid if valid under the domestic law of any state having a sufficient contact with the parties or transaction to make its policies relevant—unless another state would advance its policies by invalidating the contract *and* one or more of the following factors suggest that the conflict should be resolved in favor of invalidity:

   a/   The invalidating rule reflects a *viable, current trend* in the law of contracts, such as the growing concern for protection of parties in an inferior bargaining position;

   b/   The invalidating rule differs from the validating rule in *basic policy*, not just in minor detail;

   c/   The parties should have *foreseen the substantial interest* that the state with the invalidating rule would have in controlling the outcome;

   d/   The context of the contract is *noncommercial*;

   e/   The courts of the state with the validating rule have *deferred in similar interstate cases* to the policies underlying the foreign invalidating rule.

(c) Criticisms of "functional analysis" [§354]

The same criticisms levied against governmental interest analysis (*see supra*, §§336-338) would apply equally to the "functional analysis" approach.

(d) Comments [§355]

The distinguishing feature of "functional analysis" is its recognition that *the law is not static* but constantly changing. By directing the forum court to consider trends in the law, as opposed to merely focusing upon existing laws of the other states, better results might be achieved.

(2) "Lex fori" (Ehrenzweig) approach—"proper law in a proper forum" [§356]

The "lex fori" approach calls for application of the "proper law in the proper forum." Basically, the proper law is determined by existing *"true rules"* (statutory or common law), which direct the court to apply the laws of a particular jurisdiction. In the absence of a true rule of choice, the law of the forum should be applied if the forum is proper (*i.e.,* if it has sufficient contacts with the parties or the transaction).

(a) Methodology [§357]

Under the "lex fori" approach, the decision whether foreign law is to be applied is a matter of forum law. If the applicable substantive rule of the forum is based on a "moral datum" or other equitable principles (*e.g.,* rejection of fraud), the forum law will not be displaced by that of other states. In the absence of moral data, the "proper law" to be applied is determined by the following procedure:

1) Identification of "true rules" [§358]

The true rules of choice determine which law will be applied to resolve a particular issue. Such rules fall into two categories:

a) Formulated rules of choice [§359]

Formulated rules may be statutory (*e.g.,* reference to the obligor's law in the Uniform Support Act), but most are based on settled common law doctrines. Examples of formulated rules would include reference to the law of the situs of the property in land cases involving security of title, the law of the domicile in succession cases (if application serves the unity of the estate), and the law of the place of the wrong in causes of action for tort (although Ehrenzweig recognizes that this rule is now being undermined).

b) Nonformulated or inchoate rules of choice [§360]

Nonformulated rules are deduced from a factual and policy-oriented analysis of judicial precedent. They are not as widely recognized as formulated true rules and their scope is still somewhat indefinite. Ehrenzweig points to at least two such nonformulated rules of choice: recognition of child custody decrees in favor of a parent having "clean hands" (although the courts here speak in terms of jurisdiction); and recognition of nonadhesion contracts, wills and trusts in the face of technical defenses—the "true rule of validation" (although the courts here speak in terms of traditional formulas about place of making, place of performance, etc.).

2) Interpretation of forum law sought to be displaced [§361]

If no true rule of choice can be discerned, the court must resort to its own domestic law. The interpretation of forum law may lead to application of the forum's own law or to application of a foreign law. Where a court determines that the forum's tort rule is designed to punish for example, it will interpret the rule to refer to the law of the place of acting rather than to the law of the place of injury.

3) Possibility of dismissal [§362]

If the policies underlying the substantive law of the forum are not applicable to the particular facts, the suit may be dismissed if no prejudice would result therefrom.

4) Application of the forum law as "residual" [§363]

Finally, where there is no true rule of choice, the forum policies are not applicable, and it is impossible to dismiss the suit without prejudice, the court will simply apply its own domestic law as a "residuary solution." Ehrenzweig refers to this as a "theory of nonchoice."

(b) Criticism of "lex fori" analysis [§364]

Emphasis on the law of the forum in the "lex fori" approach makes it difficult for parties to predict the applicable law since they may not know in advance where litigation could arise. Indeed, the approach encourages "forum shopping" to obtain the most favorable rules.

1) Response to criticism [§365]

Advocates of "lex fori" contend that "forum shopping" can be eliminated by encouraging parties to sue in the "proper forum" through use of the doctrine of forum non conveniens (*see supra*, §227)—*i.e.*, that application of an inappropriate forum law be controlled by limitations on the exercise of jurisdiction.

(3) "Principles of preference" (Cavers) approach [§366]

The "principles of preference" approach espoused by Professor David Cavers posits that courts in a federal system faced with choice-of-law problems should strive to accommodate the conflicting laws so as to optimize the working of the federation. The process of accommodation, although carried out primarily on a case-by-case basis, should be accomplished through the creation of rules—*"principles of preference"*—that will go beyond ad hoc decisions to provide guides for similar cases in the future. Cavers believes that "principles" with respect to particular fact situations should be developed by the courts over time.

(a) Methodology [§367]

Cavers accepts the basic premises of the governmental interest approach (*supra*) in its analysis of the policy or "purpose" of a particular law and the interest of a state in having its law applied. Wherever possible, cases should be disposed of by showing that the conflict is false or can be avoided by examining the purposes of the laws involved and the circumstances of the case. However, principles of preference are useful both in identifying false conflict cases and in solving true conflict situations.

1) Development of principles of preference [§368]

A principle of preference should determine when a law serving one purpose (*e.g.*, a rule designed to protect a class of people who engage in a given type of activity) should be preferred to the law of another state which serves a different purpose (*e.g.*, a law that does not protect people engaged in that activity). The principle adopted should not only achieve a desirable accommodation of the conflicting laws but also deal fairly with the parties. Such principles are to be developed through reasoned analyses of particular situations or groups of situations.

2) Illustrative principles [§369]

For purposes of illustration, Cavers has formulated the following seven principles of preference (five for tort cases and two for contract cases):

a) Torts

1/ Place of injury—higher standard [§370]

Where the laws of the state of injury impose a *higher* standard of conduct or financial protection against injury than the laws of the state where the tortious act occurred or the law of defendant's domicile, *the laws of the state of injury should determine the standard and the protection applicable to the case* (at least where the plaintiff was not so related to the defendant that the question should be relegated to the law governing their relationship).

Example: Defendant, a domiciliary of Arizona, injures a California resident in California. Defendant dies, and the question is whether an action for personal injury survives his death. California law permits survival; Arizona law does not. California law should govern, according to the principle of preference, regardless of whether the suit is brought in Arizona or California. [*Based on a variant of* **Grant v. McAuliffe,** 41 Cal. 2d 859 (1953)]

2/ Place of act and injury—lower standard [§371]

Where the laws of the state in which both the act and the injury occur establish a *lower* standard of conduct or financial protection than the laws of the plaintiff's domicile, *the laws of the state of conduct and injury should determine the applicable standards* (again, where the plaintiff was not so related to the defendant that the question should be relegated to the law governing their relationship).

Example: A tourist in State A is killed in State B by a State B defendant. Suit is brought in State A for wrongful death. State A has unlimited damages for wrongful death, while State B imposes a limit of $15,000. Application of the principle would dictate a limited recovery under the law of State B, even if suit was brought in State A. [*See* **Cipolla v. Shaposka,** 267 A.2d 854 (Pa. 1970)]

3/ Place of act—special controls [§372]

Where the state in which a defendant acts has established special controls over the kind of activities in which the defendant is engaged, the *plaintiff should be accorded the benefit of the special conduct and financial protection of those sanctions.* This is true even though plaintiff has no special relationship to defendant and the state of injury has imposed no such controls or sanctions.

Example: Minnesota has a dramshop act imposing liability on saloonkeepers who sell liquor to drunks for injuries caused by the drunk. A Minnesota saloonkeeper sells liquor to a drunken Minnesota driver who subsequently injures a Wisconsin pedestrian in Wisconsin. Even if Wisconsin has no dramshop act or other similar statutory imposition of liability on saloonkeepers, the Wisconsin plaintiff could recover against the Minnesota saloonkeeper. [*See* **Schmidt v. Driscoll Hotel, Inc.,** 82 N.W.2d 365 (Minn. 1957)]

4/ Center of relationship—higher standard [§373]

Where the law of the state in which a relationship is centered has imposed a standard of conduct or financial protection on one of the "related" parties for the benefit of the other party which is *higher* than that imposed by the state of injury, the law of the former state should determine the applicable standards for the benefit of the party protected by that state's law.

Example: A New York domiciliary in New York boards an airplane owned by a Massachusetts corporation. The airplane crashes in Massachusetts, killing the New York passenger. Massachusetts has a limit on wrongful death damages of $15,000, while New York has no limitation on damages. If suit for wrongful death is brought in a third state having no connection with the parties or the controversy, the principle would direct the forum to apply the law of New York, the state in which the relationship was centered. [*Based on a variant of* **Kilberg v. Northeast Airlines, Inc.,** 9 N.Y.2d 34 (1961)—where the true conflict is to be resolved by a disinterested forum]

5/ Center of relationship—lower standard [§374]

Similarly, where the law of a state in which a relationship is centered has imposed *lower* standards than those imposed by the state of injury, the law of the state where the relationship is centered should determine the standard of conduct or financial protection applicable to the case for the benefit of the party whose liability would be denied or limited by that state's law.

Example: Husband and Wife live in State X, which recognizes interspousal immunity in tort. Husband injures Wife in State Y, which has abolished interspousal immunity. According to this principle, the law of State X would prevent Wife's recovery.

a/ Comment

Cavers disapproves of this as a principle, and includes it in his list of seven only for purposes of illustration. However, at least one state supreme court has applied the principle. [*See* **Johnson v. Johnson,** 216 A.2d 781 (N.H. 1966)]

b) Contracts and conveyances

1/ Protective provisions [§375]

Where a state has imposed restrictions on the power to contract or to convey or encumber property for purposes of affording protection against the adverse consequences of incompetence, improvidence, ignorance, or unequal bargaining power, its protective provisions should be applied against a party to the restricted transaction where (i) the person protected is *domiciled in that state* (and comes within the "protected class"), *and* (ii) the *affected transaction or protected property interest was centered there,* or if not, the facts were simply fortuitous or were manipulated in order to evade the protective law.

---

e.g. **Example:** A Massachusetts married woman is solicited in Massachusetts by the agent of a Maine firm to sign a contract guaranteeing her husband's credit. Her husband does business in Massachusetts. Massachusetts does not permit married women to make such contracts, while Maine has recognized the full contractual capacity of married women. Since the transaction is centered in Massachusetts, the principle would require application of Massachusetts law. [**Milliken v. Pratt,** *supra,* §321]

2/ Parties' expectations [§376]

If the parties to a transaction intended that the law of a particular state which is reasonably related to the transaction should be determinative, the law of that state should be applied *if it validates* the transaction—even though neither party is domiciled in that state and the transaction is not centered there.

a/ Note

This principle will not apply where the results would violate any protective law that would be applicable under the preceding principle; nor will it apply where the transaction involves a conveyance of land and the mode of conveyance or the interests created violate the mandatory rules of the situs of the land. Also, this principle does not govern the legal effect of the transaction on third parties with independent interests.

Example: Plaintiff, a resident of State X, and Defendant, a resident of State Y, enter into a contract for the sale of goods which they agree will be governed by the law of State Z. State Z has no connection with the parties or the transaction, but its law upholds the contract. The law of State Z will be applied, unless the principle described in §375, *supra*, has been violated.

(b) Criticism of "principles" approach [§377]

The major difficulty with the principles of preference approach is that it envisions a multitude of all-embracing "principles" to be developed by the courts, and it could be decades before such principles are formulated. Moreover, such an approach, like that of the First Restatement, would ultimately become mechanical—thereby minimizing judicial flexibility and discretion. [Leflar, American Conflicts Law §95]

(4) "Better law" (Leflar) approach—"choice-influencing considerations" [§378]

While courts faced with choice-of-law problems may speak in terms of the mechanical rules and underlying policies, their ultimate decisions reflect "choice-influencing considerations"—not always recognized or identified as such, but nonetheless present and operative. These choice-influencing considerations have been cited by various scholars, and Leflar has reduced them to a manageably compact form.

(a) Methodology [§379]

The "better law" approach *rejects all "rules" and "formulas"* except for specific statutory or constitutional directives, focusing instead on five basic choice-influencing considerations (below) with a view toward effectuating justice between the parties. The forum is directed to select whichever law would best achieve this end in light of the particular problems presented in each case (the "better law").

1) Choice-influencing considerations [§380]

The court is concerned with the following considerations:

a) *Predictability of results*—to discourage forum shopping, protect the justified expectations of parties to planned transactions, and further the goal of uniform results.

b) *Maintenance of interstate and international order*—to further the free flow of persons and goods from one jurisdiction to another and thereby encourage interstate and international intercourse.

c) *Simplification of the judicial task*—to permit the forum to apply its own procedural law as a matter of judicial convenience, while recognizing that in some cases the outcome-determinative procedural law of another state should be applied (*e.g.*, Statute of Frauds, measure of damages, or survival of tort claims).

d) *Advancement of forum's governmental interests*—to permit the forum to effectuate its own legitimate interest in applying a given rule (its own or another state's) to the case, while recognizing that "governmental interests" should reflect "the total governmental concerns of a justice-dispensing court in a modern American state."

e) *Application of the better rule of law*—to recognize that choice of law should be between the particular laws involved, not between the states whose law is to be applied. Judges should prefer rules of law that make good sense for the time and place in which the court speaks, in light of the goal to do justice in the individual case.

(b) Criticism of "better law" approach [§381]

The "better law" analysis has been criticized on the ground that it is indefinite and uncertain, that the "choice-influencing considerations" may be evaluated differently by different courts, and that the "better" rule selected by the forum will usually be its own! Nevertheless, five jurisdictions (Arkansas, Minnesota, New Hampshire, Rhode Island, and Wisconsin) have adopted the "better law" approach.

3. Application of Choice-of-Law Theories in Practice

a. In general [§382]

The modern choice-of-law theories discussed above have appeared in court opinions during the last few decades. The traditional approach was first abandoned in cases that presented "false problems"—*i.e.*, situations in which only one state had an interest in the application of its law (*see supra*, §322). When more complicated cases arose, the courts experienced difficulties in distinguishing among the various approaches and applying any one of them consistently.

b. Emerging "common law" in conflicts cases [§383]

Today, only 10 states continue to follow the traditional approach in torts conflicts cases, while 11 states do so in contracts conflicts cases. The remaining states and the District of Columbia have chosen alternative modern approaches. In *torts* cases, 22 states adopt the Second Restatement approach, three follow a "significant contacts"approach, three states and the District of Columbia follow governmental interest analysis, three states follow a "lex fori" approach, five states follow Leflar's "better law" methodology, and six states use a combination of the modern approaches. In *contracts* conflicts cases, 24 states adopt the Second Restatement approach, five follow a "significant contacts" approach, the District of Columbia follows interest analysis, none follows a "lex fori" approach, two follow Leflar's "better law approach," and 10 follow a combination of the modern approaches. [Symeonides, *Choice of Law in the American Courts in 2000: As the Century Turns,* 49 Am. J. Comp. L. 1 (2001)—author stated in 2002 that this list remains current, *see* 51 Am J. Comp. L. 1 (2003)]. Despite these differences in approach, however, Professor Sedler has argued that in many typical situations, the "judicial method" used in policy-centered conflict of laws cases by courts that have abandoned the traditional approach has produced substantial uniformity of result. For example, in torts conflicts cases, he finds that the first universal rule of choice of law followed by all states that have abandoned the traditional approach is that when two residents of the forum are injured in another state, the law of the forum applies. [*See* Sedler, *A Real World Perspective on Choice of Law,* 48 Mercer L. Rev. 781 (1997)]

Chapter Five: Choice of Law in Specific Substantive Areas

CONTENTS

Chapter Approach

Some approaches to choice of law, specifically the traditional, ***vested rights approach*** of the First Restatement and the ***most significant relationship approach*** of the Second Restatement, have different rules for choice of law depending on the subject matter area in question. In answering an exam question using these two approaches to choice of law, you must indicate what those different rules are. This chapter discusses the different rules by area of law.

Other approaches to choice of law, such as Currie's governmental interest approach and, to a lesser degree, Leflar's better law approach, do not vary the analysis by subject matter. However, you will still take account of the unique aspects of the different subject matter areas when using these approaches when you analyze the ***policies underlying*** the conflicting laws.

A. Torts

1. General Approaches

a. Traditional "vested rights" approach—"place of wrong" rule [§384]
The traditional rule—now almost completely discredited—was that the existence and extent of tort liability was to be determined according to the law of the ***place of the "wrong."*** [(First) Restatement of Conflict of Laws ("Rest.") §378]

(1) Rationale
The rationale for this rule was that since tort claims are transitory (*i.e.,* a defendant may be held liable in any state where the plaintiff catches her), it was only fair that the defendant be judged according to the standards in effect where she acted rather than the standards where she was sued. [**American Banana Co. v. United Fruit Co.,** 213 U.S. 347 (1909)]

(2) Place of injury as place of "wrong" [§385]
The place of the "wrong" was generally held to be the place where the plaintiff's injuries were sustained. While this ordinarily would be the same state in which the defendant acted, it could make a difference where the defendant "acted" in one state but the injuries were received in another—*e.g.,* blasting in one state causing damage across a state line. [**Pendar v. H & B American Machine Co.,** 87 A. 1 (R.I. 1913)] The First Restatement defined the place of the "wrong" as "where the last event necessary to make the actor liable took place." [Rest. §377]

(3) Criticisms [§386]

The following criticisms were leveled at the "place of the wrong" rule:

(a) Fortuitous results

Focusing only on the law of the place of the injury (wrong) often led to entirely fortuitous results—as where injuries were sustained in an auto accident in State A involving parties who both resided in State B and were merely passing through State A.

(b) Policy of other states defeated

The rule frequently defeated the policies and laws of states having far more significant contacts with the parties and their injuries (*e.g.,* the state where the plaintiff was domiciled was no doubt far more concerned with compensation than the state where the impact took place).

(c) Other considerations

In many cases, it was more appropriate to look to the place of the defendant's conduct to determine liability (*e.g.,* where the defendant claims a privilege); and in such cases an inflexible reference to the place of the injury would result in cutting off a defense that the defendant might otherwise assert.

(4) "Exceptions" to place of wrong rule [§387]

Recognizing the validity of the above criticisms, courts used several devices to avoid such fortuitous results (*see* below, *and see supra,* §§307-311).

(a) Characterization as "procedural" [§388]

As mentioned previously (*supra,* §308), the forum ordinarily applies its own law to routine "procedural" matters but looks to appropriate foreign law on all outcome determinative ("substantive") issues. By classifying a particular aspect of a tort problem as "procedural," the court could thus avoid reference to otherwise applicable foreign law. [**Dorr Cattle Co. v. Des Moines National Bank,** 98 N.W. 918 (Iowa 1904)—recoverability of particular item of damages held "procedural" and thus governed by forum law; **Kilberg v. Northeast Airlines, Inc.,** *supra,* §373, *and see infra,* §677—characterization used to circumvent a limitation on damages imposed by the law of the place of the injury; *and see infra,* §§638 *et seq.*]

1) Criticism [§389]

This technique merely avoids the issue—paying lip service to the "place of the wrong" rule while evading it through a characterization device.

(b) Characterization as "nontort" problem [§390]

To avoid unfavorable law at the place of injury, courts might also characterize the basic problem as something other than "tort."

Example: Where the defendant negligently breached a duty of care arising from a contractual relationship, the court might choose to apply a "contracts" choice-of-law rule. [*See* **Levy v. Daniels' U-Drive Auto Renting Co.**, *supra*, §309] Similarly, the question of interspousal immunity has been characterized as a "family law" problem rather than a "torts" problem so as to justify reference to the law of the spouses' domicile rather than to the law of the place of injury. [**Haumschild v. Continental Casualty Co.**, 95 N.W.2d 814 (Wis. 1959)]

(c) Holding "wrong" to be conduct rather than injury [§391]

Particularly where the defendant's conduct is shown to be morally blameworthy, a number of courts have designated the *conduct*, rather than the injury, as the "wrong" in order to apply the law of the place where the conduct took place. [*See* **Gordon v. Parker**, 83 F. Supp. 40 (D. Mass. 1949)—forum applied its own law to hold defendant liable in alienation of affections case because adulterous conduct took place within forum, even though all the parties were domiciled in another state and any "injury" probably took place there]

(d) Public policy defense [§392]

Finally, courts have sometimes invoked "local public policy" as a last-ditch defense to application of the "place of the wrong" rule. [*See* **Mertz v. Mertz**, 271 N.Y. 466 (1936)—"local public policy" against interspousal litigation barred reference to law of place of injury which allowed such suits]

1) Criticism [§393]

Invocation of local public policy as a defense to application of a choice-of-law rule undermines any attempt at uniformity of results, and really reflects an overly rigid "rule" leading to unfair results.

EXAM TIP **gilbert**

Although Torts questions are fairly easy under the traditional approach—you generally *apply the law of the place of the wrong (injury)*—don't overlook the *escape devices*, which you should consider if the result under the traditional approach seems unjust.

---

b. Second Restatement "most significant relationship" approach [§394]

Recognizing the shortcomings of the rigid "place of the wrong" rule, a number of authorities in recent years have opted instead for a "most significant relationship" approach. Under this approach, the forum is directed to consider the "contacts" and interests of each state involved and to apply the law of the state having the most significant relationship with the parties and the transaction in light of the particular issue before the court. [Rest. 2d §145]

(1) Application

A leading case establishing this position was **Babcock v. Jackson**, *supra*, §322, in which a New York court permitted a guest to sue the driver of the car in which he was riding for injuries sustained in Canada, although Canadian law barred such actions. The court emphasized that since all parties were New York residents, the car was ordinarily garaged there, and the guest-driver relationship arose there, the "most significant contacts" with respect to the guest statute issue were in New York and therefore its law should apply.

(2) "Significant" contacts [§395]

According to the Second Restatement, the significant contacts to be isolated in a torts case are:

(i) The place of *injury*;

(ii) The place of *conduct*;

(iii) The place of *each party's residence and/or business*; and

(iv) The place where the *relationship (if any) between the parties is centered*.

[Rest. 2d §145(2)] These contacts are to be evaluated according to their relative *importance to the particular issue* involved in the case, together with the various general factors and policies discussed previously (*see supra*, §315). However, the Second Restatement retains the basic *preference* for the law of the *place of injury*, unless other factors establish a "more significant" relationship. [Rest. 2d §§146, 147]

EXAM TIP   gilbert

When answering a Torts question using the Second Restatement approach, note that **usually the place of injury will be the determinative contact**, but be sure to consider the other three "significant" contacts above because sometimes (see *infra*) one of the other three will be more important. Therefore, it is wise to consider, and at least mention, **all four contacts** in your answer, even if you decide that the usual rule applies. Finally, don't forget to include an evaluation of any relevant **policy interests** that indicate one state has a stronger interest than the other.

---

(3) Criticism [§396]

In using the "most significant relationship" approach, different courts may reach different results by "weighing" the "contacts" differently.

Example: The unpredictability of the approach is illustrated by the fact that the same court that decided *Babcock*, *supra*, reached precisely the opposite result in **Dym v. Gordon,** 16 N.Y.2d 120 (1965)—the only factual difference being that the guest and the driver, although domiciled in New York, were attending school in Colorado. The court nevertheless concluded that the guest-driver relationship "arose" in Colorado and applied its guest statute.

Compare: Later, the New York courts began to place more emphasis on the *purposes of the respective laws* in question. In **Tooker v. Lopez,** 24 N.Y.2d 569 (1969), for example, the court on substantially identical facts observed that the only apparent purpose of the guest statute in effect at the place of injury (Michigan) was to prevent fraudulent claims against local insurers and to protect local automobile owners ("hosts"), and since these purposes were not involved where both the host and guest were residents of another state, only the state of residence (New York) had any "real interest" in whether recovery should be granted and its law should be applied. (This is substantially the "governmental interest" approach; *see* below.) (*But note:* More recently, New York courts have restricted *Tooker* to cases where the host and guest were both forum residents by holding that where the passenger and driver were domiciled in different states, the law of the place where the accident occurred should be applied. [*See, e.g.,* **Neumeier v. Kuehner,** 31 N.Y.2d 121 (1972)—Ontario guest statute applied to bar recovery by Ontario resident (guest) against New York host for injuries sustained in Ontario])

c.   **"Governmental interest" approach [§397]**
Other modern decisions have adopted the "governmental interest" approach to choice of law, in which the forum applies its own law if it has an interest in doing so.

Examples: In a wrongful death action arising out of a collision in Missouri, the decedents were residents of Ohio, and the defendant-driver was a resident of California. Missouri (the place of the wrong) had a statute limiting the amount of damages in a wrongful death action; no such statute was in effect in California or Ohio. The California court held that the forum must consider all of the "interests" involved to determine the applicable law. It concluded that Missouri had no conceivable interest in having its limitation on damages applied since neither the plaintiff nor the defendant resided there. The defendant likewise had no basis to rely on a rule limiting damages, since the law in effect in his domicile (California) allowed unlimited damages. Consequently, the court chose to apply the law of Ohio, the only interested state, to permit it to implement its policies of compensation for survivors of decedents domiciled there. [**Reich v. Purcell,** *supra,* §333]

(1) Effect of post-accident changes [§398]

Several courts have held that a change of domicile by the plaintiff after the cause of action arose is *irrelevant*. [**Reich v. Purcell,** *supra*]

(a) Rationale

To apply a different rule because a party moves his residence might encourage forum shopping, or possibly subject the defendant to liabilities that could not have been foreseen when she acted.

(b) But note

Other authorities assert that post-accident changes or events (such as a change in domicile by either party) *should* be considered insofar as they affect a state interest analysis. [69 Colum. L. Rev. 865 (1969); *and see* **Miller v. Miller,** 22 N.Y.2d 12 (1968)—court disregarded limitation on recovery recognized under law of former domicile, since that state would have no further interest in having limitation applied]

2. Analysis of Specific Torts Problems [§399]

Application of the doctrines and "rules" set forth above is best illustrated by focusing on specific types of "torts" problems.

a. Wrongful death cases [§400]

All states now have wrongful death statutes, which allow a decedent's survivors to recover their damages from a tortious injury to the decedent that caused his death. Thus, there is little conflict regarding the existence of this cause of action. However, the statutes often differ significantly with respect to who may sue, measure of damages, and limitations on recovery—so that the choice of which statute applies is often crucial.

(1) Traditional approach [§401]

Courts traditionally applied the wrongful death statute of the place in which the *fatal injuries were sustained*, even where the decedent actually died elsewhere. [**Pack v. Beech Aircraft Corp.,** 132 A.2d 54 (Del. 1957)]

(a) Note

In **Kilberg v. Northeast Airlines** (*see infra,* §677), the court held that the law of the place of injury governed the right to recover for a wrongful death, but it avoided a limitation on maximum recovery in that law by characterizing the damage issue as "procedural," thereby allowing the forum to apply its own law.

EXAM TIP   **gilbert**

Again, remember that because under the traditional approach the result is often unfair, you should consider the *escape devices* (*see supra*, §§307-311) and discuss the relevant ones in your answer.

---

(2) Modern approaches [§402]

Today, the "place of injury" rule in wrongful death cases has been largely discredited, *particularly where the decedent was domiciled elsewhere at death.*

(a) "Contacts" approach [§403]

The Second Restatement would apply the law of place of injury unless another state had a "more significant relationship." [Rest. 2d §175] However, in wrongful death cases, contacts other than the place of the injury may be more significant. A New York court—as a "disinterested third state"—applied the wrongful death statute of Pennsylvania in a case stemming from a fatal air crash in Maryland on a round trip flight between Pennsylvania and Puerto Rico. The court reasoned that the *"weight of contacts"* was in Pennsylvania (*i.e.*, decedent's domicile, estate, survivors, possible creditors were there; flight began and was to end there; etc.) and rejected the law of the place of injury, which would have barred recovery. [**Long v. Pan American World Airways, Inc.**, 16 N.Y.2d 337 (1965)]

EXAM TIP   **gilbert**

Although the place of the injury is often the most significant relationship in tort cases, note that here is one type of case—and there are others (*see infra*)—where *another interest* (domicile) may be *more significant*. So don't get too mechanical in your approach to Second Restatement questions; be sure to consider *all four interests*.

(b) "Interest" approach [§404]

Courts following an "interest" approach recognize three potential interests served by wrongful death statutes: (i) *compensation* for survivors; (ii) *deterrence* of conduct; and (iii) *limitation* (or the lack thereof) on the amount of damages recoverable. In making a choice of law, the court must focus on the precise issue involved and apply whichever law best serves the interests underlying that issue.

Example: In **Reich v. Purcell**, *supra*, §397, the issue was whether the forum (California) should recognize a limit of damages in the law of the place of death (Missouri). The court concluded that the limitation was designed to protect resident defendants from excessive financial burdens, and that since the defendant was not a resident of Missouri, that state had no interest in having its limitation applied to protect him. Instead, the forum applied the law of decedent's domicile (Ohio), which imposed no such limitation.

> **cf.** **Compare:** The same issue was involved in **Hurtado v. Superior Court,** 11 Cal. 3d 574 (1974). Here, a limitation on damages existed in the plaintiff's domicile (Mexico), but there was no limitation under the law of defendant's domicile and the place of injury (California). The court concluded that Mexico had no interest in having its limitation law applied to protect a California resident against liability for wrongful conduct on California highways, and the court thus applied California law.

b. **Survival of cause of action [§405]**

States may have different laws regarding whether a tort cause of action survives the death of the tortfeasor or the victim. Generally, courts today use a policy-based approach.

(1) **Traditional approach [§406]**

Whether a tort cause of action survives the death of the tortfeasor or the victim traditionally was decided according to the law of the *place of injury*. [**Ormsby v. Chase,** 290 U.S. 387 (1933)]

(a) **Characterization as "nontort" problem [§407]**

Even under the traditional approach, a substantial minority of states avoided the rigid "place of the wrong" rule by characterizing the issue of survivability as an issue in the administration of decedents' estates, and thus governed by the law of the place where decedent's estate was being administered. [**Grant v. McAuliffe,** *supra,* §370]

1) **Note**

The same result (*i.e.,* application of forum law) was reached in other cases by characterizing the matter as "procedural." [10 Stan. L. Rev. 205 (1957)]

(2) **Modern approach [§408]**

Today, courts tend to reject the "place of the wrong" rule entirely in favor of "a more flexible approach" allowing them to *weigh the interests and policies* underlying the particular issues before the court. [*See* **Griffith v. United Air Lines, Inc.,** 203 A.2d 796 (Pa. 1964); Rest. 2d §167] Usually, this results in application of the survival statute in decedent's *domicile* (forum).

c. **Multistate injuries—defamation and invasion of privacy [§409]**

Defamation or invasion of privacy resulting from nationwide publication or broadcasts and other cases involving multistate injuries raise difficult choice-of-law problems. No clear "rules" have yet evolved, and the courts have adopted widely varying positions.

(1) Place of injury [§410]

A number of past cases adhered to the rigid "place of injury" rule, thereby concluding that it was necessary to consider the law of *each state in which injuries occurred*. [**Hartmann v. Time, Inc.,** 166 F.2d 127 (3d Cir. 1948)]

(a) Multiple causes of action [§411]

Indeed, some cases have held that there were separate causes of action in each state where an injury occurred. [*See* **Connecticut Valley Lumber Co. v. Maine Central Railroad,** 103 A. 263 (N.H. 1918)—defendant might be liable for injuries under the laws of one state, and not liable in another, even though both injuries flowed from same act]

(b) Criticism [§412]

This rule leads to obvious inconsistencies and unfair results—particularly in cases of nationwide publication where there may be "injury" in every state.

(c) Uniform Single Publication Act [§413]

A few states (*e.g.,* California) have adopted the Uniform Single Publication Act, which provides that a defamatory publication creates only a single cause of action, no matter where the damages took place. A judgment on the merits of any jurisdiction that has adopted this act thus bars suit elsewhere. [Restatement (Second) of Torts §577A]

1) Note

The single publication rule does not restrict the plaintiff's choice of a forum; *i.e.,* suit can still be maintained anywhere there are "minimum contacts." This is so even though the plaintiff may lack personal contacts with the forum and filed suit there (New Hampshire) because it was the only state in which the suit was not time-barred. [**Keeton v. Hustler Magazine, Inc.,** *supra,* §131]

(2) Place of conduct [§414]

Other courts, emphasizing the tort policy of punishing a defendant for wrongful conduct, have applied the law of the place of the defendant's act (*e.g.,* place of broadcast, publication, etc.). [**Palmisano v. News Syndicate Co.,** 130 F. Supp. 17 (S.D.N.Y. 1955)]

(3) Place of plaintiff's domicile [§415]

A number of cases have applied the law of the plaintiff's domicile or principal place of business as the place of "principal injury." [**Mattox v. News Syndicate Co.,** 176 F.2d 897 (2d Cir. 1949); Rest. 2d §150(2)]

(4) Forum law [§416]

Certain commentators have suggested that as long as the forum has any legitimate contact with the matter, it should merely apply its own laws in every case. [36 Minn. L. Rev. 1 (1951)] Some courts have adopted this position. [**Anderson v. Hearst Publishing Co.,** 120 F. Supp. 850 (S.D. Cal. 1954)]

d. Vicarious liability [§417]

Difficult conflicts questions may also arise where a plaintiff seeks to hold a defendant vicariously liable for acts committed by another in a different state— *e.g.,* in "permissive use" (auto owner's liability) or tavernkeeper's liability cases.

(1) Traditional approach [§418]

As in other torts situations, the traditional approach determined questions of vicarious liability according to the law of the place of wrong. Typically, this meant the law of the *place of injury*, but courts occasionally would characterize the wrong as the *place where the defendant acted* (*i.e.,* where she put into motion the forces that ultimately resulted in injury).

(a) Permissive use cases [§419]

Where the defendant allows another person to drive her automobile and the driver causes injury in another state, the defendant has been held liable under the permissive use statute in effect at the *place of injury*—at least where the defendant gave the driver express or implied consent to operate the auto in the state where the injury occurred. [**Scheer v. Rockne Motors Corp.,** 68 F.2d 942 (2d Cir. 1934); **Siegmann v. Meyer,** 100 F.2d 367 (2d Cir. 1938)—defendant must be shown to have "submitted" to law of place of injury]

1) Rationale

If the defendant put into motion the force that causes the injury (by allowing a negligent driver to drive into the state where the injury occurred), she should be subject to liability under the law of the place of injury. [*See* **Young v. Masci,** 289 U.S. 253 (1933)—upholding constitutionality of such application]

2) Application [§420]

If there was no permissive use statute in effect at the place of injury, the defendant owner could not be held liable for injuries caused by the driver of her car—even if there was a permissive use statute where the car was loaned to the driver (defendant's residence). [*See* **Jesselson v. Moody,** 309 N.Y. 148 (1955)]

a) But note
Some decisions have avoided this by characterizing the issue as a "nontorts" problem. [*See* **Levy v. Daniels' U-Drive Auto Renting Co.,** *supra,* §390—applicability of permissive use statute characterized as "contracts" problem, justifying reference to law where "contract" was made]

3) Criticism [§421]
The requirement of showing that the defendant "consented" to the operation of her car in the state where the accident occurred has been criticized on the ground that the defendant should be subject to liability under any law whose application was reasonably foreseeable and against which she could have insured herself. Support for this view may be found in analogous dogbite cases, where a nonresident owner may be held liable under the law of the place of injury for injuries inflicted by a dog that has run away across the state line. [**Fischl v. Chubb,** 30 Pa. D. & C. 40 (1937)]

(b) Tavernkeeper's liability cases [§422]
A number of courts held liquor sellers liable under a forum "dramshop act" for injuries inflicted by intoxicated patrons outside the state, even though no such act was in effect at the place of injury. As long as the sale occurred in the forum state, the forum has viewed itself as the place of the wrong. [**Schmidt v. Driscoll Hotel, Inc.,** *supra,* §372]

1) Note
Under the traditional approach, it was unclear whether liability should be imposed where no dramshop act was in effect where the liquor was sold, but such an act existed at the place of injury. Courts apparently would hesitate to impose liability where no such liability existed where the defendant acted (where she sold the liquor). [*See* **Waynick v. Chicago's Last Department Store,** 269 F.2d 322 (7th Cir. 1959)]

EXAM TIP   **gilbert**

Note that this is one of the areas where the *conduct*, not the injury, is the "wrong" under the traditional approach, and so the place of the conduct, rather than the place of injury, controls.

---

(2) Modern approaches [§423]

Modern decisions indicate that in situations involving vicarious liability, as in other conflicts cases, the *"most significant relationship" or "governmental interest" approach* should apply, and the defendant owner should be subject to liability under the law of any state whose application was reasonably foreseeable (and against which she might have insured herself). [Rest. 2d §174]

 Example: It has been held that a tavernkeeper's liability for injuries inflicted by an intoxicated patron upon another should be determined by a "governmental interest" analysis. Thus, where a Nevada tavernkeeper sold liquor to an intoxicated patron who caused injury in California, the California court held that California law recognizes the tavernkeeper's liability for such injuries whereas Nevada law does not. The court then applied California law because its interest would be the more impaired if not applied. [**Bernhard v. Harrah's Club,** *supra,* §328]

---

e. Products liability [§424]

In this area, more than in any other, the courts tend to apply whichever law is most favorable to the plaintiff in order to facilitate compensation, while phrasing their decision in terms of a "contacts" or "interest" approach. [*See* 78 Harv. L. Rev. 1452 (1964)]

(1) Traditional approach [§425]

Traditionally, the nature and extent of products liability (including both breach of warranty and tort liability) was determined by the *"place of the wrong."* [**Reed & Barton Corp. v. Maas,** 73 F.2d 359 (1st Cir. 1934)]

(a) "Place of wrong" [§426]

However, several past decisions held that the place of the "wrong" in such cases was the place *where the product was manufactured, sold, or repaired,* rather than the place of injury. [**Vrooman v. Beech Aircraft Corp.,** 183 F.2d 479 (10th Cir. 1950)—forum applied its own law to a claim for injury sustained in an air crash in a foreign state, because the airplane was manufactured and repaired in the forum, hence "wrong" was committed there]

(2) Modern approach [§427]

Today, courts emphasize the interest in protecting the consumer or user of any product in the "stream" of commerce, and thus tend to look to the *injured party's domicile* as the state having the "most significant" contact or interest (at least where this facilitates recovery).

 Example: A Montana family traveling in their pickup truck through Kansas was involved in an accident with a semi-tractor trailer. The minor plaintiff was the only survivor in the pickup. A Montana court allowed recovery under Montana's strict products liability statute for defectively designed products, even though neither the state of injury (Kansas) nor the state where the pickup truck was placed in the stream of commerce and subsequently sold to the plaintiff's father (North Carolina) would have permitted recovery. The court reasoned that Montana had a more significant relationship to the issue of liability than did Kansas, pointing to the residence of the family in Montana at the time of the injury, Montana's interest in fully compensating Montana residents, and Montana's interest in preventing defective products from causing injuries to Montana residents. [**Phillips v. General Motors Corp.,** 995 P.2d 1002 (Mont. 2000)]

e.g. **Example:** A California court allowed recovery under California law for injuries sustained by a California resident in Mexico due to a defective shotgun shell he had purchased in Mexico. The shotgun shell had been manufactured in Mexico by a Mexican subsidiary of Remington (a Connecticut-based corporation). While there were more "contacts" in Mexico than in California, the court stressed California's interest in assuring compensation to residents for injuries from defective products, and Mexican law would have prevented such recovery (since it did not recognize strict tort liability). [**Kasel v. Remington Arms Co.,** 24 Cal. App. 3d 711 (1972)]

e.g. **Example:** Similarly, a New Hampshire court applied its own law to allow recovery by a local resident for injuries caused by a defective power saw manufactured by a Michigan defendant, purchased from a dealer in Georgia, and delivered in Florida to the plaintiff, who later brought it to his home in New Hampshire. [**Stephen v. Sears, Roebuck & Co.,** 266 A.2d 855 (N.H. 1970)]

f. Privileges [§428]

Where the issue is whether the defendant's conduct was privileged (*e.g.,* to save the life or property of another), courts may hold that the "most significant relationship" is with the law of the place *where the conduct took place*, rather than with the place of injury. [Rest. 2d §163] *Rationale:* If the defendant's conduct was privileged where committed, she should not be held liable for it elsewhere.

g. Immunities [§429]

A great body of conflicts law has developed in the area of tort immunities. For example, Husband and Wife, domiciled in State X, take a short drive into State Y, where Wife is injured because of Husband's negligent driving. The law of the domicile (State X) permits Wife to sue Husband for negligence, but

State Y has interspousal tort immunity. If Wife files suit in State X, should State Y immunity apply?

(1) Interspousal and parental immunity

(a) Traditional approach [§430]
In the past, some courts rigidly applied the "place of the wrong" (injury) rule and barred suit if immunity was recognized at that place—regardless of any statutes at the parties' domicile. [**Straw v. Lee,** 129 S.E.2d 288 (N.C. 1963)]

1) Characterization device [§431]
Other courts avoided the "place of the wrong" rule by characterizing the question of interspousal or parental immunity as a "family relations" problem, which justified reference to the law of the parties' domicile. [**Haumschild v. Continental Casualty Co.,** *supra,* §390]

(b) Modern approach [§432]
Most courts today regard the state of the *parties' domicile* as having the "most significant relationship" to the immunity issue and apply that state's law, flatly rejecting the "place of the wrong" rule. [**Thompson v. Thompson,** 193 A.2d 439 (N.H. 1963); *and see* Rest. 2d §169]

1) Rationale
In the situation above (§429), the purpose of State Y's immunity statute is to preserve marriages and prevent collusive suits. However, *State Y has no legitimate interest* in protecting marital harmony or preventing collusive suits with respect to parties domiciled in State X—particularly since their marital domicile does not find this kind of protection necessary. On the other hand, *State X (the domicile) has a legitimate interest* in providing compensation to prevent hardship to local domiciliaries and protect local creditors who render services to injured domiciliaries. Finally, the rights and immunities of spouses domiciled in one state should not change constantly as family members cross state boundaries during temporary absences from their homes. [*See* **Emery v. Emery,** 45 Cal. 2d 421 (1955)]

(2) Charitable immunity [§433]
In the past, charitable corporations have been protected if an immunity statute was in effect at the *place of injury.* Today, however, the whole concept of charitable immunity is waning. Hence, courts are less concerned with protecting the charity and tend to apply the law of the state

having the "most significant relationship" with the question of liability, so as to facilitate compensation to the plaintiff. [**Rosenthal v. Warren,** 475 F.2d 438 (2d Cir. 1973)—New York court refused to apply Massachusetts charitable immunity doctrine in action for wrongful death of New York resident allegedly resulting from malpractice in Massachusetts by residents of that state; *and see* Rest. 2d §168]

h. Guest statutes [§434]

A guest statute bars a nonpaying passenger ("guest") in a noncommercial vehicle from suing the driver ("host") for damages due to the driver's ordinary negligence. The issue (and the development of law) in this area is similar to that in the interspousal immunity cases (above). Typically, the plaintiff and the defendant—*both domiciled* in State X—drive in the defendant's car into State Y, where the plaintiff ("guest") is injured due to the defendant's ("host") negligent driving. Should State Y's "guest statute" bar recovery where no such statute exists under the law of the domicile-forum (State X)?

(1) Traditional approach [§435]

Earlier cases mechanically applied the "place of injury" rule in this situation.

(2) Modern approach [§436]

However, in the leading case of **Babcock v. Jackson** (*supra,* §394), the New York Court of Appeals rejected the "place of injury" rule in favor of a "predominant concern" ("most significant relationship") test which indicated that reference should be to the law of the *domicile-forum,* where the host-guest relationship was entered into and where the car regularly was garaged. Most subsequent cases have used this approach. [*See, e.g.,* **Wilcox v. Wilcox,** 133 N.W.2d 408 (Wis. 1965); **Clark v. Clark,** 222 A.2d 205 (N.H. 1966); *and see* 29 A.L.R.3d 603]

(a) "Principles of preference" approach [§437]

A few decisions have adopted something like the "principles of preference" approach, holding that the guest can recover if suits are allowed at the place where the guest-host relationship was entered into *or* at the place of injury, whichever state imposes the higher standard of care. [**Kell v. Henderson,** 26 App. Div. 595 (1966)—suit between Ontario residents in which New York court applied forum law to permit recovery because of forum's policy to compensate persons injured on local roads, even though parties' domicile would not have permitted such lawsuits]

(b) "Split domicile" cases [§438]

The result may be different where the host and guest are domiciled in different states ("split domicile" cases).

1) Host residing at place of injury [§439]

Where a guest statute exists at the place of injury and the *host* resides there, recovery probably will be *denied*—even where the domicile of the injured guest would permit recovery and the parties were en route to that state. *Rationale:* A defendant should be able to rely on protections in the law of the state in which she resides and acts. [**Cipolla v. Shaposka,** *supra,* §371— Pennsylvania court applied Delaware guest statute to protect a Delaware host against liability, even though injured guest was Pennsylvania resident, parties were en route to Pennsylvania, and Pennsylvania law would have allowed recovery]

2) Guest residing at place of injury [§440]

There is also some authority for applying the guest statute in effect at the place of injury if the *guest* resides there, even though no guest statute exists where the defendant (host) was domiciled. [**Neumeier v. Kuehner,** *supra* §396—New York court applied Ontario guest statute to deny recovery against New York host, even though New York law would have permitted such recovery]

a)

The *Neumeier* decision has been criticized by several commentators as a "retreat" to the lex loci delicti ("place of injury") rule.

b)

And even in New York, courts may refuse to apply a guest statute in effect at the place of injury if both host and guest are from different states, neither of which has a guest statute. [**Chila v. Owens,** 348 F. Supp. 1207 (S.D.N.Y. 1972)— injury occurred in Ohio (which had guest statute) but driver was from New York and injured guest from New Jersey, neither of which had a guest statute; court reasoned that applying Ohio guest statute would defeat common policy of both New Jersey and New York in allowing unlimited recovery]

i. Comparative negligence [§441]

The comparative negligence rule *reduces* a plaintiff's tort recovery if she is partly at fault; under the older, contributory negligence rule, the plaintiff's recovery *is barred* if she is at all at fault. Significant problems arise where injuries occur in a contributory negligence jurisdiction but involve residents of states where comparative negligence has been adopted (or vice versa). This area is rather unsettled, and relevant choice-of-law rules are still emerging. However, a forum that has adopted comparative negligence will probably apply that doctrine to litigation involving forum residents, even though the injuries occur in a contributory negligence jurisdiction. [*See* **Schwartz v. Consolidated Freightways Corp.**, 221 N.W.2d 665 (Minn. 1974)]

j. "No-fault" insurance [§442]

No-fault insurance allows recovery from one's own insurer regardless of who is at fault, while under the traditional, fault-based system recovery is available only from the other party or her insurance and only if the damages were due to the other party's negligence. Similar choice-of-law problems arise where a "no-fault" system has been adopted in the state where one or both parties reside but the injuries occur in a state without "no-fault" (or vice versa). As with comparative negligence, this area likewise is unsettled.

(1) Note

If the forum has a "no-fault" insurance system, it will probably apply the doctrine to immunize a defendant forum resident from tort liability for injuries inflicted within the state—even if the injured party resides in a state that would permit a tort action against the defendant. [**Johnson v. Liberty Mutual Insurance Co.**, 297 So. 2d 858 (Fla. 1974)]

k. Damages [§443]

The law to be applied with respect to damage issues in torts cases is discussed *infra*, §§676-678.

l. Contribution among tortfeasors [§444]

In deciding whether one of several joint tortfeasors can compel contribution from the other tortfeasors, modern courts tend to follow a "contacts" or "governmental interest" analysis. Under this approach, it has been held that the law of the state where the defendant tortfeasors reside should govern, rather than the law of the state in which judgment was entered but in which the defendants had no continuing presence. [*See, e.g.,* **Caterpillar Tractor Co. v. Teledyne Industries, Inc.**, 53 Cal. App. 3d 693 (1975)—Florida judgment was rendered against two California corporations, and one corporation paid entire judgment and sought contribution from other in California court; contribution among tortfeasors was not permitted under Florida law, but Florida had no "interest" in application of its rule to nonresidents since judgment was paid, and hence, court applied California law permitting contribution]

B. Contracts

1. In General [§445]

Problems involving construction and enforcement of contracts are among those most frequently litigated in the choice-of-laws area. Although numerous theories and "rules" have been formulated, the courts generally have attempted to develop

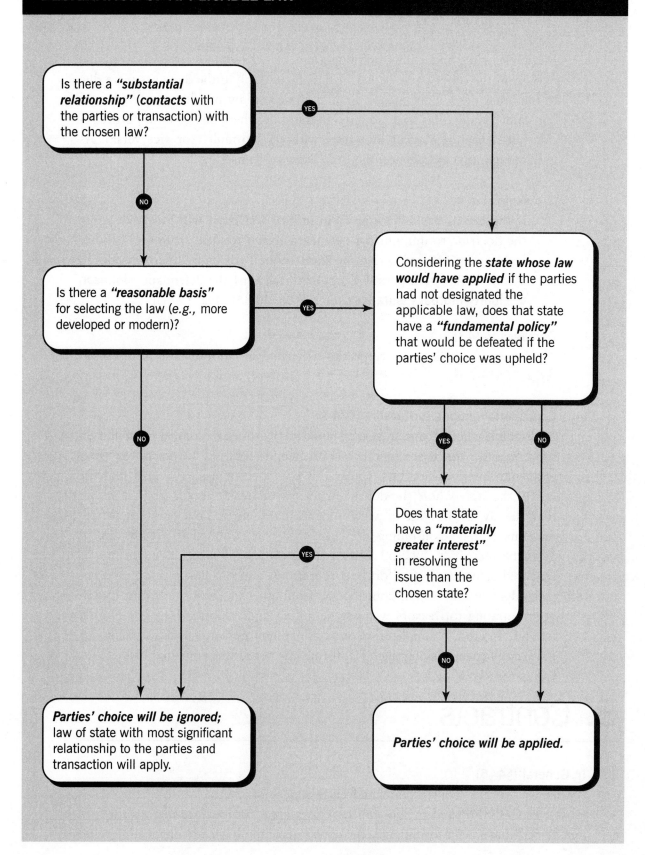

Is there a *"substantial relationship"* (**contacts** with the parties or transaction) with the chosen law?

YES →

NO ↓

Is there a *"reasonable basis"* for selecting the law (*e.g.,* more developed or modern)?

YES →

NO ↓

Considering the **state whose law would have applied** if the parties had not designated the applicable law, does that state have a *"fundamental policy"* that would be defeated if the parties' choice was upheld?

YES ↓   **NO** ↓

Does that state have a *"materially greater interest"* in resolving the issue than the chosen state?

YES ←

NO ↓

Parties' choice will be ignored; law of state with most significant relationship to the parties and transaction will apply.

Parties' choice will be applied.

principles that give effect to the *expectations of the contracting parties* unless these are clearly outweighed by the interests or policies of a state having a direct and immediate relationship with the transaction.

2. Effect of Parties' Express Designation of Applicable Law [§446]

Contracting parties often expressly stipulate that the law of a particular state (or country) shall govern all rights and obligations arising under the contract. What is the effect of such stipulations?

a. Early view [§447]

Early decisions stressed a "vested rights" rationale and held that parties were precluded from designating any different law; the law of the place of contracting applied. The view was that if the contract was made in one state, "it should not do the parties any good to wish they were in another." [**Gerli & Co. v. Cunard Steamship Co.**, 48 F.2d 115 (2d Cir. 1931)] This is clearly *not the law today*, except in a few states that adhere to the traditional approach.

b. Modern view [§448]

Modern courts recognize that, as long as it is not against public policy, the parties may expressly incorporate some foreign law into their contract as a "shorthand" to including other provisions or interpreting provisions already contained in their agreement. [**Duskin v. Pennsylvania-Central Airlines Corp.**, 167 F.2d 727 (6th Cir. 1948)]

(1) No "contacts" [§449]

Some courts even allow the parties to designate the law of a state with which there are no "contacts" at all. [*See* **Ringling Brothers-Barnum & Bailey, Inc. v. Olvera**, 119 F.2d 584 (9th Cir. 1941)]

(2) Distinguish—Restatement view [§450]

Under the Second Restatement, however, parties may designate the law to be applied *unless* (i) there is *no "substantial relationship"* with the chosen law and *no other "reasonable basis"* for selecting that law; or (ii) application of the chosen law would be *contrary to a "fundamental policy"* of a state that has a *"materially greater interest"* in determining the issue. [Rest. 2d §187(2)]

(a) Application

1) Substantial relationship or reasonable basis

A court following the Second Restatement must determine whether a "substantial relationship" (*i.e.*, *contacts* with the parties or transaction) or a "reasonable basis" for applying that law (*e.g.*, that state's law is *well-developed or follows a modern view*) exists. If not, the law of the state with the most significant relationship to the parties and transaction will be applied and the parties' choice will be disregarded.

2) Fundamental policy of state with materially greater interest

If there is a substantial relationship or reasonable basis for applying the state's law, the court must then determine: (i) what state's law *would have applied* in the absence of party choice; (ii) whether that state has a *"fundamental policy"* that would be defeated if the parties' choice were upheld; and (iii) whether that state has a *"materially greater interest"* in resolving the issue than the state chosen by the parties. This determination thus prevents parties to a contract from evading a fundamental policy of a materially interested state that would have been the state whose law would be applicable in the absence of party choice.

Example: Minor and Merchant are both State A domiciliaries. State A law prohibits a minor from selling his property without his parents' consent. State B, following the more modern view, allows such agreements. Clearly the parties (Minor and Merchant) could not avoid State A law by inserting a provision in the sales contract designating State B's law as controlling. Because both Minor and Merchant are domiciled in State A and the contract was made there, State A would be the state of governing law in the absence of party choice, and its law protecting minors in these circumstances would represent a fundamental policy. On these facts, State A has a materially greater interest in the matter than State B, and thus its law would apply.

(b) Uniform Commercial Code [§451]

The U.C.C. position is similar in that it permits the parties to non-consumer contracts to agree to the governing law, unless application of the designated law would be contrary to a fundamental policy of the state or country whose law would govern in the absence of an agreement. [U.C.C. §1-301 (c), (f)] If a consumer is a party to the transaction, however, the chosen law must bear a "reasonable relation" to the transaction. (*See supra,* §§298-300.)

c. Exception—adhesion contracts [§452]

The modern rule recognizing the contracting parties' right to designate which law will control their rights and obligations will *not apply* where the parties did *not have equal bargaining positions* in choosing such law. Thus, where the designation is incorporated as a fine-print provision of an adhesion contract to which one party has no real bargaining power (*e.g.,* employment, insurance, suretyship, loan agreements), courts are reluctant to uphold the designation, particularly where to do so would evade forum laws for the protection of that party. [**Zogg v. Pennsylvania Mutual Insurance Co.**, 276 F.2d 861 (2d Cir. 1960)]

3. General Approaches [§453]

If there is no express designation by the parties of the law that will govern their contract, the courts must make this determination. While there are various "approaches" in this area, the basic policy behind each is to obtain a result that is consistent with the *presumed intention of the parties—i.e.,* what they would have done had they considered the problem.

a. Traditional "vested rights" approach [§454]

Traditionally, courts applied separate choice-of-law rules to problems concerning the *validity* of the contract as opposed to problems concerning the *performance* of the contract.

(1) Validity problems—"place of making" rule [§455]

According to the traditional approach, all problems relating to the validity of a contract were to be determined by reference to the law of the *place where the contract was "made."* [**Milliken v. Pratt,** *supra,* §375]

(a) Note

This position was adopted by section 332 of the First Restatement, and by many of the early decisions. Indeed, some courts asserted this "rule" even against the parties' expressed intention.

(b) What constitutes a "validity" problem [§456]

The above rule applied to issues involving formalities of the contract; sufficiency of consideration; the parties' capacity; fraud, illegality, or other defenses making the contract voidable; nature and extent of duty; and the like.

(c) Determining "place of making" [§457]

The forum reached its own determination of where the contract was "made," although generally this was where the *offer was accepted.*

> **e.g.** **Example—mail:** For contracts negotiated by mail, therefore, the place where acceptance was posted was considered the place of making, since such posting is the last event necessary to create a binding contract. (*See* Contracts Summary.)

> **e.g.** **Example—telephone:** For contracts negotiated in an interstate telephone call, the place of "making" was where the accepting party spoke. [**Linn v. Employers Reinsurance Corp.,** 139 A.2d 638 (Pa. 1958)]

(2) "Performance" problems—"place of performance" rule [§458]

"Performance" problems (as distinguished from "validity" problems) were traditionally governed by the law of the *place at which performance is called for in the contract.* [Rest. §358; **Scudder v. Union National Bank,** 91 U.S. 406 (1875)]

(a) Rationale

The parties presumably intended to resolve performance disputes with reference to the laws of the place where performance was to be rendered. Also, the place where the contract was to be performed creates the rights and duties flowing therefrom—the "vested rights" rationale.

(b) What constitutes a "performance" problem [§459]

"Performance" problems would include sufficiency of performance; manner of performance; excuses for nonperformance; existence and materiality of breach; questions relating to damages (measure, amount, etc.); and the right to rescind, where based on performance issues.

(3) Criticisms of "vested rights" analysis

(a) Characterization difficult [§460]

The characterization of issues as "validity" or "performance" problems was difficult, since the two areas frequently overlapped. Thus, for example, questions as to interpretation of contract provisions relating to performance were classified as "validity" problems without an adequate explanation. [*See* **Aluminum Co. v. Hully**, 200 F.2d 257 (8th Cir. 1952)]

(b) Intent of parties [§461]

There was no reason to assume that contracting parties intended different states' laws to apply to "validity" and "performance" issues. Indeed, it is more logical to assume that they intended the same laws to apply to both, ". . . performance being merely the other side of the obligation coin." [*See* **Jacobs, Marcus & Co. v. Credit Lyonnaise**, [1884] 12 Q.B.D. 589]

(c) Arbitrary result [§462]

Finally, and most importantly, reliance on what may have been purely fortuitous "contacts" sometimes led to arbitrary results. For instance, the mere fact that the contracting parties happened to reach agreement while passing through State A hardly justified reference to State A laws to interpret their agreement, where every other "contact" was with other states.

EXAM TIP   gilbert

Remember that for contracts cases, the traditional approach requires you to think a little before you apply a mechanical rule: You have to decide if you are dealing with a *"validity" problem* or a *"performance" problem*. Once you have made that decision, you know which rule to apply. Of course, once again, if the result seems unjust, consider the *escape devices*, especially seeing if you can recharacterize the case as, for example, a "performance" problem rather than a "validity" problem or as a tort rather than a contract.

CHARACTERIZATION UNDER TRADITIONAL APPROACH IN CONTRACTS CASES

gilbert

"VALIDITY" PROBLEMS

☑ Formalities of the contract (*e.g.*, acceptance of offer)

☑ Sufficiency of consideration

☑ Capacity of parties (*e.g.*, a minor or otherwise incompetent party)

☑ Defenses to formation of contract (*e.g.*, fraud or illegality)

☑ Nature and extent of duty

"PERFORMANCE" PROBLEMS

☑ Sufficiency of performance

☑ Manner of performance

☑ Excuses for nonperformance

☑ Breach of contract issues (*e.g.*, existence and materiality of breach)

☑ Damages issues (*e.g.*, measure, amount)

☑ Right to rescind based on performance

b. Modern approaches [§463]

Recognizing the shortcomings of a "vested rights" approach, most modern courts have abandoned the "validity" vs. "performance" distinction in favor of more policy-oriented approaches.

(1) Grouping of contacts—"center of gravity" approach [§464]

A number of cases have employed the quasi-mechanical approach of "grouping" the various "contacts" in the case and applying the law of the resultant "center of gravity"—*i.e.*, the state *with a preponderance of "contacts."* [*See, e.g.*, **Auten v. Auten**, 308 N.Y. 155 (1954)—court applied law of England as "center of gravity" to sustain a support agreement between English nationals, even though contract was made in New York and was to be performed (payments made) there]

(a) Criticisms [§465]

The primary objection to this approach is that it is too mechanical. The mere fact that more "contacts" occur in one state than another is not always sufficient reason to apply the former state's law. In one case, for example, the court ended up invalidating a contract that was valid where entered into simply because more "contacts" occurred in a different state. [**Rubin v. Irving Trust Co.**, 305 N.Y. 288 (1953)—oral promise to make a will held unenforceable even though promise was enforceable under law of place where made]

1) And note

The approach breaks down where there is no preponderance of "contacts" in one state or the other. In such cases, the forum's determination of the "center of gravity" is often merely a legal conclusion disguising its actual choice-influencing considerations.

(2) "Most significant relationship" approach [§466]

The Second Restatement approach applies the law of the state having the *"most significant relationship"* to the transaction and the parties with respect to the particular issue or type of contract involved. The Uniform Commercial Code also adopts this approach, section 1-105 specifying that reference is to be made to the law of the state with "appropriate relations" to the transaction.

(a) Determinative factors [§467]

In deciding which state has the "most significant" relationship, the courts should consider the principles enumerated in §315, *supra*, together with the following "contacts" specifically applicable to contracts problems:

(i) The place of *contracting*;

(ii) The place of *negotiation*;

(iii) The place of *performance*;

(iv) The location of *subject matter* of the contract; and

(v) The *domicile, residence, nationality, place of incorporation and place of business* of each party to the contract.

[Rest. 2d §206]

(b) Exception regarding "minor details of performance" [§468]

For "minor" details of performance under a contract (*e.g.*, time, manner, and place of performance not provided for in the contract), the Second Restatement retains the "place of performance" rule (above). [Rest. 2d §206] This reflects the strong policy in negotiable instrument cases (*see infra*, §488) to apply the law of the place of performance to all questions of performance due under bills and notes (*i.e.*, presentment, notice of dishonor, days of grace, currency payable, etc.).

EXAM TIP   **gilbert**

When trying to decide how a court using the Second Restatement approach would rule in a contracts case, you need to consider the general choice-of-law principles (*e.g.*, interstate concerns, uniformity of results, forum's policies, etc.—*see supra*, §315). But note that **one of these principles**—protection of justified expectations—**is specifically for contracts cases**. Therefore, when you consider the specific contracts contacts (*supra*, §467), keep in mind that the court will try to protect the contracting parties' expectations and **apply the law that would uphold** the contract or its term if it can do so without violating an important policy of an interested state.

---

4. Analysis of Specific Contracts Problems

a. Capacity to contract—minors, incompetents, married women, etc.

(1) Traditional approach [§469]

Under the traditional "vested rights" approach, a party's capacity to contract was considered to be a "validity" problem to be determined by reference to the law of the *place of making*.

(a) Criticism [§470]

This inflexible rule sometimes operated unfairly, forcing the forum court to impose contractual liabilities against a local domiciliary who lacked capacity under local law, simply because he had been outside the state when he entered into a contract. [**Milliken v. Pratt**, *supra*, §455] Note that other courts refused to reach such results, on the ground the forum should never be required to deprive a local domiciliary of the protection he would receive under local capacity laws. [**Union Trust Co. v. Grosman**, 245 U.S. 412 (1918)]

(2) Modern approach [§471]

Today, the *forum usually applies its own rules* to determine the capacity of a party domiciled within the forum.

(a) Second Restatement approach [§472]

Under the Second Restatement approach, the forum would conclude that since the party is a local domiciliary, the "most significant relationship" is with forum law. [Rest. 2d §198]

(b) "Governmental interest" approach [§473]

Alternatively, a court using a "governmental interest" approach would simply assert its interest in the capacity of local domiciliaries and apply its own law, even where the contract was executed and to be performed in another state. [**Lilienthal v. Kaufman,** *supra,* §327—Oregon spendthrift protected against contract he had negotiated and executed in California]

(3) Nonresident party [§474]

Where the party is not domiciled within the forum, there would be less preference for the application of forum law and reference might be made to the laws of that party's domicile or some other law (*e.g.,* where contract executed) to uphold the contract. [*See* **Mayer v. Roche,** 75 A. 235 (N.J. 1909)]

b. Sufficiency of consideration [§475]

Under the traditional approach, sufficiency of consideration issues would be a "validity" problem and thus the law of the place of making would apply. Under the modern approach, courts tend to apply whichever law would *uphold the sufficiency of consideration*, provided the parties could reasonably be assumed to have contracted with reference to that law. The rationale is that the parties cannot be presumed to have contemplated a law that would defeat their promises. [**Pritchard v. Norton,** 106 U.S. 124 (1882)]

c. Legality of contract [§476]

Under the traditional approach, legality issues would point to a "validity" problem, and thus the law of the place of making would apply. Courts using the modern approaches consider the nature of the grounds upon which legality is challenged.

(1) Regulatory matters [§477]

Where the claimed illegality consists of the alleged violation of a statute (in the forum or elsewhere) aimed at *regulating business transactions* (*e.g.,* liquor sales, financing contracts, etc.), the courts generally refer to a law that would *uphold the validity* of the contract, provided it is reasonably applicable. [**Intercontinental Hotel Corp. v. Golden,** 15 N.Y.2d 9 (1964)]

(a) Usury cases [§478]

In the case of contracts alleged to be usurious, courts tend to apply whichever law would hold the contract valid (nonusurious) *if there is a reasonable relationship* with the transaction and the *parties were in equal bargaining positions*. [**Seeman v. Philadelphia Warehouse Co.,** 274 U.S. 403 (1927); Rest. 2d §203]

1) Rationale

The general presumption of validity is even more necessary in these cases, to encourage the free flow of trade and commerce across state lines. Otherwise, lenders might hesitate to make out-of-state loans. [**Green v. Northwestern Trust Co.,** 150 N.W. 229 (Minn. 1914)]

2) Limitations [§479]

However, a presumption of validity should not apply where the parties were not acting in good faith or where the lender merely erected a "front" in another state so as to avoid usury restrictions under local law. [**Ury v. Jewelers Acceptance Corp.,** 227 Cal. App. 2d 11 (1964)]

a) And note

Where the "overwhelming" weight of contacts is in the forum state, the forum probably will apply its own usury law even if this invalidates the contract. [**Rochester Capital Leasing Corp. v. K & L Litho Corp.,** 13 Cal. App. 3d 697 (1970)—where only contact with New York was that loan payments were to be made there, and loan had been negotiated in California to a California resident and secured by collateral located in California, California court refused to apply New York law to uphold contract]

3) Contractual stipulations of validity [§480]

Loan agreements frequently designate a controlling state law so as to avoid claims of usury. Such stipulations are usually enforceable as long as there is a "reasonable" relationship with the law designated [**Bigelow v. Burnham,** 49 N.W. 104 (Iowa 1891)]; but this may not be true in the case of "adhesion contracts" (*see supra,* §452).

(2) Matters that violate forum public policy [§481]

Where the claimed illegality is more than a mere regulatory measure—*i.e.,* an alleged violation of some strong local policy—the *forum will probably apply its own law.*

Examples: The forum will generally invalidate contracts that violate local statutes concerning sale of securities, fair trade practices, marriage and divorce, and the like.

> **cf. Compare:** A number of courts have applied a foreign law to uphold gambling contracts that were illegal in the forum but legal where made. [**Intercontinental Hotel Corp. v. Golden,** *supra,* §477]

(3) Matters that violate only foreign law [§482]

The forum is less concerned with enforcing the public policy of another jurisdiction, and unless the clear preponderance of "contacts" is in that state, a court will generally **uphold a contract valid under forum law** that violates foreign law.

(4) Second Restatement approach [§483]

Restatement (Second) section 202 refers courts to the law of the place of performance to determine whether **performance** of a contract would be illegal. All other questions of legality (*e.g.,* whether promise itself is legal) would be determined by the law of the state having "the most significant relationship" to the transaction and parties. [Rest. 2d §188]

d. Formalities—Statute of Frauds [§484]

The trend in this area is to use the general contracts choice-of-law rules.

(1) Traditional approach [§485]

Under the traditional approach, whether the forum would apply its own Statute of Frauds or look to some reasonably applicable foreign law depended on whether the Statute was characterized as *"substantive" or "procedural."* (*See infra,* §§642-644.)

(a) Analysis

Statute of Frauds provisions were deemed "substantive" if they went to essential validity of the contract (such as those declaring that "no contract shall be valid" unless in writing). On the other hand, provisions declaring that "no action shall be brought" on an oral contract were held "procedural," so that the characterization depended on the wording of the provision in question.

(b) Effect

Results in these cases were often arbitrary. For instance, in **Marie v. Garrison,** 13 Abb. N. Cas. 210 (N.Y. 1883), the contract in question failed to satisfy the requirements of the forum Statute of Frauds or that of the place of contracting but was nevertheless enforced, because the Statute of the place of contracting was construed as procedural and that of the forum as substantive, so that neither Statute applied!

(2) Modern approach [§486]

Today, most commentators and courts disregard the antiquated "substance" vs. "procedure" distinction and assert that Statute of Frauds issues should be decided under the choice-of-law rules applicable to contracts generally. [**Bernkrant v. Fowler,** 55 Cal. 2d 588 (1961); *and see* Rest. 2d §199]

---

e.g. **Example:** Decedent sold Nevada land to Nevada residents, maintaining a security interest in the property. Later, he made an oral promise to the purchasers that if they would refinance their obligation and pay him a substantial amount immediately, he would include a provision in his will to cancel any unpaid indebtedness for the land at his death. The purchasers refinanced and made the payment to Decedent. Decedent then died in California without including such a provision in his will. Nevada law would enforce such an oral agreement, but California's Statute of Frauds made such agreements unenforceable. The record did not show where Decedent was domiciled at the time the agreement to refinance was made. The court held that, even if Decedent was domiciled in California at that time, because the purchasers were Nevada residents, the contract involved Nevada land and was made and performed by the purchasers there, Nevada had a substantial interest in the contract and in protecting the rights of its residents. This would also protect the reasonable expectations of the parties to the contract. Therefore, Nevada law should be applied. [**Bernkrant v. Fowler,** *supra*]

---

e. **Negotiable instruments [§487]**

The law to be applied in cases involving negotiable instruments depends on whether the conflict concerns *performance issues* or whether it concerns *another issue*, such as negotiability, ownership, or possession.

(1) Performance issues [§488]

Courts are strongly inclined to refer to the law of the *place of payment* (performance) in deciding questions concerning the performance due under negotiable instruments. [Rest. 2d §214; **United States v. Guaranty Trust Co.,** 293 U.S. 340 (1934)] Thus, on questions of tender, payment, defenses to payment, transfer, or warranties, most courts would refer to the law of the place where the instrument is made payable.

(2) Other issues [§489]

However, where the issue at hand involves the original negotiability of the instrument, or ownership or possession of the instrument, courts tend to look to the law of the place *where the instrument was executed or is located.* In these cases, the place of ultimate payment is considered less significant. [**McCornick & Co. v. Tolmie Brothers,** 269 P. 96 (Idaho 1928); Rest. 2d §216] Thus, questions concerning the validity or effect of negotiation on transfer are generally referred to the place of transfer. [*See* **Citizens Bank v. National Bank of Commerce,** 334 F.2d 257 (10th Cir. 1964)]

f. Insurance contracts [§490]

The courts have developed special rules for insurance cases.

(1) Policy designations rejected [§491]

First of all, although courts today usually recognize a contract term designating which law will control (*see supra,* §§448-451), in insurance cases, courts tend to *disregard such terms* on the ground that the parties do not have equal bargaining positions (*i.e.,* it is an adhesion contract; *see supra,* §452).

(2) Life and casualty insurance [§492]

The "most significant contact" with respect to life and casualty insurance policies is generally held to be the *location of the risk* (*i.e.,* the domicile of the insured or the situs of property), and reference is usually made to the law of that place—regardless of whether the "place of making" or "center of gravity" is elsewhere. [*See* **Zogg v. Pennsylvania Mutual Insurance Co.,** *supra,* §452]

(a) Note

The usual outcome is that the forum will apply its own law, since the insured generally sues in her own state.

(3) Liability insurance [§493]

In claims involving tort liability insurance, courts usually refer to whatever law would otherwise govern the *tort liability* of the parties. [**Castorri v. Milbrand,** 118 So. 2d 563 (Fla. 1960)]

(a) Distinguish—compliance [§494]

However, questions involving compliance with contractual provisions (*e.g.,* giving notice of loss) are generally governed by the applicable *contracts* choice-of-law rule. [**Rittersbusch v. Sexsmith,** 41 N.W.2d 611 (Wis. 1950)]

(b) Direct action [§495]

And the question of whether a direct action is permitted by the injured party against the insurer (without first obtaining judgment against the insured) is treated as a "procedural" issue, so that the forum applies *its own law* regardless of contrary provisions in the insurance policy. [*See* **Watson v. Employers Liability Assurance Corp.,** 348 U.S. 66 (1954); *and see infra,* §679]

g. Employment and agency contracts [§496]

In this area, courts generally apply the law of the *place of performance* in resolving questions involving "performance." [Rest. 2d §205]

(1) Licensing [§497]

To determine the applicability of local statutes regulating or requiring licensing of agents, courts usually look to *where the services were rendered.* [**Cochran v. Ellsworth,** 126 Cal. App. 2d 429 (1954)]

(2) Wages, hours [§498]

However, where the issue concerns wages, hours, or working conditions in an employment contract, the place of performance is given less weight. More frequently, the court will refer to the law of the *place of contracting or of the employee's domicile* (particularly if there are protective statutes in effect there).

h. Rights of third parties [§499]

Issues addressing the rights of third parties to a contract include contracts entered into by an agent, third-party beneficiaries, and assignments.

(1) Contracts executed by agent [§500]

There are very few cases in this area, but it appears that the rights and liabilities of third persons who deal with the agents of another should be determined by the law *where the transaction takes place*, whether the agent had actual or apparent authority from the principal. [Rest. 2d §§292, 293]

(2) Third-party beneficiaries [§501]

Case law in this area is also rather scant. In **Brown v. Ford Motor Co.,** 48 F.2d 732 (10th Cir. 1931), the court rigidly applied the "place of making" rule—thereby invalidating the third-party beneficiary's rights under the contract even though such rights could have been upheld by reference to law of the forum (which was also the place of performance).

(a) Criticism [§502]

In view of the modern policy to uphold and enforce the rights of third-party beneficiaries wherever possible (*see* Contracts Summary), the *Brown* case has been criticized. Some commentators have proposed a reference to whatever reasonably applicable law would accomplish this underlying policy.

(3) Assignments [§503]

Choice-of-law rules concerning assignments vary with the type of problem involved.

(a) Basic rights of assignees [§504]

In determining the basic rights of a third-party assignee, courts generally look to the law *where the assignment takes place*. [Rest. 2d §209]

(b) Assignability of contract [§505]

On the other hand, questions as to the assignability of the underlying contract should be determined by the law that would govern the *"validity" of the contract*. [Rest. 2d §208]

(c) Priority of assignees [§506]

And in determining priority among successive assignees of the same debt, reference generally should be made to the place *where the performance is due* (*e.g.,* where the assigned debt is to be paid). [Rest. 2d §211]

i. Quasi-contracts [§507]

A plaintiff may seek to maintain an action in quasi-contract (restitution) where the basic right to relief is alleged to grow out of contract, tort (plaintiff "waiving the tort and suing in assumpsit"), or neither—as where an alleged right to restitution arises from benefits conferred by mistake, etc. In such cases, the courts usually tend simply to apply their own laws. Nevertheless, certain choice-of-law rules have been formulated:

(1) Benefit conferred [§508]

Where the plaintiff has conferred a benefit on the defendant (by contract, mistake, or duress), the forum should refer to the law of the place *where the benefit was conferred* to determine if the plaintiff has any right to be compensated therefor. [Rest. 2d §221]

(2) Unjust enrichment [§509]

But where the right to relief is based on a theory of unjust enrichment (*e.g.,* tort cases), the Restatement refers courts to the law of the place *where the benefit was received* to determine whether there is any duty to repay. [Rest. 2d §221]

(3) Underlying obligation [§510]

Alternatively, the court could look to the law from which the *quasi-contractual obligation arose*; *i.e.,* if the obligation arose in connection with a contract, the forum would apply the choice-of-law rule applicable to contract problems, and if the obligation arose in tort, it would apply the rule applicable to tort liability.

C. Property

1. Characterization [§511]

In property cases, characterization is a two-step process: First, the court must decide whether or not the case presents a *property problem*. (Many issues could be characterized as contracts—*e.g.,* contracts to sell land.) Then the court must determine whether the property interest involved is a *"movable"* or an *"immovable."*

a. Test for distinguishing "movables" and "immovables" [§512]

Land obviously is "immovable," and so issues pertaining to ownership of land are governed by the *law of the situs of land,* but what about other interests pertaining to land? The basic test for distinguishing "movables" and "immovables" is how closely the particular interest is connected with land. If the

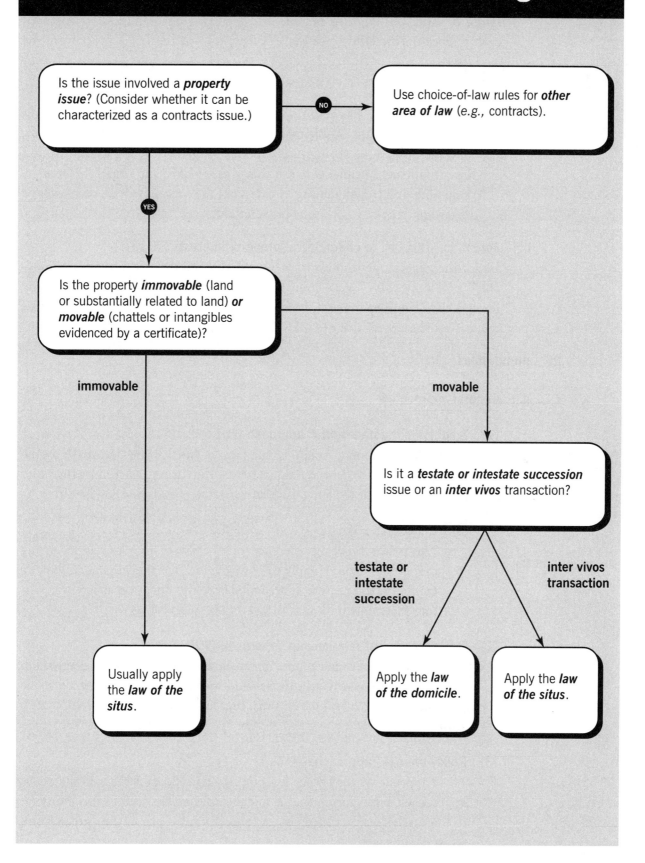

Is the issue involved a **property issue**? (Consider whether it can be characterized as a contracts issue.)

NO → Use choice-of-law rules for **other area of law** (e.g., contracts).

YES ↓

Is the property **immovable** (land or substantially related to land) **or movable** (chattels or intangibles evidenced by a certificate)?

immovable → Usually apply the **law of the situs**.

movable → Is it a **testate or intestate succession** issue or an **inter vivos** transaction?

testate or intestate succession → Apply the **law of the domicile**.

inter vivos transaction → Apply the **law of the situs**.

interest has any substantial relation to land, it is classified as an "immovable" and the *law of the situs of the land* is applied. Thus, the following interests may be classified as "immovables": (i) *leaseholds*; (ii) *proceeds from sale or rental* of land; (iii) *right to income and profits* from land; and (iv) perhaps even a *fence* on the land since there is little use for the fence apart from the land itself.

(1) Rationale

The situs of land has traditionally been the most important and prevailing "contact" with problems involving land or interests related thereto, and there is a *very strong public policy* favoring the application of that law to all such problems (since that state is most interested in the marketability and transferability of titles and the accuracy of its own records regarding property within its jurisdiction).

b. Forum vs. situs law to characterize property interests [§513]

Under the general view, the forum would characterize an interest as "movable" or "immovable" according to *its own law*, without reference to any foreign law. The Restatement, however, provides that the law of the situs of the interest should control even the characterization issue.

2. Immovables

a. General approaches

(1) Traditional "vested rights" approach [§514]

Under the traditional rule, all rights are deemed to be "created" by the *law of the situs*. To enforce those rights, the forum court must therefore refer to the law of the situs. [**Clarke v. Clarke**, 178 U.S. 186 (1900)]

(a) Renvoi [§515]

The policy favoring reference to the law of the situs is so strong that courts usually apply the "whole law" of the situs, including its conflict rules; *i.e.,* the court will decide the litigation as if it were sitting as a court in the situs. (*See supra*, §§257-266.)

(2) "Most significant relationship" approach [§516]

In practically all instances, the "most significant" contact or relationship to any problem involving title to immovables is likewise deemed to be with the *situs of the property*; thus, that law is applied. [Rest. 2d §§222, 236]

(3) Policy-oriented approaches [§517]

These approaches may place less emphasis on the situs than do the above approaches, but a forum that is not the situs of the land is also more apt to find itself "disinterested" so as to justify reference to the "greater" interest of situs law.

EXAM TIP **gilbert**

When your exam question concerns immovable property, you will almost always end up applying the *law of the situs*. However, if the particular jurisdiction uses the Second Restatement approach or especially if it uses one of the policy-oriented approaches, you should still mention the **contacts and policies involved**, even though you will most likely end up applying the law of the situs.

b. Specific applications

(1) Testate and intestate succession [§518]

Normally, all questions with respect to testate or intestate succession *to land* are determined by reference to the *law of the situs*. Indeed, this is perhaps the strongest choice-of-law rule in existence, being grounded on fundamental policies and interests of a sovereign to control the disposition of local land.

Examples: Orders of descent, validity and construction of devices of real property, capacity of heirs to inherit land, and marital property rights in land, etc., all are determined according to the law of the situs.

(2) Conveyances [§519]

The validity and effect of conveyances of immovables are determined *strictly* according to the *laws of the situs*. Thus, a conveyance made in F1 as to land located in F2 must be in the form required by F2 and its effect will be determined by F2 laws. Likewise, the capacity of the grantor to convey, and of the grantee to take title, must be determined by F2 law.

(a) Mortgages [§520]

Although mortgages, like other conveyances, involve elements of contract, they are still deemed to be so closely connected to land that they are construed according to the law of the *situs*. [Rest. 2d §228]

1) Distinguish—note securing mortgage [§521]

But the validity and effect of the promissory note or other obligation which the mortgage *secures* may be considered a "contracts" rather than a "property" problem, and thus justify the use of a different choice-of-law rule.

2) Deficiency judgment [§522]

The courts have split on whether a mortgagee's right to a deficiency judgment against the mortgagor is a "contracts" or "property" problem—*i.e.,* whether it is more closely related to a mortgagor's contractual undertakings or to the security transaction involving the property. [*See* **Younker v. Reseda Manor,** 255 Cal. App. 2d 431 (1967)—California court insisted on applying own law to protect a California resident from a deficiency judgment following foreclosure of a trust deed on Nevada land, even though promissory note and trust deed had been executed and "made payable" in Nevada]

(3) Contracts to convey, executory land sale contracts, etc. [§523]

Most courts treat these issues as "contracts" problems, and a choice of law is made according to appropriate *contracts rules*. The importance of the contractual undertaking is deemed to outweigh the property factors involved—even in cases where the contract operates as a conveyance of equitable title. [**Polson v. Stewart,** 45 N.E. 737 (Mass. 1897); Rest. 2d §189]

(a) Covenants [§524]

Covenants and agreements contained in deeds are treated like other land contracts (*contracts* rules apply), except that those found to *run with the land* (*i.e.,* burdens and/or benefits of the covenant pass to successive owners of the land) are always subject to the law of the *situs*. [**Platner v. Vincent,** 187 Cal. 443 (1921)]

(b) Forfeiture clause in executory land sale contract [§525]

The Supreme Court has held that problems involving forfeiture clauses may be properly characterized as either "contracts" *or* "property" questions; thus it is not unconstitutional to apply a "contract" choice-of-law rule in such cases. [**Kryger v. Wilson,** 242 U.S. 171 (1916)]

1) But note

Most authorities suggest that the law of the situs *ought* to be applied in this situation because of the vital interest of the situs in rights to local land and the need for uniformity of decisions.

(4) Marital property rights [§526]

Issues concerning dower, community property, or other marital rights in land are determined by reference to the *law of the situs* of the land. Again, that reference is to the "whole" law of the situs, and it is possible that in determining marital rights, the situs law may refer to the law of the *spouses' domicile* at the time of acquisition. [Rest. 2d §233]

(a) Community property [§527]

Thus, even where land is acquired in a community property state, the marital property rights in such land are usually determined by reference to the law of the spouses' domicile at the time of acquisition.

(5) Recovery of real estate commissions [§528]

Many states have statutes prohibiting any recovery for services as a real estate broker unless the recipient is licensed. The question arises whether a broker suing for a commission (or even a "finder's fee") must be licensed under the laws of the state where the land is located, where the contract of employment was executed, or where her services were rendered.

(a) Land outside forum [§529]

Where the forum is not the situs of the land, most courts tend to characterize this issue as a "contracts" problem and apply the law of the state that has the greater "interest" or "relationship" with the transaction—generally tending to uphold the validity of the parties' fee agreements whenever possible. [*See* **Cochran v. Ellsworth,** *supra,* §497—allowing broker licensed in California to recover for services performed in California although land in Arizona]

(b) Land within forum [§530]

But where the land is located in the forum state, some courts feel compelled to apply the law of the situs (forum), even where this would deny recovery to a broker not licensed locally who may nevertheless be licensed where she performed the services. The overriding interest in regulating activities relating to local land is thought to justify this approach. [50 Colum. L. Rev. 303 (1959)]

3. Movables

a. General approaches

(1) Traditional "vested rights" approach [§531]

Historically, either of two different rules was applied to choice-of-law problems involving movables, depending upon the nature of the problem.

(a) Testate and intestate succession [§532]

All questions relating to testate or intestate succession of *movable chattels* were determined by reference to the law of the *owner's domicile* at death. [**Bullen v. Wisconsin,** 240 U.S. 623 (1915); Rest. 1st §300]

1) Rationale

Since chattels are generally capable of being transported freely from state to state, it was felt that the governing law should be that of the owner's domicile at death (rather than the situs of the property), since this is presumably what the decedent would have intended.

EXAM TIP   gilbert

Note the difference under the traditional approach for testate and intestate succession of immovable and movable property: Issues involving the inheritance of the decedent's **land and other immovables** are governed by the law of the **situs**, because the state where the land is located is deemed to have control over it. Issues involving the decedent's **movables (chattels)** are governed by the law of the decedent's **domicile**; because the decedent had control over the movable items (think of it as he could move them wherever he wanted), the law where he lives (*i.e.*, of his domicile) controls.

(b) Inter vivos transactions [§533]

All other questions relating to conveyances, mortgages, sales, etc., of movable chattels are determined by reference to the law of the *situs of the chattel at the time of the transaction* in question. [Rest. 1st §255]

(2) "Most significant relationship" approach [§534]

The Second Restatement reframes the above choice-of-law rules by providing that *domicile* is usually the "most significant" contact or relationship with respect to *succession and marital property questions*, and *situs* the "most significant" contact or relationship with respect to *inter vivos transactions involving movables*. [Rest. 2d §§244, 260]

(a) Uniform Commercial Code [§535]

The U.C.C. (which covers all sales and secured transactions in movables) refers courts in cases where a consumer is a party to the transaction for the sale of goods to the law of the state or country in which the consumer both makes the contract and takes delivery of the goods, if that state or country is not the one in which the consumer principally resides. (*See supra*, §299.) [U.C.C. §301(e)(2)(B)]

(3) Policy-oriented approaches [§536]

These approaches treat choice-of-law issues arising from the transfer of movables the same as other choice-of-law questions.

b. Specific applications

(1) Conveyances [§537]

The validity and effect of the conveyance of a movable is determined by the *law of the situs of the chattel at the time of conveyance*. [*See* Rest. 2d §244]

(2) Contracts of sale [§538]

The same *"law of situs"* rule applies to contracts of sale or conditional sales contracts pertaining to chattels. [Rest. 2d §251]

(a) Distinguish

Problems distinct from the question of title to the movable—such as questions regarding the vendor's warranties as to quality—may be regarded as "contracts" problems and reference is to the appropriate law for contracts questions. [**Hutchison v. Ross,** 262 N.Y. 381 (1933); Rest. 2d §191]

(b) But note

Even so, in transactions subject to the U.C.C., the outcome should be the same—since the U.C.C. has been adopted in nearly all states (*see* above).

(3) Priorities in secured transactions [§539]

The typical situation here is Buyer gives Seller a security interest in movables (*e.g.,* machinery) located in F1, and Seller duly files a financing statement in F1 as required by the U.C.C. Buyer then takes the machinery to F2 (where Seller's interest is not recorded), and either sells it outright or mortgages it for value to an innocent purchaser for value (a BFP). Who prevails?

(a) Uniform Commercial Code [§540]

Section 9-316 provides an arbitrary *four-month period* during which a security interest duly executed and recorded in F1 will protect the secured party (mortgagee) in any other state. During this period, not even a bona fide purchaser without notice (BFP) can acquire priority, and this is true whether or not the secured party (mortgagee) consented to or had knowledge of the debtor's taking the machinery out of F1. If the secured party fails to file or record his interest in the state to which the chattel has been removed (F2) during the four-month period, however, his interest is subordinated to that of any BFP who purchases (or acquires a perfected security interest in) the chattel. (A different rule applies to automobiles or other property covered by a certificate of title; *see* Secured Transactions Summary.)

(4) Testamentary or inter vivos trusts [§541]

Courts have tended to depart from ordinary choice-of-law rules when dealing with trusts involving movables. The underlying policy is to uphold the trust and the exercise of any power thereunder if possible. [Rest. 2d §268] Thus, courts may refer to the law of *whatever state would uphold validity*, provided there are sufficient "contacts" with that state. In identical fact situations, courts have referred to the law of the situs, the place of administration [**Hope v. Brewer,** 136 N.Y. 126 (1892)], or domicile of the settlor, whichever would uphold the trust.

(a) Future interests [§542]

The same approach applies to transfers of future interests in movables. [64 Nw. U. L. Rev. 388 (1969)]

(5) Marital property rights [§543]

Community property or other marital property rights in movables are usually determined by reference to the law of the property *owner's domicile* at the time of acquisition.

(a) Rationale

Once acquired, marital rights are not lost or changed merely because the spouses move to another state. [Rest. 2d §259]

(b) But note

The state of the spouses' new domicile may apply its own concepts to such property for certain purposes; *e.g.,* property acquired in non-community-property states may be distributed on death as if it were community property. (*See* discussion of "quasi-community property" in Community Property Summary.)

(6) Intangibles [§544]

Generally, an intangible (*i.e.,* a chose in action) has no "situs," and so there can be no reference to the law of situs. However, if there is a document representing the intangible (*i.e.,* a token chose), this may provide a situs.

(a) No document [§545]

Where there is no document, questions as to *assignability* of the right involved should be governed by the law of the place of transfer—although some courts refer to the "situs of the debt" (domicile of the debtor). Questions regarding the *effect of assignment*, or the *validity of the particular mode of transfer*, are "contracts" problems and should be governed by contract choice-of-law principles.

(b) Some document [§546]

Where some document represents the chose in action and the document is fully negotiable, the intangible rights are taken to be *embodied in the instrument* because people deal with the instrument as if dealing with the rights themselves. The document thus becomes a tangible "res" that justifies reference to the law of situs. [**First Trust Co. v. Matheson,** 246 N.W. 1 (Minn. 1932)]

 Example: Under the U.C.C., a stock certificate represents the intangible shares of stock in the corporation and thus is treated as a fully negotiable instrument. Accordingly, reference should be made to the law of the situs of the certificate in questions involving title to the shares, etc. [*Cf.* **Morson v. Second National Bank of Boston,** 29 N.E.2d 19 (Mass. 1940)]

---

(7) Administration of decedents' estates—jurisdictional issues [§547]

The choice-of-law rules governing succession of property upon the death of the owner have been discussed above. The following issues relate primarily to *jurisdiction* and the *effect of judgments* in probate proceedings involving local and foreign administrations.

(a) Place for administration [§548]

A decedent's will may be probated and an executor appointed (or an administrator appointed for an intestate) in any of the following places:

1) Decedent's domicile [§549]

A decedent's estate is always subject to administration at the place of her domicile *at the time of death*. This is true regardless of whether any assets are located in that state (although there would be little reason for such administration without assets). [Rest. 2d §315]

a) "Principal" administration [§550]

The administration at the domicile is referred to as the "principal" administration. Administration of assets at any other place (*see* below) is referred to as "ancillary" administration.

b) Domicile characterized by forum [§551]

As discussed earlier, one state is not bound by the findings of another as to "domicile" (*see supra,* §§37-39), and it is therefore conceivable that more than one state might find a decedent to have been domiciled there at the time of death (and thus subject the estate to taxation). But this rarely happens, at least where the same parties are litigating the question in each state, because the first finding as to domicile is res judicata and binds the parties in any subsequent proceeding.

2) Situs of assets—"ancillary" administration [§552]

There may also be an administration wherever the decedent left any property (whether movable or immovable). Any administration of assets outside the decedent's domicile is considered an "ancillary" administration. The person appointed as ancillary administrator or executor may (but need not) be the same person as the principal (domiciliary) administrator. (Many states require administrators to be local residents but permit executors to be nonresidents [*see* Cal. Prob. Code §420].)

a) Immovable and movable property [§553]

Usually there is an ancillary administration when the decedent left real property outside the state of his domicile. Even where he left *movable property* outside the domiciliary state, there may be an ancillary administration where the property is located. However, the situs state of movable property will normally apply the law of the *decedent's domicile* to dispose of the property (*see supra,* §532).

b) No minimum amount or type of property [§554]

Generally, no minimum amount or type of property is required for administration.

1/ A debt (intangible) owed to the decedent is traditionally held to be a sufficient "asset" for the appointment of an administrator, wherever the debtor is subject to jurisdiction. [**Gordon v. Shea,** 14 N.E.2d 105 (Mass. 1938)]

2/ Likewise, when a wrongful death claim is made on account of decedent's death, administration is proper wherever jurisdiction over the defendant tortfeasor can be obtained. [Rest. 2d §314(c)]

(b) Power of administrator outside state [§555]

Each administration is deemed separate and distinct from all others, and an administrator appointed in one state usually has no power to act outside the state in which she was appointed.

1) Taking possession of assets [§556]

However, if no ancillary administrator has been appointed, it is proper for the domiciliary administrator to take possession of decedent's personal property, and her possession thereof will be recognized and protected in any other state. [Rest. 2d §319]

2) No power to sue or be sued [§557]

The common law rule provides that an administrator or executor appointed in one state cannot sue or be sued in her representative capacity in the courts of another state. [56 Colum. L. Rev. 915 (1968)]

a) Effect

Denying the domiciliary administrator power to sue outside the state often operates harshly. Particularly where the decedent had interests in other parts of the country, it significantly increases the expense and difficulty of winding up the estate, and may impose a tremendous economic burden on a small estate.

b) Statutes [§558]

Today, statutes in some states allow foreign administrators to sue locally. Other statutes adhere to the common law rule but permit a foreign administrator to secure local appointment without elaborate proceedings, so that she can maintain an action in local courts. [54 Mich. L. Rev. 821 (1956)]

c) Distinguish—long arm statutes [§559]

Various state long arm statutes confer jurisdiction against the personal representative (executor or administrator) of a nonresident whose conduct or act has brought him within the statute. And others, while not expressly so providing, have been construed to permit jurisdiction. (*See supra,* §§142 *et seq.*)

(c) No res judicata effect of judgments in actions by or against administrator [§560]

In accordance with the common law rule that an administrator in one state could not sue or be sued in another, each administration is deemed separate and no privity between administrators is recognized. Hence, res judicata does not apply.

1) Result [§561]

Judgments for or against an administrator in F1 are generally of *no effect* in litigation involving an administrator appointed in F2. [**Nash v. Benari**, 105 A. 107 (Me. 1918); Rest. 2d §356]

Example: If the plaintiff wins a judgment against the F1 administrator, she can enforce it only against assets of the decedent being administered in F1. Conversely, if the defendant loses the suit against the F1 administrator, this does not bar a later suit against an administrator in a different state.

---

a) Criticism [§562]

Where a creditor has presented a claim against the decedent's estate in F1 and loses, it would seem that the judgment (in favor of the F1 administrator) should be entitled to collateral estoppel in subsequent proceedings on the same claim in F2, but the Restatement position, at least, is to the contrary. [*See* Rest. 2d §357]

2) Exceptions [§563]

Various exceptions to the above rule have developed over time:

a) Executor [§564]

Sufficient privity has been found where the same person or persons are appointed as *executors* in several states, so that a judgment against an executor in F1 *is conclusive* in F2. [**Carpenter v. Strange,** 141 U.S. 87 (1891)—an executor is named by decedent as his representative, whereas an administrator is merely appointed by probate judge]

b) Administrator [§565]

Moreover, where the *same administrator* sued or was sued outside the state of appointment, the judgment rendered *may be binding* in later proceedings inside the state; *i.e.,* courts have recognized that even though the administrator sued in different states, she is the same legal person and should not be entitled to relitigate. [**Peare v. Griggs,** 8 N.Y.2d 44 (1960)]

c) Merger [§566]

And a judgment in favor of an F1 administrator will operate as a merger. Thus, where the administrator in F1 recovers judgment against a debtor there, that judgment "merges" the claim so there is nothing left to sue upon. This prevents administrators in other states from *relitigating the same claim* or collecting twice on the same debt. [**Lewis v. Adams,** 70 Cal. 403 (1886)]

1/ On the other hand, if the F1 administrator loses the suit against the debtor, there is no bar; *i.e.,* other administrators may sue the same debtor on the same claim.

3) Comment [§567]

Most commentators today argue that a judgment for or against an administrator in one state *should* be held binding on every other administrator in order to terminate litigation and avoid inconsistent results. The notion that each administration is "separate and independent" is not realistic in practice, since the same parties usually stand to benefit from each and a substantial degree of intercommunication and control exists. The courts, however, have not yet accepted this view.

D. Corporations

1. General Approaches

a. Traditional "vested rights" approach [§568]

Traditionally, all rights and obligations respecting a corporation were deemed to be "created" by the law of the *place of incorporation*, and reference was therefore made to such law. [**Knights of Honor v. Nairn,** 26 N.W. 826 (Mich. 1886)]

b. "Most significant relationship" approach [§569]

The Second Restatement also refers to the law of the *state of incorporation* for many conflicts questions, *e.g.,* creation and dissolution of the corporation and shareholder liability for assessments.

c. Policy-oriented approaches [§570]

These approaches would treat choice-of-law issues respecting corporations the same as other conflicts issues.

EXAM TIP **gilbert**

For corporations questions, under any approach, the law to be applied is *usually* going to be that of the *state of incorporation*. However, don't forget to consider *escape devices* to avoid an unjust result under the traditional approach, and when using the Second Restatement and policy-oriented approaches, keep in mind that for some issues such as *corporate transactions* (as opposed to issues of corporate structure and power), the *statutes and policies of other interested states*, especially the forum, may be the proper law to apply.

---

2. Specific Applications

a. Corporate powers and liabilities [§571]

Most questions regarding corporate powers, purposes, capacity to contract or hold title to property, regulation of internal affairs, etc., are decided by reference to the law of the *place of incorporation.* [Rest. 2d §302]

b. Capacity to sue [§572]

Capacity to sue is likewise determined by the law of the *state of incorporation.* [*See* Fed. R. Civ. P. 17(b)]

(1) State "qualification" requirements [§573]

Keep in mind that if a foreign corporation is doing business locally, it must "qualify" in the state (pay local filing fees, etc.) and comply with nondiscriminatory local regulations. If it fails to do so, the corporation may be denied the right to sue or defend itself in local courts. [*See* **Textile Banking Co. v. Colonial Chemical Co.,** 285 F. Supp. 824 (N.D. Ga. 1967)]

(2) Constitutional limitation [§574]

Note, however, that such regulations *cannot* constitutionally be applied to corporations that do not operate regularly within the state and whose intrastate activities are merely "fleeting events" in otherwise purely interstate business transactions. [**Allenberg Cotton Co. v. Pittman**, *supra*, §244]

c. Liabilities of officers, directors, or controlling shareholders [§575]

The law of the *state of incorporation* governs issues relating to the corporate *structure* (*e.g.*, liability for issuing "watered" stock or dividends from illegal source). [Rest. 2d §309] However, where claims involve *transactions* (*e.g.*, seizing a corporate opportunity, making a contract, or committing a tort), the *forum* or some other state may have an interest in regulating this conduct and the law of that state may be applied. [Rest. 2d §301]

---

e.g. **Example:** Questions of alter ego (*i.e.*, whether officers and directors are personally liable for corporate debts) are usually decided by referring to the law of the place of contracting rather than the place of incorporation. [Rest. 2d §302]

---

3. Limitation—Forum Statutes or Public Policy [§576]

The general "state of incorporation" rule will not be applied to uphold a transaction contrary to the forum's own statutes or strong public policy. This limitation reflects the development of case law recognizing that a state other than that of incorporation may have a legitimate interest in regulating the affairs of a foreign corporation. [**White v. Howard**, 46 N.Y. 144 (1871)]

---

e.g. **Example:** A California court has refused to permit a Delaware corporation to solicit shareholder approval for an amendment to its articles of incorporation that would have eliminated cumulative voting for directors. Even though the amendment would have been permitted under Delaware law, California had a *legitimate interest* in the matter, since the corporation's principal business was in California and many shareholders resided there. Hence, the court insisted upon applying its own laws (prohibiting amendment). [**Western Air Lines, Inc. v. Sobieski**, 191 Cal. App. 2d 399 (1961)]

---

a. Distinguish—statutory limitation [§577]

A few states now have statutes that regulate the choice of law in litigation involving corporations. Under the California statute, a foreign corporation that does more than half its business in California and more than half of whose shareholders reside there is treated as a *"pseudo-foreign"* corporation, which allows California courts to apply California law with respect to certain major corporate issues (*e.g.*, directors' liability, shareholders' voting rights, rights on merger and reorganization). [Cal. Corp. Code §2115(b); *and see* N.Y. Bus. Corp. Law §1306]

E. Workers' Compensation

1. In General [§578]

Workers' compensation statutes provide benefits to an employee injured within the scope of employment. Usually, this is the employee's exclusive remedy against the employer. Early choice-of-law decisions attempted to characterize workers' compensation claims as "tort" or "contracts" actions. It is generally recognized today that such actions fall into **neither category**, although elements of both areas are involved.

a. Problems [§579]

Workers' compensation claims present some unique problems (both jurisdictional and choice of law) due to the fact that the "contacts" involved—place of injury, place of employee's residence, place of employer's business, and place where employee was hired—frequently transcend state boundaries.

b. Policy [§580]

If a state takes jurisdiction over a workers' compensation claim, it usually applies its **own workers' compensation statute**—since such claims are generally processed by administrative agencies that operate under local statutes (below). The basic policy in this area is to afford to an injured worker the most favorable recovery possible, and jurisdiction and choice-of-law rules have been framed to achieve this end.

2. Jurisdiction [§581]

Workers' compensation proceedings are statutory in nature, and most statutes provide coverage for injuries sustained outside the state. Thus, an injured worker may file a claim in any state where the **employer is subject to jurisdiction** and where the forum has a **legitimate interest** in regulating the employment relationship involved. [**Alaska Packers Association v. Industrial Accident Commission**, 294 U.S. 532 (1935)]

3. Choice of Law [§582]

As noted above, most workers' compensation boards simply apply **their own local laws** (ignoring any foreign "contacts" in the case). This has been upheld as constitutional, as long as the forum has some legitimate interest in regulating the employment relationship; *i.e.,* the forum is the place of injury, hiring, employee's residence, or employer's place of business.

Example: A nonresident may file a compensation claim in the state where he was hired, and that state may apply its own laws to the claim, regardless of the fact that the injuries were sustained outside the state. [**Alaska Packers Association v. Industrial Accident Commission,** *supra*]

Example: Likewise, the forum may apply its own laws on a compensation claim arising from injuries sustained within the forum, even though the claimant is a nonresident and was hired outside the state. [**Pacific Employers Insurance Co. v. Industrial Accident Commission,** 306 U.S. 493 (1939)]

EXAM TIP	gilbert

In a workers' compensation case, don't be fooled by a fact situation where most of the facts relate to State A but the employee files her claim in State B. If State B (i) *has jurisdiction over the employer* and (ii) *has a legitimate interest in regulating the employment relationship* (*i.e.,* at least one major contact is there), it can apply its own law, despite any interest of State A in the case.

---

4.   **Multiple Awards [§583]**

In **Industrial Accident Commission v. McCartin,** 330 U.S. 622 (1947), the Court held that an injured worker may file a claim and recover an award under the compensation statutes of several states having a "legitimate interest" in regulating the employment relationship unless the statute in one of the states makes its award the "exclusive" remedy (*i.e.,* barring award by any other state), in which event multiple recovery will not be allowed. In **Thomas v. Washington Gas Light Co.,** 448 U.S. 261 (1980), a plurality of the Court reaffirmed the *McCartin* result for a different reason: Treating workers' compensation awards as different from court judgments, the plurality view was that no state has a *legitimate interest in preventing* a supplemental workers' compensation award by a state that would have had the power to apply its workers' compensation law in the first instance. (*See also infra,* §781.)

a.   **Further limitation against multiple recoveries [§584]**

Even where multiple recoveries are permitted, any prior award must be *credited against the amount recovered in subsequent proceedings* so that the worker is limited to the *largest* award she would have been entitled to under any of the applicable acts.

b.   **Independent tort actions permitted [§585]**

However, the limitation against multiple recoveries does *not* apply to an independent tort (or wrongful death) action against the employer or any third person, if such action is permitted under forum law. This is true even where the injured worker previously recovered a workers' compensation award from the employer in another state whose compensation laws purported to prohibit any independent action for industrial injuries. [*See* **Carroll v. Lanza,** 349 U.S. 408 (1955)]

F.   Family Law

1. **Introduction [§586]**

   Choice-of-law problems in the area of domestic relations are relatively simple in comparison with those encountered in torts, contracts, or property. The following section discusses problems relating to marriage, adoption, and status of children. Divorce, annulment, and custody are treated in connection with recognition and enforcement of judgments (*see infra*, §§834 *et seq.*).

2. **Marriage**

   a. **Choice of law regarding validity of marriage [§587]**

      The validity of a marriage is determined by the law of the *place of celebration* (*i.e.*, where the marriage relationship was entered into) at the time of the marriage—at least where the marriage can be *upheld* by reference to that law and there is no problem of remarriage following divorce. This rule will be applied whether the matter is litigated at the parties' domicile, at the place of celebration, or in some third state. [Rest. 2d §283(2); 71 A.L.R.2d 687]

      (1) **Rationale**

         There is a strong interest in upholding marriages. Since people frequently marry in places other than their domicile, the courts usually uphold a marriage that is valid where entered into unless the relationship violates some fundamental interest of the domicile concerning the health, mores, welfare, or family characteristics of its domiciliaries.

      (2) **Reference to law of domicile to uphold marriage [§588]**

         Conversely, where a marriage would *not be valid* under the law of the place of celebration but would be recognized under the law of the parties' domicile, courts will apply the *law of the domicile*—again, provided this is not grossly offensive to the public policy or mores of the forum. [**Applebaum v. Applebaum,** 9 Misc. 2d 677 (1957); Rest. 2d §283, comment i]

         (a) **Comment**

            A number of authorities urge that the parties' domicile at time of marriage has the paramount interest and that reference should always be made to its law, except that the law of the place of celebration may control questions of *mere form* (license, capacity of person performing the ceremony, etc.). However, difficulties would arise where the husband and wife were domiciled in different states prior to marriage. And in any case, the courts have not adopted this position.

      (3) **Statutes regulating choice of law [§589]**

         Under some state statutes, marriages by local residents entered into outside the state are invalid if contrary to the laws of the place of marriage—even where the marriage would have been valid under local (domicile) law. [**Estate of Levie,** 50 Cal. App. 3d 572 (1975)—marriage between first cousins held void because it violated Nevada law (where marriage was entered into), even though spouses were at all times domiciled in California and marriage between first cousins would have been permitted under California law]

EXAM TIP   **gilbert**

In answering choice-of-law questions regarding the validity of marriage, be sure to keep in mind the **strong policy interest courts have in upholding marriages**. This means that they will try to find the marriage valid if at all possible. So if the law of the place of **celebration** doesn't work to uphold the marriage, try the law of the parties' **domicile** to see if it will do so. If so, that is the law the courts would apply unless there is some fundamental interest that will be violated.

---

b. **Specific applications**

(1) **Formal requirements of marriage [§590]**
Marriages valid at the place of celebration are generally upheld against any law of the parties' domicile that would invalidate the marriage for non-compliance with formal requirements: *e.g.,* necessity for license, health certificate, proper solemnization, validity of proxy marriage, etc. [**Barrons v. United States,** 191 F.2d 92 (9th Cir. 1951)]

(2) **Capacity [§591]**
Even questions as to the parties' capacity to marry or the necessity of parental consent are usually decided by reference to the law of place of celebration if this would uphold the marriage. [**State v. Graves,** 307 S.W.2d 545 (Ark. 1957)]

(a) **But note**
There are cases that hold that the "paramount interest" of the parties' domicile should require that its law determine questions of capacity. [*See, e.g.,* **Ross v. Bryant,** 217 P. 364 (Okla. 1923)]

(3) **Common law marriages [§592]**
The validity of these relationships is governed by the law of the place *where the relationship was entered into—i.e.,* where the parties commenced cohabitation. If valid under that law, the common law marriage will be upheld even where the forum would not otherwise recognize the marriage. [*See* **Boltz v. Boltz,** 92 N.E.2d 365 (Mass. 1950)]

(4) **Exception—marriages contravening "laws of nature" [§593]**
The policy of upholding marriages valid under the law of the place of celebration may be outweighed in certain cases. Thus, courts in other states may refuse to uphold marriages that are grossly offensive to their own public policy because they are contrary to the "laws of nature"

(*e.g.,* polygamous, incestuous, etc.). [117 A.L.R. 186; *and see infra,* §609]

(a) Law of domicile governs [§594]

According to the Second Restatement, a marriage that is incestuous or polygamous under the law of the place where the parties were ***domiciled at the time of the marriage*** and where ***they intend to make their home thereafter*** is invalid everywhere on the rationale that that state has the "paramount interest" in the marriage. [Rest. 2d §283, comment k]

(b) "Status" vs. "incidents" distinction [§595]

However, even a polygamous or incestuous marriage may be upheld where the court is not called upon to sanction the "unnatural" cohabitation. Particularly after the death of one of the parties, courts may recognize and uphold such marriages for the purpose of determining property or other rights as "incidents" of the relationship. [*See, e.g.,* ***In re* May's Estate,** 305 N.Y. 486 (1953)—marriage between uncle and niece, valid where consummated but incestuous under domicile-forum law, upheld in probate proceedings on issue of whether survivor had right to administer decedent spouse's estate]

c. Validity of remarriage following divorce [§596]

A problem frequently arises where either or both spouses in a marriage were under a prohibition against remarriage for a certain period following a divorce in another state. Here, no strong policy exists to uphold the validity of the second marriage, and the courts' willingness to do so will depend on several factors.

(1) Remarriage before final decree [§597]

If the divorce is by interlocutory decree only (*i.e.,* a waiting period must expire before the final decree can be obtained) and either party remarries outside the state before the final decree is obtained, the marriage is ***usually void***. This is because until the final decree is obtained, the first marriage still exists and neither party has the capacity to remarry. [**Earle v. Earle,** 141 App. Div. 611 (1910)]

(2) Split of authority where divorce final [§598]

Where the divorce is absolute but the law of the parties' domicile imposes a prohibition against remarriage for a certain period of time, and one of the spouses remarries outside the state within the prohibited time, the authorities are split.

(a) Majority view [§599]

Most courts ***would uphold*** the second marriage if it is valid under the law of the place of celebration. [*See* **Pickard v. Pickard,** 45 N.W.2d 269 (Iowa 1950)]

(b) Minority view [§600]

However, some cases have held the new marriage *void* because it violates the law of the parties' domicile. [**Lanham v. Lanham,** 117 N.W. 787 (Wis. 1908)]

(c) Determinative factors [§601]

In deciding which law to apply, the following factors are significant [Rest. 2d §283, comment 1]:

1) Effect of new domicile [§602]

If either of the divorced spouses has acquired a new domicile following the divorce and has entered into a valid marriage in the new domicile, the courts are more likely to uphold the second marriage. [**Loughran v. Loughran,** 292 U.S. 216 (1934)]

2) Type of proceeding in which raised [§603]

The second marriage is more likely to be upheld in an inheritance proceeding than in a bigamy prosecution or divorce action. [*In re* **Miller's Estate,** 214 N.W. 428 (Mich. 1927)]

3) Where suit is brought [§604]

Courts in the place of celebration or some state other than the domicile are also more inclined to uphold the marriage than to enforce the prohibitions of the domiciliary law. [**Adams v. Hutchinson,** 167 S.E. 135 (W. Va. 1933)]

4) Length of marriage [§605]

Finally, where there has been extensive cohabitation, property accumulations, children born, etc., the courts are much more inclined to apply the law of the parties' domicile and less inclined to follow the law of the place of celebration in determining the validity of the marriage.

d. Statutes [§606]

In some states, recognition of foreign marriages is governed by statute.

(1) Former view—Uniform Marriage Evasion Act [§607]

The Uniform Marriage Evasion Act provided that if the parties to a marriage are domiciled and intend to remain domiciled in a particular state, and if their marriage would be *void* (not merely voidable) under the law of the domicile, the marriage is void regardless of the law of the place of celebration. Only a few states ever enacted this statute, and even in those states, the statute was not literally applied in all cases. [*See* 9 V. and. L. Rev. 607 (1956)] The Commissioners on Uniform State Laws withdrew their approval of this Act in 1973 and instead promulgated a different rule in the Uniform Marriage and Divorce Act (*see* below).

(2) Modern view—Uniform Marriage and Divorce Act [§608]

The Uniform Marriage and Divorce Act provides in section 210 that marriages validly contracted outside a state will be valid in the state of the parties' domicile. However, section 207 prohibits certain marriages that are bigamous or incestuous no matter where celebrated. This position is consistent with statutes already enacted in some states. For example, California Family Code section 308 provides: "A marriage contracted outside this state that would be valid by the laws of the jurisdiction in which the marriage was contracted is valid in this state." As in the Uniform Act, marriages that are bigamous or incestuous are void. [*See* Cal. Fam. Code §§2200-2201] Both the Uniform Act and the California statute negate any attempt to assert local public policy over domiciliaries whose out-of-state marriages would have been invalid if entered into in California—whether a question of "form" or "capacity" is involved, and even where local domiciliaries marry outside the state for the specific purpose of evading local laws.

(3) Defense of Marriage Act [§609]

The federal Defense of Marriage Act ("DOMA") permits states to refuse to recognize same-sex marriages validly performed in other states. DOMA provides that no state "shall be required to give effect to" such marriages. The Act has not yet been tested by the courts, and it has been widely criticized as both unnecessary (because of the public policy exception noted in §593, *supra*) and unconstitutional (because of its invidious purpose of discriminating against gays and lesbians who wish to marry). (*See also infra*, §816.) Many states have enacted their own versions of DOMA. For example, California Family Code section 308.5, which was added by an Initiative Measure in 2000, provides that "[o]nly marriage between a man and a woman is valid or recognized in California."

3. Change in Status of Children

a. Status of child at birth [§610]

The status of a child at birth as marital or nonmarital is governed strictly by whether it is born during a lawful marriage. This is a "marriage validity" problem and is thus determined in accordance with the rules and policies discussed *supra*, §§587-591.

(1) Statutes [§611]

However, many states today have statutes that provide that children of void or voidable marriages are "marital" so that the "validity" of the parents' marriage (or even a judicial decree of nullity) will not affect the child's status at birth. [*See* Cal. Civ. Code §4453; 87 A.L.R.2d 1294]

b. Change in status after birth

(1) By marriage of parents [§612]

In most states, a subsequent marriage of the parents will serve to change the status of a nonmarital child. (*Note:* Some states require additional acts such as the recognition of the child; *see* below.)

(2) By recognition [§613]

The natural father can also perform certain acts (*e.g.,* admit in open court that he fathered the child) which may change the child's status ("recognition"). Choice-of-law problems may arise when the sufficiency of these acts is questioned. (*See* below.)

(3) Choice of law governing change in status after birth [§614]

Where a child was nonmarital at birth under the appropriate law but it is claimed that the child's status was subsequently changed by the father (*e.g.,* by recognition), what law should determine the sufficiency of the subsequent acts relied upon to effect the change in status of the child? (This question is usually raised in heirship proceedings against the father's estate.)

(a) Probate weight of authority [§615]

The law of the father's domicile at the time the acts were performed governs the sufficiency of the acts, even though the acts were done outside the state and even if the child was domiciled elsewhere. [**Blythe v. Ayres,** 96 Cal. 532 (1892); Rest. 2d §287(2)]

1) Note

Some courts apply the law of the father's domicile at the time of the father's death, rather than at the time of acts. [*In re* **Lund's Estate,** 26 Cal. App. 2d 472 (1945)]

(b) Comment

The general policy of the law favors a finding of the child's status as marital; thus, some commentators argue that whichever law would achieve this end (the domicile of the child or the domicile of the father) should control.

c. Basis for jurisdiction

(1) Inheritance (heirship) proceedings [§616]

Where the child's status as a marital child is at issue in inheritance proceedings, the court's jurisdiction is based on its power over the assets involved in the inheritance proceedings (in rem).

(2) Support proceedings [§617]

But where the child's status as a marital child is asserted as the "springboard" for a support obligation against the father during his lifetime, most courts hold that personal jurisdiction over the father is required. [**Hartford v. Superior Court,** 47 Cal. 2d 447 (1956)]

(a) But note

A few authorities are contrary, arguing that such an action merely seeks a declaration of status that is in rem in nature, just as in the divorce cases. [*See* 20 S.C. L. Rev. 339 (1947)]

4. Adoption

a. Choice of law [§618]

Adoption is a wholly statutory proceeding. There are no choice-of-law problems, since the *forum always applies its own law.*

EXAM TIP **gilbert**

Because in adoption cases the *forum always applies its own law*, if you see a question about adoption on your Conflicts exam, it will most likely require you to discuss jurisdictional or due process issues rather than choice-of-law issues (see below).

---

b. Basis for jurisdiction [§619]

Several bases for jurisdiction in adoption proceedings have been suggested.

(1) "Status" of child [§620]

A number of courts have held that residence of the child within the state, plus domicile of the adoptive parents, is a sufficient basis for jurisdiction—even though no personal jurisdiction is obtained over the natural parents. [**Woodward's Appeal,** 70 A. 453 (Conn. 1908)] *Rationale:* The court is deciding a question of "status" (parent-child), and the presence of the child within the state brings the status (a "res") before the court. The court can then handle the matter as a proceeding in rem, without personal jurisdiction over the natural parents.

(2) Restatement view [§621]

The Second Restatement requires *either* domicile of the child (which is that of the parents, *see supra,* §30) or domicile of the adoptive parents, *plus* personal jurisdiction over the child or person having custody thereof. [Rest. 2d §78]

(3) State's interest in child [§622]

Finally, some commentators suggest that mere residence of the child—as distinguished from domicile—should be a sufficient basis for jurisdiction. *Rationale:* A state in which the child is physically present has a paramount interest in his welfare, education, support, etc., even though he may be technically domiciled elsewhere.

c. Requirement of notice to natural parents [§623]

In any event, due process requires that the natural parents be given adequate notice and an opportunity to be heard in such proceedings. [**Armstrong v. Manzo,** 380 U.S. 545 (1965)]

(1) Adequate notice [§624]

Precisely what sort of notice is required has not been specified. Apparently, a natural parent within the state should be served personally with notice of the proceedings; whereas for a nonresident, the "next best" type of service (*i.e.,* substituted service, *see supra,* §206) would be necessary.

d. Inheritance rights of adopted child [§625]

The fact that the forum has jurisdiction to decree an adoption does not mean that the forum's law should apply to the inheritance rights of the child. Such rights are determined strictly by the law governing the distribution of the estate of the child's natural or adoptive parents at the time of their death (*see supra,* §549).

CHOICE-OF-LAW RULES FOR SPECIFIC AREAS OF SUBSTANTIVE LAW

gilbert

SUBSTANTIVE AREA OF LAW	"VESTED RIGHTS" APPROACH	"MOST SIGNIFICANT RELATIONSHIP" APPROACH
TORTS	Place of the wrong (injury).	Consider the place of: - Injury; - Conduct causing the injury; - Residence and/or business of parties; - Center of parties' relationship.
CONTRACTS	*Validity problem*—place of making. *Performance problem*—place of performance.	Consider the place of: - Contracting; - Negotiation; - Performance; - Location of subject matter; - Domicile, residence, nationality, incorporation and business of parties.
PROPERTY	*Immovable property*—situs. *Movable property:* Testamentary and intestate transfer—domicile of owner at time of death. Inter vivos transactions—situs of property at the time of the relevant transaction.	
CORPORATIONS	Place of incorporation.	
WORKERS' COMPENSATION	Forum.	
FAMILY LAW	*Marriage*—place of celebration (if marriage can be upheld under that law). *Change in nonmarital child's status after birth*—father's domicile. *Adoption*—forum.	

Note: The "governmental interest" approach does not vary according to the substantive area of law.

Chapter Six: Traditional Defenses Against Application of Foreign Law

CONTENTS

Chapter Approach

Chapter Approach

In choice-of-law questions, after you have decided which law should be applied, you need to analyze whether there are any reasons *not to apply* the foreign law. A defense to application of the foreign law might be that such application would violate the forum's local *public policy* or that the foreign law is a *penal law* or *revenue law* and thus unenforceable. Courts may also avoid application of a state's law by characterizing it as *"procedural"* (forum's law applies) *or "substantive"* (foreign law applies).

These defenses are more commonly used in connection with the traditional "vested rights" approach to choice of law (to avoid the somewhat rigid rules producing inequitable results) than they are with the more modern, policy-oriented approaches. In all cases, remember that use of these defenses is *limited*.

A. Local Public Policy, Penal Laws, and Revenue Laws

1. Local Public Policy

a. Traditional "vested rights" rule [§626]
The First Restatement provided that a forum state was not required to entertain foreign causes of action that were contrary to its strong public policy. Since the general First Restatement approach to choice of law was based on the theory that courts *would* enforce rights that had "vested" under the law of another state, the public policy exception was minimized by stating that it was *extremely limited*—*i.e.,* applicable only when enforcement of the foreign right would violate some "fundamental principle of justice, good morals, or deep-rooted tradition of the local jurisdiction." [**Loucks v. Standard Oil Co.,** 224 N.Y. 99 (1918)]

(1) Application [§627]
Thus, forum courts generally permitted recovery on debts arising from *gambling* activities that were legal where performed (*e.g.,* in Nevada, Puerto Rico, etc.), even though they would have been criminal acts in the forum. [**Caribe Hilton Hotel v. Toland,** 307 A.2d 85 (N.J. 1973)—forum not a sanctuary for those who would "play but not pay"; **Intercontinental Hotel Corp. v. Golden,** 15 N.Y.2d 9 (1964)]

(a) But note

In some cases, courts have refused to enforce rights *arising under foreign law* on the ground that they violate local public policy.

Example: The court held that the local public policy against spouses suing each other in tort barred a suit by a wife against her husband for damages due to a car accident, even though the injuries occurred in a state where such suits were permitted, and the forum choice-of-law rule otherwise required reference to the law of the place of injury. [**Mertz v. Mertz**, *supra*, §392]

(b) And note

Several decisions have used "local public policy" as grounds for refusing to *recognize limitation on recovery* under foreign wrongful death statutes in actions based on the death of local residents.

Example: Kilberg, a New York (forum) resident, died of injuries inflicted in Massachusetts. His administrator sued for wrongful death filed in New York. New York choice-of-law rule looks to place of injury, but the court held that "local public policy" assuring full compensation to a forum resident's estate justifies a refusal to apply limitations on recovery under law of place of injury. [*See* **Kilberg v. Northeast Airlines**, *supra*, §401; *and see infra*, §677]

---

(2) Distinguish—dissimilarity of laws [§628]

Note that the mere lack of any similar cause of action in the forum would *not* justify its refusal to enforce a foreign right. If the forum's choice-of-law rule refers to a foreign law for determination of the case, the fact that the foreign law creates rights different from or dissimilar to those recognized in the forum is immaterial.

b. "Most significant relationship" approach [§629]

The Second Restatement continues the flat prohibition against enforcement of foreign law contrary to the forum's strong public policy—with the same narrow scope of application as the First Restatement (*see supra*, §626).

c. Policy-oriented approaches [§630]

These approaches do not use public policy as a "defense" against enforcement of foreign law. Instead, "public policy" is used *affirmatively* to determine whether forum law should be applied in the first place.

Example: A Wisconsin woman remarried in Michigan within a year after receiving a Wisconsin divorce from another man. The general rule provided that a marriage valid where celebrated is valid everywhere. However, Wisconsin has a policy prohibiting remarriage for one year following divorce, and since Wisconsin had an interest in applying that policy (the divorcee and the new spouse both being Wisconsin residents), its policy was applied directly to hold the remarriage void. (Basically, this presents a "false conflicts" case—since Wisconsin is the only state interested in the marriage status of its domiciliaries and the incidents thereof.) [**Lanham v. Lanham,** *supra,* §600]

EXAM TIP   **gilbert**

Resort to the "local public policy" doctrine is necessary only where courts feel compelled to employ rigid choice-of-law rules to the problem at hand. Where such rules are flexible (as in the policy-oriented approaches), local public policy is simply a *factor in selecting* (rather than correcting) the rule to be applied. Therefore, use this defense sparingly on an exam.

---

2. Penal Laws

a. Traditional "vested rights" approach [§631]

Historically, the forum has refused to enforce claims arising under the *penal laws* of another state. A "penal" law in the conflicts sense is one in which a penalty is awarded *to the state* as compensation for some *public wrong*, as distinguished from damages as redress for private wrongs. [**Huntington v. Attrill,** 146 U.S. 657 (1892)]

(1) Limitation [§632]

Under this definition, very few noncriminal claims can be refused enforcement on the ground that they are "penal."

---

e.g. **Example:** A New York statute making corporate directors liable to creditors for debts of the company upon failure to file required reports was held *not* to be "penal" because the purpose of the statute was to grant a private remedy to corporate creditors, not to compensate a public wrong. [**Huntington v. Attrill,** *supra*]

---

e.g. **Example:** A state law allowing punitive damages to a plaintiff for injuries sustained in another state has been held *not* to be penal in the conflicts sense. There is no public wrong committed, and the penalty does not go to the state. [**Roseberry v. Scott,** 244 P. 1063 (Kan. 1926)]

---

(2) Characterization [§633]

Whether or not the foreign statute is "penal" is *determined by the forum*; *i.e.,* it is not bound by the characterization of the enacting state.

b. "Most significant relationship" approach [§634]

The Second Restatement contains the same prohibition against enforcement of foreign penal laws and the same distinction between punishment for public wrongs and compensation for private injuries.

EXAM TIP	gilbert

Although it is not usually a common exam topic, you may see a choice-of-law question that raises a subissue of whether a law is "penal" and thus the forum need not enforce it. If so, recall that the key is to check **who is getting the money**—if it is **not the state**, it cannot be a "penal" law.

3. Revenue Laws [§635]

Foreign revenue laws were traditionally treated the same as "penal" laws; *i.e.,* they were not enforceable in the forum state. This rule developed in England and originally applied only to the revenue claims of foreign nations.

a. Supreme Court [§636]

The Supreme Court has not ruled on the matter. In **Milwaukee County v. M.E. White Co.,** 296 U.S. 268 (1935), the Court held that full faith and credit had to be given to a foreign *judgment* for taxes due, but left open whether a tax *claim* arising under foreign law could be rejected in another state.

b. State courts [§637]

However, many state courts have entertained actions brought by another state to collect taxes, stressing the need for reciprocal relations among the states. [**Oklahoma Tax Commission v. Rodgers,** 193 S.W.2d 919 (Mo. 1946)] And more than half the states have enacted "reciprocal" statutes requiring their courts to entertain foreign tax claims where the sister state extends the same privilege to the forum.

EXAM TIP	gilbert

If faced with an issue about whether a foreign tax law must be applied by the forum, note that although traditionally such laws were treated the same as penal laws, today most states **will enforce another state's revenue laws**.

B. "Substance" vs. "Procedure"

1. In General [§638]

If the forum determines that reference should be made to a foreign law, the traditional rule provides that such reference need only be to *"substantive" matters.* The law of the forum will govern all "procedural" matters. [39 Mich. L. Rev. 392 (1940)]

a. Characterization [§639]

The determination of what is "substance" and what is "procedure" is *made by the forum* according to its own standards.

b. Criticism [§640]

In matters of pleading, service of process, and evidence—*i.e.*, issues that affect only the way in which a case is presented to the court—it is sensible to apply forum law. However, the characterization of certain issues as "procedural" has often been a means for the forum to apply its own law and avoid the impact of a rigid or overly broad choice-of-law rule to which it still felt compelled to pay lip service. [*See, e.g.*, **Kilberg v. Northeast Airlines**, *infra*, §677]

c. Constitutional limitations [§641]

Arbitrary classification of issues as "procedural" may also raise constitutional problems. In **John Hancock Mutual Life Insurance Co. v. Yates**, 299 U.S. 178 (1936), for example, the Supreme Court held that the forum had violated the Full Faith and Credit Clause in refusing to apply a foreign statute to a particular issue by illogically classifying the issue as "procedural." However, this holding is probably limited to cases in which the forum has no significant contacts at all with the parties or transaction. (*See infra*, §§690-692.)

2. Definitions [§642]

The purpose of distinguishing between "substance" and "procedure" is to "draw the line" on what issues the forum is justified in deciding according to local law. Because uniformity of results has long been the major goal of choice-of-law methodology, this line should be drawn so as to encourage to the greatest extent possible application of the appropriate foreign law. [42 Yale L.J. 333 (1933)]

a. "Substance" [§643]

All issues that might *materially affect the outcome* of a case have been classified as substantive.

b. "Procedure" [§644]

On the other hand, the *house rules of the litigation*—aspects of the case that will have little bearing on the outcome—can be governed by forum law, for reasons of convenience and practicality and to insure the proper administration of justice.

EXAM TIP   **gilbert**

When you are deciding which state's law should be applied in an exam question, don't forget about the *substance-procedure distinction*, as it may affect the law to be applied. The first rule here is easy: The *forum characterizes* the law as substantive or procedural. It doesn't matter what the other state thinks about the rule; the forum decides this issue. The second rule—that if the law is procedural, the *forum law* applies; if it is substantive the *other state's law* applies—is easy to state, but a little harder to apply because whether a law is procedural or substantive is not always clear. Things such as the burden of proof can be either substantive or procedural, depending on the particular case. The test is whether the law would *materially affect the outcome* of the case. If so, it is substantive. Procedural rules, on the other hand, are the "house rules of litigation" that have little effect on the outcome. (See the chart at the end of the chapter for examples.)

---

3. Applications [§645]

Routine matters relating to service of process, sufficiency of pleadings, procedural capacity of the parties, forms of actions, and the like obviously can be classified as "procedural" although the forum may still refer to foreign law on such matters if it chooses. [*See, e.g.,* Cal. Civ. Proc. Code §417.20—permits service of process outside the state "in the manner prescribed by the law of the place where the person is served"] However, many other issues are not so easily categorized.

a. Rules of evidence

(1) Burden of proof [§646]

The "burden of proof" may require a party to (i) present certain elements of evidence with respect to a particular issue or lose on that issue, or (ii) raise the issue and go forward with the evidence. Burden of proof in the first sense clearly has a profound effect on the outcome of the case, and should therefore be considered a *"substantive" matter* for choice-of-law purposes. [**Fitzpatrick v. International Railway,** 252 N.Y. 127 (1929)] However, burden of proof in the second sense generally does not affect the outcome of the case and can be treated as *"procedural"* to justify application of the law of the forum. [**Levy v. Steiger,** 124 N.E. 477 (Mass. 1919)]

(a) Second Restatement [§647]

Under the Second Restatement, burden of proof issues are to be decided under forum law (*i.e.,* considered "procedural") unless the court finds that the primary purpose of the other state's rule is to affect decision of the issue (as where the other state has enacted a statute changing the common law rule on burden of proof in a particular type of action).

(2) Presumptions [§648]

Presumptions involve the same problems as burden of proof.

(a) "Procedural" [§649]

If a presumption *merely relates to the manner in which facts may be proved,* it is clearly "procedural."

(b) "Substantive" [§650]

However, if the presumption would *materially affect the outcome of a case*—as in the case of "conclusive presumption" such as the presumption of due care in a negligence case—it should be considered "substantive" and governed by the appropriate foreign law up to the point that such application becomes impractical or inconvenient for the forum. [**Rodney v. Stamen,** 89 A.2d 313 (Pa. 1952)]

(c) Res ipsa loquitur [§651]

Under the tort doctrine of res ipsa loquitur, a presumption that the defendant was negligent may arise from the mere fact that the injury occurred. (*See* Torts Summary.) Whether res ipsa loquitur applies in a given fact situation will frequently have a material effect on the outcome and would therefore appear to be "substantive." However, at least one court has reached a contrary conclusion on this point. [*See* **United Air Lines, Inc. v. Wiener,** 335 F.2d 379 (9th Cir. 1964)]

(3) Proof of facts [§652]

Rules of evidence, competency, and credibility of witnesses are generally deemed *procedural* and thus governed by the forum's own law. [Rest. 2d §135; 58 Harv. L. Rev. 153 (1944)] Again, however, if such matters would have a material effect on the outcome of the case, foreign law should control up to the point of inconvenience, etc.

(4) Privileged testimony [§653]

The purpose of allowing privileged testimony is to protect the underlying relationship of the parties and to encourage their full and free communication. An interesting question arises where a communication is made in one state (*e.g.,* between husband and wife, or between attorney and client), it is called into question in a suit brought in another state, and it appears that the communication would be privileged under the law of one state but not the other.

(a) Traditional approach [§654]

Traditionally, privileged testimony was considered "*procedural*" and forum law controlled.

(b) "Most significant relationship" approach

1) Testimony privileged under forum law but not under foreign law [§655]

The Second Restatement focuses on the law of the state that has the most significant relationship with the communication. If the communication is not privileged under that law, the forum should not treat it as privileged, unless introduction of the evidence would be contrary to the forum's strong public policy.

2) Testimony privileged under foreign law but not under forum law [§656]

Here, the law of the state having the most significant relationship with the communication protects the testimony. *Rationale:* Insofar as the parties govern their relationship according to the law of the place where they normally communicate, they may have relied on that law and their reliance deserves protection. Nevertheless, according to the Second Restatement, the forum should admit the testimony (*i.e.,* apply its own law) "unless there is some special reason why the forum policy favoring admission should not be given effect" (*e.g.,* the forum's contacts with the parties are insignificant or the testimony is relatively immaterial).

(c) Policy-oriented approaches [§657]

The policy-oriented approaches can be very useful in this area, since they cut through verbiage to analyze the competing policies and interests.

(5) Parol evidence rule [§658]

Many authorities view this rule as a principle of *substantive law* rather than a mere rule of evidence. [Wigmore §2400] Where this is the case, the appropriate foreign law will govern. [**Smith v. Bear,** 237 F.2d 79 (2d Cir. 1956)]

b. Formalities—Statute of Frauds [§659]

As a general proposition, the Statute of Frauds usually has profound effect on the outcome of the case and could be applied with little inconvenience, so that the forum ought to apply the foreign law.

(1) Early law [§660]

As discussed *supra,* §485, many earlier decisions expressed a great deal of concern over the wording of the forum's own Statute of Frauds. Where the statute read, "No action shall be brought . . ." the courts for many years followed an English case [**Leroux v. Brown,** 138 Eng. Rep. 1119 (1852)] which interpreted such statutes as "procedural" and thus applied it to all contracts sued upon in the forum. On the other hand, a provision that "No contract shall be valid (or allowed to be good) . . ." was considered "substantive" allowing reference to the foreign Statute of Frauds.

(a) Criticism [§661]

This is not a problem of statutory interpretation, and the wording of the forum Statute should not control the choice-of-law decision.

(2) Modern view [§662]

Modern cases treat the question of formalities as one of *"substance," particularly where necessary to uphold a contract.* The courts thus apply the Statute in effect in the state that has the most significant "interest" in or "relationship" to the formalities issue. [49 Cal. L. Rev. 962 (1961)]

(a) Application

Many courts have reached this result by interpreting the forum Statute of Frauds as to contracts having their principal "contacts" outside the forum, or by adopting new choice-of-law rules allowing reference to whichever law will uphold the contract. [**Bernkrant v. Fowler,** *supra,* §486]

(b) Distinguish—Uniform Commercial Code [§663]

In transactions subject to the U.C.C., formalities are governed by the Statute of Frauds in effect in the state chosen by the parties as identified in U.C.C. section 1-301 (*see supra,* §298).

c. Time limitations—statute of limitations

(1) Traditional approach [§664]

A statute of limitations usually has a material effect on the outcome of a case and thus ought to be treated as a matter of "substance" for choice-of-law purposes. However, the courts traditionally have not followed this reasoning but have adopted the English rule that the statute of limitations is "*procedural*" and thus governed by forum law. [63 Harv. L. Rev. 1177 (1950)] A majority of the Supreme Court relied on the traditional characterization of statutes of limitation as "procedural" in holding that a forum state court does not violate either the Full Faith and Credit or Due Process Clause by applying its own statute of limitations to cases governed by another state's substantive law. [**Sun Oil Co. v. Wortman,** 486 U.S. 717 (1988)]

(a) Rationale

The only explanation or rationale advanced for this result is that time limitations involve a strong public policy warranting an exception to the general rule favoring application of foreign law to the greatest extent possible.

(b) Application [§665]

The rule that the statute of limitations is "procedural," and hence governed by forum law, applies to all issues related to the statute. For example, the appropriate limitations period may depend on whether the action is characterized as "tort" or "contract" (since a shorter period usually applies in tort actions). Such characterization is made according to forum law, and it is immaterial how the action would be characterized where the cause of action arose (*i.e.,* where the transaction took place). [**Mahalsky v. Salem Tool Co.,** 461 F.2d 581 (6th Cir. 1972)]

1) Foreign judgments [§666]

The forum statute of limitations applies not only to causes of action arising under foreign law but also to suits to enforce foreign judgments. Thus, whether such a suit is timely depends on the *forum's* limitations period for suits on judgments—*not* on the statute in effect where the judgment was rendered. [**Watkins v. Conway,** 385 U.S. 188 (1966)]

(c) Criticisms

1) Forum shopping [§667]
Applying forum law encourages "forum shopping" since it allows a plaintiff who is barred in one forum to take the case to any other forum with a longer statute in which jurisdiction over the defendant can be obtained.

2) Unfair to defendant [§668]
Applying a shorter forum limitations period to a cause of action arising under foreign law merely bars the action locally (while not affecting the plaintiff's right to sue elsewhere). However, where the forum's longer limitations period is applied—allowing suit on a claim on which the foreign statute has already run—it cuts off a defense the defendant would have had if sued where the cause of action arose. This, of course, operates extremely unfairly on the defendant.

(d) Exceptions [§669]
Recognizing the possibility of unfair results under the general rule, various "exceptions" have been devised to prevent application of a longer forum limitations period.

1) "Special" limitations periods [§670]
When an action is based on a claim created by a foreign statute that contains *its own specific limitations rule*, the forum may treat the foreign limitations period as "substantive"—*i.e.,* "barring the right, not merely the remedy." [**Davis v. Mills,** 194 U.S. 451 (1904); Rest. 2d §143]

---

e.g. **Example:** Suit is filed in F2 to enforce a wage claim arising under a statute in F1. The F1 statute contains a one-year statute of limitations on any claim thereunder. F2 will treat the F1 limitations as "substantive." [**Bournias v. Atlantic Maritime Co.,** 220 F.2d 152 (2d Cir. 1955)]

---

a) Note
The "special" limitations period need not be set forth in the statute creating the cause of action. It can be included in a separate statute or code, as long as it limits the specific cause of action in question (as opposed to any general category of actions). [**Davis v. Mills,** *supra*]

2) "Borrowing statutes" [§671]
Many states also have enacted special statutes that provide that where a cause of action "arises" under the law of a foreign state and is also barred by the statute of limitations in that state, no action can be maintained in the forum, *except* by a citizen of the forum who has held the cause of action from the time it accrued. [*See, e.g.,* Cal. Civ. Proc. Code §361]

a) Note
Problems are often encountered with "borrowing statutes" in determining the state in which a cause of action "arose," where events occurred in several different states. [*See* **George v. Douglas Aircraft Co.**, 332 F.2d 73 (2d Cir. 1964)]

3) "Tolling statutes" [§672]
In addition to borrowing statutes, most states today have statutes that "toll" (*i.e.,* extend) the statutory period if the defendant was not subject to service. Thus, the forum may conclude that a foreign statute of limitations has not yet run if defendant was not subject to service in the foreign state.

a) Caution—effect of long arm statutes [§673]
The mere fact that the defendant was not physically present in the foreign state does not necessarily mean that he was not subject to service there. The foreign state may have a long arm statute authorizing service on the defendant outside the state, and if so, the tolling statute would not operate (since the defendant would have been subject to service there).

(e) Adverse possession [§674]
Due to the strong interests of the "situs" of property, it is recognized that if real or personal property is held in adverse possession for the period of limitation *in the situs*, the holder acquires title that will be recognized in any other state—regardless of the limitations period in the forum or any other state. [Rest. 2d §227]

(2) Modern approach [§675]
The modern trend is to reject the "substance" vs. "procedure" dichotomy, and determine which state has the "most significant relationship" or "interest" concerning the statute of limitations issue—the same as with any other choice-of-law problem. [**Dindo v. Whitney**, 429 F.2d 25 (1st Cir. 1970)] This is the approach that the Second Restatement takes.

Example: A Quebec infant filed suit in New Jersey against a New York drug manufacturer for birth defects resulting from the infant's mother having taken the drug thalidomide. The action was barred by the limitations period under Quebec law but not under New Jersey law. The New Jersey court applied the shorter Quebec statute because of Quebec's "interest" in regulating conduct affecting local sales and residents. [**Henry v. Richardson-Merrell, Inc.,** 508 F.2d 28 (3d Cir. 1975)]

(a) Note

A few courts have reached the same result under the "substance" vs. "procedure" approach by characterizing the statute of limitations as "substantive." [**Heavner v. Uniroyal, Inc.,** *supra,* §296] The Uniform Conflict of Laws Limitations Act (1982) takes a similar approach by applying, in most cases, the limitations period of the state whose law is chosen to govern the substantive claim.

PROCEDURE VS. SUBSTANCE—EXAMPLES — gilbert

PROCEDURAL	SUBSTANTIVE
• Civil practice rules in general	• Civil practice rules that would change outcome
• Burden of proof requiring party to present certain elements of evidence	• Burden of proof requiring party to raise issue and go forward with evidence
• Presumptions relating to manner in which facts may be proved (rebuttable presumptions)	• Conclusive (irrebuttable) presumptions
• Rules of evidence, competency, and credibility of witnesses	• Parol evidence rule
	• Statute of Frauds
• Statutes of limitations in general	• Statutes of limitations that condition a substantive right or set period of limitation for adverse possession, or borrowing statutes

d. Measure of damages

(1) Traditional approach [§676]

The measure of damages, and any conditions or limitations on the recoverability of damages, obviously will have an important effect on the outcome of the action. Thus, such matters *ordinarily* are classified as "*substantive*" and governed by the appropriate foreign law. [**Bowles v. Zimmer Manufacturing Co.**, 277 F.2d 868 (7th Cir. 1960)]

(a) "Public policy" limitation [§677]

However, a number of cases have reached an opposite conclusion to avoid restrictive foreign laws. In **Kilberg v. Northeast Airlines**, *supra*, §627, for example, a New York court heard a wrongful death action for the death of a New York resident in Massachusetts and allowed full recovery of damages notwithstanding a $15,000 limitation on recoveries in such actions under Massachusetts law. To do so, the court asserted that the measure of damages was a "procedural" or remedial issue, and hence governed by the law of the forum.

1) Rationale for holding

The real reason for this characterization, of course, was the forum's public policy against such limitations on recovery. The New York Court of Appeals later admitted as much by retracting the procedural basis of *Kilberg*. [**Davenport v. Webb**, 11 N.Y.2d 292 (1962)] The Second Circuit followed this shift of position in a later case that held that the New York public policy against limitations on damages would be applied whenever suit was brought by a New York domiciliary, regardless of conflicting policies in sister states. [**Rosenthal v. Warren**, *supra*, §433]

(b) Criticism

Cases such as *Kilberg* illustrate the courts' "unacknowledged" attempts to avoid overly restrictive and out-of-date choice-of-law rules. It would be more realistic simply to discard the old "place of injury" torts rule (*see supra*, §406), rather than arbitrarily classify vital matters such as damages as "procedural."

(2) Modern approaches [§678]

The modern trend in this area is to refer to the law of the state that has the ***most significant "interest"*** in or "relationship" to the question of damages. [*See* **Reich v. Purcell**, *supra*, §404]

e. Direct action against insurer [§679]

Whether a direct action can be maintained against an insurance company for injuries inflicted by its insured has been held to be a "*substantive*" issue because it is outcome determinative. Consequently, even where no such action is permitted under forum law, the forum court may allow a direct action against an insurance company if this is permitted under the law of the place where the policy was issued and the accident occurred. [*See* **Roberts v. Home Insurance Indemnity Co.**, 48 Cal. App. 3d 313 (1975)—California resident sued for injuries suffered in Louisiana where insurance policy issued; Louisiana statute permitting direct action against insurer held a "substantive" right enforceable in California]

Chapter Seven: Constitutional Limitations and Overriding Federal Law

CONTENTS

Chapter Approach

Occasionally, a choice-of-law question will involve the conflicting laws of two states subject to the United States Constitution. In answering a question involving *constitutional limitations*, you should ask:

1. Is the forum's application of its own law *forbidden by the Due Process Clause*; or

2. Is application of another state's law *required by the Full Faith and Credit Clause*?

The answer to both questions will almost always be "no," except where the forum has *no contact of significance* to the transaction or to the parties, either at the time of the transaction or at the time of the suit. But constitutional limits to the application of forum law do exist, however rarely invoked, and your answer should examine that possibility as an initial matter.

Sometimes a question will involve a possible *conflict between state and federal law*. Remember that where a *federal right* is involved, federal law applies. Where *no federal right* is involved (in diversity cases brought in federal court), the federal court must apply *state* law as well as state choice-of-law approaches, if the choice between state and federal law is *"outcome determinative."* However, the modern view is that the "outcome determinative" test is somewhat restricted; thus, your analysis of whether state law will determine the outcome of the case must take into account that:

1. *Federal Rules of Civil Procedure prevail* over conflicting state law; and

2. *Other federal policies* may prevail over state law.

A. Influence of the United States Constitution

1. **In General [§680]**

    The resolution of choice-of-law problems is primarily a matter of judicial discretion. Occasionally, however, there may be constitutional limitations that will affect the choice-of-law decision. At one time, the United States Constitution was interpreted to require the application of a particular law in certain cases. However, the modern view is that the Constitution merely *sets limits* on the extent to which states may apply their own law in conflicts cases.

2. **Fourteenth Amendment Due Process Clause**

a. Early view [§681]

In a series of insurance cases, the Supreme Court suggested that the Due Process Clause required the application of the law of the place where the contract was made to determine the validity and consequences of the contract. Had this suggestion been followed, it would have written the "vested rights" choice-of-law theory into the Constitution. [**New York Life Insurance Co. v. Dodge,** 246 U.S. 357 (1918); **Mutual Life Insurance Co. v. Liebing,** 259 U.S. 209 (1922); *and see supra,* §§302-312]

b. Present view [§682]

Today, however, the question is not whether due process compels the application of a particular law but how it *limits* the choice-of-law decision.

(1) Whether forum *may* apply its own law [§683]

In **Home Insurance Co. v. Dick,** *supra,* §282, the Court held that it is a violation of the Fourteenth Amendment Due Process Clause for the forum to apply its own laws when the *only* contact it has with the problem being litigated is that it is the forum. Therefore, if *all* the other contacts are with another state or states, the forum cannot constitutionally refuse to make reference to the appropriate foreign law. This decision was reaffirmed in **Allstate Insurance Co. v. Hague,** 449 U.S. 302 (1981), a plurality of the Court stating that "for a state's substantive law to be selected in a constitutionally permissible manner, that state must have a significant contact or significant aggregation of contacts, creating state interests, such that choice of its law is neither arbitrary nor fundamentally unfair."

(a) Rationale

Due process requires "fundamental fairness"; thus, if there is no reasonable relationship between the forum and the parties or the cause of action, application of forum law would be fundamentally unfair; *i.e.,* it is not something that the parties could have foreseen or intended.

(b) Application [§684]

In **Allstate Insurance Co. v. Hague,** *supra,* the plurality relied on three contacts between the forum (Minnesota) and the parties and occurrence that, in the aggregate, were enough to permit Minnesota to apply its own law rather than that of Wisconsin, where the parties all resided at the time of the accident and where the accident occurred. The three contacts were: (i) decedent was employed in Minnesota prior to his death and commuted there from Wisconsin daily to work; (ii) the defendant (Allstate Insurance Company) did business in Minnesota and could not claim that it was surprised by the application of Minnesota law; and (iii) the plaintiff (decedent's widow) had moved to Minnesota after the accident but prior to the institution of suit.

1) Note

The plurality declined to say that any one of these three contacts, standing alone, would have been sufficient. A concurring opinion by Justice Stevens thought application of Minnesota law was not fundamentally unfair to either litigant without regard to the three contacts. A dissent by three justices agreed to the significant contacts test for applying forum law, but found the three contacts relied on by the majority to be "trivial," and not related to the substantive policy of the law Minnesota sought to apply—its rule allowing "stacking" of insurance policies placed on different vehicles to add up to one cumulative amount.

2) *Hague* test reaffirmed

The *Hague* test was reaffirmed in **Phillips Petroleum Co. v. Shutts,** 472 U.S. 797 (1985). There the majority of the Court held that a Kansas court's application of Kansas law to all claims in a class action suit involving interest payments on suspended royalties arising from the sale of natural gas violated due process, because over 99% of the gas leases and about 97% of the plaintiffs had no connection to Kansas (apart from the suit) and the states with which they had connections (Texas and Oklahoma) had laws that were potentially in conflict with those of Kansas.

(2) Whether forum *must* apply any particular foreign law [§685]

On the other hand, due process *cannot* be invoked *to compel* the forum to apply some particular foreign law; *i.e.,* no affirmative choice-of-law rules are required by the Due Process Clause. [**Hoopeston Canning Co. v. Cullen,** 318 U.S. 313 (1943)]

 Example: In **Watson v. Employers Liability Assurance Corp.,** *supra,* §496, a resident of Louisiana brought suit in that state against a British liability insurer for injuries sustained through use of a home permanent manufactured by an Illinois subsidiary of a Massachusetts corporation, which was insured by the British firm. The Louisiana court permitted the action under a local statute permitting an injured party to sue the defendant's liability insurer directly, and this was upheld by the Supreme Court. The Court rejected the argument that due process required the Louisiana court to refer to the laws of Massachusetts and Illinois (where the insurance policy had been negotiated and issued, and which did not permit "direct actions").

Example: And in **Clay v. Sun Insurance Office, Ltd.,** 377 U.S. 179 (1964), the Supreme Court specifically held that in the absence of some enforceable contractual or statutory limitation, the forum is free to apply the law of any state with which the transaction has a reasonable relationship ("minimum contacts").

(3) Effect [§686]

As long as the forum state has *any reasonable relationship* to the parties or the cause of action, it may reject all foreign law in favor of its own law. Only where there are no such "contacts" does due process impose limits—on the same rationale of fairness and substantial justice that underlies the "minimum contacts" doctrine for jurisdiction (*see supra*, §116).

EXAM TIP   **gilbert**

The key thing to remember in a *due process* question is that just because a foreign state has more contacts with the action than the forum does, this does not automatically dictate that the foreign law must apply. (Otherwise, the vested rights approach would be the only relevant approach to determining which law to apply.) Instead, you need to check to see if the forum has *any reasonable relationship* with the action other than just being the place where the action is brought. If so, the forum may apply its own law regardless of how many contacts the other state has.

---

3. Full Faith and Credit Clause [§687]

Article IV, Section 1 of the Constitution requires that each state give "full faith and credit" to the "public acts, records and judicial proceedings" of every other state. The question is the extent to which this limits the choice-of-law rules that a state may adopt.

a. Definitions

(1) "Judicial proceedings" [§688]

"Judicial proceedings" refers to the *judgments* of sister state courts, and has also been construed to include awards made by certain quasi-judicial state tribunals (*e.g.,* workers' compensation awards). However, the Supreme Court has not yet indicated the extent to which awards by other administrative agencies and tribunals are entitled to full faith and credit in proceedings in other states. (The enforcement of sister state judgments is discussed *infra*, §§729 *et seq.*)

(2) "Public acts" [§689]

"Public acts" has been construed to mean both *statutes and case law* of sister states. *Rationale:* There is no logical or constitutional basis for discriminating in favor of claims arising under state statutes as opposed to those arising under judge-made law. [**Carroll v. Lanza,** *supra*, §585]

b. Effect on choice-of-law process [§690]

The requirement that courts in one state give "full faith and credit" to the "public acts" (statutes and case law) of another does not compel the forum to adopt and apply the laws of other states in every case. Indeed, where there are multistate contacts, a forum court probably could not apply the law of every state involved if it wanted to. Hence, the choice of which state's "public acts" should be applied is still primarily a matter of judicial discretion.

(1) Earlier view [§691]

In **Order of United Commercial Travelers v. Wolfe,** 331 U.S. 586 (1947), the Court indicated that where the weight of public policy behind a foreign law clearly outweighed the public policy behind the law of the forum, full faith and credit would compel reference to the *foreign* law.

(2) Modern view [§692]

Today, however, the Court's position is clearly contrary; *i.e.,* a *forum may apply its own rules of law* as long as *some reasonable relationship* exists between the forum and the parties or the transaction, so that the forum has a *legitimate interest* in doing so. [**Allstate Insurance Co. v. Hague,** *supra,* §683—*reaffirmed by a unanimous court in* **Franchise Tax Board v. Hyatt,** 123 S. Ct. 1683 (2003)]

(a) Applications

1) Statute of limitations cases [§693]

In **Wells v. Simonds Abrasive Co.,** 345 U.S. 514 (1953), the Supreme Court upheld the forum's application of its own shorter statute of limitations (which had the effect of barring suit locally on a foreign claim), since the forum had reasonable "contacts" with the subject of the litigation.

a) Note

In **Sun Oil Co. v. Wortman,** *supra,* §664, the Supreme Court upheld the forum's application of its own longer statute of limitations even though its contacts with the dispute were *limited to its status as the forum.* (This decision was based on the traditional classification of statutes of limitation as procedural.)

b) And note

The only apparent restriction on the forum's right to apply its own law is that the forum law may not discriminate against foreign judgments or claims arising under foreign law; *i.e.,* a statute that would provide a shorter limitations period for bringing suit on a foreign judgment than on domestic judgments would violate the Full Faith and Credit Clause. [*See* **Watkins v. Conway,** *supra,* §666]

2) Workers' compensation cases [§694]

Initially, it appeared that the Full Faith and Credit Clause required the forum court in workers' compensation cases to apply the law of the place of employment. [**Bradford Electric Light Co. v. Clapper,** 286 U.S. 145 (1932)] Later cases, however, upheld a reference to other laws where the interest of the place of employment was outweighed by the interest of the place of injury [**Alaska Packers Association v. Industrial Accident Commission,** *supra,* §582] or the place of the claimant's residence [**Pacific Employers Insurance Co. v. Industrial Accident Commission,** *supra,* §582]. Finally, the Court in **Carroll v. Lanza,** *supra,* §689, disapproved its earlier decisions and held that full faith and credit *did not require the forum to adopt any particular choice-of-law rule* in workers' compensation suits. This result left the forum free to apply its own workers' compensation law in cases of overlapping coverage.

c. Full faith and credit as limitation on forum's power to exclude foreign claims [§695]

Although the Full Faith and Credit Clause does not generally compel a forum to apply foreign law, it does limit the use of local public policy as a *defense* to the application of foreign law. The national interest in uniformity of decisions and the policies behind res judicata (both of which underlie full faith and credit) are held to outweigh local policies against recognition of the "public acts" or judgments of sister states in most cases.

(1) Application

In **Hughes v. Fetter,** *supra,* §232, the Supreme Court held invalid a forum statute that withdrew jurisdiction from its courts to hear wrongful death actions arising under foreign statutes. The court ruled that "at least where *all* elements of the wrong occurred in the sister state, the forum cannot refuse to recognize the existence of a cause of action created under that state's statute." [*See also* **Kenney v. Order of Moose,** 252 U.S. 411 (1920); *see infra,* §806]

(a) Note

This type of statute may also violate the interstate privileges and immunities of national citizenship, since it discriminates against persons injured or killed outside the forum. [*See* **Shapiro v. Thompson,** 394 U.S. 618 (1969); *and see also* Constitutional Law Summary]

(2) Comment

An incidental effect of the *Hughes* case is that it may weaken the doctrine of forum non conveniens (*see supra,* §§227-232) and the theory that a forum state need not enforce the penal or revenue laws of another state (*see supra,* §§631-637). If F2 cannot constitutionally refuse to recognize a cause of action created under a foreign statute or a foreign judgment, the discretion of F2 courts to refuse to hear certain causes of action (on the theory of forum non conveniens, etc.) would also seem to be limited. Thus far, however, the holding of *Hughes* has been limited to its particular facts and is *not* authority for the proposition that full faith and credit requires a state to provide a forum for all foreign causes of action.

EXAM TIP   **gilbert**

It seems clear that the Full Faith and Credit Clause—like the Fourteenth Amendment Due Process Clause—does not compel a forum to adopt any particular choice-of-law rule. As long as the forum state itself has some *reasonable relationship* (*i.e.,* "minimum contacts") with the matter in dispute, choice of law remains largely a matter of *judicial discretion*, rather than constitutional compulsion.

---

d. Criticism of approach to full faith and credit [§696]

Many commentators blame the divergence in choice-of-law decisions on the Supreme Court's failure to provide constitutional standards in this area. Instead of 50 different sovereignties searching for a unifying choice-of-law "approach" or "theory," these commentators urge that the Full Faith and Credit and/or Commerce Clauses be invoked to establish uniform federal rules and standards for litigation touching two or more states. [58 A.B.A. J. 874 (1972)]

4. Privileges and Immunities Clause [§697]

Article IV, Section 2 of the Constitution provides that "[t]he citizens of each state shall be entitled to all privileges and immunities of citizens in the several states." In the past, this Clause has had little impact on choice of law. Recently, however, a few decisions have dealt with the question of when a state may limit the benefits available within its territory to its own residents.

a. "Essential" activities and "basic" rights approach [§698]

In **Baldwin v. Fish & Game Commission,** 436 U.S. 371 (1978), the Supreme Court permitted the state of Montana to impose a substantially higher hunting license fee on nonresidents than on residents. The Court held that *only "essential" activities* and *"basic" rights* were encompassed by the Privileges and Immunities Clause, and found that elk hunting (for recreation and sport) did not fall within either of those categories.

(1) Dissent

In a dissenting opinion, Justice Brennan rejected the "essential" activity/ "basic" right test in favor of a more pragmatic approach. In his view, discrimination against nonresidents should be permissible under the Privileges and Immunities Clause where: (i) the presence or activity of nonresidents is the *source or cause of the problem* with which the state seeks to deal, and (ii) the discrimination practiced against nonresidents *bears a substantial relation to the problem* they present.

b. **"Leeway to solve nonresident problems" [§699]**

Although Justice Brennan's test was not accepted by the majority in *Baldwin*, a unanimous Court used it in **Hicklin v. Orbeck**, 437 U.S. 518 (1978), to invalidate an Alaska statute that required preference to qualified Alaska residents over nonresidents for employment on the Trans-Alaska pipeline. The Court found that the problem Alaska sought to solve (high unemployment) was not caused by an influx of nonresidents seeking jobs, and that the proposed remedy did not bear a substantial relation to the real problem of poorly educated and trained residents.

(1) Note

Since the right of nonresidents to seek employment in the state is an "essential" activity under the *Baldwin* test, the two cases are not formally inconsistent. However, the *Hicklin* approach is much broader and, as a practical matter, would prevent state limitation of benefits in more cases. The *Baldwin* and *Hicklin* tests were used in combination in two subsequent cases. One held that the Privileges and Immunities Clause invalidated a Camden, New Jersey, municipal ordinance that required at least 40% of the employees of contractors and subcontractors working on city construction projects to be residents of Camden. [**United Building Construction Trades Council v. Mayor & Council of Camden**, 465 U.S. 208 (1984)] The other case held that the Clause invalidated a New Hampshire requirement that all lawyers who were members of the New Hampshire bar must be New Hampshire residents. [**Supreme Court of New Hampshire v. Piper**, 470 U.S. 274 (1985)]

c. **"A substantial reason for the difference in treatment of nonresidents" apart from mere fact of lack of state citizenship [§700]**

In **Lundig v. New York Tax Appeals Tribunal**, 522 U.S. 287 (1998), a majority of the Court held that New York had violated the Privileges and Immunities Clause because it had not "adequately justified" its denial of an alimony deduction to nonresidents by characterizing alimony payments as expenses wholly linked to personal activities carried on outside the state. New York's requirement that nonresidents pay more tax than residents merely because they are liable for alimony violates the rule of "substantial equality of treatment" for resident and nonresident taxpayers announced in **Austin v. New Hampshire**, 420 U.S. 656 (1975).

(1) Dissent

Justice Ginsburg pointed out in dissent that since the petitioner's income was not taxed in his state of residence, he was seeking a windfall to escape any tax on that portion of this income devoted to alimony payments, not equality of treatment with New York taxpayers. She found New York's attribution of income to some taxpayer—either the alimony payer or the alimony recipient—"hardly unfair," and concluded that New York's decision to refer a decision as to deductibility of "personal life expenses" to the taxpayer's state of residence was a sufficient articulation of a policy basis for its action to satisfy the Privileges and Immunities Clause.

B. Conflict Between Federal and State Law

1. Problem [§701]

If the case is one in which there is *concurrent* federal and state court jurisdiction, certain additional choice-of-law questions must be considered. If the action is filed in a state court, to what extent is the state court bound to apply federal law? Conversely, if suit is filed in a federal court, will that court apply the laws (including the choice-of-law rules) of the state in which it is located or some other "federal" rules?

2. Where Federal Right Involved [§702]

If the litigation involves any claim arising under the United States Constitution, statutes, or treaties, *federal law alone* will be applied to that issue. This follows from the Supremacy Clause of the United States Constitution (article VI) which provides: "This Constitution and the Laws of the United States which shall be made in pursuance thereof . . . shall be the supreme law of the land; and the judges in every State shall be bound thereby."

a. Effect [§703]

Federal law alone is applied to any issue arising in the fields in which federal power is *"exclusive"* (*e.g.*, admiralty, foreign commerce, national banking, etc.) or in which Congress has *"preempted"* the field (*e.g.*, most of interstate commerce; *see* Constitutional Law Summary). Conflicting state rules are irrelevant in this situation, even if the case is being litigated in state courts. [82 Harv. L. Rev. 1512 (1969)]

> **Example:** In litigation over the ownership of U.S. bonds, federal statutes and regulations specifying the rights of persons claiming title will control over any conflicting state rules. Consequently, state courts must defer to the federal rules, disregarding any local rules which might otherwise apply. [**Free v. Bland,** 369 U.S. 663 (1962)—rejecting application of community property concepts to federally created rights]

b. "Federal law" defined [§704]

The "federal law" to be applied to any federally created right includes not only the United States Constitution and all statutes and administrative orders or regulations pursuant thereto, but also the decisions of federal courts ultimately required to interpret, implement, and enforce the same—*i.e.,* the so-called federal common law. [**Bank of America National Trust & Savings Association v. Parnell,** 352 U.S. 29 (1956)]

c. State "procedural" rules [§705]

If the suit is brought in state court, the procedural rules of that state normally will apply, subject to the limitation that novel rules of pleading and practice cannot be invoked to defeat a claimant's rights under federal law. [**Brown v. Western Railway**, 338 U.S. 294 (1949)—reversing state court dismissal of claim under Federal Employers' Liability Act which resulted from state court's narrow construction of pleadings]

3. Where No Federal Right Involved [§706]

If the claim in the lawsuit does not turn on any issue of federal law, the Supremacy Clause does not apply, and the question is whether the plaintiff can expect more favorable treatment in state or federal court; *i.e.*, in the typical *diversity-of-citizenship* lawsuit, can the plaintiff expect the federal court to apply different, and perhaps better, rules of law than would be applied in the local state court?

a. Background

(1) Judiciary Act [§707]

In the Judiciary Act of 1789, Congress required the federal courts to apply "the laws of the several states" as "rules of decision" in common law actions in federal courts.

(2) Swift v. Tyson [§708]

The Supreme Court first construed the Act as applying only to state statutes and not state case law, so that on all matters not specifically regulated by local statutes, federal courts were free to adopt and apply "general principles of federal common law." [**Swift v. Tyson**, 41 U.S. 1 (1842)]

(a) Effect—forum shopping [§709]

This meant that in major areas of litigation not generally regulated by local statute (*e.g.*, commercial law, torts, etc.), there were two separate systems of law—state and federal. In turn, this led to "forum shopping" for the most advantageous rules of law in each particular case.

(3) Erie Railroad v. Tompkins [§710]

Ultimately, the Court reversed *Swift* and held that the Judiciary Act merely stated the constitutional obligation of federal courts to apply state substantive law on nonfederal questions—*i.e.*, that the act applied to *both state statutory and case law*. [**Erie Railroad v. Tompkins**, 304 U.S. 64 (1938)]

(a) Purpose

The purpose of the *Erie* decision was to eliminate uncontrolled "forum shopping" between state and federal courts by compelling federal courts to reach the same result as state courts on nonfederal questions.

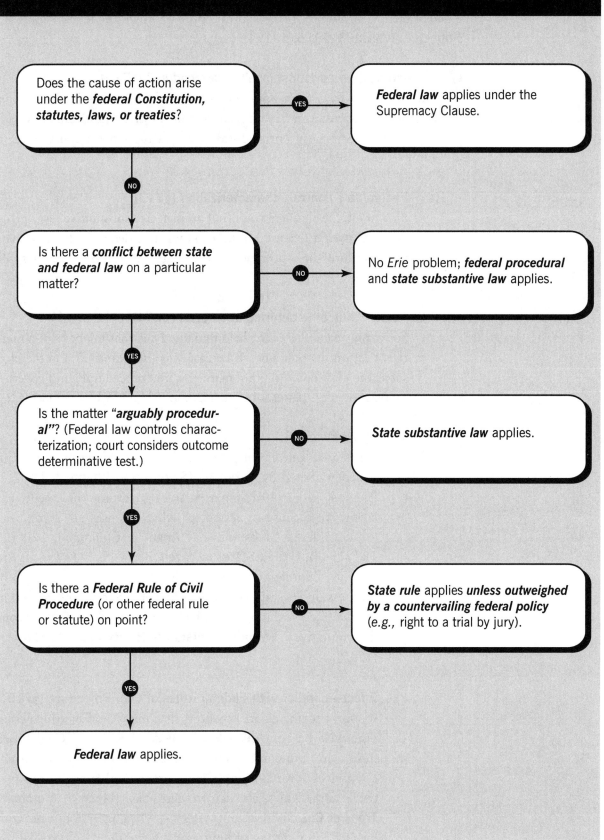

Does the cause of action arise under the *federal Constitution, statutes, laws, or treaties*?

YES → *Federal law* applies under the Supremacy Clause.

NO ↓

Is there a *conflict between state and federal law* on a particular matter?

NO → No *Erie* problem; *federal procedural* and *state substantive law* applies.

YES ↓

Is the matter *"arguably procedural"*? (Federal law controls characterization; court considers outcome determinative test.)

NO → *State substantive law* applies.

YES ↓

Is there a *Federal Rule of Civil Procedure* (or other federal rule or statute) on point?

NO → *State rule* applies *unless outweighed by a countervailing federal policy* (e.g., right to a trial by jury).

YES ↓

Federal law applies.

b. **Scope of *Erie* doctrine [§711]**

Under *Erie*, federal courts are free to apply their *own rules of "procedure"* but any issue of *"substantive" law* (other than a "federal question," above) must be determined according to the laws of the *state* in which the federal court sits. [**Sibbach v. Wilson,** 312 U.S. 1 (1941)]

(1) Characterization as "substance" or "procedure" [§712]

The obvious difficulty in applying the *Erie* doctrine lies in determining whether a particular matter or issue is "substantive" (and thus governed by state law) or merely "procedural" (so that the federal court is free to apply its own rules).

(a) Federal law controls characterization [§713]

First of all, the characterization of an issue as "substantive" or "procedural" is *itself* a *federal question* so that state determinations on what is "procedure" or "substance" are immaterial. [**Hanna v. Plumer,** 380 U.S. 460 (1965)]

(b) Former "outcome determinative test" [§714]

For many years, the Court held that any issue that might have a material effect on the outcome of the case was "substantive" and therefore subject to state law. All other matters were "procedural" and governed by federal rules. [**Guaranty Trust Co. v. York,** 326 U.S. 99 (1945)]

1) Application

Rules as to burden of proof are "outcome determinative" and hence governed by state law. [**Sampson v. Channell,** 110 F.2d 754 (1st Cir. 1940)] Similarly, rules governing the essential elements of a cause of action, or what defenses are recognized, are considered "substantive." [**Angel v. Bullington,** 330 U.S. 183 (1947); **United States v. Yazell,** 382 U.S. 341 (1966)] And whether a foreign corporation that had not "qualified" to do business under state law should be permitted to enforce a contract entered within the state has also been held to be "outcome determinative." [**Woods v. Interstate Realty Co.,** 337 U.S. 535 (1949)]

2) Effect—conflict with Federal Rules of Civil Procedure [§715]

It soon became clear, however, that many matters that would otherwise be controlled by the Federal Rules of Civil Procedure were "outcome determinative" and federal courts found themselves forced to apply state procedural rules, rather than the Federal Rules, to such matters. [*See* **Ragan v. Merchants Transfer Co.,** 337 U.S. 530 (1949)—when an action was "commenced," for statute of limitations purposes, should be decided under state law because issue was outcome determinative; the Court rejected contrary rule under the Federal Rules (apparently now overruled by **Hanna v. Plumer,** below)]

(c) Modern test [§716]

The modern position of the Court appears to restrict the "outcome determinative" test.

1) Federal Rules prevail [§717]

First of all, the Court has held that in any conflict between the Federal Rules of Civil Procedure and state law, *the Federal Rules control; i.e.,* all such matters are presumptively "procedural" so that they need not yield to state law under *Erie.* [**Hanna v. Plumer,** *supra*—sufficiency of service in federal action determined by Federal Rules of Civil Procedure; contrary state rules disregarded]

a) Rationale

Although the 1789 Judiciary Act compels reference to state law (*supra*), the 1934 Rules Enabling Act [28 U.S.C. §2072] authorizes the adoption of procedural rules for federal courts. This latter Act is said to "amend" the former, thereby establishing the supremacy of the Federal Rules over state law wherever the two conflict.

2) Other federal policies may also outweigh [§718]

The Court has likewise indicated that other constitutional doctrines or federal policies may occasionally prevail over the *Erie* doctrine in determining whether state or federal law will be applied. [82 Harv. L. Rev. 1512 (1969)]

---

e.g. **Example:** In **Byrd v. Blue Ridge Rural Electric Cooperative, Inc.,** 356 U.S. 525 (1958), the Supreme Court held that federal law controlled as to the right to jury trial in federal courts—regardless of whether the state rule (which provided for trial by judge only) was "outcome determinative." *Rationale:* The Seventh Amendment guarantees a jury trial in federal court, and this provision is "essential to the integrity of the federal judiciary."

---

c. How state law is determined [§719]

If the federal court finds that the issue involved is "substantive" and that state law should be applied, it will look to all applicable statutes and to opinions of the highest state courts that have dealt with that issue. [**West v. American Telephone & Telegraph Co.,** 311 U.S. 223 (1940)]

(1) State law uncertain [§720]

However, the federal court cannot refuse to exercise jurisdiction merely because state law in the area is uncertain. If there is no statute or case law on point, the federal court must attempt to *predict* what position the state appeals court would take in such a case—giving the federal court as much discretion as the state appellate courts. [**Polk County v. Lincoln National Life Insurance Co.**, 262 F.2d 486 (5th Cir. 1959)]

(a) Certification to state court [§721]

Some states permit local federal courts to certify questions of state law to state courts for decision where state law is uncertain. [*See* Fla. Stat. Ann. §25.031] But such a procedure is not obligatory; *i.e.,* the federal court cannot be forced to certify such questions to the state court. [**Lehman Brothers v. Schein**, 416 U.S. 386 (1974)]

(2) "Abstention" doctrine [§722]

Where a crucial question of state law will be controlling in a federal diversity case, and that same question is *pending in the state appellate courts* (in related or separate litigation), the federal court must "abstain"; *i.e.,* it must stay the diversity action pending a state court determination of the state law issue involved. [**Kaiser Steel Corp. v. W.S. Ranch Co.**, 391 U.S. 593 (1968)]

d. Effect of *Erie* doctrine on choice of law [§723]

A federal district court effectively sits as a trial court of the state in deciding "substantive" issues. Accordingly, it must adopt the state's choice-of-law rules and apply them as its own; there are *no federal choice-of-law rules.* [**Klaxon Co. v. Stentor Electric Manufacturing Co.**, *supra,* §328]

Example: A federal court in State A must apply whatever choice-of-law rules the courts of State A would apply: If the courts of State A would look to the law of State B, then the federal court in State A must also apply State B law. This is true even where the action is *transferred* from the federal court in State A to another federal court in State B under the federal transfer statute. [28 U.S.C. §1404(a); *see supra,* §235] The transferee district court in State B must apply the choice-of-law rules of State A (rather than the choice-of-law rules in State B). [**Van Dusen v. Barrack**, *supra,* §235]

---

(1) Court cannot modify rules [§724]

The federal court must apply the state's choice-of-law rules *then in existence; i.e.,* it is not allowed to create "exceptions" or to update or "modernize" the state rules. [**Day & Zimmerman, Inc. v. Challoner**, 423 U.S. 3 (1975)]

(2) Characterization [§725]

And the federal court must characterize the issue as the state court would for choice-of-law purposes. *Note:* In determining whether the issue is "substantive" or "procedural" *for choice-of-law purposes*, it is immaterial that the federal court has *already characterized it as "substantive" for purposes of the Erie doctrine.*

EXAM TIP	gilbert

Note that in an *Erie* question, a court may have to do **two characterizations** as to substance or procedure: The first characterization as to whether the matter is substantive or procedural is to determine whether **federal or state law** applies. If state law is to be applied, then the second characterization as substantive or procedural is to determine **which state's law** will be applied. Note that these are two independent characterizations and can have different results.

Example: In **Sampson v. Channell** (*supra*, §714), a federal district court in Massachusetts applied the Massachusetts rule regarding burden of proof in a negligence case involving an accident in Maine. It did so because it concluded that Massachusetts courts would have characterized burden of proof as a "procedural" issue governed by forum law, even though for *Erie* purposes the issue was clearly "substantive" and state rather than federal law applied.

---

(3) Comment—exceptional cases [§726]

While there is little authority at present, it seems likely that in exceptional cases a federal choice of law will be recognized.

(a) "Prevailing" federal interest [§727]

In at least one air disaster case, a federal court has chosen to apply federal rather than state law in determining whether indemnity and contribution should be allowed among the defendants. This was held to be justified because of the "prevailing" federal interest in uniform air regulation. [**Kohr v. Allegheny Airlines, Inc.**, 504 F.2d 400 (7th Cir. 1974)]

(b) Need for uniformity [§728]

Likewise, in multiparty cases involving many different states, each with a different standard of liability, the need for a uniform liability standard in order to dispose of the case may well outweigh all other "interests" or "contacts" and justify the use of a federal choice-of-law rule.

Example: A federal trial court in California heard wrongful death actions against a California aircraft manufacturer and others growing out of the crash of a Turkish airliner in Paris. Over 300 persons were killed in the crash, most of whom were foreign nationals, and the Americans aboard came from 12 different states. The laws of these foreign countries and states differed widely on the standard of tort liability and measure of damages to be applied. The federal court followed an "interests" analysis in holding that *both* California and federal law applied: California's interest was in preventing manufacture and sale of defective aircraft within its borders, while the federal interest was based on extensive federal regulation and design of aircraft and the need for a uniform rule of liability in such multiparty cases. [*In re* **Paris Air Crash,** 399 F. Supp. 732 (C.D. Cal. 1975)]

Chapter Eight: Recognition and Enforcement of Foreign Judgments

---

CONTENTS

Chapter Approach

Chapter Approach

This chapter covers various issues pertaining to foreign judgments, "foreign" meaning a judgment of another state *or* of a foreign country.

1. **Sister-State Judgment**

    A question that raises an issue of whether the judgment of another American court is entitled to recognition or enforcement will usually turn on one or more of the following factors:

    (i)   Whether the court that entered the judgment had *proper jurisdiction over the parties or the subject matter* (but recall that if the question was litigated by the parties and determined by the court in the prior proceeding, jurisdiction cannot later be challenged);

    (ii)   Whether the *judgment is final* (the more difficult issues concern alimony and child support decrees); and

    (iii) Whether the *judgment is on the merits*.

    A judgment is entitled to full faith and credit (or comity) *only if* the above three factors are met.

2. **Foreign Country Judgment**

    If the judgment to be recognized or enforced is that of a foreign nation, the Full Faith and Credit Clause that compels recognition of sister-state judgments is *not* applicable. Therefore, you need to discuss the possibility of *voluntary recognition* or *comity principles*.

A. Underlying Policies

1. **State Court Judgments**

    a. **Full Faith and Credit Clause [§729]**

       Recognition and enforcement by one state of a judgment rendered in any other is compelled by the Full Faith and Credit Clause of the United States Constitution (article IV, section 1). This Clause requires a court in a second state ("F2") to give a judgment from the first state ("F1") the same effect it would receive in the first state. [*See* **Fauntleroy v. Lum,** 210 U.S. 230 (1908)]

(1) Impact—national unifying force [§730]

Since this Clause insured that a state court judgment entitled to full faith and credit (*see infra*, §§741 *et seq.*) would be recognized and enforceable in other states as a *matter of right*, it became a "national unifying force" helping to change the status of the several states from independent sovereignties to integral parts of a single nation.

b. Enforcement procedure [§731]

Although the *effect* of an F1 judgment is determined by F1 law, *enforcement procedures* are governed by the *law of the forum* (F2). Thus, the plaintiff is entitled only to those procedures (execution, sequestration, contempt, etc.) allowed in F2—even if the judgment would have been enforceable by additional or different procedures in F1.

(1) Note

In most states, the judgment creditor must file a new lawsuit in F2 to enforce the F1 judgment; *i.e.*, she has to file a complaint, obtain service of summons, etc. Personal jurisdiction over the defendant must be obtained if in personam relief is sought. Only when an F2 judgment is obtained can the creditor proceed to levy execution against the judgment debtor.

(2) Distinguish

A growing number of states permit sister-state money judgments simply to be "filed" or "registered" in local courts, and execution can issue thereon without a new action. [Uniform Enforcement of Foreign Judgments Act; Cal. Civ. Proc. Code §§1710.10 *et seq.*] (This procedure also governs enforcement of a federal judgment in another federal district; *see* below.)

2. Federal Court Judgments

a. Federal implementing statute [§732]

Although the Full Faith and Credit Clause applies only where a *state* court judgment is sought to be enforced in another state, an implementing federal statute provides that judicial proceedings "shall have the same full faith and credit in every court within the United States and its Territories and Possessions as they have by law or usage in the courts of such State, Territory or Possession from which they are taken." [28 U.S.C. §1738] Thus, recognition of judgments is also required between state and federal courts and between federal courts. [*See, e.g.*, **Kremer v. Chemical Construction Corp.**, 456 U.S. 461 (1982)—state court judgment affirming a state agency's finding of no employment discrimination against P must be recognized and thus barred P from federal employment discrimination proceedings]

b. Enforcement procedure [§733]

Congress has provided that a final judgment rendered by a federal district court in an action for recovery of money or property may simply be *registered* in any other federal district court (by filing a certified copy of the original judgment in the second district). Once registered, the judgment has the same effect as a judgment of the district in which it was rendered and may be enforced directly (*i.e.,* no new action need be filed on the judgment, and no jurisdiction over the defendant need be obtained). [28 U.S.C. §1963]

(1) State court enforcement [§734]

Because of this simple procedure, there is rarely any reason to seek enforcement of a federal judgment in state courts. Where such enforcement is sought, however, it must be in compliance with the procedures of the state court; *i.e.,* it may require filing a new action, obtaining jurisdiction over the defendant, etc.

3. Judgments of Foreign Countries [§735]

The Full Faith and Credit Clause does *not apply* to judgments rendered in a foreign country. However, many foreign countries have entered into treaties with the United States providing for mutual recognition and enforcement of judgments. Even in the absence of such treaties, foreign judgments have been recognized in American courts under two theories:

a. Reciprocity doctrine [§736]

In **Hilton v. Guyot,** 159 U.S. 113 (1895), the Supreme Court held that *federal courts* should recognize and enforce judgments of a foreign country if the foreign country would subject an American judgment to similar treatment. This doctrine is *not binding on the states* and has been expressly rejected by New York.

(1) Note

Federal courts in diversity cases apply the recognition law of the states in which they sit, under the *Erie* doctrine (*see supra,* §711).

b. Comity [§737]

Most states will recognize the judgments of a foreign country as a matter of "comity" (*i.e.,* mutual respect and cooperation among sovereign nations)—*provided* that the foreign court had *proper jurisdiction* and that it *employed fair procedures* in adjudicating the case.

(1) Standards for recognition [§738]

The *recognizing state* determines whether the foreign court had jurisdiction and whether fair procedures were employed, according to its own law.

(2) Uniform Foreign Money-Judgments Recognition Act [§739]

Also, several states have enacted the Uniform Foreign Money-Judgments Recognition Act, which recognizes final foreign country *money* judgments where jurisdiction was based on personal service, consent, domicile, doing business, or use of a motor vehicle or an airplane where the cause of action arises out of such use in that country. (In addition, an open-ended section permits the state to recognize other bases of jurisdiction.) The Act applies to judgments granting or denying *recovery of money*—except tax, penal, alimony, and child support judgments.

4. Doctrine of Res Judicata [§740]

The rationale underlying both the Full Faith and Credit Clause and recognition by "comity" of the judgments of foreign nations is the doctrine of res judicata: If a person has had his day in a court with valid jurisdiction, the judgment of that court should be conclusive as to that person in any future suit on the same cause of action, so as to: (i) prevent waste of judicial machinery and expense to both parties in relitigating the case, and (ii) avoid the problem of inconsistent judgments in different jurisdictions. (*See infra,* §§765-771; *and see* Civil Procedure Summary.)

B. Requirements for Recognition of Foreign Judgments

1. In General [§741]

Before the F1 judgment is entitled to full faith and credit (or "comity") recognition, it must appear that the F1 court had *proper jurisdiction* (*i.e.,* an adequate basis for jurisdiction, competency of court, and adequate notice; *see supra,* §§42-47) and that the F1 judgment is a *"final" judgment "on the merits"* (*see* below).

2. Requirement that Foreign Judgment Be "Final"

a. F1 law governs "finality" [§742]

A judgment is "final" if no further judicial action by the rendering court is necessary to resolve the litigation. The determination of "finality" is governed by the law of the *state rendering the judgment* (F1). [**Paine v. Schenectady Insurance Co.,** 11 R.I. 411 (1876)]

b. "Finality" as affected by appeal [§743]

Problems of "finality" frequently arise where an F1 judgment is sought to be enforced in F2 while an appeal from the judgment is still pending in F1.

(1) Not final judgment [§744]

If F1 takes the position that an appeal *vacates* a lower court judgment, then there is no final judgment within the meaning of full faith and credit, and the judgment is not entitled to recognition or enforcement in F2.

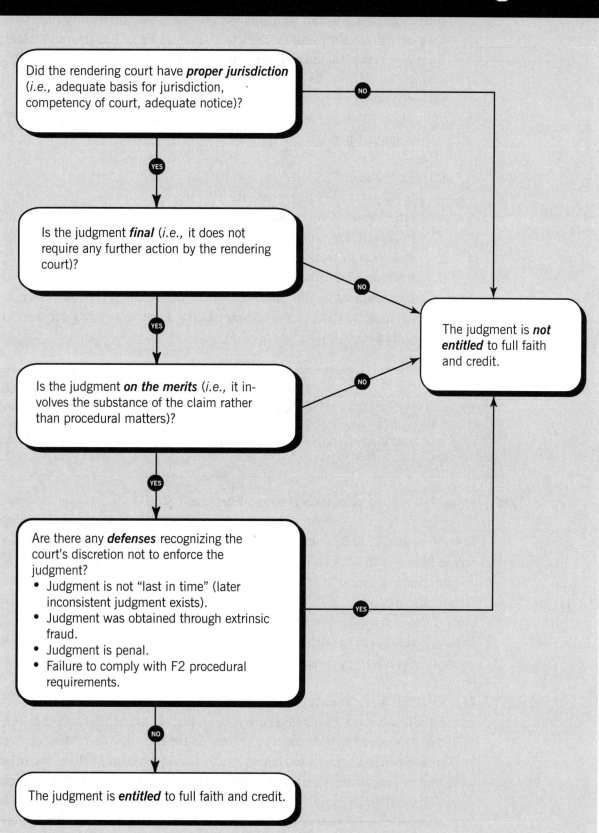

Did the rendering court have ***proper jurisdiction*** (*i.e.,* adequate basis for jurisdiction, competency of court, adequate notice)?

NO

YES

Is the judgment ***final*** (*i.e.,* it does not require any further action by the rendering court)?

NO

YES

The judgment is ***not entitled*** to full faith and credit.

Is the judgment ***on the merits*** (*i.e.,* it involves the substance of the claim rather than procedural matters)?

NO

YES

Are there any ***defenses*** recognizing the court's discretion not to enforce the judgment?
- Judgment is not "last in time" (later inconsistent judgment exists).
- Judgment was obtained through extrinsic fraud.
- Judgment is penal.
- Failure to comply with F2 procedural requirements.

YES

NO

The judgment is ***entitled*** to full faith and credit.

(2) Final judgment [§745]

However, if F1 takes the position that the judgments of its lower courts are valid and binding *until actually overturned* on the appellate level, such a judgment—even though appealed from—is sufficiently final to be entitled to full faith and credit when sued upon in F2. [**Huron Holding Corp. v. Lincoln Mine Operating Co.**, 312 U.S. 183 (1941)]

(a) But note

Most F2 courts will nevertheless *delay enforcement* of such an F1 judgment pending the outcome of the F1 appeal.

(b) And note

If F2 proceeded to enforce the F1 judgment and that judgment was later reversed on appeal, this would *not ipso facto destroy* the F2 judgment. Assuming the latter judgment was based on sufficient jurisdiction, it would remain valid in F2 despite reversal of the F1 judgment upon which it was based. (As a practical matter, of course, the party injured by this "mix-up" undoubtedly could get equitable relief by suing to enjoin enforcement of the F2 judgment.) [Restatement of Judgments §44]

EXAM TIP   gilbert

With so many other issues discussed previously, the forum (F2) makes preliminary determinations, such as how to characterize the area of law, whether the matter is substantive or procedural, etc. Note that there is a different rule for *full faith and credit issues*—it is the *state rendering the judgment* (F1) that decides whether it is final.

---

c. "Finality" of spousal and child support decrees [§746]

A difficult issue as to "finality" occurs when an F1 decree for spousal or child support is sought to be enforced in F2 and it appears that the decree is subject to modification in F1. (Those few spousal support decrees that are not subject to modification are treated as "final" judgments and hence enforceable in F2 as to amounts already due thereunder and as to all future payments.) Since most such decrees are subject to modification on a showing of "changed circumstances," the question is to what extent the forum should enforce the foreign spousal or child support decree.

(1) Past due installments [§747]

Usually accrued installments are not modifiable under F1 laws; therefore, these *amounts past due* will be treated as *sufficiently "final"* for full faith and credit purposes—so that they can be enforced in F2 like any other money judgments. [**Sistare v. Sistare**, 218 U.S. 1 (1910)] (*But note:* If the judgment was rendered in a state that allows retroactive modification of spousal or child support orders, the result might be different. [*See* **Sistare v. Sistare**, *supra*])

(2) Future installments [§748]

From a constitutional standpoint, full faith and credit need *not* be given to *future modifiable installments* under an F1 spousal or child support order. *Rationale:* The fact that F1 reserved the power to modify its decree as to future installments means that the order is *not* "final" in F1. [*See* **Griffin v. Griffin,** 327 U.S. 220 (1946)]

(3) Discretionary enforcement [§749]

Even where full faith and credit does not apply, many states today—as a matter of judicial policy—will recognize and enforce sister-state spousal and child support decrees as to modifiable installments past due or payments to become due in the future. [**Worthley v. Worthley,** 44 Cal. 2d 465 (1955)—California court modified New Jersey support decree both prospectively and retroactively, in accordance with provisions of New Jersey law]

(a) Rationale

Most courts taking this position assert that the F1 decree should be given the same treatment in F2 that it would receive in F1, and thus should be modifiable in F2 on the same conditions as F1 would impose. [**Worthley v. Worthley,** *supra*]

(b) Distinguish

But some courts hold that F2 is free to apply its own standards in modifying the F1 decree—*i.e.,* that the determination of "changed circumstances" should be made with reference to F2, not F1, law. [**Petersen v. Petersen,** 24 Cal. App. 3d 201 (1972); *and see* Rest. 2d §109, comment c]

(4) Statutes [§750]

The Uniform Interstate Family Support Act ("UIFSA") and its predecessors (URESA and RURESA) have eliminated much of the above problem. For example, one spouse (Wife) no longer has to go to the other's (Husband's) domicile (F2) and try to enforce the F1 decree against him there. Wife may now register the F1 support order with the F2 court by initiating an F1 court action. F1 sends the order to the F2 court and the order may be enforced as if it had been issued by F2.

(a) Note

Alternatively, Wife may bypass the F2 court and mail an income-withholding order directly to Husband's employer, who must then withhold wages unless Husband makes a timely objection, or may mail the order to the support enforcement agency in F2 to seek administrative enforcement.

(b) But note

While UIFSA simplifies enforcement of support orders, it limits the ability of another court to *modify* the original support order. The role of F2 is only to *enforce* the original order, unless the parties no longer reside in the issuing state or the parties agree in writing that the nonissuing court may assert jurisdiction to modify the order.

EXAM TIP   gilbert

An exam question may arise about enforcement of spousal support decrees. If you see such a question, you should mention that such decrees are usually **subject to modification** and so there is an issue of whether they are "final" for purposes of full faith and credit. You should then see if there is **past due support** owed. If so, note that past due amounts are usually **not modifiable** and thus are "final" and may be enforced. Be sure to distinguish **future** support payments, which usually **are modifiable** and thus not "final." Also, remember that uniform law (UIFSA) allows enforcement of support orders even if they are not afforded full faith and credit.

---

d. "Finality" of child custody decrees [§751]

By its very nature, a decree awarding custody of a child is nonfinal. Because of its paramount concern for the welfare of the child, the court making such a decree reserves the power to modify it at any time upon a showing of changed circumstances (*see* below). The question then arises whether custody decrees (being nonfinal) are entitled to full faith and credit in other states. The issue is critical, because the parent who loses the custody battle in F1 may be tempted to abscond with the child to F2 and hope for a different result there. Congress resolved this issue by enacting the "Parental Kidnapping Prevention Act" in 1980 (*see infra*).

(1) Majority view—limited full faith and credit [§752]

Because of the nature of child custody decrees, most state courts hold that such decrees are entitled to only *limited* full faith and credit; *i.e.*, the decree is "final" only as to the facts and circumstances existing at the time of the decree. For example, if the issue of a parent's fitness was litigated in F1, the F1 determination will be given effect in F2 but only as to factors existing or brought into issue at the time of the F1 hearing. [44 A.L.R.2d 1085]

(a) "Changed circumstances" doctrine [§753]

Because the welfare of the child is the paramount consideration, changed circumstances *subsequent* to the F1 decree will justify F2 in modifying or completely ignoring the decree and making its own determination of custody. [**Mylius v. Cargill**, 142 P. 918 (N.M. 1914)]

1) Note

It is unclear whether F1 or F2 law should govern what constitutes sufficient "changed circumstances" and the manner in which the decree is modifiable. Using full faith and credit principles (judgment to receive same effect in F2 as it would have received in F1), it would seem that F1 standards should be applied. [*See* **New York *ex rel.* Halvey v. Halvey,** 330 U.S. 610 (1947)]

(b) Comment [§754]

There may be some constitutional limitation on what are sufficiently "changed circumstances" to ignore the F1 decree. Some courts are so vitally concerned with the welfare of children within their state that they have held that a change in residence—*i.e.,* merely bringing the child into the state—is a sufficiently "changed circumstance" to justify modification of a prior F1 custody decree. [**Security Savings & Trust Co. v. Evans,** 21 P.2d 782 (Or. 1933)]

(2) No full faith and credit [§755]

A few states have taken the position that full faith and credit simply does not apply to child custody decrees, and that F2 is free to disregard any F1 decision whether or not there have been changed circumstances. *Rationale:* The paramount concern of the state is for the welfare of the child. [**Bachman v. Mejias,** 1 N.Y.2d 575 (1956)]

(3) Refusal to exercise jurisdiction [§756]

Other courts take a directly opposite approach: As a matter of judicial discretion, they may refuse to exercise jurisdiction in child custody disputes whenever there is a prior F1 custody decree in effect, thereby forcing the parent dissatisfied with the F1 decree to seek modification from the F1 court. [62 Mich. L. Rev. 795 (1964), *and see* **Ferreira v. Ferreira,** 9 Cal. 3d 824 (1973)]

(a) Note

This position is often rationalized on the ground that the petitioning parent in F2 lacks "clean hands" (having absconded with the child, etc.) and sometimes on the basis of forum non conveniens. [*See* **Hawkins v. Hawkins,** 504 P.2d 709 (Or. 1972)]

(b) Uniform Act [§757]

The Uniform Child Custody Jurisdiction and Enforcement Act ("UCCJEA"), which replaced the Uniform Child Custody Jurisdiction Act ("UCCJA") in 1998, provides that the courts of F1 have *exclusive, continuing jurisdiction* over a custody determination and no other state may modify that determination unless: (i) neither the child, the child and one parent, nor the child and a person acting as a parent have a significant connection with F1 and substantial evidence concerning the child's care, protection, training, and personal relationships is no longer available in F1; or (ii) at the time the modification is sought, none of these persons presently resides in F1. (*See also infra,* §905.)

1) Rationale

States adopting the UCCJA had in effect concluded that it is better to close their courts to this kind of case rather than to allow modification and never-ending litigation between parents seeking to obtain changes of custody decrees made in other states. However, because the UCCJA permitted overlapping jurisdiction between the child's "home state" and a state having "significant connections" with the child and at least one contestant, courts in F2 frequently declared themselves competent to modify the F1 decree if the child and one parent or person acting as a parent had established residence there. To remedy this situation, the UCCJEA unambiguously gives *jurisdictional priority to the "home state"* and thus is consistent with the Parental Kidnapping Prevention Act (*see* below).

2) Parental Kidnapping Prevention Act [§758]

The Parental Kidnapping Prevention Act ("PKPA") is a federal statute [28 U.S.C. §1738A] that requires that full faith and credit be given in every state to the determinations of a state acting in accordance with the UCCJA, but gives priority to the "home state." The home state's custody determination may be modified only if the modifying state has jurisdiction to act under the UCCJA, *and* the first state no longer has jurisdiction under the Act *or* it has declined to exercise its jurisdiction. The UCCJEA's modification provision is in conformity with the PKPA (*see* above, *and see infra,* §900).

a) Note

The PKPA does not confer jurisdiction on the federal courts to enforce its terms directly by determining which of two conflicting state court custody determinations is valid. The matter would have to be appealed in the state court system and review sought thereafter by certiorari to the United States Supreme Court. [**Thompson v. Thompson,** 484 U.S. 174 (1988)]

EXAM TIP   **gilbert**

If you get a question about modifying custody determination, you should point out that for full faith and credit purposes, most states do *not consider a child custody decree to be final*. Because the welfare of the child is the most important issue, custody can be modified if there has been a subsequent change in circumstances. However, you should also point out that most states have adopted the UCCJEA, and under that act the original forum (F1) has *exclusive and continuing jurisdiction* as long as it has significant connections with the child.

3. **Requirement that F1 Judgment Be "On the Merits" [§759]**

In addition to being "final," the F1 judgment must be "on the merits" in order to entitle it to recognition and enforcement in F2.

a. **Definition [§760]**

A judgment is "on the merits" where the court by rendering judgment has extinguished the cause of action (the cause of action merging into the judgment); *i.e.*, the judgment must *involve the "substance" of the plaintiff's claim(s)*. [Restatement of Judgments §48]

(1) **Note**

Where the court merely holds that there is some technical reason why plaintiff cannot recover on the cause of action, admitting the existence of the cause but not deciding the matter, the judgment is *not* "on the merits."

b. **Application**

(1) **"Not on the merits" [§761]**

Dismissals for lack of jurisdiction, improper venue, lack of capacity to sue, failure to join an indispensable party, and forum non conveniens are not judgments "on the merits." [Rest. 2d §110] Likewise, the prevailing view is that dismissals on the ground of laches or because the statute of limitations has run are not judgments "on the merits." [*See* **Warner v. Buffalo Drydock Co.,** 67 F.2d 540 (2d Cir. 1933)]

(2) **Demurrer or motion to strike [§762]**

If a demurrer is sustained or a motion to strike granted because of plaintiff's failure to state a cause of action, the judgment is "not on the merits"—except where plaintiff cannot amend to allege a cause of action (in which case it would be "on the merits").

c. **Distinguish—direct estoppel [§763]**

Even though a judgment is not on the merits, whatever matters have been fully litigated and decided *will be conclusive* in subsequent litigation between the same parties under the concept of "direct estoppel" (*see* below) and thereby entitled to full faith and credit in other states. [**Angel v. Bullington,** *supra*, §714—F1 suit dismissed because F1 court determined that a special statute barred recovery; plaintiff could not relitigate in F2 the applicability of that statute]

(1) **Default and consent judgments [§764]**

Likewise, default and consent judgments are not really adjudications "on the merits," but are binding on the parties and entitled to full faith and credit in other states in any attempt to relitigate the same claim.

C. Effect to Be Given to Foreign Judgments

1. Res Judicata Effects [§765]

If the F1 judgment is "final" and "on the merits," it is entitled to any or all of the following res judicata effects in F2 (just as it would receive in F1):

a. Merger [§766]

Plaintiff's original cause of action is *merged into the final judgment*. Thereafter, the plaintiff cannot sue on the original cause of action, but can only sue on the judgment itself. As a corollary, the defendant is precluded from relitigating the merits since the original cause of action no longer exists. The Restatement (Second) of Judgments refers to merger as *"claim preclusion."*

b. Bar [§767]

A judgment for the defendant will bar the plaintiff from later suing on the same cause of action—even on new grounds that might have been raised in the original action. With merger and bar combined, the result is that the first final judgment is conclusive as to all matters that *were or could have been litigated* in the first proceedings. The Restatement (Second) of Judgments refers to bar as *"claim preclusion."*

c. Direct estoppel [§768]

Even where the first judgment is not "final" or is not a judgment "on the merits," whatever has been *fully litigated* in the first proceedings will be conclusive in subsequent proceedings between the *same parties* on the *same cause of action*. The Restatement (Second) of Judgments refers to direct estoppel as *"issue preclusion."*

d. Collateral estoppel [§769]

Finally, any issue *actually litigated and essential* to the judgment in the first action is binding on the parties or their privies if that issue is raised in a subsequent lawsuit—*even on a different cause of action*. The Restatement (Second) of Judgments refers to collateral estoppel as *"issue preclusion."*

(1) "Mutuality" [§770]

The older cases required "mutuality" here—*i.e.*, that the subsequent lawsuit be between the same parties or their privies.

(2) Modern views [§771]

However, most modern jurisdictions recognize the prior judgment as binding *against* (but not in favor of) any party to the present suit who was a party to the prior litigation—even though the *other party* to the present action was not involved in the earlier suit. (*See* further discussion in Civil Procedure Summary.)

2. Persons Affected by F1 Judgment

a. Privies [§772]

Not only the parties to the F1 action, but also all persons "in privity" with them are bound by the F1 judgment. A question may arise as to what persons are parties and "privies." To decide that question, F1 law is generally binding on F2. [Rest. 2d §94]

(1) Constitutionality [§773]

However, the Supreme Court in **Bigelow v. Old Dominion Copper Mining & Smelting Co.,** 225 U.S. 111 (1912), refused to take a position on this point. It seemed to suggest that there may be constitutional limits on how far F1's judgment would be conclusive on persons not subject to F1's personal jurisdiction at the time judgment was rendered. In the *Bigelow* case, the Court would not allow the defendant to assert rights under an F1 judgment because he was not bound by it—the Court insisting upon "mutuality" before a person could be deemed a "privy."

(2) Due process limitation [§774]

Also, no person will be bound by an F1 judgment where to do so would violate the Due Process Clause of the Fourteenth Amendment—as where a nonresident who is sought to be bound had no notice of the suit, no representation in the F1 court, etc. [**Riley v. New York Trust Co.,** 315 U.S. 343 (1941)]

b. Successors in interest [§775]

A transferee or successor in interest of a res that was the subject of litigation in F1, and in which the transferor was a party, generally will be bound by the F1 judgment. [Restatement of Judgments §89]

c. Class suits [§776]

An F1 judgment in a class action will be binding on all members of the class wherever they may later bring suit on the same cause of action, provided that: (i) the absent members of the class were *adequately represented* in the F1 class suit, and (ii) a *"reasonable" number* of the class (not necessarily every member) were given *adequate notice* of the F1 suit *and an opportunity to be heard* therein. [**Sovereign Camp v. Bolin,** 305 U.S. 66 (1938)]

(1) Rationale

It is a question of convenience and practical necessity where class rights are in dispute and the class is composed of many members of different states, etc. [**Hansberry v. Lee,** 311 U.S. 32 (1940)]

(2) Comment

The only real explanation is that it is an outright exception to the **Pennover v. Neff** doctrine that personal rights can only be determined when the individual is before the court—a policy conflict in which the interest of res judicata (here, in settling class litigation) prevails.

3. Scope of Relief [§777]

Ordinarily, the F1 judgment merges the plaintiff's cause of action, so that the plaintiff can seek only the relief granted in the F1 judgment. He cannot seek any other or supplemental relief in F2.

a. Exception—workers' compensation awards [§778]

An injured worker may have a right to recover under the compensation laws of the place of injury, the place of residence, the employer's principal place of business, or the like (*see supra*, §583).

(1) Early view [§779]

Earlier decisions took the position that if an injured worker once obtained recovery (under the law of F1), he could not obtain supplemental relief in any other state; *i.e.*, full faith and credit barred any such "double recovery." [*See* **Magnolia Petroleum Co. v. Hunt**, 320 U.S. 430 (1943)]

(2) *McCartin* [§780]

Later, it was recognized that an injured worker could file a claim and recover an award under the compensation awards of several "interested" states **unless** the statute in one of the states made its award the **exclusive remedy**. [**Industrial Accident Commission v. McCartin**, *supra*, §583]

(3) Modern view [§781]

The modern position of the Supreme Court is to uphold F2's right to grant a workers' compensation award **in addition** to that previously granted in F1, if F2 could have made a worker's compensation award in the first instance. [**Thomas v. Washington Gas Light Co.**, *supra*, §583]

(a) Rationale

The plurality in *Thomas* believed that *Magnolia Petroleum* was overruled—that **no state had a legitimate interest** in preventing another state with sufficient interest in the employment situation from applying its own law.

1) But note

Five Justices (two dissenting and three concurring) disagreed that

Magnolia Petroleum was overruled. The concurring Justices still support *McCartin*. Thus, the Court's position on *McCartin* is uncertain, although hearing was denied in a later case that treated *McCartin* as good law. [*See* **Landry v. Carlson Mooring Service,** 643 F.2d 1080 (5th Cir.), *cert. denied,* 454 U.S. 1123 (1981)]

(b) Result—"highest" but not "double" recovery [§782]

Although a worker may recover awards in both F1 and F2, amounts paid under the F1 award are *credited against the F2 recovery*. The effect is to insure an injured worker the *highest* recovery to which he would have been entitled under the laws of any state having jurisdiction.

4. Effect of Foreign Decree Concerning Title to Local Land [§783]

As discussed *supra,* §172, an F1 court does not have power to enter a decree in rem as to F2 lands, and any F1 judgment that purported to do so would be void for lack of jurisdiction. However, where the F1 court had personal jurisdiction over both parties, it could enter a decree in personam commanding the owner to convey title, etc.—thereby indirectly affecting title to the F2 lands. If the parties obey the decree of the F1 court, there are no problems. However, difficulties arise where the owner of the F2 land fails to execute the conveyance or otherwise abide by the F1 decree. If the adverse party then brings suit in F2 to enforce the F1 decree, what effect will the F2 courts give to the decree? The courts are split on this point:

a. No full faith and credit [§784]

The traditional view is that F1's decree is not entitled to any full faith and credit in F2, so that F2 is free to fully relitigate the matter. *Rationale:* Only the situs of land has subject matter jurisdiction to affect title to land. Rights in local land are of such paramount importance that local courts will not give res judicata or other effect to a foreign decree pertaining thereto. [*See* **Fall v. Eastin,** 215 U.S. 1 (1909)]

b. Comity recognition [§785]

Another view is that F1's decree should, and ordinarily will, be given recognition in State Y—but as a matter of "comity," and not as compelled by full faith and credit. In other words, only the respect and cooperation that one sovereign owes to another warrants recognition, and even then the decree will be recognized only where not offensive to local (F2) laws or public policy. [**Clouse v. Clouse,** 207 S.W.2d 576 (Tenn. 1948)]

c. Limited full faith and credit [§786]

A growing number of cases have held that F2's courts should be compelled to give full faith and credit to the *facts* as found by the F1 court, although F2 should be free to make its own determination as to the decree. [**Matson v. Matson,** 173 N.W. 127 (Iowa 1919)]

d. Total full faith and credit [§787]

Finally, some courts have held that the F1 decree is entitled to full faith and credit in F2 without reservation, and that the F1 decree is therefore enforceable in F2. [**Redwood Investment Co. v. Exley,** 64 Cal. App. 455 (1923); *and see* **Varone v. Varone,** 359 F.2d 769 (7th Cir. 1966)—Michigan decree in divorce action requiring husband to convey Illinois land entitled to full faith and credit in Illinois]

(1) Rationale

Parties who are personally before a competent court ought to be bound by its determination as to their rights in sister-state land as fully as they are bound by its adjudication of any other matter. [Rest. 2d §102, comment d]

(2) Criticism

Several authorities point out that this result is inconsistent with the well-established rule in equity that the F1 court cannot affect title to lands in F2, *i.e.,* that equity cannot act in rem as to foreign lands. To assert that F2 is compelled to enforce F1's decree as to land located in F2 is to say that the F1 decree can operate to transfer title to land in F2. If the proceedings in F2 are merely "rubber-stamp approvals" by which the F1 decree is enforced, it becomes apparent that the F1 decree is operating in rem—something courts have continually asserted it was beyond their power to do. [21 U. Chi. L. Rev. 620 (1954)]

5. Effect of F1 Decree Enjoining Suit in F2

a. Power to enjoin suit [§788]

Within the limits of "equity and good conscience" and when required to prevent fraud, oppression, or a miscarriage of justice, a court has the power to *enjoin the parties* before it from proceeding in an action in any other court, domestic or foreign.

(1) No effect on F2 jurisdiction [§789]

However, such an injunction does ***not destroy the jurisdiction*** of the other court or prevent jurisdiction from attaching. If the party at whom the injunction is aimed prosecutes the action in spite of the injunction, a judgment in her favor is ***not void*** for lack of jurisdiction. Such party, however, may be imprisoned *for contempt* by the court that granted the injunction and may also be compelled to surrender whatever she recovered by way of judgment in the other proceeding. [**Platt v. Woodruff,** 61 N.Y. 378 (1875)]

EXAM TIP **gilbert**

Be sure you understand how the F1 injunction against suit in F2 works. Although we say that the *suit* is enjoined, it is really the *party that is enjoined*. The injunction orders the party not to proceed with the suit; it cannot order the F2 court to stop. If the party continues, the F2 judgment is valid, but the party can be held in contempt of court for violating the injunction.

---

(2) When foreign suit will be enjoined [§790]

Enjoining an action pending before another court is an extreme remedy available in only limited situations.

(a) Prevention of fraud [§791]

Suppose Husband commences a divorce action in Nebraska, falsely claiming that he is domiciled there (domicile being a requisite basis for jurisdiction in divorce actions; *see infra*, §842). If Wife obtains personal jurisdiction over Husband in New Jersey, his real domicile, New Jersey courts can restrain his further prosecution of the Nebraska action. To allow Husband to proceed with the Nebraska divorce suit would be to propagate a fraud on the Nebraska courts; they would be deceived by his claims that he is domiciled there since Wife is not there to contest same and should not be forced to go to Nebraska to litigate. [**Kempson v. Kempson**, 43 A. 97 (N.J. 1899)]

(b) Prevention of oppressive suits abroad [§792]

Similarly, an injunction may be granted where a party goes to a foreign jurisdiction for the purpose of avoiding local laws or creating hardships on the other party. However, the courts proceed with caution here; it must clearly appear that both parties are local domiciliaries and that the foreign suit would be "oppressive"—*i.e., grossly unfair* to the other party or *violative of local public policy.*

---

e.g. **Example:** A domestic creditor may be enjoined from suing outside the jurisdiction to reach property of a domestic debtor if such property would be protected by exemption statutes in a domestic suit. [**Jones v. Hughes**, 137 N.W. 1023 (Iowa 1912)]

---

e.g. **Example:** A few courts have enjoined foreign suits instituted in distant jurisdictions for the clear purpose of making it impossible for the defendant to compel the attendance of witnesses or properly present evidence to defend himself.

---

cf. **Compare:** Suits in a foreign state by local creditors will not be enjoined merely because the foreign state recognizes a more stringent collection procedure than is allowed locally.

(c) Concurrent litigation dealing with same res [§793]

When an action in F2 deals with a specific res or property that is before an F1 court in a pending proceeding (*e.g.*, property brought before the court by writ of attachment or garnishment), F1 may enjoin the parties from proceeding further with the F2 litigation regardless of which action was filed or commenced first. *Rationale:* In reaching its determination of the merits, the court having custody of the property should not be concerned about being embarrassed by a contrary decision of a foreign court.

b. Limitations on power to enjoin foreign suits [§794]

There are, however, certain limitations on the states' power to enjoin foreign suits.

(1) Federal court proceedings [§795]

A state court *cannot enjoin* the parties from proceeding before a federal court, regardless of the type of proceeding involved. [**Baltimore & Ohio Railroad v. Kemper,** 314 U.S. 44 (1941)]

(2) Congressional grant of concurrent jurisdiction [§796]

And in situations where Congress has specifically provided that all states have concurrent jurisdiction (*e.g.*, Federal Employers' Liability Act), no state court can enjoin a party's proceeding in any other state. *Rationale:* Congress must have intended that considerations of oppression, inconvenience, or expense to one party should not govern since they gave every state concurrent jurisdiction. [**Miles v. Illinois Central Railroad,** 315 U.S. 698 (1942)]

c. Distinguish—forum non conveniens [§797]

Closely allied to the problem of when a local court may enjoin a suit pending in a foreign jurisdiction is the question of whether the court in which the action is brought may *refuse to exercise jurisdiction* simply because it would be *unfair or inconvenient* to hear the action locally. (This is the doctrine of forum non conveniens, discussed *supra*, §§227-236.) Wherever F1 might enjoin the further prosecution of a suit pending in F2, it would also be appropriate for F2 to dismiss the suit on the basis of forum non conveniens.

6. Effect of F1 Decree Enjoining a Party from Testifying in Other Action

a. Power to enjoin testimony [§798]

A state court may enjoin a party, as part of an agreed upon settlement, from voluntarily testifying against the other party in actions filed against it. [**Baker v. General Motors Corp.,** 522 U.S. 222 (1998)]

(1) No effect on F2 jurisdiction [§799]

However, such an injunction does not prevent a court in F2 from ordering the party to testify in an **unrelated** action brought by plaintiffs who were **not parties or privies** to the F1 action. [**Baker v. General Motors Corp.,** *supra*—former GM employee's settlement agreement in employment dispute not to voluntarily testify against GM in other actions did not prevent his subpoenaed testimony in a wrongful death case against GM brought in another state by plaintiffs unrelated to the employment dispute]

(2) F2 plaintiffs not subject to F1 jurisdiction [§800]

The injunction does not affect the F2 plaintiffs because neither they nor their cause of action were subject to F1's judicial power.

b. No full faith and credit due [§801]

The Court in *Baker, supra,* held that the F2 court, in ordering the party to testify in the F2 proceeding, did not deny full faith and credit to the F1 decree because: (i) the F1 decree was not self-executing in F2—F1's enforcement mechanisms did not travel with its decree into other jurisdictions; and (ii) F1's decree could not determine evidentiary issues such as whether to admit or exclude evidence in a lawsuit brought in F2 by plaintiffs who were not subject to F1's jurisdiction.

D. Defenses to Recognition or Enforcement of Foreign Judgments

1. Introduction [§802]

There are certain situations in which the policies behind the doctrine of res judicata (which underlie both the Full Faith and Credit Clause and the comity principle) may be outweighed by other policies that dictate against recognition of the foreign judgment. In such cases, the forum may assert its right to **relitigate the cause** and render an independent judgment.

2. State Court Judgments

a. Defenses raising invalidity of judgment

(1) Lack of jurisdiction in F1 [§803]

As noted previously, a judgment rendered without proper jurisdiction is **void** and not entitled to full faith and credit. Lack of jurisdiction is therefore the most important defense in F2 against enforcement of an F1 judgment.

(a) Where defendant did not appear in F1 [§804]

As a general rule, where defendant has **not appeared** in the F1 proceedings, F2 can inquire into the sufficiency of F1 jurisdiction regardless of F1's findings; *i.e.,* F2 does not have to accord full faith and credit to F1's findings as to its own jurisdiction. [**Thompson v. Whitman,** *supra,* §204]

1) F1 standards govern [§805]

However, the sufficiency of F1 jurisdiction is measured by due process and *F1's* own standards. Thus, for example, it is no defense to enforcement of an F1 judgment that service of process or the basis for jurisdiction failed to meet F2 standards—as long as these met F1 standards and minimum due process requirements. [**Bay Plaza Management Co. v. Estep,** 525 P.2d 56 (Or. 1974)]

(b) Where defendant appeared in F1—"bootstrap doctrine" [§806]

If defendant *appeared* in the F1 proceedings—by a general appearance or even solely for the purpose of contesting jurisdiction—F1's findings as to its own jurisdiction ordinarily *will be binding* on F2; *i.e.,* by defendant's appearing (even specially to contest jurisdiction), the F1 jurisdictional findings become entitled to full faith and credit. If the defendant had *not* appeared, the F1 judgment would always be subject to collateral attack in F2 on the issue of jurisdiction (above). This is known as the "bootstrap doctrine." [**Baldwin v. Iowa State Traveling Men's Association,** 283 U.S. 522 (1931)]

1) Rationale

The policy behind res judicata (estopping parties from relitigating issues previously adjudicated) simply outweighs the policy against enforcing judgments of a court without jurisdiction.

2) Applies even where jurisdiction not challenged in F1 [§807]

F1's findings as to the sufficiency of its own jurisdiction may be conclusive even where the issue was not actually raised in the F1 proceedings. As long as both parties were before the court and the issue *could* have been litigated therein, the F1 judgment bars the parties from later raising any jurisdictional defect. [**Chicot County Drainage District v. Baxter State Bank,** 308 U.S. 371 (1940)]

a) Rationale

This is an application of the res judicata effect of bar; *i.e.,* the parties are barred from relitigating issues that were or could have been fully litigated in the F1 proceeding (*see supra,* §767).

b) Effect

This enables parties to "confer" jurisdiction on the court—something courts do not ordinarily allow; *i.e.,* if both parties appear and collusively agree not to raise any issue as to jurisdiction, F1's judgment (which expressly or impliedly asserts the sufficiency of its own jurisdiction) bars litigation of this issue in any later proceedings in F2. (And this is frequently the exact maneuver undertaken in collusive divorce proceedings.)

EXAM TIP   **gilbert**

This is an important point to remember: If the defendant **appeared in F1**, she cannot claim lack of jurisdiction later, even if the issue of jurisdiction was not actually litigated. (The key is she **could have** raised the issue.) If she did **not appear** (*i.e.,* there was a default judgment), the defendant can raise jurisdictional issues in F2 but the F2 court must use the F1 standards.

---

3) Applies to jurisdiction over person and subject matter [§808]

According to modern authority, the "bootstrap doctrine" applies to F1's findings as to its jurisdiction over the parties *and* jurisdiction over the subject matter. [Rest. 2d §97]

Example: In **Durfee v. Duke,** 375 U.S. 106 (1963), the Court held that where both parties were before the court, F1 findings as to location of land in a quiet title action were binding and conclusive in later litigation in F2; *i.e.,* the parties having appeared and litigated that issue in F1, the matter could not be relitigated in F2 even though the F2 court disagreed with F1's findings as to the location of the land (the land being in the middle of a river forming the boundary between the two states). [*See also* **Underwriters National Assurance Co. v. North Carolina Life & Accident & Health Insurance,** 455 U.S. 691 (1982)]

(c) Limitations [§809]

There may be situations in which F1's findings as to its own jurisdiction would not be given effect regardless of whether the issue was litigated in F1 or whether defendant appeared therein. Other policies and interests occasionally may prevail over the doctrines of res judicata and full faith and credit. [*See* Rest. Judgments §10]

Example: A state court's decision that it had jurisdiction to dispose of property that is the subject of bankruptcy proceedings in a federal court clearly is not entitled to res judicata effect, because the federal Bankruptcy Act provides an overriding policy in favor of the orderly administration of the bankrupt's estate, which outweighs the policies of res judicata.

Example: Similarly, a state court's decision that it had jurisdiction to render a judgment in a suit against a foreign ambassador or consul would also be subject to collateral attack in a federal court because of the overriding policy of having such actions litigated in federal courts.

---

(2) Judgment lacks "finality" or is "not on the merits" [§810]

If the judgment sought to be enforced is not "final" under the law of the rendering state or is "not on the merits," it is not entitled to full faith and credit and its enforcement in another state may be resisted on such grounds.

b. Defenses recognizing court's discretion not to enforce valid judgments

(1) F1 judgment not "last in time" [§811]

An F1 judgment will not be enforced if there is a later, inconsistent judgment between the same parties relating to the same cause of action; *i.e.,* the judgment *"last in time" supersedes* any earlier, inconsistent judgment. [**Perkins v. Benguet Consolidated Mining Co.,** *supra,* §123; Rest. 2d §114]

Example: In **Treinies v. Sunshine Mining Co.,** 308 U.S. 66 (1939), a Washington probate court determined that certain stock belonged to Plaintiff. This decree was challenged in Idaho on the ground that Washington had no jurisdiction over the subject matter (the stock). The Idaho court agreed and refused to give full faith and credit to the Washington decree, instead awarding the stock to Defendant. Instead of appealing the issue through the Idaho courts, Plaintiff filed an interpleader action in federal court. However, the Idaho judgment had become final, and the Supreme Court held that the second judgment prevailed over any earlier inconsistent judgment regardless of the correctness of either determination (*i.e.,* even though it appeared that Idaho had erroneously failed to give full faith and credit to the earlier Washington decree). *Rationale:* If Idaho made an error in failing to give full faith and credit to the Washington decree, that error should have been appealed through the Idaho state courts to the United States Supreme Court, if necessary. Having failed to appeal—and the Idaho judgment having become final in the process—Plaintiff was bound by it.

(a) Enforceable in F1? [§812]

If the later F2 judgment is sought to be enforced in F1, F1 theoretically would have to disregard its earlier judgment and enforce the inconsistent F2 judgment. However, there is very little authority to this effect. Indeed, most F1 courts would probably insist that the enforceability of F1 judgments in F1 cannot be affected by happenings in F2. [*See* **Tarnoff v. Jones**, 497 P.2d 60 (Ariz. 1972)—F2 rendered judgment enforcing earlier F1 decree; later, the F1 court reexamined and invalidated the original F1 decree, ignoring the intervening F2 judgment]

(2) Fraud in procurement of F1 judgment [§813]

Early cases held that fraud in the procurement of the F1 judgment was not a legal defense to its enforcement in F2, but that the injured party could seek equitable intervention to enjoin enforcement of the judgment. [**Christmas v. Russell**, 72 U.S. 290 (1866)] The *better view*, however, is that if the judgment is subject to the equitable defense of fraud in F1, the fraud should be a defense to recognition or enforcement of the judgment in F2 as well. [Rest. 2d §115, comment d]

(a) Rationale

First of all, law and equity have been merged in most jurisdictions, and any ground for equitable intervention is recognized as a legal defense today. Furthermore, since a judgment obtained by fraud is subject to being set aside in F1, it should certainly be impeachable in F2; full faith and credit requires only that the judgment be given the same effect in F2 as it would receive in F1. [**Levin v. Gladstein**, 55 S.E. 371 (N.C. 1906)]

(b) What constitutes "fraud" [§814]

In most states, only *extrinsic fraud—i.e.,* fraud that prevented the party from having a fair opportunity to present her case—constitutes a defense to enforcement of a judgment. Examples would include bribery of a judge, collusion to prevent defendant's appearance, and breach of plaintiff's promise not to take judgment. *Intrinsic fraud*—such as perjury of witnesses, forged documents in evidence, or malpractice of counsel—generally is *not* a defense, on the theory that a party is deemed to have sufficient opportunity to protect herself against such fraud by proper preparation of her case and effective cross-examination at trial.

1) Note

Some courts (including federal courts) refuse to enforce judgments obtained by *any* fraud—whether extrinsic or intrinsic.

(3) Defense based on nature of original cause of action

(a) Contrary to public policy of F2 [§815]

As a general rule, the scope of a defense based on public policy is **very limited**. The F2 court ordinarily cannot go behind the F1 judgment to look at the nature of the original cause of action because of the requirements of full faith and credit and the doctrine of res judicata. Thus, even though it would have violated F2 public policy to permit an original suit on the cause of action, this is no defense to the F1 judgment; it is entitled to the same effect it would receive in F1. [**Fauntleroy v. Lum,** *supra,* §729; Rest. 2d §117]

Example: A New York court was required to enforce a foreign judgment for damages based on alienation of affections and "criminal conversation," even though this particular cause of action had been abolished in New York and even though most of the acts alleged as the basis for the foreign judgment took place in New York. [**Parker v. Hoefer,** 2 N.Y.2d 612 (1957)]

---

1) But see—Defense of Marriage Act [§816]

The federal Defense of Marriage Act ("DOMA") creates an exception from the duty to give effect to "any public act, record, or judicial proceeding of any other state" respecting "a relationship between persons of the same sex that is treated as a marriage under the laws of such other state . . . ." This unique congressionally mandated exception from the Full Faith and Credit Clause has not yet been judicially interpreted. (*See also supra,* §609.)

(b) Claim barred by statute of limitations in F2 [§817]

F2 **may not refuse to enforce** an F1 judgment on the ground that it had been rendered on a claim arising under F2 law and as to which the statute of limitations had run in F2. Even after the F2 statute has run, the plaintiff may (if she can get jurisdiction) commence proceedings on the claim in F1, and if she obtains judgment there, the F2 courts will have to enforce it. [**Roche v. McDonald,** 275 U.S. 449 (1928)]

1) Distinguish

It is not clear whether the above principle can be extended to permit revival of an "old" judgment. For example, suppose F1 renders a judgment against Defendant, which remains outstanding for five years; an F1 statute provides that no action may be brought in F1 to enforce any judgment more than five years old.

Plaintiff takes the F1 judgment into F2 and commences a new action there against Defendant, based on the F1 judgment (F2 permitting suits on judgments more than five years after entry). Plaintiff then takes the judgment she obtains in F2 back to F1, and brings suit on it there. Will F1 be required to enforce the F2 judgment even though it is based on an earlier F1 judgment which could not be enforced in F1? There is little known authority on the point. The Second Restatement section 118(2) indicates that F1 should give full faith and credit to the F2 judgment as long as the nature of the proceedings in F2 was to create a "new" judgment (rather than merely extend the effective life of the original F1 judgment).

(c) Claim based on tax or penal liabilities [§818]

There may be exceptional situations in which the F2 court may "look behind" the F1 judgment to the nature of the original cause of action. However, this would only be permitted where there was an F2 policy sufficiently strong to outweigh the basic policy of res judicata.

1) Penal judgments [§819]

It is well settled that F2 will not enforce F1's "penal" laws (*see supra,* §631). In **Huntington v. Attrill**, *supra,* §631, the Supreme Court seemed to indicate that F2 might inquire if an F1 judgment was based on penal law—thus looking behind the F1 judgment.

a) *A "penal law"* in the conflicts sense is one designed to punish (by fine and/or imprisonment) an offense against the public justice—*i.e.,* a ***wrong to the public*** as a whole. (*See supra,* §631.)

b) *But a judgment for "punitive" (exemplary) damages* recovered by an individual as a remedy for a wrong done to her individually or as a member of a group is ***not*** a "penal" judgment in the conflicts sense, and full faith and credit thus applies. [**Huntington v. Attrill**, *supra*—punitive damages judgment against director who falsely certified corporation's financial position to prejudice of its creditors, held not a "penal" judgment]

2) Judgments for taxes [§820]

In **Milwaukee County v. M.E. White Co.**, *supra,* §636, the Supreme Court sidestepped another established conflicts rule—that F2 will not enforce F1's revenue laws—by compelling enforcement in F2 of an F1 judgment for taxes owed, on the rationale that the F2 court was being compelled to enforce an F1 judgment (not F1's revenue laws). In dictum, the Court questioned whether an F2 court could even look behind an F1 judgment to see if it were based on a "penal law," thus casting doubt on the inference previously drawn from the *Huntington* case, above.

(d) Second Restatement [§821]

The Restatement proposed to allow public policy as a defense to enforcement of a foreign judgment in a greater range of cases. Section 103 provides that a judgment of F1 need not be recognized in F2 "if it would involve an *improper* interference with *important interests* of (F2)." However, this proposal has been criticized as endangering full faith and credit. [54 Cal. L. Rev. 282 (1966)]

(4) Failure to comply with F2 procedure [§822]

F2 does not have to enforce an F1 judgment where the holder of the F1 judgment has failed to comply with F2 procedural requirements, provided that such requirements are not discriminatory against F1 judgments.

(a) Forum statute of limitations applies [§823]

Accordingly, F2 may apply its own statute of limitations in suits to enforce foreign judgments (where not unreasonable) even though the F2 statute is shorter than F1's statute of limitations on suits on F1 judgments. [**McElmoyle v. Cohen,** 38 U.S. 312 (1839)]

1) And note

There is apparently no violation of full faith and credit even where the forum statute of limitations for suits on foreign judgments is shorter than that applicable to suits on domestic judgments if the foreign judgment, after revival in the foreign state, can be enforced under the forum statute of limitations. [**Watkins v. Conway,** *supra,* §693]

(b) Effect of contempt [§824]

Some cases have held that where the judgment holder is in contempt of the F2 courts—even though the contempt relates to a separate and independent action—F2 may refuse him any judicial relief, including enforcement of foreign judgments. [**Kubon v. Kubon,** 51 Cal. 2d 229 (1958)] (This holding, however, has been criticized as violating the full faith and credit mandate that F2 give the judgment the same effect it would receive in F1.)

(5) Distinguish—error or mistake in F1 proceedings is no defense [§825]

The F1 judgment *cannot* be attacked in F2 on the basis of some mistake or error in the proceedings in F1. Any such error, judicial or otherwise, must be raised by appeal in F1 and cannot serve as the basis for collateral attack on the judgment in F2. [**Milliken v. Meyer,** *supra,* §85]

(a) Note

The result is the same even where the mistake alleged is the erroneous application by F1 of what it considered to be F2's law. For example, suppose a contract action is brought in F1. In deciding the case, the F1 court chooses to apply the laws of F2 to interpret the contract because the contract was entered into there. The F1 court misconstrues the F2 law and arrives at a clearly erroneous judgment, but the judgment becomes final in F1. If plaintiff brings the judgment into F2 to enforce it, F2 must enforce the erroneous interpretation of its own laws because of the conclusive effect of F1's judgment. [Rest. 2d §106; **In re Morgan Guaranty Trust Co.,** 28 N.Y.2d 155 (1971)]

(6) Forum law preventing courts from enforcing foreign judgment is no defense [§826]

Clearly, a state cannot escape its constitutional obligation to give full faith and credit to the judgments of sister states by denying or withdrawing jurisdiction from otherwise competent courts to entertain suits on foreign judgments.

---

e.g. **Example:** In **Kenney v. Order of Moose,** *supra,* §695, the Supreme Court invalidated an Illinois law that provided that local courts could not entertain a suit for wrongful death occurring outside the state, which law the Illinois courts had interpreted as barring enforcement of any judgment rendered by courts of other states in wrongful death actions. The Court held that the statute violated full faith and credit in that it attempted to close Illinois courts to the enforcement of valid judgments rendered by sister states.

(a) Rationale

The rationale is really an extension of **Fauntleroy v. Lum,** *supra,* §815; *i.e.,* F2 must give the same effect to an F1 judgment as it would have received in F1, regardless how much this offends F2 public policy.

3. Defenses Arising If F1 Is a Foreign Country

a. Retaliation [§827]

As discussed *supra,* §736, the Supreme Court in **Hilton v. Guyot** held that res judicata effect need not be given to the judgment of a foreign country if that country refused to give such effect to United States judgments. In such event, the merits of the case could be relitigated completely.

(1) Criticism

Most authorities criticize "retaliation" as a defense on grounds that the United States would be adopting a conflict-of-laws principle designed to coerce other nations into giving conclusive effect to our judgments. [34 Yale L.J. 549 (1924-25)]

(2) Modern view [§828]

Accordingly, the modern trend is to *reject* this "reciprocity" defense.

---

e.g. **Example:** In **Cowans v. Ticonderoga Pulp & Paper Co.,** 219 App. Div. 120 (1927), the Court went against the *Hilton* principle and enforced a Quebec judgment on straight principles of res judicata, even though Quebec permitted relitigation on the merits of United States judgments.

---

b. Other defenses [§829]

Defenses may be permissible against judgments of a foreign country that are not available against judgments rendered by sister states. The doctrine of "comity" under which judgments of foreign countries are recognized (*see supra,* §737) does not carry the same constitutional compulsion as the doctrine of full faith and credit—so that foreign country public policy, tax, and "penal" judgments (among others) may be denied enforcement.

(1) Jurisdiction of foreign court must meet due process standards [§830]

A judgment rendered by the court of a foreign nation will not be enforced if the means used to acquire jurisdiction fall short of federal due process standards; *i.e.,* the foreign nation's jurisdiction must comport with that required in the forum. (*See supra,* §774.)

(2) Uniform Act [§831]

Under the Uniform Foreign Money-Judgments Recognition Act (*see supra,* §739), in effect in a growing number of states, various factors besides lack of jurisdiction may be asserted as defenses to actions to enforce judgments rendered by a foreign country. Such defenses are classified as "discretionary" or "mandatory," as follows:

(a) "Discretionary" defenses [§832]

The Uniform Act lists various defenses that a state *may* recognize to deny enforcement of a foreign country money judgment, including fraud, public policy, and inconvenient forum.

(b) "Mandatory" defenses [§833]

Moreover, the Uniform Act *forbids* recognition of a foreign country money judgment if:

(i) The judgment was rendered under a system that does not provide impartial tribunals or procedures *compatible with due process of law*;

(ii) The court *lacked personal jurisdiction* over the defendant; or

(iii) The court *lacked jurisdiction over the subject matter.*

Note: A judgment that does not meet these standards would violate due process, if rendered in this country. Hence, recognizing such a judgment might itself violate due process.

E. Family Law Judgments

1. General Problems [§834]

The choice-of-law problems relating to dissolution of marriage, annulment, and custody are twofold: (i) what is the *jurisdictional basis* necessary to affect family rights and status; and (ii) assuming an appropriate jurisdictional basis, *which state's law should control* in a case with multistate contacts?

2. Divorce (Dissolution of Marriage)

a. Choice-of-law rule [§835]

In a divorce action, the law of the plaintiff's domicile determines the grounds for divorce; *i.e.,* the *law of the forum* governs (*see* below). [**Toth v. Toth**, 178 A.2d 542 (Conn. 1962); Rest. 2d §285]

(1) Application

It is immaterial that the acts relied on as grounds for divorce would not have been sufficient under the law of the place where committed or the place where the spouses last lived together. [**Stewart v. Stewart**, 180 P. 165 (Idaho 1919)]

(2) Effect—encouragement for "migratory divorces" [§836]

The result of the above rule is that spouses living in states having restrictive grounds for divorce can simply go to states having more liberal grounds and obtain their divorces there—provided that a proper basis for jurisdiction is established (*see* below).

b. Basis for jurisdiction to dissolve marriage [§837]

A court in a divorce case may be asked to provide several different kinds of relief: to declare a dissolution of the marriage, to determine the spouses' property rights, to make orders for the support and maintenance of one spouse and the children, to enjoin transfers of property, to award custody of children, etc. This section treats the court's power to *grant a divorce*—to dissolve the marriage relationship (a status). As discussed *infra*, entirely different jurisdictional requirements and problems are encountered where the court seeks to grant *other or additional relief* (*e.g.*, regarding personal or property rights).

(1) Historical background [§838]

The early decisions disagreed on what (beyond mere residence domicile of the plaintiff spouse) was required to vest a court with the power to grant a valid divorce.

(a) Local domicile of both parties [§839]

Some courts required that both spouses be domiciled locally. [52 Am. Rep. 617]

(b) Matrimonial domicile [§840]

Others accepted the "matrimonial domicile"—the last domicile in which the parties lived together as husband and wife—as sufficient basis for jurisdiction, even if one spouse was no longer in the state when the action was brought. [**Atherton v. Atherton**, 181 U.S. 155 (1901)]

(c) Plaintiff spouse's domicile [§841]

Still other courts recognized domicile of the plaintiff spouse alone if personal jurisdiction was obtained over the defendant spouse or if the plaintiff spouse's separate domicile in the forum was acquired with the consent, or due to the fault (desertion, etc.), of the defendant spouse. [**Haddock v. Haddock**, 201 U.S. 562 (1906)]

(2) Modern rule [§842]

These conflicting positions were resolved by the Supreme Court in **Williams v. North Carolina**, 317 U.S. 287 (1942) (**"Williams #1"**), which held that the *domicile of the plaintiff spouse* alone provided a sufficient basis for divorce jurisdiction. Thus, a divorce granted by any state in which the plaintiff spouse was then domiciled is entitled to full faith and credit in every other state.

(a) Rationale—in rem jurisdiction [§843]

The court reasoned that a divorce action is a proceeding "in rem"; *i.e.*, the plaintiff spouse brings the marital relationship (the res) with her when establishing domicile locally. Having jurisdiction over the res, the local courts can therefore dissolve or otherwise adjudicate questions as to the marital relationship.

1) "Minimum contacts" requirement [§844]

As discussed earlier (*supra*, §173), all assertions of state jurisdiction—including in rem jurisdiction—must now be evaluated according to a single "minimum contacts" standard. However, this does not necessarily mean that the jurisdictional rules governing the adjudication of status are inconsistent with the new standard of fairness. [**Shaffer v. Heitner**, *supra*, §173]

(b) Effect—"ex parte divorces" [§845]

Since domicile of the plaintiff spouse is a valid basis for divorce jurisdiction, it follows that courts in that domicile have the power to grant a divorce ex parte—*i.e., without personal jurisdiction over the defendant spouse.*

1) Note

This is true even where the plaintiff spouse has been enjoined by the courts of the former domicile from proceeding with the divorce suit in the new domicile. [**Keck v. Keck**, 290 N.E.2d 385 (Ill. 1972)—F2 must give full faith and credit to F1 divorce decree (F1's jurisdiction having been established), even though plaintiff violated an F2 injunction in proceeding with the suit in F1]

EXAM TIP   **gilbert**

Note that under the doctrine of "divisible divorce," a divorce can be granted to the plaintiff spouse ex parte—*i.e., without the court having jurisdiction over the other spouse.* This allows, for example, a spouse who cannot find the other spouse to end the marriage. But remember that that is all an ex parte divorce can do—*end the marriage.* The court has no power to order spousal support, divide property, etc., unless it has jurisdiction over the other spouse. (See *infra*, §873.)

---

(3) Is anything less than domicile constitutionally sufficient?

(a) Residence [§846]

Several authorities have urged the substitution of residence (tangible, physical presence in the forum) for the "shadowy yardstick" of domicile as the basis for divorce jurisdiction. [*See* **Williams #1**, *supra*—Rutledge's concurring opinion]

1) State statutes [§847]

Some states have enacted statutes authorizing residence for a specified period as the sole basis for such jurisdiction, regardless of domicile. [**Wheat v. Wheat,** 318 S.W.2d 793 (Ark. 1958)]

a) And note
Under the proposed Uniform Marriage and Divorce Act, 90 days' residence by either spouse would be sufficient basis for jurisdiction to dissolve the marriage. [Rest. 2d §302(a)]

2) Statutes regarding military personnel [§848]
Other state statutes provide that persons in military service who are stationed within the state for a specified period (usually one year) are "conclusively presumed" to be domiciled within the state for purposes of conferring jurisdiction to dissolve the marriage.

a) Note
A few courts have upheld such jurisdiction without such statutes, on the ground that "domicile is not the sole jurisdictional basis for divorce" (at least for those in the service). [**Lauterbach v. Lauterbach,** 392 P.2d 24 (Alaska 1964)]

(b) Place where married [§849]
In New York, courts are authorized to assert divorce jurisdiction as to parties married in New York, regardless of the parties' domicile at the time of divorce. [**David-Zieseniss v. Zieseniss,** 205 Misc. 836 (1954)]

1) Note
New York courts will also recognize Mexico's "quickie" divorces, at least where one of the parties is physically present in Mexico when the decree is granted and the other has submitted to jurisdiction through appearance of local counsel. [**Rosentiel v. Rosentiel,** 16 N.Y.2d 64 (1965)]

(c) Constitutionality? [§850]
The United States Supreme Court has yet to rule on the constitutionality of such state laws. However, the court has never held that domicile of the plaintiff spouse is the *only* sufficient basis for divorce jurisdiction. And in view of the Court's tendency to uphold personal jurisdiction on the basis of "minimum contacts" (*see supra,* §110), it would probably uphold state laws substituting other "contacts" besides domicile as a sufficient basis for divorce jurisdiction.

(d) Comment [§851]

It is not clear what effect the substitution of residence (or some other "contact") for domicile would have on the applicable choice-of-law rule; *i.e.,* would the plaintiff still be limited to the grounds for divorce recognized in her domicile, or would the forum apply its own rules with respect to grounds for divorce? The latter approach might be objectionable since it would encourage the dissolution of marriages on grounds not recognized at the parties' domicile. [*See* **Rosentiel v. Rosentiel,** *supra*—parties were domiciled in New York but went to Mexico and obtained a divorce on grounds not allowed in New York]

(4) Limitations on ex parte divorces [§852]

The very fact that a divorce can be obtained without personal jurisdiction over the defendant spouse [**Williams #1,** *supra*] has led to serious problems, such as migratory divorces in inconvenient forums and the like. In response thereto, certain limitations have been imposed.

(a) Limitation—forum residence requirements [§853]

Plaintiff's domicile must be established in accordance with the law of the forum (*see supra,* §37). Also, most states have established, by statute, some minimum period of actual residence (*e.g.,* six months, one year, etc.) to establish "domicile" for purposes of divorce.

1) Constitutionality [§854]

The Supreme Court has upheld a one-year residence requirement for divorce. Such a requirement does not violate equal protection or a citizen's right of interstate travel (discriminating against newer residents), because it serves two legitimate state interests: (i) insuring that divorce seekers are "genuinely attached" to the state, so that state courts will not become divorce mills for unhappy spouses residing elsewhere; and (ii) providing state divorce decrees with greater protection against collateral attack in other states (*see* below). [**Sosna v. Iowa,** *supra,* §5]

a) But note

The Court has not passed on the validity of durational residence requirements *longer than one year.* Arguably, no legitimate state interest could justify an appreciably longer requirement. [*See* 51 Tex. L. Rev. 585]

(b) Limitation—sufficiency of plaintiff's domicile subject to collateral attack in F2 [§855]

Due to the strong interest of the domicile of the defendant spouse, the determination of the plaintiff's domicile in F1 (and thus the validity of F1 divorce jurisdiction) may be collaterally attacked and reexamined in F2. [**Williams v. North Carolina,** 325 U.S. 226 (1945) (**"Williams #2"**)]

1) Rationale

The holding in *Williams #2* exemplifies the principle that where the defendant has not appeared in the F1 proceedings, F1's findings as to its own jurisdiction may always be reexamined in F2 (*see supra,* §804).

2) Effect

Williams #2 also undermines to some degree the decision in *Williams #1,* which requires that full faith and credit be given to sister states' divorce decrees. And it renders "ex parte divorce proceedings" in F1 subject to the great infirmity that there may always be a subsequent collateral attack on the issue of jurisdiction.

3) Determining sufficiency of plaintiff's domicile in F1 [§856]

The Supreme Court has refrained from establishing any constitutional definition of "domicile" for divorce purposes. Rather, "domicile" is treated as any other jurisdictional fact so that the forum (F2) will usually apply its own standards and concepts in testing the sufficiency of the plaintiff's domicile in F1 (under the doctrine of characterization, *see supra,* §37).

a) Presumption of validity [§857]

However, F1's findings as to the plaintiff's domicile are entitled to a *presumption of validity,* and it would violate full faith and credit for F2 to apply some novel or arbitrarily high standard of "domicile" solely to invalidate out-of-state divorces. [**Williams #2,** *supra*]

b) Distinguish—Uniform Act [§858]

The Uniform Divorce Recognition Act embodies a *conflicting presumption*—that any person domiciled in F2 for at least a year previously, and who resumed residence in F2 within 18 months after departing to F1 to obtain the divorce, was at all times still domiciled in F2; and the same presumption applies to any person who maintained a residence in F2 during the period of time that he was in F1 obtaining the divorce. This presumption offsets any presumption of validity as to the F1 decree. *But note:* The Uniform Act is presently in force in only seven states, and it has been officially withdrawn by the Commissioners on Uniform State Laws.

4) Who may collaterally attack [§859]

A collateral attack in F2 on the validity of the F1 decree ordinarily may be made by *any interested person who is not bound by the F1 decree*—*e.g.,* the defendant spouse (assuming he was not subject to F1 personal jurisdiction), a child or heir in a probate proceeding, or the state in a bigamy prosecution.

5) Persons barred from collateral attack [§860]

Certain individuals will not be allowed to make such an attack. Because of their relationship to the F1 proceedings, they will either be bound by the F1 decree under the doctrine of res judicata or will be equitably estopped to attack it. Thus, even though the F1 divorce is based on defective jurisdiction, it may still be binding against these persons.

a) Plaintiff in F1 [§861]

Whichever spouse obtained the F1 divorce decree is bound thereby under res judicata and cannot collaterally attack it in F2. Thus, the spouse cannot remarry and later seek to annul the marriage on the ground that the F1 divorce was invalid. [**Krause v. Krause**, 282 N.Y. 355 (1940)]

b) Defendant who "participated" in F1 proceeding [§862]

Likewise, a defendant spouse who files a general appearance or otherwise "participates" in the F1 proceedings will be bound by the F1 decree on principles of res judicata, because the matter is then no longer an "ex parte" proceeding; the defendant had a chance to fully litigate all issues of the case, including jurisdiction, and is therefore bound by the F1 judgment, whether the issue of jurisdiction was actually litigated or not. [**Sherrer v. Sherrer**, 334 U.S. 343 (1948)]

1/ What constitutes "participation" [§863]

The Supreme Court has never defined the term "participation," nor set any minimal standards on the issue. Seemingly, all that is required is an appearance that affords the opportunity to raise the jurisdiction issue. [**Cook v. Cook**, 342 U.S. 126 (1951)]

a/ *A general appearance filed by authorized counsel* on behalf of a nonresident defendant spouse has been held sufficient "participation" to bar the defendant from later collaterally attacking the F1 decree. [**Johnson v. Muelberger**, 340 U.S. 581 (1951)]

b/ *But appearances that are sham or are coerced* may be disregarded by the court.

2/ Effect—"collusive divorces" [§864]

Spouses wishing a "quickie" divorce may proceed in a forum that is not the real domicile of either spouse (and which therefore has no divorce jurisdiction), and if both "participate" in the F1 proceeding, the F1 judgment is binding on them under res judicata and cannot be attacked by either of them in subsequent proceedings. The parties thus can effectively "confer jurisdiction" on the F1 court. [**Johnson v. Muelberger,** *supra*]

c) Privies [§865]

Persons who are in "privity" with either of the parties before the F1 court will also be bound by the F1 decree. [**Johnson v. Muelberger,** *supra; and see supra,* §§772-774]

1/ Note

In determining which persons are in "privity" with the parties before the F1 court, the law of F1 applies; *i.e.,* the F1 decree must receive the same effect in F2 as it would have received in F1. [**Johnson v. Muelberger,** *supra*]

2/ Distinguish

States vary in their rules on privity. For example, some courts hold that a child of the divorced parents is "privy" to the F1 decree, and thus barred from attacking it later in a probate proceeding in F2. [**Johnson v. Muelberger,** *supra*] But there are also contrary decisions on this point. [*See, e.g.,* **Lindgren's Estate,** 293 N.Y. 18 (1944)]

d) "Strangers"

1/ Nonappearing spouse [§866]

A defendant spouse not subject to the personal jurisdiction of the F1 court is not bound by res judicata—but may nevertheless be equitably estopped from challenging the F1 decree if he instigated the F1 proceedings (*e.g.,* Husband pays Wife to go to Nevada and get the divorce) or if he has remarried in reliance on the F1 decree, knowing it to be defective. [**Carbulon v. Carbulon,** 293 N.Y. 375 (1944)]

2/ Third parties [§867]

If both spouses are bound by a divorce decree and there is no fraud involved, third persons generally will **not** be permitted to attack the decree.

Example: The Supreme Court refused to permit a second husband to attack his wife's divorce from her first husband where the first husband had appeared and was personally bound by the decree. [**Cook v. Cook,** *supra*] (On the other hand, such an attack would have been permitted had the divorce been ex parte.)

Compare: Even where the divorce is *ex parte*, a third party may be equitably estopped from challenging the decree if he instigated the F1 proceeding. Thus if X induces Wife to divorce Husband and pays all her costs in moving to Nevada and obtaining a divorce there, and X then marries Wife, X will be estopped from later challenging the validity of the F1 divorce decree, in an attempt to claim that his marriage to Wife is invalid. [**Goodloe v. Hawk,** 113 F.2d 753 (D.C. Cir. 1940)]

---

a/ Note

The courts are split as to whether a prospective spouse will be estopped from challenging the F1 divorce merely because she knew of the circumstances casting doubt on the validity of the plaintiff spouse's "domicile" there and nevertheless married the spouse in reliance on the decree. While some courts have invoked an estoppel in such cases [**Dietrich v. Dietrich,** 41 Cal. 2d 497 (1953)], others have not [**Wood v. Wood,** 16 N.Y.2d 64 (1965)].

3/ State [§868]

The state of the spouse's real matrimonial domicile is clearly **not** a party or privy to the proceedings in another state. Thus, the state is not bound by res judicata, nor is there usually any basis for invoking equitable estoppel against it. The state, then, may treat the spouses as still validly married to each other; *i.e.,* the state would not be barred from prosecuting for bigamy either spouse who remarries following the F1 decree. [**Williams #2,** *supra*, §855]

a/ And note

This would probably be true even where the bigamy prosecution is based on the testimony and complaint of the spouse who "procured" the F1 decree or "participated" therein. However, there is little authority on this point.

e) Effect of statutes [§869]

The above rules have been modified by statutes in some states.

1/ Uniform Divorce Recognition Act [§870]

The Act apparently permits *anyone* to collaterally attack a foreign divorce decree. It provides that if both spouses were in fact domiciled locally when the out-of-state divorce was obtained, the divorce "shall be of no force or effect in this state."

a/ But note

It is questionable whether this Act could constitutionally be applied to allow a person who had appeared in the F1 proceedings to collaterally attack the F1 decree in F2. It would seem that under *Sherrer* (*supra,* §862) F2 would be required to hold the decree binding on all persons who "participated" therein. (*See also supra,* §858.)

2/ Distinguish

Some states (*e.g.,* Nevada) simply do not allow any third-party collateral attacks on foreign divorce decrees.

(c) Effect of F2 decree setting aside F1 divorce [§871]

If F2 allows a collateral attack on the F1 decree and determines that the plaintiff was not in fact validly "domiciled" in F1 (so that F1 lacked divorce jurisdiction), F2 will not give full faith and credit to the F1 divorce.

1) Effect of F2 decree outside F2 [§872]

Assuming both spouses were subject to the personal jurisdiction of F2, it would seem that F2's determination (invalidating the F1 divorce) would be res judicata and thus binding on both parties in any further litigation involving the F1 divorce—in F1 or any other state. [*See* **Sutton v. Leib,** 342 U.S. 402 (1952)—dictum to this effect]

a) Comment

Such a result would also be in accord with the principle that as between two inconsistent judgments, the "last in time" prevails (*see supra*, §811).

b) But note

The Supreme Court has declined to decide whether an F1 court is constitutionally bound to recognize an F2 judgment that invalidates an earlier F1 decree. In **Colby v. Colby**, 369 P.2d 1019 (Nev. 1962), Nevada had granted Wife an ex parte divorce, which was declared void in subsequent proceedings in Maryland (where both parties were subject to jurisdiction). Husband then took the Maryland decree to Nevada in an attempt to have Nevada set aside its divorce decree. But Nevada refused to do so, reasoning that its own prior judgment was entitled to as much credit as Maryland's, and the Supreme Court refused certiorari.

c. Basis for jurisdiction as to property or support rights—"divisible divorce" doctrine [§873]

Without personal jurisdiction over the defendant spouse, a court in the plaintiff spouse's domicile may validly dissolve the marriage (marital res, *see* above) but it *cannot grant in personam relief* against the absent spouse—*e.g.*, alimony, support, orders to convey property, etc. In other words, the court may have valid jurisdiction for one purpose (to dissolve the marriage) but not for another (awarding support, etc.). This is known as the doctrine of *"divisible divorce."* [**Estin v. Estin**, 334 U.S. 541 (1948); *and see infra*, §§877-878]

(1) Jurisdiction as to support obligations

(a) Personal jurisdiction over obligor spouse required [§874]

As indicated above, the court generally must have personal jurisdiction over the defendant spouse in order to impose an enforceable alimony or support obligation. [**Armstrong v. Armstrong**, 350 U.S. 568 (1956)]

1) Basis of personal jurisdiction [§875]

Personal jurisdiction may be based on a valid application of an appropriate forum long arm statute. For example, several statutes provide that jurisdiction may be exercised over a nonresident spouse if the forum was the matrimonial domicile (*see supra*, §164). [73 Colum. L. Rev. 289 (1973)]

2) Continuing jurisdiction [§876]

Once personal jurisdiction is obtained, it "continues" as long as the action is pending—enabling a court in a domestic relations case to modify or increase support years later without new personal service on the defendant spouse. (*See* doctrine of "continuing jurisdiction," *supra*, §§217-219.) [**Varone v. Varone,** *supra*, §787]

(b) Rights of obligee spouse cannot be affected without personal jurisdiction [§877]

Similarly, a divorce decree obtained by one spouse without personal jurisdiction over the other spouse may not be effective to terminate a spouse's duty to support the other. [**Estin v. Estin,** *supra*]

Example: In *Estin,* Husband had been ordered by a New York court (having personal jurisdiction over him) to make monthly payments to Wife for separate maintenance. Husband then went to Nevada and obtained an ex parte divorce decree that purported to terminate any future support obligation to Wife. In subsequent proceedings in New York, Husband asserted that the Nevada decree freed him from any further obligation to Wife. However, the Supreme Court held that the Nevada decree was "divisible": It was entitled to full faith and credit in New York insofar as it terminated the marital status; but it was ineffective to cut off Wife's support rights because she was not subject to personal jurisdiction in the Nevada court.

---

1) Note—doctrine extended [§878]

The *Estin* doctrine has been extended to protect an absent wife from ex parte determinations of her rights—even when there was no prior support order, and even where the prior ex parte divorce purported to cut off any alimony obligation to the wife.

Example: In **Vanderbilt v. Vanderbilt,** 354 U.S. 416 (1957), a married couple had been domiciled in California. When they separated, Wife moved to New York, while Husband moved to Nevada where he obtained an ex parte divorce. Later, Wife sued Husband for support in New York. The Supreme Court held that the Nevada decree had no effect on Wife's right to alimony (a "personal" right) because she was not subject to personal jurisdiction of that court. Consequently, alimony could be granted by New York after the marriage had been effectively terminated by the Nevada ex parte decree.

---

a)   But note

In *Vanderbilt, supra,* a New York statute expressly authorized alimony awards after the parties had been divorced. Not all states have such statutes. [*See* **Gosselin v. Gosselin,** 294 N.E.2d 555 (Mass. 1973)] And some states that would otherwise allow alimony under such circumstances might be unwilling to impose that obligation against a resident husband in favor of a nonresident wife. In those states, a wife's support rights *could* be jeopardized by an ex parte decree. [**Estin v. Estin,** *supra*]

(2)   Jurisdiction as to property rights

(a)   In personam jurisdiction gives court power to order conveyances of property anywhere [§879]

If the court has personal jurisdiction over *both* spouses, it can make a *complete disposition* of the spouses' property claims, including assets in other states; *i.e.,* it can order either spouse to make whatever conveyances of title are required, and enforce such orders by contempt proceedings if necessary. (As to whether an F1 decree by itself is effective as to land in F2, *see supra,* §783.)

(b)   In rem or quasi in rem jurisdiction [§880]

Without personal jurisdiction over the defendant spouse, however, a local court can exercise in rem or quasi in rem jurisdiction as to the defendant's local property only if the forum state is shown to have sufficient "minimum contact" with the defendant and the subject of the litigation.

(c)   Effect of ex parte divorce on property rights [§881]

Remember that even without personal jurisdiction over the defendant spouse, an ex parte divorce is entitled to full faith and credit insofar as it terminates the marriage. [**Williams #1,** *supra,* §852] Hence, if Wife's property rights depend on her being married to Husband (*i.e.,* being his "wife" or "widow"), the ex parte divorce will effectively cut off such rights. [**Simons v. Miami Beach First National Bank,** 381 U.S. 81 (1965)]

Example: Husband obtained an ex parte divorce from Wife and later died. Wife was held not entitled to dower rights in Husband's property because she was not his "wife" at the time of death (a prerequisite to dower). [**Simons v. Miami Beach First National Bank,** *supra*]

---

(3) Impact [§882]

Other than the limited relief available through in rem or quasi in rem jurisdiction, the court in divorce proceedings must have personal jurisdiction over the defendant spouse in order to grant effective remedies as to support and property rights. This has always been a problem where the defendant flees the state. Under modern law, however, the problem is being alleviated.

(a) UIFSA [§883]

First of all, the Uniform Interstate Family Support Act ("UIFSA") provides the means to enforce support obligations to the other spouse and children, even though the obligor spouse is out of state and not subject to the personal jurisdiction of the courts of the obligee spouse or child's domicile (*see supra*, §750).

(b) Long arm statutes [§884]

Furthermore, several states have enacted long arm statutes authorizing the exercise of personal jurisdiction in divorce or separate maintenance actions against a nonresident spouse whose last matrimonial domicile was within the state (*see supra*, §164).

1) Constitutionality [§885]

The constitutionality of such statutes has not been finally determined. However, marital domicile would seem to have a sufficient "nexus" with a defendant spouse who has left the state, that the exercise of personal jurisdiction over the defendant in actions related to the marriage would not offend "traditional notions of fair play and substantial justice." (*See supra*, §111.)

3. Annulment [§886]

An annulment is a judicial declaration that the marriage itself was ***never valid*** because of factors existing at the time of the marriage ceremony.

a. Applicable choice-of-law rule [§887]

Annulment actions are governed by the law that would determine the validity of the marriage for any other purpose (*see supra*, §587)—*i.e.,* the law of the place of celebration, except where the marriage is contrary to the "laws of nature" or otherwise contravenes some overriding policy of the parties' domicile.

b. Basis for jurisdiction to annul marriage [§888]

There is disagreement as to what factors are required to give a court jurisdiction to annul a marriage.

(1) Place of celebration plus personal jurisdiction [§889]

The early cases held that since annulments are based on factors existing at the time of marriage, *only the place of celebration* should have the power to determine the validity of the marriage (since it "brought the marriage into existence")—and then *only if it had personal jurisdiction over both spouses*. This is still the law in a number of states today. [**Titus v. Titus,** 174 S.E. 874 (W. Va. 1934); Rest. 2d §76(b)]

(2) Domicile of plaintiff spouse alone [§890]

However, many states hold that the *domicile of the plaintiff spouse alone* is a sufficient basis for jurisdiction to annul a marriage—allowing ex parte annulments, the same as ex parte divorces. [**Roth v. Roth,** 104 Ill. 35 (1882); Rest. 2d §76(a)]

(a) Rationale

This result is based on analogies to the divorce cases; *i.e.,* plaintiff spouse brings the marital relationship (a res) with her when entering the state and establishing domicile therein.

(b) Criticism

However, it has been argued that no analogies should be drawn to divorce cases because the theory of an annulment is that there never was a valid marriage, and hence there was never a marital res for plaintiff to bring into the state.

(3) Personal jurisdiction alone [§891]

A few courts have allowed mere *residence of or appearance by the plaintiff spouse* and *personal service on the defendant* as a sufficient basis for jurisdiction to annul—*i.e.,* treating annulment as a transitory, in personam action. [**Avakian v. Avakian,** 60 A. 521 (N.J. 1905)]

(a) Rationale

An annulment differs conceptually from a divorce in that a divorce terminates a legal status (and hence some sort of jurisdiction over that status is required), whereas an annulment establishes that no such status ever existed. Consequently, simple in personam jurisdiction should be sufficient in the latter case. [**Whealton v. Whealton,** 67 Cal. 2d 656 (1967)]

4. Judicial Separation—"Limited Divorce" and Separate Maintenance [§892]

A limited divorce is a judicial decree that relieves the petitioning spouse from the rights and duties of cohabitation but *does not terminate* the marital status. Provisions for support and maintenance may also be involved.

a. Applicable choice-of-law rule [§893]

The forum (usually the domicile of plaintiff) normally applies its own law with respect to grounds for judicial separation, which are usually the same as those for divorce.

b. Basis for jurisdiction

(1) As to support or property rights [§894]

Where the plaintiff seeks to establish support or maintenance obligations on the part of the defendant spouse, *personal jurisdiction over the defendant* is necessary.

(a) Rationale

As already discussed, rights and duties in "property" (support) cannot be affected without personal jurisdiction over the parties; whereas rights and duties in "status" may be affected without such jurisdiction. [*See* **Estin v. Estin,** *supra,* §877]

(2) As to cohabitation [§895]

Where only the rights and duties of cohabitation are at issue, there is a split of authority as to the requisite basis for jurisdiction:

(a) Early view [§896]

The early view, still followed in some jurisdictions, was that a decree of judicial separation did not go to "status" but merely affected personal rights and duties between two parties. Accordingly, personal jurisdiction over both parties was required. [**Pettis v. Pettis,** 101 A. 13 (Conn. 1917)]

(b) Modern view [§897]

However, this rule has been rejected in many jurisdictions. Although there is no current authority from the United States Supreme Court, it seems probable that the Court today would uphold domicile of the plaintiff spouse (or other "contacts") alone as a sufficient basis for jurisdiction. Earlier decisions of the Court analogized separation cases to divorce cases with respect to the basis for jurisdiction. [**Thompson v. Thompson,** 226 U.S. 551 (1913); *see* Rest. 2d §75(b)]

5. Custody of Children

a. Choice-of-law rule [§898]

There are really *no choice-of-law rules* here. Courts will apply whatever law they feel best serves the *interests and welfare* of the child.

b. Basis for jurisdiction

(1) Early view [§899]

Early cases held that domicile of the child within the state was the only sufficient basis for jurisdiction in custody cases. [**State *ex rel.* Larson v. Larson,** 252 N.W. 329 (Minn. 1934)]

(a) Criticism

A child's "domicile" is often difficult to determine (*see supra*, §§30-33), and this approach can therefore lead to unfair results.

(2) Modern view [§900]

More than half the states have now adopted the Uniform Child Custody Jurisdiction and Enforcement Act ("UCCJEA"), which replaces the earlier Uniform Child Custody Jurisdiction Act ("UCCJA"). Unlike the UCCJA, the UCCJEA accords primary jurisdiction to make an initial custody determination to the *"home state,"* defined as the state "in which a child lived with a parent or a person acting as a parent for at least six consecutive months immediately before the commencement of a child-custody proceeding." (If a child is less than six months old, the home state is the state in which the child lived "from birth" with any of the persons mentioned above.) By giving priority to the home state, the UCCJEA is in conformity with the earlier federal Parental Kidnapping Prevention Act ("PKPA"), which had elevated the home state to priority over states that had a "significant connection" with the custody dispute. The PKPA required that full faith and credit be given to the home state's determinations, and that recognition be accorded to the contacts state only if there is no home state. (*See supra*, §758.) Thus, under both the PKPA and the UCCJEA, other states are required to *defer to the home state's jurisdiction*—both for the initial award and for later modifications (as long as the "home state" retains that status and does not relinquish jurisdiction). (*See supra*, §758.)

(3) Constitutional requirements [§901]

The Supreme Court has not ruled clearly on what constitutes a sufficient basis for jurisdiction to determine custody. In fact, its decision in **May v. Anderson,** 345 U.S. 528 (1953), merely served to confuse the matter. There was no majority opinion, and the justices merely set forth various differing views:

(a) Personal jurisdiction [§902]

Four justices took the position that child custody proceedings are primarily disputes between the parents concerning custody of the child, which is an in personam right. Thus, personal jurisdiction over both parents was deemed to be the requisite basis for jurisdiction, the domicile of the child being irrelevant.

1) Criticism

This position encourages "child snatching" by the parent out of custody who can then safely retain the child as long as she can avoid being personally served.

(b) No personal jurisdiction [§903]

Three of the justices took the position that the prime concern in child custody proceedings should be the welfare of the child. This would justify treating a child within the state as a res and allowing the state in which the child is domiciled or physically present to deal with custody without personal jurisdiction over the parents.

c. Requirement of notice and hearing [§904]

Regardless of the basis for jurisdiction, the relationship between parent and child (legitimate or otherwise) is protected by due process guarantees. Hence, the natural parent must be afforded *notice and a hearing* in any proceedings affecting custody of the child. [**Stanley v. Illinois**, 405 U.S. 645 (1972)—unwed father entitled to notice and hearing on his fitness as a parent, in determining custody of child on death of mother]

d. Continuance of jurisdiction [§905]

Custody is an area in which the doctrine of "continuing jurisdiction" (*see supra*, §217) is put to the greatest test; *i.e.,* does a court have the power to modify a custody award after the child has been taken from the state? Most courts hold that the "continuing jurisdiction" rule applies and assert that they do have such power, even though the child is no longer within the state. [**Berlin v. Berlin**, *supra*, §217]

e. Effect of F1 custody decree in F2 [§906]

The enforceability of an F1 custody decree in subsequent custody proceedings in F2, with regard to whether F2 can modify or disregard the prior determination, is now governed by the PKPA, and in states that have enacted it, by the UCCJEA (*see supra*, §758).

6. Paternity Actions [§907]

An action to establish the paternity of a child is ordinarily treated as in personam in nature, since the usual purpose of the proceeding is to subject the alleged father to a support obligation. Accordingly, personal jurisdiction over the father is required. [**Hartford v. Superior Court**, *supra*, §617]

SUFFICIENT JURISDICTIONAL BASES FOR FAMILY LAW JUDGMENTS

gilbert

TYPE OF CASE	BASIS FOR JURISDICTION
DIVORCE	
• **To grant a divorce**	*Domicile of plaintiff spouse* (in some states residence is enough) + *in most states residence for a certain period* (generally 6 months - 1 year)
• **To grant support**	*Personal jurisdiction over defendant spouse* by valid long arm statute
• **To divide property**	*Personal jurisdiction over both parties* (see above) or *in rem* or *quasi in rem jurisdiction over defendant spouse's local property* (must be minimum contacts with defendant and local property)
ANNULMENT	Differing views: (i) *domicile of plaintiff spouse;* (ii) *place of celebration + personal service on both spouses;* or (iii) *residence or appearance of plaintiff spouse + personal service on defendant*
LIMITED DIVORCE OR SEPARATE MAINTENANCE	
• **To grant support or divide property**	*Personal jurisdiction over defendant spouse*
• **To determine rights and duties of cohabitation**	*Personal jurisdiction over both spouses,* or under modern view, *domicile of plaintiff spouse*
CHILD CUSTODY	Under the UCCJEA, the *home state of the child*
PATERNITY	*Personal jurisdiction over alleged father*

Review Questions
and Answers

Review Questions

DOMICILE

1. Hal obtains a new job in State B, rents an apartment there, and returns home to State A to help his family pack and move. While en route to State B, the family is killed in an auto accident in State C. In probate proceedings, where would Hal's wife, Winnie, be held domiciled? _____

2. Assume instead that Hal obtains a new job in State B and asks Winnie to join him there, but she refuses, insisting that she does not want to leave her career in State A. She agrees to spend her vacations with Hal in State B. Where is Winnie domiciled? _____

3. A family has been domiciled in State A. Father obtains new employment and moves to State B. Son, a minor, remains in State A to finish the school year. Is Son domiciled in State B? _____

4. Same facts as in previous question, except that Son has attained majority when Father moves. Son remains in State A, and thereafter is drafted into the army and stationed in State C. Where is Son domiciled? _____

JURISDICTION

5. In which of the following actions is in personam jurisdiction *not* required? _____

   (A) Plaintiff sues Defendant for personal injuries.

   (B) Plaintiff sues Defendant for conversion of personal property.

   (C) Plaintiff sues Defendant for trespass to real property.

   (D) Wife sues Husband for spousal and child support.

   (E) Plaintiff sues Defendant for an injunction against continuing trespass on land in another state.

   (F) Vendor sues to require Purchaser to pay the purchase price for land in a foreign jurisdiction.

   (G) Purchaser sues to compel Vendor to execute and deliver a deed to property in a foreign jurisdiction.

(H)   Vendor sues Purchaser to quiet title to local land.

(I)   State sues Defendant to condemn local property.

(J)   Plaintiff sues Defendant for payment of a promissory note.

6.   First Heartless Bank sues to foreclose a mortgage on land in the forum state. Debtor (the mortgagor) is a nonresident and is not subject to personal jurisdiction. Can a forum court grant a decree foreclosing the mortgage and grant a deficiency judgment against Debtor?

7.   Lotta Landowner files suit in State A for damages caused by Terry Trespasser to Lotta's real estate located in State B. Does the State A court have subject matter jurisdiction?

8.   Will the following types of personal service generally be upheld as valid bases for in personam jurisdiction over a nonresident individual defendant?

a.   Defendant is served with process in the forum state while on vacation, being neither a resident nor a domiciliary of the state.

b.   Defendant is served with process while on an airplane flying five miles above the forum state, but which did not take off from or land in the forum state.

c.   Defendant is served with process in the forum state by Plaintiff, after Plaintiff—secretly intending to serve Defendant—had invited him to the forum state, ostensibly to try to resolve their differences without legal action.

d.   Defendant is served within the forum state while en route to testify voluntarily (not under subpoena) as a witness in a civil trial.

9.   Plaintiff and Defendant are both domiciled in the forum state. Plaintiff sues for damages, leaving copies of the complaint with Defendant's wife, pursuant to a forum statute that provides that a complaint may be either served on a defendant personally or left with any person of suitable age at the defendant's residence. Does the statute violate Defendant's due process rights?

10.   Danielle Touriste is domiciled in State A, but is touring Europe for a year. If a suit against Danielle is filed in State A during her absence, would the court have a valid basis for personal jurisdiction over her?

11.   A nonresident defendant who sends an attorney to represent him in an action, but who himself never personally appears, may not thereafter collaterally attack the judgment by alleging a lack of jurisdiction. True or false?

12. A forum statute provides: "Any foreign corporation doing business in this state is hereby required to appoint a resident of this state as its agent for receipt of process in any action brought against it in the courts of this state." XYZ Co., a foreign corporation, is doing business locally but has never appointed a local agent for receipt of process.

    a.   The statute is unconstitutional as an unreasonable burden on XYZ's right to engage in interstate commerce. True or false?   _____

    b.   The fact that XYZ failed to appoint a local agent for service of process effectively prevents courts from asserting personal jurisdiction over XYZ. True or false?   _____

    c.   The forum courts would probably exercise jurisdiction over XYZ only on causes of action arising from the business done by XYZ within the state. True or false?   _____

13. Which of the following factors would be *irrelevant* in determining whether maintenance of jurisdiction in local courts over a foreign corporation can be sustained under the *International Shoe* standard?   _____

    (A)   The corporation incorporated in another state.

    (B)   Witnesses reside in another state.

    (C)   The cause of action arose in another state.

    (D)   The corporation maintains no office, personnel, or property in the forum state.

    (E)   The corporation is not licensed to do business in the forum state.

    (F)   "Fair play and substantial justice."

    (G)   The corporation did not *purposefully* act so as to engage in business in the forum state.

14. The *International Shoe* standard for personal jurisdiction applies only to foreign corporations and not to nonresident individuals. True or false?   _____

15. Plaintiff has funds on deposit in Bank in State A. Plaintiff moves from State A to State B, and Bank thereafter sends all its statements to Plaintiff in State B, and receives correspondence and deposits from him in State B. On these facts alone, Bank is *not* subject to personal jurisdiction in State B. True or false?   _____

16. A forum statute provides that "all foreign corporations doing business within the state" are subject to the personal jurisdiction of local courts. XYZ Co., a foreign

corporation, is involved in a single, isolated business transaction with a local resident. Suit follows in local courts. Which of the following statements are true? _____

(A) Whether the statute applies to a single transaction is, first of all, a question of statutory construction by local courts.

(B) If local courts have construed the statute to apply even to an isolated business transaction, the statute would be unconstitutional on its face as violating the Fourteenth Amendment's Due Process Clause.

(C) The ultimate test of the statute's constitutionality is whether its application in the present case would "offend traditional notions of fair play and substantial justice."

(D) XYZ would be subject to suit locally on any and all causes of action—whether or not related to the isolated business transaction that occurred in the forum.

17. In the absence of statute, state courts have no inherent power over persons outside the state. True or false? _____

18. Pardner and Deadwood each claim ownership of a herd of cattle. The cattle are being shipped to market. Pardner files a quiet title action in the forum state (where Deadwood is not subject to personal jurisdiction), and causes a court seizure order to be levied on the herd of cattle. Is the presence of cattle in the state (even though they are only passing through) a sufficient basis for jurisdiction in a quiet title action? _____

19. Purchaser and Seller enter into a contract for the purchase/sale of Seller's home in the forum state. Before the closing, the estranged wife of Seller makes a claim to the property. Purchaser then reneges, and Seller sues Purchaser. Neither Purchaser nor Seller's wife is subject to personal jurisdiction in the forum. Can the forum grant *any* relief to Seller? _____

20. Aldo executes a *negotiable* promissory note to Bahar in California. Bahar takes the note to New York, where she indorses and delivers it to her Bank. Later, a dispute arises between Bahar and Bank, and she demands the note back but Bank refuses. Bahar thereupon returns to California and causes a garnishment to be levied on Aldo, attaching all monies owed under the note. Can the California court decide, without personal jurisdiction over Bank, whether the money is payable to Bahar or Bank? _____

21. Augustus owes Brutus $1,000. Brutus owes Cassius $1,500. While Augustus is present in State V, Cassius files suit there against Brutus and causes a garnishment to be levied on Augustus, attaching the $1,000 debt owed to Brutus. Brutus is not otherwise subject to the court's personal jurisdiction. Is the garnishment levied on Augustus a valid basis for State V's exercise of quasi in rem jurisdiction with respect to Cassius's claim against Brutus? _____

22. A court's "competence" is ultimately determined by federal constitutional standards. True or false? _____

23. A court's subject matter jurisdiction is determined primarily by local statutes, rather than by rules of federal constitutional law. True or false? _____

24. Filing an action in the wrong court may involve improper venue, but is never a jurisdictional defect. True or false? _____

25. State A initiates condemnation proceedings against Blackacre, which is owned by D. Procedural due process is satisfied if: _____

    (A) D resides on Blackacre and the state mails the summons and complaint to him by registered mail.

    (B) D does not reside on Blackacre but does live in the same city, and the state posts the summons and complaint on the property.

    (C) D resides outside the state and notice is published in the local newspaper.

    (D) D is given whatever form of notice is reasonable under the circumstances.

26. In an action for damages against a nonresident motorist, the forum state requires personal service of pleadings on a state official. Which of the following statements is true? _____

    (A) The statute is unconstitutional if it does not *also* require the state official to communicate notice of the action to the nonresident defendant.

    (B) If the nonresident's out-of-state address is known, it is sufficient if he is notified by personal delivery of pleadings, by registered mail, or by publication of summons in a newspaper in the community in which he lives.

    (C) The form of notice to be given to the nonresident is that required by the laws of the state in which the nonresident resides.

27. Bessie Businessperson purchases a machine in California from a sales representative of Machine Co., a New York corporation maintaining its principal office in New York. A provision of the installment contract provides that in the event of default, Bessie consents to service of process by delivery to John Jones in New York. Bessie has never met John (who in fact is an employee in the office of Machine Co.'s attorney). Machine Co. brings suit in New York, and serves John, who then notifies Bessie. Which of the following statements is true? _____

    (A) The New York court would have to dismiss the action because John Jones is not a bona fide agent or employee of Bessie Businessperson.

    (B) The New York court would have no personal jurisdiction because the contract did not actually require John Jones to notify Bessie Businessperson.

(C) The New York court probably would have no personal jurisdiction if John Jones had neglected to notify Bessie Businessperson.

(D) Assuming jurisdiction is established, if the contract contained a cognovit, New York would refuse to enforce it, as a matter of law.

28. A nonresident individual who is served with process while in the forum state, in a lawsuit having no other "contact" with that state, would be best advised to (choose one of the following):

(A) Make a special appearance.

(B) Make a limited appearance.

(C) Move to dismiss on the ground of forum non conveniens.

(D) Move to dismiss for lack of jurisdiction.

29. Pauline, a Nevada resident, brings an action in California against D Corp., a Delaware corporation, for damages caused by a fire that occurred in Nevada allegedly through D Corp.'s negligence.

a. Assuming D Corp. is subject to personal jurisdiction in California, on what ground can D Corp. best oppose the maintenance of the action in California courts?

b. Which of the following facts should the court consider in ruling on D Corp.'s motion?

(A) Costs and expenses to each party of litigating in California.

(B) Whether D Corp. is amenable to suit in Nevada.

(C) The convenience of witnesses.

(D) Whether court calendars in California are congested.

(E) Whether it will be necessary for jurors physically to inspect the damaged property.

c. The fact that Pauline chose to file the action in California is entitled to *great* weight in ruling on D Corp.'s motion. True or false?

d. If D Corp.'s motion is granted, what action will the California court take?

e. If the action had been filed in *federal* court, it could be transferred to any other federal district court in which it could have been filed originally, and on a *lesser* showing of inconvenience to the parties and witnesses. True or false?

f. If transferred from the federal district court in California to the federal district court in Nevada, the transferee court would apply Nevada's *choice-of-law* rules in the case, rather than California's choice-of-law rules. True or false? _____

30. As long as there are "minimum contacts," due process is satisfied, and it is immaterial whether assertion of jurisdiction over a foreign corporation would impose any "burden" on interstate commerce. True or false? _____

31. State A has a statute that provides that all claims arising out of auto accidents within the state must be referred to a special tribunal and cannot be litigated in other courts or in any other state. If P has an auto accident in State A, but files suit thereon in State B, the State B court must give full faith and credit to the laws of the state where the accident occurred (State A), and therefore must dismiss P's action. True or false? _____

RENVOI

32. Courts are more apt to apply the "whole" law of the other state where the choice-of-law rule is rigid—*e.g.*, where the issue is one of title to land, and the other state is the situs of the land. True or false? _____

33. Having decided to apply the law of some other state or country, most American courts look only to the internal rules of the other state or country and pay no attention to its conflicts rules. True or false? _____

34. If uniformity of decisions is the only consideration, the "whole renvoi" position would be most likely to achieve that end. True or false? _____

CHOICE-OF-LAW APPROACHES

35. Current choice-of-law approaches recognize that legal rights always arise under the law of some particular jurisdiction and follow the individuals involved wherever they go so that the forum must always identify the jurisdiction where the cause of action arose and apply its laws. True or false? _____

36. Under the Second Restatement "most significant relationship" approach, courts isolate the "contacts" that occur in each state, and then make reference to the law of the state in which the "balance (gravity) of contacts" occurs. True or false? _____

37. Under the "governmental interest" approach, the forum court will always advance its own governmental interests and hence apply its own law—over the law of any other state—unless it is a "disinterested" forum, in which case reference to another state's law is proper. True or false? _____

38. Under the "governmental interest" approach, the forum court will concern itself primarily with the policies behind the conflicting rules of law. True or false? _____

39. With respect to determining whether a guest statute should be applied to bar an injured guest's claims against the driver of the car in which he is riding—

    a.   The traditional "vested rights" approach is to look to the law of the place where the parties were domiciled when their ride commenced. True or false?   _____

    b.   The forum could, if it chose, simply apply its own law in these cases, as long as it had some contact with the parties or occurrence. True or false?   _____

    c.   If there was a guest statute in effect where the accident occurred, but no such statute where the parties were domiciled, this would be a "false problem" case under the "governmental interest" approach, and the forum should apply the law of the parties' domicile as that of the only interested state. True or false?   _____

    d.   Under the facts stated in the previous paragraph, it should make no difference whether the litigation occurs at the place of the accident, the place where the parties were domiciled, or in some third state. True or false?   _____

40. Amelia, a resident of State A, was vacationing in State B when she was injured in an automobile accident with Chauncey, a resident of State C. Suit is brought in State B. An issue is raised as to what law the forum should apply in determining whether Chauncey's conduct was negligent.

    a.   This is a question of "procedure," and the forum always applies its own procedural rules. True or false?   _____

    b.   Under the "vested rights" approach, the first step would be to characterize the problem as a "torts" problem; then look to the law of the place of "wrong" (*i.e.,* injury). True or false?   _____

    c.   Under the Second Restatement approach, the law of the place of wrong is applied in personal injury cases **unless** some other state has a more significant relationship to the parties or the occurrence. True or false?   _____

    d.   If Chauncey's conduct was privileged where he acted (in State B), this would be an absolute defense to the application of any other state's law under the modern approaches. True or false?   _____

41. Lewis and Clark enter into a contract that states that all issues arising thereunder shall be decided by the law of State X. Neither party resides in State X.

    a.   The designation of X law as controlling will not be given effect if suit is filed outside State X, because jurisdiction "springs from the law." True or false?   _____

    b.   The parties' agreement that the laws of State X shall govern the interpretation of their contract will generally be respected. True or false?   _____

c. The parties' designation of State X law as controlling would not be given effect if it violated some "fundamental" policy of the state in which the parties were domiciled. True or false? _____

d. If the contract called for interest payments which were lawful under the law of State X, but usurious under the law of the state in which the parties were domiciled, the parties' designation of X law should be invalid. True or false? _____

42. Korngrower purchases a tractor from a Butterfly dealer in State A, for use on Korngrower's farm in State B. Later, Korngrower sues to recover her money, claiming the tractor does not work properly.

a. Under the traditional "vested rights" approach, the court should apply the law of the place where the contract was "made" (State A). True or false? _____

b. Under the Second Restatement approach, in determining the state of the "most significant relationship" it would be material whether the dealer made delivery of the tractor to Korngrower in State B, or otherwise knew it was to be used there. True or false? _____

c. Under the "governmental interest" approach, if the lawsuit was filed in any state other than State A or State B, the state of filing would probably deem itself a "disinterested forum." True or false? _____

d. If, instead of suing for her money, Korngrower had made a *gift* of the tractor to Soyman, and later tried to revoke her gift and get the tractor back, the court would probably apply the law of the place where the tractor was when the gift was made. True or false? _____

43. P and D, domiciled in State A, orally agree on a two-year lease of land located in State B. Suit is filed in State A to enforce this lease; D raises the Statute of Frauds as a defense.

a. The enforceability of such a lease is a "property" issue to be determined by the law of the situs. True or false? _____

b. Traditionally, the forum always applied its own Statute of Frauds if the forum's statute was worded, "No action shall be brought . . ." on an oral contract. True or false? _____

c. Under modern approaches, it is proper to consider whether either state has an interest in upholding the oral agreement, as well as reasonable party expectations. True or false? _____

44. Vendor executes and delivers to Purchaser, in State X, a deed to land located in State Y. State Y has a statute requiring that the delivery of the deed be witnessed,

but this was not done (nor was it required under State X law). Litigation concerning the validity of the deed arises in State Z.

a. The validity of a deed is determined by the law of the place of making, and since it was executed and delivered in accordance with State X law, it is sufficient although unwitnessed. True or false? _____

b. Modern approaches have almost uniformly rejected the law of the situs in choice-of-law issues involving land. True or false? _____

c. If the situs (Y) had a law validating deeds executed and delivered in compliance with the law of the place where executed, the forum (Z) would (under Restatement approaches) apply the "whole law" of Y, and hence validate the deed. True or false? _____

d. If Purchaser had died intestate, and the question was which of his heirs was entitled to his interest in the property, reference would be made to the law of his domicile at the time of death. True or false? _____

45. Harry and Wanda marry and live in State A (which is not a community property state) for many years. Later, they move to State B, a community property state. Wanda now sues for divorce in State B.

a. Whether Wanda has any marital interest in Harry's farm in State A is determined solely by the law of the situs (State A). True or false? _____

b. Whether Wanda has any marital interest in Harry's sportscar depends on the law of the spouses' domicile at the time of acquisition. True or false? _____

c. If Harry died after the divorce, and the question arose whether the divorce revoked his earlier will leaving everything to Wanda, the forum would probably apply the law of Harry's domicile at the time he executed the will. True or false? _____

46. Decedent dies leaving property in State A and State B. An administrator is appointed in each state. Administrator A sues Debtor in State A to collect money due Decedent.

a. If A wins the lawsuit, but is unable to collect from Debtor, Administrator B can sue Debtor in State B on the same debt in order to collect. True or false? _____

b. If A loses the lawsuit against Debtor, in most cases there is no bar to Administrator B's suing Debtor again on the same debt in State B. True or false? _____

c. The result in the previous paragraph would be different if A had been an executor (instead of an administrator) and had been appointed to act in both states. True or false? _____

47. Dorothy died while domiciled in State A, owning real property in State B, stock certificates held in escrow in State C, and cash in various banks in States A, B, and C. Is all such property subject to probate administration in State A, where Dorothy was domiciled?

48. Goodworker, a resident of State A, is employed there by Contractor but is sent to State B temporarily to work on a construction project. Goodworker is injured while in State B.

   a.   If Goodworker returns home and files a workers' compensation claim, the State A workers' compensation commission would have no authority to make an award for injuries sustained outside the state. True or false?

   b.   If Goodworker filed a claim with the State A commission, it would make an award according to whatever level of compensation is authorized under State B's compensation laws. True or false?

   c.   If the State A commission made an award according to its laws, it would be possible for Goodworker to go back to State B and file another claim there for any higher level of compensation provided by State B law. True or false?

49. Romeo and Juliet, both age 18, reside in State A, which requires parental consent to marriage if the parties are under age 21. State B permits marriage of 18-year-olds without such consent. The couple go to State B, get married there, and return to live in State A.

   a.   If Juliet later seeks an annulment in State A, the court would probably uphold the marriage. True or false?

   b.   If both spouses were under age 18, the State A court would be less likely to invalidate the marriage in annulment proceedings. True or false?

   c.   If Juliet had been under age, but she died (before any annulment), Romeo would probably be allowed to inherit as her intestate heir. True or false?

TRADITIONAL DEFENSES TO APPLICATION OF FOREIGN LAW

50. Heartbroken sues Cad for "alienation of affections" based on conduct that occurred in F2, involving parties who were at all times domiciled there. A cause of action for alienation of affections is allowed under F2 law, but is not allowed under F1 law.

   a.   The Full Faith and Credit Clause (requiring each state to give "full faith and credit" to the "public acts, records and proceedings" of sister states) requires F1 to enforce the cause of action, regardless of its own policy with regard thereto. True or false?

b.	F1 should enforce the cause of action unless it violates some "fundamental principle and deep-rooted tradition" of F1 law. True or false? _____

c.	Under modern approaches, forum public policy may be taken into account in *choosing* which law to apply rather than invoking it as a defense to the application of foreign law. True or false? _____

d.	If Heartbroken had obtained a judgment on the above cause of action in F2, F1 would be required to enforce the F2 judgment, without regard to the nature of the action involved. True or false? _____

51.	Which, if any, of the following would be valid reasons for the forum (F1) to refuse application of F2 law? _____

(A)	The F2 law is part of a statute that expressly provides that any suit to enforce rights thereunder must be litigated in F2 and not elsewhere.

(B)	The cause of action sued upon is for a wrongful death which occurred in F2, and the F2 wrongful death statute provides an arbitrary amount of damages ($50,000) for every wrongful death.

(C)	The cause of action sued upon is for a penalty for an offense against the public (*e.g.*, $50,000 for causing a public nuisance in F2).

(D)	The cause of action sued upon is for taxes owed to F2.

52.	A court would probably apply its own local rules of law, as "procedural," to which of the following issues? _____

(A)	Whether the summons and complaint have been properly served.

(B)	What constitutes a proper pleading of defensive matter.

(C)	The admissibility of hearsay evidence.

(D)	Whether testimony privileged under the law of another state, but not under forum law, is admissible.

(E)	Presumptions shifting the burden of proof from one party to another.

(F)	The measure of damages.

53.	Assume that an auto accident occurs in State A, but suit is filed in State B.

a.	If the applicable statute of limitations in State A is two years, but is only one year in State B (the forum), the forum will have to apply the State A statute. True or false? _____

b.   If the State A statute of limitations is one year, but the forum statute is two years, the forum may permit suit even though the action would be barred in the state where the injuries occurred. True or false?   _____

c.   If the State A statute of limitations is one year, and the forum has a "borrowing statute" in effect, then the action would be barred in the forum after one year—even though the forum's own (two-year) statute had not yet run. True or false?   _____

d.   If the injured party had obtained a *judgment* in State A, full faith and credit requires the forum to allow a suit to enforce the judgment during whatever period is permitted under State A law. True or false?   _____

CONSTITUTIONAL LIMITATIONS

54.   A forum court is **never required** to make reference to foreign law in cases having foreign contacts. True or false?   _____

55.   It is constitutionally permissible for the forum to apply the law of **any** state having a reasonable relationship to the parties and transaction involved. True or false?   _____

56.   Statutes in effect at the place where the cause of action arose must be given full faith and credit, and must be applied if the action is filed in another state. True or false?   _____

57.   The forum is required under the Full Faith and Credit Clause to allow suit on a cause of action arising under another state's laws. True or false?   _____

58.   Unless a state has sufficient "contacts" with the case to allow application of its own laws under the Due Process Clause, it violates full faith and credit by refusing to apply an appropriate foreign rule. True or false?   _____

59.   If Congress establishes a private cause of action and provides that suit may be brought in either federal or state courts, state courts are **constitutionally** required to enforce that cause of action. True or false?   _____

60.   Under the *Erie* doctrine, federal courts may apply state law to any issue in the case which might have a material effect on the outcome of the case. True or false?   _____

61.   Federal courts are required to apply not only the conflict-of-laws rules of the state in which they are located, but also the conflicts rules of the state in which the case was *first* filed, if it was transferred from one federal district to another. True or false?   _____

RECOGNITION OF FOREIGN JUDGMENTS

62. If a State A court lacks subject matter jurisdiction, but nevertheless tries the case and renders a judgment, the validity of its judgment is determined by State A law rather than by the law of State B where the judgment is ultimately sought to be enforced. True or false? _____

63. A judgment rendered by a state court is not entitled to full faith and credit in a federal court. True or false? _____

64. A judgment rendered in one federal district is automatically entitled to registry and enforcement in any other federal district. True or false? _____

65. A judgment rendered by a state court is entitled to recognition in any other state if it is a final judgment, on the merits, by a court of competent jurisdiction. True or false? _____

66. Winnie obtains a divorce from Hector in State A where they had lived together with their children during the marriage and immediately before the divorce. The State A court orders Hector to pay Winnie $1,000 per month as spousal support. Hector then moves to State B. Winnie now sues in State B to recover payments past due, and to obtain a State B judgment ordering Hector to make all future payments. Which of the following statements are true? _____

    (A) If State A law does **not** allow retroactive modification of past due spousal support installments, Hector cannot obtain retroactive modification, even though this is allowed under State B's law.

    (B) If State A law **allows** retroactive modification, the State B court cannot enforce the order because it is not a "final" judgment.

    (C) It would be proper for State B to order Hector to make future payments of spousal support to Winnie, without any showing other than the State A decree.

    (D) If Hector claims he is entitled to a reduction because of changed circumstances, the court in State B must apply State A law in determining whether the changes are sufficient to justify modification.

67. Under the Uniform Interstate Family Support Act, Winnie (in the question above) would not have to bring suit in State B to enforce her right to spousal support. True or false? _____

68. Suppose that the State A divorce decree above awarded Winnie custody of the couple's minor children. Can State B, at Hector's request, reexamine the custody issue and make a different award? _____

69. Which, if any, of the following types of judgments is **not** entitled to full faith and credit in another state? _____

    (A)   A default judgment.

    (B)   A cognovit judgment.

    (C)   A judgment sustaining a demurrer without leave to amend.

    (D)   A judgment dismissing the action for lack of jurisdiction.

70. Pike brings an action in California for specific performance of a contract for the sale of land in Iowa. DesMoines is personally served in California. Pike prevails on the merits, and the court orders DesMoines to convey title to Pike.

    a.   If DesMoines refuses, and the court then directs a commissioner to execute a deed in DesMoines's name, will the deed be effective to transfer title to land in Iowa? _____

    b.   If Pike takes the California decree to Iowa and files suit there against Des-Moines, is the Iowa court constitutionally required to give full faith and credit to the decree? _____

    c.   Even if DesMoines is not subject to personal jurisdiction in Iowa, can the courts there award effective relief? _____

71. Axel, a State A resident, files suit in that state against Bertram, a State B resident. At the same time, Axel files a separate suit against Bertram in the courts of State B. Which of the following statements are true? _____

    (A)   The court in State A may properly refuse to exercise jurisdiction because of the pendency of the action in State B.

    (B)   If Bertram goes into the State B court and obtains an injunction against Axel's proceeding further with the action in State A, State A's jurisdiction will not be affected.

    (C)   If such an injunction were issued, and the State A court proceeded to render judgment in Axel's favor, Bertram could have no remedy against Axel.

    (D)   If the State A court rendered judgment in Axel's favor, but the State B court rendered judgment in Bertram's favor, the judgment rendered in State A would prevail if Axel had commenced the State A action prior to the State B action.

72. Plaintiff sues in State B to enforce a judgment that she had earlier recovered against Defendant in State A. Defendant defends on the ground that the State A court had no jurisdiction over him. Which of the following statements are true? _____

(A) Whether Defendant is permitted to challenge State A's jurisdiction depends on whether he appeared in the State A proceedings.

(B) If Defendant did appear in State A, he is barred from relitigating the issue of jurisdiction in State B.

(C) Defendant is barred from relitigating the issue of jurisdiction in State B only if that issue was in fact litigated in State A.

(D) If Defendant did not appear in State A, he is free to attack the judgment on any ground.

73. If a defendant fails to attack the jurisdiction of the court before a default judgment is rendered against her, can she still raise the jurisdictional issue in a subsequent proceeding? _____

74. Plaintiff files suit against Defendant in State A. Defendant makes a "special appearance," in which he only contests the jurisdiction of State A, but loses. He makes no further appearance in the case, and a judgment is subsequently returned against him. Plaintiff now seeks to enforce that judgment against Defendant in State B. Which of the following statements is true? _____

(A) Since Defendant never made a general appearance in State A, he never submitted to its jurisdiction, and therefore is free to challenge the judgment for lack of jurisdiction.

(B) Defendant cannot challenge the judgment by alleging a lack of jurisdiction; having raised the issue once (in State A), he is bound by the outcome and cannot relitigate the issue.

75. Following an ex parte Nevada divorce decree brought by Wendy, Howey brings an action against Wendy in California, obtaining personal jurisdiction over her, to have the Nevada decree declared void on the ground that Wendy never established a bona fide domicile in Nevada. Howey wins in the California action. Both judgments become final.

a. If Wendy later dies, leaving property in Arizona, and Howey claims the property as Wendy's intestate heir (surviving "husband"), the Arizona court will recognize the California judgment (nullifying the Nevada divorce). True or false? _____

b. If Wendy died leaving property in Nevada, and Howey claimed such property as Wendy's intestate heir, the Nevada court would recognize the California judgment (nullifying the Nevada divorce). True or false? _____

76. Which, if any, of the following facts should the courts in State B recognize as a valid defense to enforcement of a judgment rendered by the courts of State A? _____

(A) The judgment is sought to be enforced against a person who is a "privy" to the judgment under the laws of State A, but not under the laws of State B.

(B) The cause of action sued upon in State A was for taxes owed to that state.

(C) The cause of action sued upon in State A was for a gambling debt.

(D) The judgment includes a recovery of punitive damages on a tort claim.

(E) The judgment was obtained through perjured testimony (not a defense in State A).

(F) The judgment was obtained through inadvertence or neglect on the part of the defendant's attorney.

77. Which, if any, of the following facts should the courts in State B regard as a valid defense to the enforcement of a judgment rendered by the courts of a foreign nation? _____

(A) The foreign court lacked jurisdiction in accordance with its own standards.

(B) The foreign court lacked jurisdiction in accordance with (United States) constitutional due process standards.

(C) The foreign country does not recognize or enforce American judgments.

(D) The judgment was for taxes due the foreign government.

78. Heinrich and Wilhelmina were married in California and have resided there for five years. Wilhelmina goes to Nevada, remains there for the required six-week residency period, and obtains a Nevada divorce decree. Copies of the summons and complaint were mailed to Heinrich in California.

a. The Nevada decree is invalid because the court had no basis for divorce jurisdiction. True or false? _____

b. The Nevada decree is invalid insofar as it attempts to impose any spousal or child support obligation on Heinrich. True or false? _____

c. The Nevada decree is invalid insofar as it purports to award to Wilhelmina, as support, title to real property held jointly by the couple and located in Nevada. True or false? _____

d. The Nevada decree will be regarded as *prima facie valid* in the courts of every other state. True or false? _____

e. If Wilhelmina dies shortly afterwards, the Nevada decree will be effective to prevent Heinrich from claiming as her intestate heir (surviving "husband"). True or false? _____

f.   If Heinrich was given adequate notice of the Nevada proceedings and failed to appear and contest the validity of Wilhelmina's domicile in Nevada, he will be estopped to challenge the Nevada decree on this ground in any later proceedings. True or false?   _____

g.   If Wilhelmina immediately returns to California after obtaining the Nevada decree, this fact is admissible evidence in any later proceedings involving the validity of her domicile in Nevada at the time of the decree. True or false?   _____

h.   If Wilhelmina returns to California and remarries, her second husband cannot later seek annulment on the ground that the Nevada decree divorcing her from Heinrich was invalid. True or false?   _____

i.   If Wilhelmina's second husband had induced her to obtain the Nevada decree and had married her in reliance thereon, he might be equitably estopped to challenge the validity of the decree. True or false?   _____

j.   If the state of California prosecutes Wilhelmina for bigamy because of her remarriage, the Nevada decree is an absolute defense because California must give full faith and credit to the Nevada decree. True or false?   _____

79.   Assume that Heinrich had been *personally served* in Nevada, prior to the entry of the Nevada decree.

a.   If Heinrich let the action go by default, it would still be an ex parte decree and he could challenge the validity of the Nevada court's jurisdiction later in California. True or false?   _____

b.   If Heinrich appeared in the Nevada action and defended only against Wilhelmina's claims for spousal support, he would be allowed to challenge the validity of the Nevada divorce in later proceedings in California. True or false?   _____

c.   If Heinrich did in fact litigate the validity of Wilhelmina's domicile in the Nevada proceedings and lost on this issue, the Nevada judgment would then be binding on him and all persons in privity with him as determined by the law of Nevada. True or false?   _____

80.   Wallace obtains a legal separation and spousal support order in California. Edward, her husband, then goes to Nevada and obtains a Nevada divorce, serving Wallace by registered mail. The Nevada decree eliminates any spousal support payable to Wallace. Edward returns to California, and refuses to make any further payments to Wallace. She sues in California for arrearages. He defends on the basis of the Nevada decree.

a.   The California court can ignore the Nevada decree because Edward returned to California immediately after its entry. True or false?   _____

b. The Nevada decree may be upheld as valid to terminate the marriage, and still held invalid insofar as affecting Wallace's right to spousal support. True or false? _____

c. Wallace's right to spousal support under the earlier California decree cannot be cut off by a later decree of a court of another state. True or false? _____

d. Wallace's right to spousal support cannot be affected by a court that does not have personal jurisdiction over her. True or false? _____

e. If Wallace had not obtained the prior spousal support order in California, the Nevada decree would have been effective to terminate her marriage to Edward, and thereafter no court (in California or elsewhere) could impose a support obligation on Edward. True or false? _____

Answers to Review Questions

1. **STATE B**   A married woman living with her husband normally takes her husband's domicile, and Husband had been physically present in State B with the intent to remain there. [§28]

2. **STATE A**   The modern view is that a wife can obtain a separate domicile of choice, even without separating from or divorcing her husband. [§29]

3. **YES**   A minor has the father's domicile by operation of law. [§30]

4. **STATE A**   Upon majority, Son acquired a domicile by choice in State A; soldiers do not usually acquire a domicile where stationed. [§§33, 24-25]

5. **(H) and (I)**   These actions are in rem. [§§54-55, 57-59, 66]

6. **NO**   Although the forum court can foreclose the mortgage on local land, it **cannot** enter an in personam judgment against a nonresident. Nor would the court's decree concerning the balance owing on the mortgage be binding on Debtor in subsequent proceedings. [§§59-62]

7. **NO**   Actions for damages to land were deemed "local actions" at common law, but there is some modern authority contra. [§§67-68]

8.a. **YES**   Under the traditional rule, reaffirmed in **Burnham v. Superior Court,** transient service is sufficient. [§§70-76]

  b. **YES**   State's boundaries include air space. (But the constitutionality of this is questionable, even after *Burnham,* since Defendant was not intentionally present in the state.) [§§72-76]

  c. **NO**   This would probably be regarded as "fraud," causing the court to decline jurisdiction. [§§78-79]

  d. **NO**   Immunity of parties is recognized in most states. [§§80-84]

9. **NO**   The basis for jurisdiction is established by Defendant's domicile. Procedural due process does not absolutely require personal delivery if other methods reasonably assure notice and an opportunity to be heard. [§§89, 205-206]

10. **YES**   Most states have statutes authorizing local courts to exercise jurisdiction over domiciliaries wherever they are, and domicile alone is a constitutionally sufficient basis for personal jurisdiction. However, Danielle would have to be given reasonable notice and an opportunity to defend. [§§85-89]

11. **TRUE**   *Any* general appearance, whether or not in person, is sufficient as a basis for in personam jurisdiction. [§§92-93]

12.a. **FALSE**   Unless XYZ's "contacts" with the forum are really minimal, the Commerce Clause is no limitation to this requirement. [§§237-238]

  b. **FALSE**   The "contacts," rather than the formality of consent, constitute the basis of jurisdiction. [§§110, 116-117]

  c. **TRUE**   But the greater the "contacts," the more likely the corporation would be deemed "present" and hence could be sued on any transitory action. [§123]

13. **(B) and (E)**   The test is sufficiency of "contacts" between the forum and parties and/or the transaction involved. Convenience of witnesses is immaterial to jurisdiction, as is the nonlicensed status of party. [§116]

14. **FALSE**   Modern decisions indicate the test is the same for individuals and corporations. [§118]

15. **TRUE**   This is basically **Hanson v. Denckla**. [§§125-129]

16. **(A) and (C)**   (B) is wrong because the *quality* of the "contact" is the significant factor [**McGee v. International Life Insurance**], so that even an isolated transaction may be sufficient for due process purposes. [§§125-130] (D) is wrong because where a defendant is not "present" in the forum state in any realistic sense, it would probably offend "traditional standards of fair play and substantial justice" to hold it subject to jurisdiction on causes of action *unrelated* to the business done in the forum state. [§§139-141]

17. **TRUE**   The court cannot expand its jurisdiction without statutory authority. [§143]

18. **YES**   But arguably, suit would constitute interference with interstate commerce, in which event the court could not exercise jurisdiction. [§§237-238] (Note that adequate notice to Deadwood and a hearing must have preceded the seizure order. [§§177-178])

19. **YES**   No personal judgment can be awarded, but the court could *quiet title* against any claim Purchaser or Seller's wife might have to the property (in rem relief). [§§176-178]

20. **NO**   Where an instrument embodies all intangible rights and claims associated therewith, the court must have jurisdiction over the instrument in order to adjudicate such claims. [§§179-182]

21. **NO**   The mere presence of the defendant's property (the $1,000 debt) within the state does not indicate adequate "contacts" for quasi in rem jurisdiction. [§§185-188]

22.	**FALSE**	"Competence" is determined strictly by local statutes. [§197]
23.	**TRUE**	State statutes allocate types of cases among state courts. [§§197-200]
24.	**FALSE**	By statute, certain kinds of actions *(e.g.,* those involving real estate) are often jurisdictionally required to be filed in certain courts. [§§200, 202]
25.	**(A) and (D)**	(A) Although personal service is preferred, registered mail to D at his home is a method reasonably calculated to give notice. [§§206, 207]

(B) is wrong because modern cases usually require personal service for resident defendants or at least some other method that better assures actual notice. [§207]

(C) is wrong because publication is not sufficient where a nonresident's whereabouts are known or reasonably ascertainable. [§§208-211]

(D) is, in effect, the rule of **Mullane v. Central Hanover Bank & Trust Co.** [§210]

26.	**(A)**	(A) is true even where the defendant was actually notified [**Wuchter v. Pizzatti**]. [§212]

(B) is wrong because where the defendant's address is known, publication alone would not suffice. [§§210-213]

(C) is wrong because the forum's statutes control. [§212]

27.	**ONLY (C)**	(A) is false because the Supreme Court has even upheld the appointment of the plaintiff's wife as defendant's agent for service of process. [*See* **National Equipment Rental Ltd. v. Szukhent**] [§215]

(B) is false because the contract provision is immaterial as long as notice is actually given in a reasonable time and manner. [*See* **National Equipment Rental Ltd. v. Szukhent**] [§215]

(D) is false because cognovits are *not* per se unconstitutional. [**Overmyer Co. v. Frick Co.**] [§216]

28.	**(C)**	Since jurisdiction exists (service within state), the best bet is to get the court to decline to exercise its jurisdiction. [§§72, 227]
29.a.	**FORUM NON CONVENIENS**	D Corp. should argue that the California forum is an unfair or seriously inconvenient place for trial. [§§227 *et seq.*]
b.	**ALL**	All factors relating to "appropriateness" and "fairness" of maintaining the action locally should be considered. [§231]

c.	**TRUE**	Unless factors enumerated in part b., above, are strongly in D Corp.'s favor, its motion will be denied. [§231]
d.	**STAY OR DISMISSAL**	The action may be stayed or dismissed. [§§227, 230]
e.	**TRUE**	Federal statute provides for transfer where the court determines it is not a "fair and appropriate" venue. But action can be transferred only to a district in which federal jurisdiction could have been established if suit had been filed there originally. [§§233-234]
f.	**FALSE**	Transfer does not result in a change of law. [§235]
30.	**FALSE**	Indeed, the Commerce Clause may impose higher requirements. [§§237-238]
31.	**FALSE**	Each state determines the competency of its courts, and State B does not have to follow the State A statute. [*See* **Tennessee Coal, Iron & Railroad v. George**] [§§240-242]
32.	**TRUE**	Renvoi is rejected by both the First and Second Restatements except for a few situations such as title to land and testate or intestate succession to movables. [§§257-260, 266]
33.	**TRUE**	When a court decides to apply only the internal law of the other state, the renvoi problem is avoided. [§259]
34.	**TRUE**	Because it requires the forum to resolve the case exactly as the foreign court would. [§§262, 266]
35.	**FALSE**	This is the "vested rights" approach, which is no longer accepted by most courts. [§§302, 312]
36.	**FALSE**	Weighing contacts is only part of the approach; various policy-oriented factors are also considered. [§§313-316]
37.	**FALSE**	Although under this approach the forum usually applies its own law when it has a legitimate interest in doing so, it must determine the relative interests of each interested state and may choose to apply the law of another interested state as to a particular issue. [§§319-321]
38.	**TRUE**	This approach examines policies rather than merely physical contact. [§§319-321]
39.a.	**FALSE**	The place of injury controls. [§§302-305, 435]
b.	**FALSE**	In order to apply its substantive law, a forum must have a *significant* contact with the litigation so as to comply with the fundamental fairness standard. [§§682-683]

c. **TRUE** This would be a false conflict because the place of injury would have no real interest in having its law applied. [§322]

d. **TRUE** If each court recognized that the domicile forum was the only "interested" state, they would defer to its law. [§§320-322]

40.a. **FALSE** The law determining the ultimate outcome of the case is regarded as "substantive" (when this classification is still retained). [§§388-389, 642-644]

b. **TRUE** Characterization is always the first step under the "vested rights" approach. [§§304-305, 384-385]

c. **TRUE** Other factors include the place of conduct leading up to injury, where the relationship is centered, and the domicile of parties. [§§313, 394-395]

d. **FALSE** It would **not** be a defense, but it would be an extremely relevant factor and the forum would most likely find that this was the most significant "contact" or "interest." [§428]

41.a. **FALSE** Generally, courts look to whether there is a significant relationship or reasonable basis with the law chosen, even when parties do not reside in the state whose law was chosen. [§§450-451] Some courts do not require any contacts. [§449]

b. **TRUE** On the theory that it is a shorthand method of spelling out the rules they have agreed upon. [§448]

c. **TRUE** And the state of parties' domicile has a "materially greater interest" in determining the issue. [§450]

d. **FALSE** In "good faith" usury cases, courts tend to apply the law that upholds validity of the contract if there is a reasonable relationship with the forum. [§§478-480]

42.a. **FALSE** It would be treated as a "performance" issue, to be decided under law of place of performance. [§§458-459]

b. **TRUE** Specific contacts to be taken into account include the place of contracting, the place of negotiation, the place of performance, the location of the subject matter of the contract. [§§466-467]

c. **TRUE** The forum is disinterested when it has no interest in applying its law and two other states have competing interests. [§§331-333]

d. **TRUE** Both the First and Second Restatements the court would look to the situs of the chattel at the time of the transaction. [§§533-534]

43.a. **FALSE** Despite the effect on title or possession, most courts treat this as a "contracts" issue. [§484]

b.	**TRUE**	This is the "substance vs. procedure" distinction. [§485]
c.	**TRUE**	Today, most courts decide Statute of Frauds issues under the choice-of-law rules applicable to contracts. [§486]
44.a.	**FALSE**	Both Restatements permit the situs of land to control the validity and effect of a deed conveying land. [§519]
b.	**FALSE**	Both Restatements follow law of the situs. [§§514-517]
c.	**TRUE**	The First Restatement's use of renvoi has been retained by the Second Restatement. [§515]
d.	**FALSE**	The law of the situs would prevail. [§518]
45.a.	**TRUE**	The basic choice-of-law rule is that the status of real property is determined by the law of the situs. [§526]
b.	**TRUE**	But remember that on divorce, courts may order division of Harry's separate property as if it were community (quasi-community) property. [§543]
c.	**FALSE**	The law of decedent's *last* domicile normally applies; however, situs law applies if application of domicile law would affect testamentary gifts of land in other states. [§§518, 549]
46.a.	**FALSE**	The claim is merged by first judgment. B must sue on the judgment. [§566]
b.	**TRUE**	If A loses, there is no bar against suits by other administrators. [§§560-562, 566]
c.	**TRUE**	On theory that an executor is the decedent's appointed representative. Thus judgments for and against the executor are binding. [§564]
47.	**NO**	Probate proceedings are in rem; the domiciliary state has jurisdiction only over property within its borders. An ancillary proceeding would be required in States B and C. [§§535-555]
48.a.	**FALSE**	Any state having a legitimate interest in regulating the employment relationship can make the award. [§581]
b.	**FALSE**	Workers' compensation commissions apply their own laws. [§582]
c.	**TRUE**	As long as credit is given for amounts already received in the State A proceedings. [§§583-584]
49.a.	**TRUE**	Probably so; lack of parental consent is not a serious violation of a domicile's public policy. [§§587, 591]
b.	**FALSE**	More domicile policy considerations are involved. [§§587, 591]

c. **TRUE**   This is the status-incidents distinction: Although the court may not uphold the marriage generally, it may do so for the purpose of deciding property rights or other "incidents" of the marriage. [§595]

50.a. **FALSE**   The requirement of full faith and credit to statutes is interpreted very narrowly to permit the forum to apply its own statutes. [§§690-692]

b. **TRUE**   But the public policy is a very *limited defense* to choice of law. [§§626-630]

c. **TRUE**   The governmental interest approach uses public policy affirmatively. [§630]

d. **TRUE**   Full faith and credit compels recognition of the judgment. [§§687-688]

51. **(C) AND POSSIBLY (D)**   (A) is invalid as an attempt to "localize" the cause of action. [§240] (B) does not fit the definition of a "penal" law. [§§631-632] (D)—some states now allow enforcement of foreign tax claims. [§§635-637]

52. **ALL EXCEPT (F)**   (A), (B), and (C) are clearly "procedural" and hence forum rules apply. [§§645, 652] (D) is also, unless there is some special reason why the forum should respect the privilege. [§§653-656] (E) is less clear but the Second Restatement would also treat this as "procedural." [§§646-649] (F) should *not* be treated as "procedural," despite *Kilberg*. [§§676-678]

53.a. **FALSE**   There is no constitutional compulsion; it is still a choice-of-law decision. [§693]

b. **TRUE**   With some exception, the forum may apply its own statute of limitations. [§§664, 669-674] The modern trend rejects the "substance/procedure" dichotomy and determines which state has the most significant relationship or interest concerning the limitations issue. [§675]

c. **TRUE**   Because the effect of the borrowing statute is to adopt the limitations period of the place where the cause of action arose. [§671]

d. **FALSE**   The forum enforces foreign judgments according to its own judgment remedies. [§666]

54. **FALSE**   Application of forum law violates due process if there are *no* contacts with the forum. [§§685-686]

55. **TRUE**   There must be a "significant contact," similar to the "minimum contacts" test. [§§683-686]

56. **FALSE**   Full faith and credit as applied to statutes is interpreted narrowly. [§§690-692]

57. **FALSE**   Subject to the **Hughes v. Fetter** exception, a forum can refuse to hear a case. [§§695-696]

58.	**TRUE**	Due process and full faith and credit have come to mean the same thing in choice of law. [§§695-696]
59.	**TRUE**	Because of the Supremacy Clause—at least where the state court enforces an analogous state-created right. [§§702, 705]
60.	**FALSE**	This is an overstatement. Federal courts will not apply state law that conflicts with the Federal Rules of Civil Procedure regardless of effect on "outcome"; also there may be other considerations where federal policies prevail over the *Erie* doctrine. [§§714-718]
61.	**TRUE**	*See* **Klaxon Co. v. Stentor Electric Manufacturing Co.** and **Van Dusen v. Barrack.** [§723]
62.	**TRUE**	A judgment valid where rendered is valid everywhere. [§§729-730, 806-808]
63.	**TRUE**	Full faith and credit does not apply, but a federal implementing statute does. [§732]
64.	**TRUE**	By statute. [§733]
65.	**TRUE**	This is the doctrine of full faith and credit. [§741]
66.	**(A) and (D)**	(A) is true because the law of the state where judgment was rendered determines the extent to which it is modifiable. [§747]

(B) is false because although the order may not be entitled to full faith and credit, the State B court may still give it voluntary recognition. [§§746, 749]

(C) is false because, again, full faith and credit does not apply. But voluntary recognition is generally accorded. (Hector would be entitled to seek reduction by showing "changed circumstances.") [§§748-749]

(D) is true in most states, although there is some authority for the forum's applying its own law. [§749] |
67.	**TRUE**	Under UIFSA, a support order can be registered with the State B court and it will be enforced as if it were a State B order, or an income-withholding order may be sent directly to Hector's employer, who must then withhold wages. [§750]
68.	**NO**	Under the Uniform Child Custody Jurisdiction Act, State A retains jurisdiction over the case because it is the "home state" of Winnie and the children, who continued to live in State A after the divorce. [§757]
69.	**(D)**	A dismissal for lack of jurisdiction is not "on the merits" and thus not entitled to full faith and credit. [§761] As to (A) and (B), default and cognovit judgments may not be entitled to collateral estoppel, but merger and bar may

still apply. [§§764-771] As for (C), because plaintiff cannot amend, this decision would be "on the merits." [§762]

70.a. **NO** A California court cannot enter an in rem decree as to Iowa land. [§783]

b. **NO** *See* **Fall v. Eastin.** (But most courts will give res judicata effect to the *facts* determined in the California decree, and some courts will voluntarily give the decree full faith and credit.) [§§783-787]

c. **YES** Presence of the property would probably indicate sufficient contacts to justify in rem jurisdiction. [§§55-56]

71. **(A) and (B)** (A) is true because it is within State A's discretion. [§797]

(B) is true because State A is not required to recognize the injunction. [§789]

(C) is false because Bertram's remedy would be to initiate contempt proceedings against Axel in State B. [§789]

(D) is false because the judgment *last in time* supersedes any earlier, inconsistent judgment; the date of filing the lawsuit does not control. [§811]

72. **(A) and (B)** (A) is true because, if Defendant did not appear, the court's jurisdiction is subject to collateral attack. [§804]

(B) is true because Defendant has had his "day in court." [§806]

(C) is false; Defendant would also be barred if he was subject to its personal jurisdiction and failed to raise the challenge. [§807]

(D) is false; attack is permitted only on jurisdictional grounds. [§§803-805]

73. **YES** A defendant may collaterally attack the judgment at subsequent proceedings. [§806]

74. **(B)** Once litigated, the decision regarding the court's jurisdiction is final and cannot be challenged later. Defendant has had his day in court. [§§806-807]

75.a. **TRUE** On res judicata grounds since the California decree was last in time. [§793]

b. **UNCLEAR** The last judgment in point of time should prevail, but so far, forum courts uphold their own judgments whether or not they are chronologically last. [§§811-812]

76. **NONE OF THESE** Defenses to enforcement of judgments of sister courts are strictly limited by effects of the Full Faith and Credit Clause. [§§815-821]

77. **(A) and (B)** (A) and (B) are valid defenses, but (C) and (D) might also be regarded as valid defenses by some state courts. [§§827-833]

78.a.	**FALSE**	Domicile of the plaintiff spouse alone is sufficient to confer jurisdiction over marital status. [§§842-845, 853]
b.	**TRUE**	These are in personam obligations and personal jurisdiction is required. [§873]
c.	**DEPENDS**	On whether Nevada has sufficient "contacts" to exercise quasi in rem jurisdiction. [§880]
d.	**TRUE**	Attackers must establish lack of jurisdiction by ample evidence. [§§855-858]
e.	**TRUE**	The ex parte divorce has the power to terminate Heinrich's property rights. [§881]
f.	**FALSE**	Heinrich was never personally before the court. [§859]
g.	**TRUE**	Heinrich may show facts occurring *after* the divorce which cast doubt on her intent. [§§855-858]
h.	**FALSE**	But the answer would be true in Nevada. [§§866-870]
i.	**TRUE**	The doctrine of equitable estoppel prevents husband #2 from challenging the validity of the divorce, but does not validate the divorce or the subsequent marriage. [§867]
j.	**FALSE**	This is *Williams #2*. [§868]
79.a.	**FALSE**	An ex parte divorce is one rendered *without personal jurisdiction* over the defendant; the Nevada court had jurisdiction over Heinrich. [§845]
b.	**FALSE**	He had "his day in court." [§§862-863]
c.	**TRUE**	This is the *Sherrer* doctrine. [§§862, 865]
80.a.	**FALSE**	California can ignore the spousal support provisions because Nevada had no personal jurisdiction over Wallace. [§877]
b.	**TRUE**	Divorce is divisible. [§873]
c.	**FALSE**	It is the absence of personal jurisdiction, not the sequence of the decrees, that controls. [§877]
d.	**TRUE**	Because spousal support is a personal right. [§878]
e.	**FALSE**	Post-divorce spousal support is authorized in some states [*see* **Vanderbilt v. Vanderbilt**]. [§878]

Exam Questions
and Answers

Question 1
driving - bridge issue
TORT issue

Question 2
buy sell property
3 jurisdictions
(R) ase / property

Question 3
plane crash
TORT

Question 4
Dram Shop Law
TORT

Question 5
Products Liability

Question 6
(R) oral & written
☆   ☆

Question 7
Title of property
DP analysis (service)

Question 8
Charitable Immunity from Liability

Question 9
Dram Shop Person Liability / Minors

QUESTION I

The center of the Ippimissi River forms the boundary between the states of Black and White. The river is spanned by the Bridge. The Bridge is owned by Black, but nominal title is held by Bridge Commission, a nonprofit corporation chartered by Black and charged with the operation and maintenance of the Bridge. A Black statute provides:

> The Bridge Commission shall have power to sue and be sued in its own name; provided, however, that any suit against the Commission shall be brought in the Courts of this State, irrespective of the place where the obligation arose.

Recently, the Bridge collapsed. Among those killed was Husband, who was returning to his home in White from his job in Black. Where Husband was on the Bridge at the time of its collapse will never be known, except that he was far enough from either bank to have landed in the water. The wrongful death statutes of White and Black are identical except that White's statute permits a recovery of $75,000 whereas Black's statute limits recovery to $50,000. White's long arm statute authorizes its courts to exercise jurisdiction over any person ". . . who does any of the acts hereafter enumerated, as to any cause of action arising out of the doing of said acts within this state: (1) The transaction of any business; (2) The commission of a tortious act; (3) The ownership, use, or possession of any real estate; . . . ."

In representing Widow, Husband's surviving spouse who is a lifelong resident of White, should an action on her behalf be instituted in White or in Black? Discuss, indicating the relative advantage of the procedure recommended over others that may be available.

QUESTION II

Petunia is one of the prize bulls owned by Able, who lives and raises cattle in the state of Red. Able has entered Petunia and his other prize bulls in livestock shows in every state in the United States, including Red, White, Blue, and Green. During a show in White, Baker, a resident of Green, offered to buy Petunia for $500. Able replies that he would sell Petunia to Baker for that price only if Baker's prize bull beats Petunia. Able has received numerous offers to buy Petunia, the least of such offers being $20,000.

Baker's prize bull is awarded first place and Petunia is placed second. Immediately thereafter, Baker tenders Able $500 in cash and asks Able to sign a bill of sale. Able refuses and returns to Red with Petunia.

Red and Blue's statutes provide that oral contracts for the sale of personal property at a price of more than $400 "shall not be valid." White's statute provides that "no action shall be brought" on oral contracts for the sale of personal property at a price of more than $400.

1. Baker, while temporarily in Blue, sues Able in Blue court for damages for breach of contract, personally serving him in the state of Red in compliance with a Blue statute. Able specially appears to contest jurisdiction. What result and why?

2. Assume Able loses and decides to contest the action on its merits. Who will prevail, and why?

QUESTION III

Clara Client, who was in the state of Black on a business trip, contracted with Flying Service, a Black corporation, to take her home to the state of White. Flying Service owns a fleet of aircraft and an airport, and is engaged in the business of making charter flights. Flying Service requires all of its employee-pilots to carry liability insurance in the face amount of $100,000. Flying Service assigned Pierre Pilot, one of its employees, to make the trip. The plane crashed into Client's home while trying to land, killing Pilot, seriously injuring Client, and extensively damaging Client's house. Client was asleep at the time of the crash and does not know what happened.

A White statute imposes strict liability upon the owner of an aircraft that causes damage to structures on the ground; Black has no such statute. White also has a statute permitting its courts to exercise jurisdiction over "any nonresident as to any cause of action arising from an injury suffered in this state."

Client asks for advice as to her rights against each possible party and whether she may enforce such rights in White. Discuss.

QUESTION IV

The highest court of State X recently held that a social host who furnishes alcoholic beverages to an obviously intoxicated guest, under circumstances creating a reasonably foreseeable risk of harm to others, may be held legally responsible to third persons who are injured by the guest. Neighboring State Y has no such law. Its highest court recently refused to impose civil liability on a tavern owner whose bartender served drinks to an obviously intoxicated patron.

On New Year's Eve, a party was given in State Y by a State Y resident who lived just over the state line from State X. Guests were invited from both states. When the final glass of champagne had been drunk to welcome in the New Year, all guests were thoroughly and obviously intoxicated. Nevertheless, the hostess urged her guests to have "one more for the road." After the party, Richard Roe, a State Y resident, climbed unsteadily into his car to drive home. On the way, he collided in State Y with a car driven by Peter Poe, a resident of State X. Peter Poe was severely injured.

1. Peter filed suit in State X against the hostess, serving her personally in State X. Does State X have jurisdiction over the hostess?

2. Assume that State X decided it has jurisdiction over the hostess. Peter Poe relies on State X law. The hostess urges that application of State X law would violate due process. What result and why?

3. Assume that State X is constitutionally permitted to apply its own law, should it do so?

QUESTION V

Pauline, a Nevada domiciliary, purchased a bottle of hair shampoo in Oregon while visiting the state. Allegedly as a result of using the shampoo, she lost her hair. The shampoo was prepared by Dandeter, a corporation having its principal place of business in Colorado, but incorporated in Delaware.

Dandeter does not sell its shampoo in Nevada, but it does advertise in magazines which are circulated in Nevada as well as co-sponsor a national television program which is viewable in Nevada. Pauline, wishing to sue in the forum most convenient to her (*i.e.,* in Nevada) wishes to attach in Nevada certain raw materials in the hands of a common carrier, which materials are in transit through Nevada and for which the carrier had given Dandeter a bill of lading in Colorado.

Pauline also wishes to use a statute of Nevada that provides that the secretary of state can be served when no agent has been appointed to receive service for any cause of action against a foreign corporation doing business in the state, or against a foreign corporation that has done business in the state even if the corporation has now withdrawn from the state. Until two years ago, in fact, Dandeter did sell the shampoo in Nevada.

Can jurisdiction be acquired over Dandeter in Nevada? Discuss fully.

QUESTION VI

P and D, both residents of State X, were in an auto collision in State X. P asserted a claim against D for personal injuries allegedly suffered in the collision. D denied liability. Subsequently D moved to State F, and in F he and P made a written contract, called a "release," under which P agreed to relinquish all claims against D arising out of the collision in return for a promise made by D to pay P $5,000 in cash within three months. D did not make any payment within the three months, and about six weeks after that time expired P orally agreed in State X to accept $2,000, then paid to her in cash, in full satisfaction of her claim against D. P thereafter sued D in State F for $3,000, alleging this amount to be still due under the written contract. At the trial, D offered evidence of the oral agreement, but the evidence was excluded, and judgment was for P as prayed.

By the law of State X, a subsequent oral, executed agreement of this character and with these terms is effective to supersede a prior written contract, but by the law of State F the transaction operates only as a payment on the prior obligation, and parol evidence may not be given to prove a subsequent oral agreement superseding a prior written contract.

On appeal, what result? Discuss.

QUESTION VII

Perry, the buyer, sued Sylvia, the seller, in equity for specific performance of a contract for the sale of Blackacre. The suit was in State A, where both parties resided, and there was personal service of process upon Sylvia in State A. Blackacre is in State B.

In another suit in the same equity court, Perry, the buyer, sued Sam, the seller, for specific enforcement of a contract for the sale of Greenacre, located in State A. Sam was in State B and there was only constructive service upon him by publishing a notice in a newspaper in State A and delivery to him of a copy of the summons by registered mail. A statute in State A provided for such service against nonresident defendants in actions affecting title to real property within the state, including equity suits for specific performance of contracts for the sale of such property. Another State A statute provided that if a defendant refused or neglected to convey land as required by an equity decree for specific performance, the decree itself would operate as a conveyance.

In the third suit in the same equity court Perry, the seller, sued Susan, the buyer, to require her to pay the purchase price agreed in a contract for the sale of Whiteacre, which was located in State A. Susan was in State X and there was only constructive service upon her, under the State A statute.

In all three cases, Perry performed all of his part of the contracts, or tendered performance thereof, and there was no legal or equitable defense to the actions. In all three cases, the respective defendants did not appear, except specially to contest the court's jurisdiction.

What result in (1) *Perry v. Sylvia*; (2) *Perry v. Susan*; and (3) *Perry v. Sam*?

QUESTION VIII

Charity, a charitable corporation in State A, rented in State C from Trucker, a State A resident, a truck habitually kept by Trucker in State A. While Charity's employees were negligently operating the truck in State C, Plaintiff, a resident of A and a passenger in the truck, suffered severe injuries. By statute in State A, the bailor of a rented vehicle is liable for all negligence of the bailee in operating it. C has no such statute.

Plaintiff sued Charity and Trucker in State A where Charity mainly used the truck. By statute in State A, the immunity of charitable corporations for torts has been abolished, but the doctrine is still effective in State C. Prior to the accident, Plaintiff executed in State C a paper purporting to release Charity from all liability in case Plaintiff suffered any harm while being transported by Charity employees. This release is valid in State C but void as contrary to public policy in State A.

Charity moved to dismiss the action as to it because of the release and its charitable functions. Trucker moved to dismiss on the ground that the statute of State A imposing liability on the bailor is not applicable.

What ruling on each motion and why?

QUESTION IX

Xavier Jones, a resident of State X, Yancy Smith, a resident of neighboring State Y, and Yolanda Brown, also a resident of State Y, were all minors who lived at home with their respective parents. One evening, Yancy borrowed his father's car and drove to State X to pick up Xavier. The boys bought several six-packs of beer at a State X market, then drove back to State Y to visit Yolanda. After consuming more beer, they went for a drive. All three were intoxicated when Yancy, driving his father's car in State Y, struck a stone wall, killing Xavier and Yolanda.

It is unlawful in both states for merchants to sell alcoholic beverages to minors. State X, but not State Y, has a dramshop act that creates a civil cause of action on behalf of persons injured by an intoxicated person against the merchant who sold the liquor unlawfully. State Y, but not State X, views a parent's failure to supervise his child's conduct as contributory negligence, which may bar the parent's recovery in tort. State X, but not State Y, has abandoned the common law rule of contributory negligence in favor of comparative negligence.

Xavier's parents and Yolanda's parents have independently filed suit in State X against the market that sold the beer to Xavier and Yancy, seeking to recover for the wrongful death of their children. The market seeks to defend on the ground of parental failure to supervise the children. How and why should the cases be decided?

ANSWER TO QUESTION I

To decide whether Widow should institute an action in Black or in White, it is necessary to consider questions of jurisdiction, choice of law, and enforcement of judgments.

1. **Jurisdiction**

   a. **Do any of the three provisions of White's long arm statute apply to this case?**

      (1) **Did the cause of action arise out of the "transaction of business" within the state of White?** The Bridge Commission was engaged in activities within White that related to the maintenance and operation of its Bridge, which was partly located in White. It can be argued that the cause of action for wrongful death "arose out of" the activity of maintaining the Bridge; if the Bridge had not collapsed, the cause of action would not have arisen. To argue that the cause of action specifically arose out of activity within the state of White is tenuous, at best, since there is no indication that the Bridge fell because of anything the Commission did or failed to do within White. However, it could be argued that Husband's presence on the Bridge was directly related to the Commission's actions in making a thoroughfare available between Black and White which encouraged White residents like Husband to work in Black. The cause of action arose out of Husband's use of that facility and was thus related to activity occurring in White.

      An additional problem is raised by the fact that Commission is a nonprofit corporation. Is a nonprofit corporation engaged in the transaction of business? The Second Restatement has suggested that "business" consists of "doing a series of similar acts for the purpose of thereby realizing pecuniary benefit, or otherwise accomplishing an object. . . ." Also, an Illinois court had no difficulty in sustaining jurisdiction over the Missouri operators of a toll bridge spanning the Mississippi River between Illinois and Missouri, even prior to the enactment of the Illinois long arm statute. The question does not indicate whether the Bridge is a toll bridge. Even if it is not, jurisdiction should nevertheless be sustained despite the fact that the Commission is not operating the Bridge for profit—since that should not serve to isolate it from suit in White's courts based on causes of action arising out of activity carried on within White and affecting White residents. Moreover, the Bridge brings consumers and workers to Black, thus contributing to its economy.

      (2) **Did the cause of action arise out of the "commission of a tortious act" within the state of White?** Jurisdiction probably cannot be sustained under this section of the statute. The Illinois [**Gray v. American Radiator & Standard Sanitary Corp.**] and New York [**Feathers v. McLucas**] cases

that arose under similar statutes both involved situations where the injury occurred within the forum state and the negligence occurred outside the state. Illinois accepted jurisdiction under these circumstances; New York did not (but its statute was later expanded to cover the case). In this case, however, it is not clear that either the negligence or the injury occurred in White. Even if the negligence arguably occurred in both states, it still cannot be determined where Husband was injured. It would seem that this case cannot be brought within the statutory language, which requires that the tortious act be committed "within this state."

(3) **Did the cause of action arise out of "the ownership, use, or possession of any real estate" within the state of White?** It is at least established that the Commission nominally owns the Bridge; presumably it also uses or possesses the land in White to which the Bridge is affixed. It may even own this land. The only question here, then, is whether the cause of action for wrongful death arose out of that ownership, use, or possession. The argument is similar to, but appears somewhat more tenuous than, the argument made under the "transaction of business" section. There is clearly some connection between the land owned in White and the Bridge, and Husband's death arose out of the collapse of the Bridge. The case would be clearer if it could be established that the Bridge collapsed as a result of the Commission's negligence (*e.g.,* failure to repair soil erosion around the Bridge's foundations in White). Short of that, the argument will necessarily have to be a general one. It appears possible, however, to sustain jurisdiction under this section of the statute.

b. **If, as a matter of statutory construction, one or more sections of White's statute do apply, would its application to this case be consistent with due process?** The constitutionality of state courts' jurisdiction over nonresidents is measured in terms of the *International Shoe* standard—*i.e.,* due process requires only that a defendant have certain "minimum contacts" with the forum state so that the maintenance of the suit does not offend traditional notions of fair play and substantial justice. If the "transaction of business" section of White's statute is relied upon, that standard appears satisfied here. As indicated earlier, Illinois upheld jurisdiction even prior to the enactment of its long arm statute over a Missouri operator of a toll bridge between Missouri and Illinois. The case relied on the general "doing business" line of cases decided prior to *International Shoe.* The Commission certainly carries on continuous activities related to the operation and maintenance of the Bridge in White, and there are no doubt many White residents who use the Bridge daily.

The "ownership, use, or possession of real estate" section of the statute is less well established and thus might cause more difficulty on the constitutional level. Even so, if the case can be made to seem analogous to cases sustaining a state's right to redress its citizens for injuries sustained from hazardous conditions maintained on real property located within the state without looking too closely at whether the actual injury occurred within the state, due process may be satisfied. But it seems that the "transaction of business" section would be the easiest to use, from the standpoint of both statutory construction and constitutional validity.

c. **Assuming White's long arm statute applies and would be constitutional as applied, does Black's statute prevent the exercise of jurisdiction in White?** State Black's statute allows the Bridge Commission to be sued, but provides that all such suits "shall be brought in the Courts of this State." Must White respect (give full faith and credit to) this statute? The United States Supreme Court has indicated that the forum is not bound to respect another state's statutory limitation of causes of action its own courts can hear. [**Tennessee Coal, Iron & Railroad v. George**] The statute in question does not create a cause of action—it simply allows the Commission to be sued. Neither of the Supreme Court cases involved a governmental entity. Is the Black statute permissible because Black can limit the conditions under which it will waive its own sovereign immunity? On these facts, White probably does not owe full faith and credit to the Black statute. First of all, the operation of a bridge may be a proprietary function and not a governmental one—so that sovereign immunity does not apply. Secondly, there are cases holding that the ownership of property by one state within the boundaries of another state subjects the owner to suit in the courts of the situs state just as if it were a private party. Thus, the Commission would not be protected by the Black statute in the courts of White.

2. **Choice of Law—Assuming White Takes Jurisdiction, Whose Law Will It Apply?** The only conflict-of-laws issue in the question concerns the difference in damages for wrongful death: White permits $75,000; Black permits only $50,000. Traditionally, the First Restatement applied the law of the place of wrong to determine damages for wrongful death. Here, since it cannot be determined where Husband was injured, it is impossible to identify the "place of wrong." Thus, the traditional test is not helpful. The Second Restatement applies the law of the place of most significant relationship. But here, since the contacts are evenly divided between Black and White, either state could claim that it is the place of most significant relationship. Under the "governmental interest" approach, this case appears to be a "true conflicts" case in which both states have an interest in applying their own law.

A long line of cases beginning with **Kilberg v. Northeast Airlines, Inc.**, and more recently culminating in California in **Reich v. Purcell,** has upheld the right of an interested state to have its own wrongful death damages applied. Since Husband and Widow were both residents of state White, White may be expected to apply its own law if the suit is brought there. (Similarly, if suit is brought in Black, Black would apply its own law.)

3. **Enforcement of Judgments**

a. **Assuming White grants a judgment for $75,000 against Commission, how can that judgment be enforced?** If the Commission appears in White, litigates the case and loses, the resulting White judgment will be final, on the merits, and entitled to full faith and credit in Black. This is true even though Black's policy of allowing the Commission to be sued only in the courts of Black was not respected by White. [*Cf.* **Fauntleroy v. Lum**] If the Commission does not appear, how can the White default judgment be enforced? One possibility is that the judgment can be satisfied out of Commission's land located in White (if Commission owns the land). But if this is not possible, the White judgment should still be enforceable in Black. The judgment can be collaterally attacked for lack of jurisdiction, but if the jurisdiction argument previously made is sound, jurisdiction should be sustained even by Black. And in determining jurisdiction, the Black court must apply White standards for sufficiency of jurisdiction. A practical problem is that Black may decide, because of its own interest in the case, that White lacked jurisdiction or that it owed full faith and credit to the Black statute. In that case, a writ of certiorari to the United States Supreme Court may be necessary.

b. **Strategy of filing in White or Black**

(1) **Factors applicable to filing in Black**

(a) **Jurisdiction:** Jurisdiction can clearly be obtained over the Commission in Black since it is a Black corporation and the statute of Black subjects it to suit in the Black courts.

(b) **Choice of law:** As previously discussed, Black would probably apply its own law, whether it followed the Second Restatement or a policy-oriented approach. Widow would therefore be limited to $50,000 in damages since Black would protect its own Commission.

(c) **Enforcement of judgments:** There would be no problem in enforcing the Black judgment in Black. The corporation's assets are located in Black and will be available for satisfaction of the judgment.

(2) **The relative advantages of filing in White and Black:** The obvious advantage of filing in White is to gain $25,000 more damages for Widow. The problem becomes one of deciding whether to risk problems of jurisdiction in White and enforcement of White's judgment, in order to gain the more favorable law in White. Filing in Black is the more cautious approach, and probably would guarantee a certain minimum recovery to Widow. Filing in White involves a gamble but, if successful, promises more of a gain. If Commission does not appear in White, it probably will

collaterally attack the White judgment in Black. A possible approach, if the statutes of limitation permit it, would be to file first in White, wait to see whether Commission appears, and, if not, then file in Black.

ANSWER TO QUESTION II

1. **Does Blue Have Jurisdiction over Able?**

   a. **Does the Blue statute provide an adequate jurisdictional basis for the suit?** Blue's statute is not described. Assuming that it is a typical "specific acts" long arm statute of the type, it would list several jurisdictional events—*e.g.*, the commission of a tortious act within the state; the doing of any business within the state; the ownership, use, or possession of real property within the state; or contracting to insure persons or property within the state. None of these events has occurred within Blue, except that Able had previously shown Petunia at livestock shows in Blue. Although this might be construed as "doing business" in Blue, that business had no connection with this lawsuit. The long arm statute would require that the cause of action arise out of the business done in the state. Thus, the Blue statute probably would not apply.

   b. **Does the Blue statute meet the constitutional standards for personal jurisdiction?** According to the facts, a resident of Green filed suit in Blue against a resident of Red to recover damages for breach of an oral contract made and to be performed in White. Defendant Able was served personally in Red, and he has no connection with Blue in any way that relates to this lawsuit. So far as the facts show, the only connection Able has ever had with Blue is that he had previously shown Petunia at livestock shows in Blue. Thus, it may be concluded that Blue's attempt to obtain personal jurisdiction over Able, under these facts, is a violation of due process. *Reason:* There are not sufficient "minimum contacts" between Able and Blue, so that maintenance of the suit would offend "traditional notions of fair play and substantial justice" within the *International Shoe* test. Nor can *McGee* be relied upon, since Able has done nothing comparable to the Insurance Company's mailing a contract of reinsurance and accepting premiums (as occurred in that case). **Hanson v. Denckla's** admonition would seem appropriate here: If there is no act by which Able has purposefully availed himself of the privilege of conducting activities within the forum state that has a connection with this particular lawsuit, he is not liable to its summons to appear. The suit, therefore, should be dismissed.

2. **Who Should Prevail on the Merits and Why?** This question relates to the Statute of Frauds provisions in effect in the states of Red, Blue, and White. The result will vary depending on which choice-of-law approach is used by the court.

a. **Traditional ("vested rights") view:** The case given is remarkably similar to the leading case of **Marie v. Garrison** (New York 1883), which followed the substance-procedure distinction for Statute of Frauds cases suggested by the leading English case of **Leroux v. Brown** (1852). In *Leroux,* it was suggested that Statutes of Frauds providing that "no action shall be brought" should be characterized as procedural, whereas those stating that "no contract shall be valid" should be characterized as substantive. The First Restatement adopted this distinction and directed the forum to apply its own "procedural" statute but to apply the "substantive" statute of another state whose law would be applied to decide the case.

Here, the forum's statute is substantive ("shall not be valid") while the statute of White—whose substantive law would be applied to decide the case, since it is the place where the contract was made and to be performed—is procedural ("no action shall be brought"). According to **Marie v. Garrison** and the First Restatement, therefore, neither statute applies. The forum cannot apply its own statute since it is substantive and it will apply White's substantive law, and it cannot apply White's statute because it is procedural. The anomalous result is that even though the contract does not conform to *either* statute, it will still be enforced. If Blue follows this approach, Baker will win. Able's only recourse is to find some other law of White which will invalidate the contract, rather than simply render it unenforceable.

b. **Second Restatement view:** The Second Restatement expressly rejects the First Restatement's distinctions based on the wording "shall not be valid" or "no action may be brought." Instead, it favors the law chosen by the parties or the law of the place with the most significant relationship. In the instant case, Able and Baker did not choose a governing law. Thus, it must be determined which state, on these facts, has the most significant relationship to the parties and the transaction with reference to the specific issue of the Statute of Frauds.

The first three contacts to be considered (the place of contracting, negotiation, and performance) all point to White. The subject matter of the contract, Petunia, was in White at the time of the alleged contract, and is now presumably in Red. Red is Able's domicile and Green is Baker's domicile. Presumably, White is the state of most significant relationship, and its Statute of Frauds invalidates the contract. This result is similar to that reached by Red and Blue. White's Statute of Frauds should be applied and Able should prevail.

c. **"Governmental interest" approach:** According to the "governmental interest" theory, Blue is a disinterested third state—*i.e.,* it has no interest in having its laws applied to this case. Its first (and, according to Currie, best) alternative is to dismiss the suit on the grounds of forum non conveniens. It has no constitutional obligation to hear a case between two nonresidents on a contract made and to be performed elsewhere, when it must apply another state's laws.

However, *if* Blue decides to hear the case, it should look to the policy and interests of the other interested states to determine whether a true conflict exists. In this case, all states have the same policy: Contracts of the type in question should not be upheld. There is no true conflict of laws in the case; it is a false problem. It is not known what Green's law would provide, but both White and Red have a common policy to protect the promisor against oral contracts to sell personal property at a price of more than $400. The common policy of both states, which Blue shares, should be applied and Able should prevail.

ANSWER TO QUESTION III

1. **Does White Have Jurisdiction over Flying Service and Pilot or his Personal Representative?**

    a. **Does the White statute apply to this case?** The White statute applies to any nonresident who causes an injury within White. In this case, Flying Service sent its employee, Pilot, into White, where he injured Client and damaged Client's property. Both these invasions of Client's rights are injuries to Client. Since they occurred in White, the statute applies. This long arm statute is more specific than the "specific acts" type statute, which requires that the tortious act occur in the state. Here, it is enough that the injury take place in the state. Since the statute applies to "any nonresident," it presumably includes Pilot's personal representative—so that Client may sue him as well as Flying Service. At this point, it is not necessary to determine whether White's statute applies to make Flying Service strictly liable for the property damage; that will be decided at the trial on the merits. To sustain jurisdiction, it is enough that Flying Service, through its employee, injured plaintiff and her property within White.

    b. **Is the White statute constitutional as applied to these facts?** This case involves a nonresident who, through an agent, entered the state and injured plaintiff. The case is similar to **Nelson v. Miller**, the first case arising under the tortious act section of the Illinois long arm statute. There, the court held its statute constitutional as applied to a nonresident individual whose agent entered Illinois and injured the plaintiff. Statutes of this kind are based on the defendant's connection with the state in entering and committing an injurious act therein. It is also similar to the typical nonresident motorist situation, where the early rationale of "implied consent" to suit by the nonresident has given way (since *International Shoe*) to a standard of the reasonableness in requiring defendant to return to the place of injury to answer for his acts.

2. **Does the White Strict Liability Statute Apply to Create a Cause of Action Against Flying Service?** Yes. White would be allowed to apply its strict liability statute in a suit in White under the traditional approach as well as the Second Restatement and governmental interest approaches.

    a. **"Vested rights" approach:** The traditional "vested rights" view applied the law of the place of wrong to determine liability. The place of wrong is White, since that is where the injury to Client's property occurred. The First Restatement explicitly required application of the law of the place of wrong in determining whether a defendant was strictly liable, even though he would not be subject to strict liability under the law of the place where he acted. Here, Flying Service knowingly sent Pilot into White and, as a result, Client's property was damaged. The fact that Flying Service may have an action against Pilot on the insurance policy does not prevent Client from suing Flying Service. White may apply its statute.

    b. **Second Restatement approach:** In tort cases, the Second Restatement applies the law of the state having the most significant relationship to the parties and the occurrence. Usually, however, the law of the place of injury will be applied to both personal injuries and injuries to tangible things. In this case, White's law would appear to be the law chosen by this standard; it is the place of injury and conduct as well as the place of Client's domicile. Black does not appear to have a more significant relationship than White. Thus, White's law would be applied.

    c. **"Governmental interest" approach:** Finally, the "governmental interest" approach would permit White to apply its own law. The policy underlying White's strict liability statute manifests a desire to protect property owners against airplane owners. Client is a White resident and her property is located in White. Thus, White has an interest in applying its statute. Black may have a contrary interest in protecting its corporation, Flying Service, but on the facts, White would seem justified in advancing its own interests at the expense of Black.

3. **Analysis of Decedent's Estates Issue:** Client requested advice as to her rights against each possible party and whether she may enforce such rights in White, her home state. One possible party might be Pilot's personal representative. If Pilot's negligence was the reason for the injury to the owner, a cause of action exists if there is a survival statute in White (under the traditional rule that the place of wrong determines whether a cause of action survives the tortfeasor's death). Assuming a personal representative has been appointed for Pilot in Black, can that person be sued in White? The White long arm statute permits suit against "any nonresident as to any cause of action arising from an injury suffered in this State." This statute would clearly apply to Pilot, had he lived. Does it apply to his personal representative as well? At common law, a Black-appointed personal representative could not be sued outside the state of his appointment, but the nonresident motorist statutes were

practically all construed to apply to the foreign administrator of a nonresident motorist. The same justification should apply equally to long arm statutes covering injuries or the commission of tortious acts within the state. Although some statutes expressly apply to personal representatives, the court in White should be able to interpret the White statute to apply to Pilot's representative. White's interest in permitting Client to sue Pilot in White for injuries suffered there extends to permitting suit against Pilot's representative. Therefore, Client ought to be able to sue Pilot's representative in White.

ANSWER TO QUESTION IV

1.   **Does State X Have Jurisdiction over Hostess?**

The hostess was served personally in State X. Under the traditional approach of **Pennoyer v. Neff,** State X may exercise jurisdiction over nonresidents who are served with process within the geographical confines of the state. But since the Supreme Court's decision in **Shaffer v. Heitner,** which extended the minimum contacts standard of **International Shoe Co. v. Washington** to quasi in rem cases, it has been questioned whether due process permits the assertion of jurisdiction based on personal service alone. In **Burnham v. Superior Court,** however, the Court upheld jurisdiction in a divorce proceeding over a nonresident defendant whose only relevant contact with the forum was his intentional presence in the state at the time of service. Like the defendant in *Burnham,* the hostess was intentionally present in State X when she was served there. It appears, therefore, that under *Burnham,* State X has jurisdiction over the hostess based on personal service alone.

Even if the minimum contacts standard of *International Shoe* is applied, the hostess's relationship with State X appears to satisfy that standard. In **Bernhard v. Harrah's Club,** jurisdiction was unquestioned over a Nevada tavern that had solicited the patronage of California residents through extensive advertising in California. Here, although the hostess's solicitation of her guests was for noncommercial purposes, she did send invitations to residents of State X. She must have foreseen that State X residents might drive from State X to State Y to attend her party and return afterwards to State X. Like the tavern in *Harrah's Club,* the hostess can be said to have placed herself within the ambit of State X's regulatory interest as far as serving alcoholic beverages is concerned. Moreover, since the hostess lived so close to the state line, she undoubtedly had many social and business affairs that were connected with State X. Her relationships with State X residents is shown by their appearance on her guest list. In **Cornelison v. Chaney,** jurisdiction was upheld in California over a nonresident defendant who injured a California resident in Nevada while en route to California on one of his periodic trucking runs to deliver merchandise within the state. Since the accident bore a "substantial nexus" to defendant's California activity, jurisdiction was held proper. Here, too, the injury to Peter Poe in State Y had a "substantial nexus" to the hostess's State X activities, and jurisdiction would be proper even if a minimum contacts rationale were applied under *Shaffer*.

2. **Would the Application of State X Law Violate Due Process?** Under **Home Insurance Co. v. Dick,** a forum state cannot apply its own law unless it has a reasonable connection with the parties or the litigation. Here, the only contact that State X has with the case is that Peter Poe was a resident of State X. The injury occurred in State Y, the acts relied on as causing the injury took place there, and the defendant hostess is a resident of State Y. In *Dick,* the plaintiff was a citizen of the forum state, but the court held this contact insufficient since the defendant was at all material times present and acting in Mexico.

But the relationships between the hostess and State X that were relied on to establish jurisdiction can also be taken into account on the choice-of-law question. This is not a case like *Dick,* where the defendant had no connection with the forum. Here, the hostess had invited guests from State X to her party, and she had social and presumably economic contacts with State X. It is fortuitous that the guest who injured Peter Poe was a State Y, rather than a State X, resident and that the injury took place in State Y instead of State X. The defendant's acts were such that residents of State X were placed at risk from the drunken drivers who would be returning to State X from the party. Under these circumstances, the regulatory and compensatory interests of State X seem sufficient to permit State X to apply its own law as a matter of constitutional law.

3. **Assuming that State X Can Apply Its Own Law, Should It Do So?** State X may choose not to apply its own law, even though constitutionally it is permitted to do so. Here, the facts present a true conflict of laws: State X wishes to apply its own law to deter social hosts from endangering its residents, and it wishes to compensate Peter Poe for his injuries since he is a State X resident. State Y wishes to protect its resident defendant against liability for conduct it does not view as tortious—the serving of alcoholic beverages to social guests. Since both the conduct and injury occurred in State Y, that state has a legitimate reason for wishing to have its law applied to protect its resident.

The solution of this true conflict would turn on which choice-of-law approach was being used. The "vested rights" approach of the First Restatement would apply the law of State Y because that is where the wrongful act occurred. The hostess would escape liability. Under the "most significant relationship" approach of the Second Restatement, it seems likely that State Y's law would also apply. Since State Y is both the place of conduct and of injury, it is presumptively the place of most significant relationship. When the residence of the defendant is added to State Y's contacts, and the only contact with State X is that it is the plaintiff's domicile, State Y emerges as the place whose law should be applied. Under the "governmental interest" analysis, however, State X should apply its own law unless a more moderate and restrained interpretation of its policy or interests or of that of State

Y might lead it to a different conclusion. Here, State X might limit its interests only to injuries to its residents occurring in State X, leaving those injured elsewhere to the law of the place of injury. But since State X's injured residents must be cared for by State X's taxpayers if they cannot care for themselves, this solution does not appear reasonable. Thus, under the "governmental interest" analysis, State X should resolve this true conflict by applying its own law.

ANSWER TO QUESTION V

1. **Does the Nevada Statute Confer Local Jurisdiction over the Case?** Nevada's statute applies only if the foreign corporation is or had been "doing business" within the state. It seems clear that the corporation's present activities in the state are not sufficient to satisfy the traditional notions of doing business. Dandeter does not sell its shampoo in Nevada; it presumably does not even directly solicit orders for the shampoo through sales representatives. Its advertising is an indirect solicitation for sales, but under traditional tests, that probably would have been insufficient. In this case, Dandeter comes within the second part of the statute: It had done business in Nevada in the past. But since this cause of action did not directly grow out of its prior business in Nevada, application of the statute to this case might cause constitutional problems (discussed below). Some states, however, have reinterpreted their old "doing business" statutes following the *International Shoe* decision to include the new minimum contacts test. California, for example, has taken the position that its "doing business" statute is equivalent to the Due Process Clause and allows local jurisdiction based on minimum contacts between the state and the defendant so that maintenance of the suit does not offend traditional notions of fair play and substantial justice. [*See* **Jahn v. Superior Court,** 49 Cal. 2d 855 (1958)] If Nevada so interprets its doing business statute, the local courts will be competent to take jurisdiction if the Due Process Clause is satisfied.

2. **Can Nevada Constitutionally Assert Jurisdiction over Dandeter?** Several theories of personal jurisdiction over foreign corporations have been used by the courts. The first theory, that of *actual consent* by the corporation to be sued, is not applicable here because the corporation did not appoint an agent to receive service of process. Presumably, then, Pauline must rely upon the *implied consent* theory, the *presence* theory, or the *minimum contacts* theory.

    The *presence* theory would not sustain jurisdiction on these facts because the corporation presumably has not done business in Nevada for the last two years. It was therefore not present at the time suit was commenced and not amenable to suit.

    The *implied consent* theory did permit suit to be brought against a foreign corporation after it had ceased to do business in the state, but this result applied only if the cause of action had arisen out of business done by the corporation within the state. If, assuming that this cause of action arose out of the corporation's business in Oregon where Pauline bought the shampoo and where the injury apparently occurred, then the implied consent theory would not sustain jurisdiction either.

The *minimum contacts* theory requires that there be sufficient contacts between defendant and Nevada so that it will be fair and reasonable to expect it to defend there. In this case, the contacts between defendant and Nevada are that defendant advertises its shampoo nationally and this advertising is read and seen on television in Nevada. Plaintiff is a resident of Nevada, and Nevada's statute evidences a policy to provide a forum for its residents against foreign corporations who have carried on activities within Nevada. It is, however, arguable whether the cause of action can be said to have arisen from the defendant's contacts with Nevada. Pauline may have bought the shampoo in Oregon as a direct result of the defendant's advertising in Nevada. If so, there is a relationship between the defendant's product and Nevada consumers, even though this particular bottle of shampoo was not actually sold to Pauline in Nevada. The minimum contacts approach, however, requires more than a simple connection between the defendant and the state seeking to acquire jurisdiction over it. There must be a relationship based on the minimum contacts of such a quality that our traditional notions of fair play and substantial justice are not offended by requiring the defendant to appear and defend. It is debatable whether this test is satisfied here. It is clear that the defendant had at one time purposefully availed itself of the privilege of selling shampoo within Nevada, thus invoking the benefits and protections of its laws. It seems possible to argue that Dandeter's continued advertising campaign in Nevada is an indication of its purposeful intent to continue its solicitation of Nevada customers. Although the case is a close one on the facts, it does not seem unfair to require defendant to come to Nevada and defend in this lawsuit if it can be established that plaintiff's purchase of the shampoo was motivated by the defendant's Nevada advertising. Thus, the minimum contacts approach would arguably sustain jurisdiction here.

3. **Has Adequate Notice Been Given to Dandeter?** The question does not state whether Nevada's statute requires the secretary of state to notify the defendant that service has been made on the secretary and that a suit is pending against it. If the statute does not expressly require that notice be sent, it may violate the requirements of due process just as the nonresident motorist statute that failed to require that notice be sent by the secretary of state to the nonresident defendant was held to do in **Wuchter v. Pizzutti**. But if there is a requirement of notice and if Dandeter was notified, then the use of the secretary of state in the absence of an appointed agent is permissible under the cases interpreting the old "doing business" statutes.

4. **Can Pauline Attach Raw Materials in Transit Through Nevada as the Basis for Quasi In Rem Jurisdiction?** This question raises the issue of an attempt to secure personal jurisdiction by means of attaching property in the state that is unrelated

to the cause of action or to underlying ownership claims between the parties. As such, the attempt would be forbidden by **Shaffer v. Heitner**. Unless Pauline could obtain personal jurisdiction over Dandeter in Nevada via an appropriate long arm statute (*see* discussion above), she cannot do so by the use of attachment.

Even prior to *Shaffer,* however, quasi in rem jurisdiction would not have been proper in this situation. Dandeter's principal place of business is in Colorado, and presumably the raw materials are going through Nevada on their way to Dandeter in Colorado. Thus, they are in transit and in interstate commerce while within the borders of Nevada. The national interest in protecting interstate commerce precludes Nevada from exercising quasi in rem jurisdiction over these raw materials even though they are property within Nevada belonging to Dandeter under the bill of lading. No urgent or pressing need exists to permit Nevada's interest in seizure of the property to overcome the national interest in interstate commerce. Pauline's attempt to satisfy her personal claim from this property belonging to Dandeter within the state through quasi in rem jurisdiction thus will not be successful.

ANSWER TO QUESTION VI

1. **The Traditional View:** This question presents two alternative solutions, depending on how the issue is characterized. If the problem is one of parol evidence being offered to show a variation from a prior written contract, the traditional approach applied the law of the place where the written contract was made—here, State F. Since F does not permit parol evidence to prove the subsequent agreement, F correctly gave judgment for P. If, on the other hand, the oral agreement is viewed as a discharge of the written contract by subsequent agreement, the traditional view applied the law of the place where the second agreement was made—here, State X. Since X's law discharged D, F should have applied that law and P should have lost. Since F will make the characterization according to its own law, and since its rule plainly expresses a policy of disallowing an oral contract to supersede a written contract, F was following its own policy when it characterized the case as one of integration rather than discharge. That view should be sustained on appeal.

2. **The Second Restatement View:** The Second Restatement looks first to the law chosen by the parties. But they have not chosen a law here, so it must next look to the law having the most significant relationship with the parties and the transaction. Here there are two contracts: the written contract and the oral one. The factors to be applied in deciding which state has the most significant relationship include the place of contracting, negotiation, performance, location of subject matter, and domicile of the parties. On the written contract, F is the place of contracting, negotiation, and D's domicile. X is P's domicile. There is no tangible subject matter; thus, that factor is not helpful. It is not clear where the place of performance is located: It is not stated where the money is to be paid, and P's refraining from suit could occur either in X (where D is probably subject to jurisdiction because he committed a

tortious act there or because he was domiciled there at the time the cause of action arose) or in F. But assuming that F is the place of performance, then F's law would apply on the written contract.

As to the oral contract, X is plainly the place of most significant relationship, for all factors except D's domicile are X factors. The Second Restatement contains the same alternatives presented by the First Restatement: Is this case to be viewed as dealing with a discharge or with the parol evidence rule? If the parol evidence characterization is emphasized, F should apply its own law; but if the discharge characterization is followed, F should apply X's law. The Second Restatement gives no clear guide as to which characterization should be used and would probably uphold F's decision to apply its own law.

3. **The "Governmental Interest" View:** In this case, F and X have conflicting policies. F prefers to safeguard the written contract, prohibiting the parties from oral agreements to vary its terms. X allows the oral contract to be effective, preferring to abide by the actual intent of the parties. On these facts, application of F's law will benefit X's resident—P, while application of X's law will benefit F's resident—D. Does F have an interest in applying its law to all written contracts made in F? Probably not. If P and D had both been residents of X, F would have only a slight interest in applying its own law to regulate their contractual relations. Here P had the power, under X law, to release D from his obligations pursuant to the written contract. P exercised that power in X. D, acting in good faith, performed his part of the oral contract in X. X law is the only law that has an interest in controlling the release, since F need not protect P more than she is protected in X. F should apply X's law and hold that P take nothing. The only argument going the other way is one that would stress that the policy of F's law is to prevent its courts from having to assess the parol evidence. But that seems not to be a problem here, since P apparently does not deny that the X contract was made. The case should be reversed on appeal.

ANSWER TO QUESTION VII

(1) *Perry v. Sylvia*

Perry seeks from Sylvia the performance of an act—namely, the execution of a deed conveying title to Blackacre to Perry. Since Sylvia was personally served in State A while present in A, she is within A's in personam jurisdiction. A may thus order her to convey the land to Perry. But since Sylvia has not appeared, can A's decree itself operate as a conveyance pursuant to the A statute? According to the case of **Fall v. Eastin**, A's decree cannot operate as a conveyance. A has no in rem jurisdiction over land situated in State B. Thus, A cannot by its decree directly affect title to land in B any more than the commissioner appointed by Washington in *Fall* could execute a deed to land in Nebraska. A has personal jurisdiction over Sylvia, however, and it should order her to convey the land to Perry. Perry can then seek contempt enforcement of the order in A by having Sylvia imprisoned until she executes the deed, or he can seek enforcement of his State A order in the courts of State B.

(2) *Perry v. Susan*

Perry is seeking a money judgment from Susan—he wants her to pay the agreed-upon purchase price for Whiteacre to him. Despite the fact that Whiteacre is located in the forum state, State A, this is not a quasi in rem action. To require Susan to pay money to Perry, State A must have personal jurisdiction over her. To decide that question, one must know whether the State A statute confers local jurisdiction (competence) on the State A courts in actions of this type, and if so, whether the statute is constitutional as applied.

(a) **Does the State A statute apply?** The State A statute confers local jurisdiction on its courts in actions affecting title to real property in the state, including equity suits for specific performance. Even though Perry's action is for money damages, if he has asked in the alternative to have the interest of Susan as purchaser foreclosed, the suit may be one to remove a cloud from Perry's title, and thus may be within the statute. But if Perry is asking only for money, then the suit is not one affecting title to Whiteacre and the statute does not apply. Since the statute is not applicable, it cannot confer personal jurisdiction over Susan on the State A courts. Also, service on Susan outside its borders does not give A jurisdiction. So the result is that A lacks personal jurisdiction over Susan.

(b) **Is the State A statute constitutional as applied?** Since the State A statute is not applicable, this issue is not raised in the suit between Perry and Susan, but it is raised in the suit between Perry and Sam and will be discussed below.

(3) *Perry v. Sam*

In this case, Perry is the buyer who seeks title to Greenacre. Since he seeks to compel Sam to execute a conveyance, personal jurisdiction is necessary over Sam. If the suit could properly have been framed as one to quiet title, personal jurisdiction over Sam would not have been necessary. The court could have acted in its quasi in rem jurisdiction. Is that jurisdiction present?

(a) **Does the State A statute apply?** Yes, it does. The statute permits constructive service on a nonresident in actions affecting title to real property within the state. This action, which will have the effect of transferring Greenacre from Sam to Perry if Perry wins, affects title to Greenacre, which is located within State A. Service by publication plus notice by registered mail is sufficient to meet due process requirements that the defendant be given a reasonable opportunity to appear and defend. The State A statute is a type of long arm statute resting on the power of the state to regulate title to property within its borders.

(b) **Is the State A statute constitutional as applied?** Yes. Sam, as the nonresident owner of property in State A, has minimum contacts with the state as to causes of action arising from his ownership of the property. His contract to sell Greenacre to Perry has created this lawsuit. There are minimum contacts making it reasonable for Sam to appear and defend in A within the meaning of *International Shoe*. Furthermore, since A has personal jurisdiction over Sam, and since Greenacre is situated within A, A's decree can act as a conveyance even if Sam refuses to convey. A's jurisdiction is proper and its decree has conveyed good title to Perry.

ANSWER TO QUESTION VIII

1. **Charity's Motion to Dismiss**

   a. **Charitable immunity:** The traditional view applies the law of C, the place of wrong. This would mean that Charity would be allowed to invoke the immunity doctrine of C and the suit should be dismissed. The Second Restatement follows this view, unless the plaintiff's domicile is in the same state as the charity's principal place of business. Here A is both Plaintiff's residence and the state of incorporation of Charity. If assuming Charity's principal place of business is also in A, then A is the state of most significant relationship and its law should apply. On a "governmental interest" analysis, this is a false conflict case. C has no interest in applying its law protecting charities to a suit between an A charity and an A resident. Thus, only A has an interest in having its law applied and the motion should be denied.

   b. **The release:** Since the release was given prior to the injury and was made in C, the traditional view would point to C as the place where the contract was made. But since the contract would be void as against A's public policy, A is not required to apply C law. A may deny the motion, even under the traditional view. The Second Restatement would agree, since the parties are apparently attempting to avoid A's law by executing the release in C and this may not be done if A is the state of most significant relationship. Here, A should be viewed as the state of most significant relationship both on the issue of charitable immunity as indicated above and on the issue of release, which is merely an attempt to avoid A's law of charitable liability. The "governmental interest" analysis would again treat this as a false conflict case: Only A has an interest in whether its resident plaintiff can make a contract releasing its local charity from liability, and A forbids such releases. The execution of the contract in C does not give C an interest in regulating the relationship between a foreign charity and its beneficiaries.

2. **Trucker's Motion to Dismiss:** In moving to dismiss, Trucker seeks to rely on the view that the place of wrong governs the issue of vicarious liability. Since he would not

be liable for Charity's negligence under the law of C, where Plaintiff was injured, he would not be liable in A under the traditional approach. Even if vicarious liability is characterized as raising a contract issue, the contract was made in C and the reference is again to C law as the place of making. Trucker is entitled to a dismissal under the traditional view.

The Second Restatement applies the law of the state of most significant relationship to determine vicarious liability. The comments indicate that the forum should consider whether the relationship between the parties is such as to make imposition of vicarious liability reasonable and whether there is an adequate relationship between the parties and the law to be applied. These tests could arguably go either way on these facts. If the factors of place of wrong and place of contract are emphasized, C law is applicable; but if the common domicile of Trucker and Charity is emphasized and the fact that the truck is primarily kept and used in A is taken into account, A law should be applied. The better view is to apply A law. The place of wrong is fortuitous and the place of contract seems arranged for the sole purpose of evading A law. Thus A is the place of most significant relationship.

The "governmental interest" analysis would again apply A law as that of the only state having an interest in the application of its policy. The vicarious liability imposed by the A statute was intended to govern the relationship between A bailors (like Trucker) and A bailees (like Charity). C has no contrary interest. Trucker's motion should be denied.

ANSWER TO QUESTION IX

The analysis of these cases will depend on which approach to choice of law State X follows. The outcome may vary in the two cases under some approaches. In this answer, three approaches will be considered: the traditional approach, the Second Restatement approach, and the "governmental interest" approach.

1. *Xavier's Parents v. Market*

    a. **The traditional approach:** Under the traditional approach, State X would apply the substantive law of the place of wrong (here, State Y) and its own procedural law as the forum. Since the injury and death occurred in State Y, which provides no civil remedy against the market, Xavier's parents could not recover.

    b. **Second Restatement approach:** The Second Restatement looks to the law of the state of most significant relationship, which is identified in light of the particular issue raised and by taking account of the general factors as well as the specific contacts of various applicable sections. Three issues are potentially raised in this case: the liability of the market; the conduct of Xavier's parents;

and the application of contributory versus comparative negligence. Each will be considered in turn.

(1) **Liability of the market:** Under the Second Restatement, the law of the place where the injury occurred is applied in wrongful death cases unless some other state has a more significant relationship to the parties and the occurrence with respect to the particular issue raised. Here, State Y has no relation to the parties or the transaction except for being the place of injury. The "conduct causing the injury" is arguably the sale of intoxicating liquor, which took place in State X. Other factors used to identify the place of most significant relationship torts include the domicile and place of business of the parties, and here, both are in State X. So State X could conclude that it has a more significant relationship to the case than does State Y, and apply its own law to establish liability by the market.

(2) **Conduct of Xavier's parents:** Since Xavier's parents did not act outside State X, and since State X does not recognize parental failure to supervise as a defense in tort, no such defense would be available.

(3) **Contributory vs. comparative negligence:** This issue is not relevant here since Xavier's parents were not negligent.

Thus, under the Second Restatement approach, Xavier's parents should recover against the market.

c. **The "governmental interest" approach:** State X as the forum would first analyze its own policy and interests. Here the dramshop act was probably designed both to deter merchants from selling beer to minors and to provide recovery to persons injured as a result of that sale. Since the market does business in State X, the deterrence policy would be accomplished if State X law were applied. And since Xavier's parents are residents of State X, the compensation policy would also be advanced by application of State X law. Therefore, State X has two interests in applying its law. State Y's policy of no civil liability for merchants is in conflict with that of State X. Does State Y also have a conflicting interest in applying its contrary law? No, because Y has no interest in protecting a State X market against liability and no reason to wish to deny recovery to parents who are not residents of State Y. This is a false conflict in governmental interest terms, and State X should apply its own law.

2. *Yolanda's Parents v. Market*

a. **The traditional approach:** Again, State Y's law would be applied to prevent recovery.

b. **Second Restatement approach:** Again, the three issues should be examined separately.

(1) **Liability of the market:** Here, it is not clear whether the law of the place of injury would control. The place of injury and the residence of Yolanda's parents are both in State Y. The market's place of business and the wrongful conduct occurred in State X. Since these factors seem evenly balanced, it does not appear that State X has a *more* significant relationship to the parties and the occurrence than does State Y, the place of injury. If not, then the preference for the place of injury would prevail, and Yolanda's parents would lose.

(2) **Conduct of Yolanda's parents:** Assuming that the law of the place of injury did not control, and that State X was found to have a more significant relationship to the issue of liability than State Y, then one must consider the effect to be given the conduct of Yolanda's parents. Their failure to supervise their daughter, if it occurred at all, took place in State Y, and would be considered to be negligent there. This defense would be available to the market in State X. The question then becomes what weight should be given to the plaintiffs' negligence in State X.

(3) **Comparative vs. contributory negligence:** The state of most significant relationship determines whether contributory negligence bars recovery in whole or in part. If State X had already found itself to be the state of most significant relationship for purposes of liability, it would probably do so again here. In that case, comparative negligence would be used to reduce the plaintiffs' recovery, but not to bar it.

c. **The "governmental interest" approach:** Here, only one of State X's policies—that of deterring the market's conduct—is applicable. But this policy, plus the market's presence in State X, is sufficient to give X an interest in applying its law. Since Yolanda's parents lived and acted in State Y, that state may also have an interest. The question is whether State Y's policy is intended to prevent parents from recovering when their injury is partly due to their own negligence in failing to supervise their children's conduct (a deterrence policy), or whether it was designed to protect defendants against liability to negligent parents. If the latter is the policy, then Y is not interested since the market does no business in Y. If the former is the policy, then Y is interested. Thus, the case could either be a false conflict (only X's interest in deterring the market is at stake), or it could be an ostensible true conflict (X's interest in allowing recovery to deter the market conflicting with Y's interest in preventing recovery to deter parental negligence). The "governmental interest" analysis approach would attempt to reexamine this ostensible true conflict in more moderate and restrained terms in order to avoid reaching the stage of true conflict. This step might lead State X to apply its dramshop act, Y's parental liability rule, and its own comparative negligence law. This would permit the plaintiffs' recovery to be reduced according to the degree of their negligence, but not eliminated entirely. This result would give appropriate weight to the conflicting interests of both states while avoiding a true conflict.

3.   **Constitutional Problems:** Under the "governmental interest" analysis, it is possible that Xavier's parents will receive their full damages from the market but that Yolanda's parents will find their recovery limited by their own negligence. Is this difference in outcome among plaintiffs in the same case a denial of equal protection to Yolanda's parents? Although such a suggestion has been made by commentators, no case has so held. Arguably, the differential treatment based on an analysis of the differing policies and interests of the two states would be sufficient to meet the rational basis standard of equal protection review.

Table of Cases

Hope v. Brewer - §541

Huck, *In re* - §32

Hughes v. Fetter - §§232, 695

Huntington v. Attrill - §§631, 632, 819, 820

Huron Holding Corp. v. Lincoln Mine Operating Co. - §745

Hurtado v. Superior Court - §404

Hutchison v. Ross - §538

I

In re—see name of party

Indiana Transportation Co., *Ex parte* - §96

Industrial Accident Commission v. McCartin - §§583, 780, 781

Insurance Corp. of Ireland v. Compagnie Des Bauxites - §124

Intercontinental Hotel Corp. v. Golden - §§477, 481, 627

Interdyne Co. v. SYS Computer Corp. - §137

International Shoe Co. v. Washington - §§49, 75, 76, 116, 117, 118, 122, 135, 173, 194, 196

J

Jacobs, Marcus & Co. v. Credit Lyonnaise - §461

Jesselson v. Moody - §420

John Hancock Mutual Life Insurance Co. v. Yates - §641

Johnson v. Johnson - §374

Johnson v. Liberty Mutual Insurance Co. - §441

Johnson v. Muelberger - §§863, 864, 865

Jones v. Hughes - §792

Jones' Estate, *In re* - §§9, 23

K

KLM v. Superior Court - §123

Kaiser Steel Corp. v. W.S. Ranch Co. - §722

Kasel v. Remington Arms Co. - §427

Keck v. Keck - §845

Keeton v. Hustler Magazine, Inc. - §§131, 413

Kell v. Henderson - §437

Kempson v. Kempson - §791

Kenney v. Order of Moose - §§695, 826

Kilberg v. Northeast Airlines, Inc. - §§373, 388, 401, 627, 640, 660, 677

Klaxon Co. v. Stentor Electric Manufacturing Co. - §§294, 328, 723

Knights of Honor v. Nairn - §568

Kohr v. Allegheny Airlines, Inc. - §727

Krause v. Krause - §861

Kremer v. Chemical Construction Corp. - §732

Kryger v. Wilson - §525

Kubon v. Kubon - §824

Kulko v. Superior Court - §138

L

Labree v. Major- §334

Lamb v. Schmitt - §81

Landry v. Carlson Mooring Service - §781

Lanham v. Lanham - §§600, 630

Lauterbach v. Lauterbach - §848

Lehman Brothers v. Schein - §721

Leighton v. Roper - §108

Leroux v. Brown - §660

Levie, Estate of - §589

Levin v. Gladstein - §813

Levy v. Daniels' U-Drive Auto Renting Co. - §§306, 309, 390, 420

Levy v. Steiger - §646

Lewis v. Adams - §566

Lewis Manufacturing Co. v. Superior Court - §118

Lilienthal v. Kaufman - §§327, 473

Lindgren's Estate - §865

Linn v. Employers Reinsurance Corp. - §457

Livingston v. Jefferson - §68

Long v. Pan American World Airways, Inc. - §403

Loucks v. Standard Oil Co. - §626

Loughran v. Loughran - §602

Lundig v. New York Tax Appeals Tribunal - §700

Lund's Estate, *In re* - §615

M

McCornick & Co. v. Tolmie Brothers - §489

McElmoyle v. Cohen - §823

McGee v. International Life Insurance Co. - §§125, 128, 130, 139, 153, 245

Magnolia Petroleum Co. v. Hunt - §§779, 781

Mahalsky v. Salem Tool Co. - §665

Marie v. Garrison - §485

Massachusetts v. Missouri - §39

Matson v. Matson - §786

Mattox v. News Syndicate Co. - §415

May v. Anderson - §901

Mayer v. Roche - §474

May's Estate, *In re* - §595

Mertz v. Mertz - §§392, 627

Metal-Matic Inc. v. Eighth Judicial District Court - §158

Michigan Trust Co. v. Ferry - §218

Miles v. Illinois Central Railroad - §796

Miller v. Miller - §398

Miller's Estate, *In re* - §603

Milliken v. Meyer - §§85, 825

Milliken v. Pratt - §§321, 375, 455, 469

Milwaukee County v. M.E. White Co. - §§636, 820

Minichiello v. Rosenberg - §§191, 195

Missouri *ex rel.* Southern Railway v. Mayfield - §228

Morgan Guaranty Trust Co., *In re* - §825

Morson v. Second National Bank of Boston - §546

Mullane v. Central Hanover Bank & Trust Co. - §§206, 210

Murphy v. Erwin-Wasey Inc. - §**158**
Mutual Life Insurance Co. v. Liebing - §**681**
Mylius v. Cargill - §**753**

N

Nash v. Benari - §**561**
Nashua River Paper Co. v. Hammermill Paper Co. - §**222**
National Equipment Rental Ltd. v. Szukhent - §§**98, 215**
Nelson v. Miller - §**155**
Neumeier v. Kuehner - §§**396, 438**
Nevada v. Hall - §**119**
New York ex rel. Halvey v. Halvey - §**753**
New York Life Insurance Co. v. Dodge - §**681**
New York Times, Inc. v. Sullivan - §**161**
Norwood v. Kirkpatrick - §**233**

O

Offshore Rental Co. v. Continental Oil Co. - §**328**
Oklahoma Tax Commission v. Rodgers - §**637**
O'Neill, Estate of - §**25**
Order of United Commercial Travelers v. Wolfe - §**691**
Ormsby v. Chase - §**406**
Overmyer Co. v. Frick Co. - §**216**
Owens v. Superior Court - §§**88, 90**

PQ

Pacific Employers Insurance Co. v. Industrial Accident
    Commission - §§**582, 694**
Pack v. Beech Aircraft Corp. - §**401**
Paine v. Schenectady Insurance Co. - §**742**
Palmisano v. News Syndicate Co. - §**414**
Paris Air Crash, In re - §**728**
Parke-Bernet Galleries, Inc. v. Franklyn - §§**137, 153**
Parker v. Hoefer - §**816**
Peare v. Griggs - §**565**
Pendar v. H & B American Machine Co. - §**385**
Pennoyer v. Neff - §§**48, 49, 70, 776**
Perkins v. Benguet Consolidated Mining Co. - §§**123,
    811**
Petersen v. Petersen - §**749**
Pettis v. Pettis - §**896**
Phillips v. General Motors Corp. - §**427**
Phillips' Estate, In re - §**13**
Phillips Petroleum Co. v. Shutts - §**683**
Pickard v. Pickard - §**599**
Piper Aircraft Co. v. Reyno - §**231**
Platner v. Vincent - §**524**
Platt v. Woodruff - §**789**
Polk County v. Lincoln National Life Insurance Co. -
    §**720**
Polson v. Stewart - §**523**
Pritchard v. Norton - §**475**

R

Ragan v. Merchants Transfer Co. - §**715**
Redwood Investment Co. v. Exley - §**787**
Reed & Barton Corp. v. Maas - §**425**
Reich v. Purcell - §§**330, 333, 397, 398, 404, 678**
Richards v. United States - §§**265, 293, 294**
Riley v. New York Trust Co. - §**774**
Ringling Brothers-Barnum & Bailey, Inc. v. Olvera - §**449**
Rittersbusch v. Sexsmith - §**494**
Roberts v. Home Insurance Indemnity Co. - §**679**
Roche v. McDonald - §**817**
Rochester Capital Leasing Corp. v. K & L Litho Corp. -
    §**479**
Rodney v. Stamen - §**650**
Roseberry v. Scott - §**632**
Rosenstiel v. Rosenstiel - §§**849, 851**
Rosenthal v. Warren - §§**433, 677**
Ross v. Bryant - §**591**
Roth v. Roth - §**890**
Rubin v. Irving Trust Co. - §**465**
Rush v. Savchuk - §§**193, 194, 195**

S

Sampson v. Channell - §§**714, 725**
Scanapico v. Richmond, Fredricksburg & Potomac
    Railroad - §**238**
Scheer v. Rockne Motors Corp. - §**419**
Schmidt v. Driscoll Hotel, Inc. - §§**372, 422**
Schneider's Estate, In re - §**263**
Schroeder v. City of New York - §**211**
Schwartz v. Consolidated Freightways Corp. - §**441**
Scudder v. Union National Bank - §**458**
Security Savings & Trust Co. v. Evans - §**754**
Seeman v. Philadelphia Warehouse Co. - §**478**
Seider v. Roth - §§**190, 194, 195, 196**
Severn v. Adidas - §**83**
Shaffer v. Heitner- §§**49, 50, 64, 75, 76, 77, 85, 135,
    162, 173, 174, 175, 176, 178, 183, 187, 194,
    844**
Shapiro v. Thompson - §**695**
Sherrer v. Sherrer - §§**862, 870**
Sibbach v. Wilson - §**711**
Siegmann v. Meyer - §**419**
Simons v. Miami Beach First National Bank - §**881**
Sistare v. Sistare - §**747**
Slater v. Mexican National Railroad - §**239**
Smith v. Bear - §**658**
Smith, Valentino & Smith, Inc. v. Superior Court - §**224**
Sniadach v. Family Finance Corp. - §**178**
Sosna v. Iowa - §§**5, 854**
Sovereign Camp v. Bolin - §**776**
Stanley v. Illinois - §**904**
State v. Graves - §**591**
State ex rel. Larson v. Larson - §**899**

Stephan v. Sears, Roebuck & Co. - §427
Stewart v. Stewart - §835
Straw v. Lee - §430
Sun Oil Co. v. Wortman - §§664, 693
Supreme Court of New Hampshire v. Piper - §699
Sutton v. Leib - §872
Swift v. Tyson - §§708, 710

T

Tallmadge, *In re* - §259
Tarnoff v. Jones - §812
Tennessee Coal, Iron & Railroad v. George - §241
Textile Banking Co. v. Colonial Chemical Co. - §573
Thomas v. Washington Gas Light Co. - §§583, 781
Thompson v. Thompson (1988) - §758
Thompson v. Thompson (1963) - §432
Thompson v. Thompson (1913) - §897
Thompson v. Whitman - §§204, 804
Titus v. Titus - §889
Tooker v. Lopez - §396
Torlonia v. Torlonia - §37
Toth v. Toth - §835
Treinies v. Sunshine Mining Co. - §811

U

Underwriters National Assurance Co. v. North Carolina
    Life & Accident & Health Insurance - §808
Union Trust Co. v. Grosman - §469
United Air Lines, Inc. v. Wiener - §651
United Building Construction Trades Council v. Mayor &
    Council of Camden - §699
United States v. Guaranty Trust Co. - §488
United States v. Montreal Trust Co. - §151
United States v. Yazell - §714
Ury v. Jewelers Acceptance Corp. - §479

V

Vanderbilt v. Vanderbilt - §878
Van Dusen v. Barrack - §§235, 723
Varone v. Varone - §§787, 876
Vrooman v. Beech Aircraft Corp. - §426

WX

WASZ, Inc. v. Lyons - §122
Walker v. City of Hutchinson - §211
Walton v. Arabian American Oil Co. - §273
Warner v. Buffalo Drydock Co. - §761
Washington v. Superior Court - §§105, 114
Watkins v. Conway - §§666, 693, 823
Watson v. Employers Liability Assurance Corp. - §§495,
    685
Waynick v. Chicago's Last Department Store - §422
Wells v. Simonds Abrasive Co. - §693
West v. American Telephone & Telegraph Co. - §719
Western Air Lines, Inc. v. Sobieski - §576
Whealton v. Whealton - §891
Wheat v. Wheat - §847
White v. Howard - §576
White v. Tennant - §8
Wilcox v. Wilcox - §436
Williams v. North Carolina (1945) - §§842, 855, 857,
    868
Williams v. North Carolina (1942) - §§842, 846, 852,
    855, 881
Williamson v. Osenton - §§12, 29
Wilson v. Wilson - §24
Winans v. Winans - §9
Womble v. Commercial Credit Corp. - §207
Wood v. Wood - §867
Woods v. Interstate Realty Co. - §714
Woodward v. Steward - §316
Woodward's Appeal - §620
World-Wide Volkswagen Corp. v. Woodson - §§134, 135
Worthley v. Worthley - §749
Wuchter v. Pizzuti - §§109, 212

Y

York v. Texas - §93
Young v. Masci - §419
Younker v. Reseda Manor - §522

Z

Zogg v. Pennsylvania Mutual Insurance Co. - §§452, 492

Index

survival of causes of action, **§409**

torts, **§§287, 388-390, 409, 420, 431**

vested rights approach, **§§302-312**

workers' compensation, **§578**

CHARITABLE IMMUNITY, §433

CHILDREN

adoption, **§§618-625**

change in status, **§§610-617**

custody, **§§751-758, 898-906**

domicile, **§§30-33**

inheritance, **§§616, 625**

paternity actions, **§§614-615, 907**

support, **§§746-750, 873-878**

CHOICE OF LAW

See also Characterization; Choice-of-law theories; Erie
doctrine; Federal and state law;
Jurisdiction

administration of estates, **§§547-567**

adoption, **§618**

and jurisdiction, **§46**

annulment, **§887**

borrowing statutes, **§§295-296**

child custody, **§898**

conflict of choice-of-law rules. See Renvoi

constitutional limitations, **§§680-700**

Fourteenth Amendment Due Process Clause, **§§681-686**

Full Faith and Credit Clause, **§§687-696**

Privileges and Immunities Clause, **§§697-700**

contracts, **§§445-510**. See also Contracts

corporations, **§§568-577**. See also Corporations

defenses. See Defenses against application of foreign law

depeçage, **§§267, 290-291**

divorce, **§§543, 835-836, 893**. See also Divorce

domestic relations, **§§586-609**. See also Domestic
relations

domicile, **§§6, 37-40**. See also Domicile

Erie doctrine, **§§710, 723-728**

escape devices, **§§307-311**

family law, **§§586-625, 834-907**. See also Domestic
relations; Family law

forum shopping, **§§281, 710**

full faith and credit, **§§690-696**

future interests, **§542**

generally, **§§246-255, 276-282**

international, **§§248-255, 271-275, 298-299**

by agreement, **§§298-299**

proof of foreign law, **§§271-275**

judicial separation, **§§892-893**

marriage, **§§587-609**

no-fault insurance, **§442**

pervasive problems, **§§256-275**

characterization, **§268**. See also Characterization

depeçage, **§267**

proof of foreign law, **§§269-275**

renvoi, **§§257-266**. See also Renvoi

Privileges and Immunities Clause, **§§697-700**

products liability, **§§424-427**

property, **§§511-567**. See also Property

remission, **§258**

renvoi, **§§257-266**. See also Renvoi

status of children, **§§610-617**

statutory directives, **§§292-300**

borrowing statutes, **§§295-296**

Federal Tort Claims Act, **§§293-294**

Uniform Commercial Code, **§§298-300**

will execution, **§297**

substance vs. procedure, **§286**. See also Substance vs.
procedure

torts, **§§384-444**. See also Torts

transmission, **§258**

trusts, **§541**

Uniform Commercial Code, **§§298-300, 535, 538, 540**

wills, **§297**

workers' compensation, **§§578-585, 694**

CHOICE-OF-LAW THEORIES

application in practice, **§§382-383**

better law approach, **§§378-381**

Leflar, Robert, **§378**

"common law," **§383**

comparative impairment, **§§327-329**

functional analysis, **§§339-355**

VonMehren and Trautman approach, **§§340-345**

Weintraub approach, **§§340, 346-353**

governmental interest analysis, **§§319-338**. See also
Governmental interest analysis

Baxter, William F., **§328**

comparative impairment approach, **§328**

Currie, Brainerd, **§§320, 335**

lex fori, **§§356-365**

Ehrenzweig approach, **§356**

true rules, **§§356, 358-360**

most significant relationship, **§§313-318**. See also Most
significant relationship approach

choice-of-law principles, **§315**

Reese, Willis, **§313**

Second Restatement, **§§313, 318**

principles of preference, **§§366-377**

Cavers, David, **§366**

contracts and conveyances, **§§375-376**

torts, **§§370-374**

traditional vested rights, **§§302-312**. See also Vested
rights approach

Beale, Joseph and Justice Holmes, **§302**

escape devices, **§§307-311**

First Restatement, **§302**

modern decline, **§312**

CHOSES IN ACTION

See Intangible property

CITIZENSHIP

See Nationality

qualification, **§573**

unqualified, **§§243-245**

COVENANTS, §524

CURRIE, BRAINERD

See Governmental interest analysis

CUSTODY

See Children, custody

D

DAMAGES

substance and procedure, **§§676-678**

tort, **§443**

DEBTORS

double liability, **§189**

jurisdiction over, **§§181-189**

DEFAMATION

choice of law, **§§409-416**

due process, **§161**

DEFENSE OF MARRIAGE ACT, §§609, 816

DEFENSES AGAINST APPLICATION OF FOREIGN LAW

See also Choice of law; Judgments, foreign

foreign judgments. *See* Judgments, foreign

generally, **§§626-627**

local public policy, **§§626-630, 815, 821**

penal laws, **§§631-634, 818-819, 821**

privilege, **§§653-657**

revenue law, **§§635-637, 820-821**

statutes of limitations, **§§664-675, 817**

substance vs. procedure, **§§308, 638-679**. *See also*
Substance vs. procedure

DEPEÇAGE, §§267, 290-291

DIPLOMACY, §249

DIRECT ACTION AGAINST INSURER, §§495, 679

DIVERSITY, §§294, 706-728

See also Erie doctrine

DIVISIBLE DIVORCE

See Divorce

DIVORCE

See also Domestic relations

child custody, **§§751-758, 898-906**

choice of law, **§§835-836, 857, 893**. *See also*
Domestic relations

collateral attack, **§§855-872**

collusive, **§864**

divisible, **§§873-885**

ex parte, **§§845, 852-872, 881**

judgments, **§§834-885**. *See also* Judgments, foreign

jurisdictional bases

constitutionality, **§§850, 885**

domicile, **§§164-165**

long arm statutes, **§§838-845**

military personnel, **§848**

place of marriage, **§§849-851**

residence, **§§846-848, 850-851**

limited. *See* Judicial separation

migratory, **§836**

"participation," **§§862-864**

privies, **§865**

property rights, **§§873, 879-885**

remarriage following, **§§596-605**

strangers, **§§866-867**

support rights, **§§873-878, 882-885**

Uniform Divorce Recognition Act, **§§858, 870**

Uniform Interstate Family Support Act, **§§750, 883**

DOING BUSINESS

See Minimum contacts

DOMESTIC RELATIONS

adoption, **§§618-625**

annulment, **§§886-891**

child custody, **§§751-758, 898-906**

choice of law, **§§586-625**

divorce, **§§835-885**. *See also* Divorce

judgments, **§§834-907**. *See also* Judgments, foreign

judicial separation, **§§892-897**

long arm statutes, **§§164-165, 884-885**

marriage, **§§587-609**. *See also* Marriage

Parental Kidnapping Prevention Act, **§§758, 900-903**

paternity actions, **§907**

children, status of, **§§610-617**

DOMICILE

and choice of law, **§§4, 37-40**. *See also* Choice of law

by operation of law, **§§6, 27-36**

incompetent, **§§34-36**

minor, **§§30-33**

wife, **§§28-29**

characterization, **§37**

decedent's, **§549**

definition, **§1**

determined by law of forum, **§§37-40**

divorce, jurisdiction, **§§835-845**

due process, **§§39, 40, 85, 89**

jurisdictional basis, **§§3, 85-89**

matrimonial, **§§164-165**. *See also* Divorce; Domestic
relations

military service, **§§24-25, 848**

modern view, **§§20-22**

multiple, **§§17, 22**

of choice, **§§6, 8-27**

acquisition of, **§§9-26**

capacity, **§§13, 27**

continuity of, **§§23-26**

intent, **§§10-18**

involuntary absence, **§§24-26**

military service, **§§24-25**

motive, **§12**

multiple dwelling places, **§§17, 22**

physical presence, **§9**

    residence compared, **§§11, 26**

of origin, **§7**

residence compared, **§§5, 11, 26**

significance, **§§2-4**

types of, **§6**

DRAMSHOP STATUTES, §§422-423

DUE PROCESS

See also Jurisdiction; Minimum contacts; Service of Process

absent defendant, **§§87-88**

California-type long arm statute, **§§145, 169-170**

choice of law, **§§681-686**

defamation, **§161**

domicile, **§§39-40, 89**

foreign judgments, **§§774, 830, 833**

implied consent, **§§107-110**

jurisdiction, **§§43-49**

long arm statutes, **§§169-170**

minimum contacts, **§§49, 79, 111-141**

notice, **§§211-213**

procedural

    class suits, **§776**

    continued jurisdiction, **§219**

    implied consent, **§109**

    nonresident defendants, **§§208-213**

    parental rights, **§904**

    quasi in rem jurisidiction, **§§61, 177-178**

    resident defendants, **§207**

    waiver, **§§98, 101-102, 214, 216**

quasi in rem jurisdiction, **§§61, 177-178**

DURESS, §§78-79

E

EHRENZWEIG, ALFRED

See Lex fori

ENFORCEMENT OF JUDGMENTS

See also Judgments, foreign

defenses. *See* Judgments, foreign

full faith and credit, **§§731, 733**

in personam, **§§52-54**

in rem, **§56**

injunctions, **§53**

jurisdiction, **§47**

money judgments, **§§54, 831-833**

quasi in rem, **§60**

ENJOINING SUIT, §§788-797

See also Judgments, foreign

ENJOINING TESTIMONY, §§798-801

ERIE DOCTRINE, §§710-728

See also Federal and state law

ESCAPE DEVICES, §§307-311

See also Choice-of-law theories, vested rights

EVIDENCE, RULES OF, §§646-659

EX PARTE DIVORCE

See Divorce

EXECUTORY LAND SALE CONTRACTS, §§523-525

EXPRESS DESIGNATION OF APPLICABLE LAW, §§446-452, 480

See also Contracts

F

FALSE CONFLICTS, §§322, 330

See also Governmental interest analysis

FAMILY LAW

See Children; Divorce; Domestic relations; Marriage

FEDERAL AND STATE LAW, §§701-728

See also Substance vs. procedure

abstention, **§722**

applicable state law, **§§719-722**

certification to state court, **§721**

characterization, **§§712-718, 725**

    modern test, **§§716-718**

choice-of-law rules, **§§723-728**

concurrent jurisdiction, **§701**

Erie doctrine, **§§710-728**

"federal law," **§704**

federal right involved, **§§702-705**

federal right not involved, **§§706-728**. *See also Erie* doctrine

Federal Rules of Civil Procedure, **§§715-717**

outcome determinative test, **§§714-715**

state procedural law, **§705**

FEDERAL RULES OF CIVIL PROCEDURE, §§715-717

FEDERAL TORT CLAIMS ACT

choice of law, **§§293-294**

renvoi, **§265**

FINALITY

See also Judgments, foreign

appeal, **§§743-745**

child custody decrees, **§§751-758**

final judgment defined, **§742**

foreign judgments, **§§741-758**

full faith and credit, **§§742-758, 810**

    limited, **§§752-754**

    not applicable, **§§749, 755, 810**

registration of federal judgments, **§§733-734**

spousal and child support decrees, **§§746-750**

FIRST RESTATEMENT

See Vested rights approach

FOREIGN JUDGMENTS

See Judgments, foreign

FOREIGN NATIONS, JUDGMENTS OF, §§735-740, 827-833

See also Judgments, foreign

savings account passbook, §184

stock certificate, §182

INTENT FOR DOMICILE, §§10-18

INTERSPOUSAL IMMUNITY, §§430-432

INTERSTATE COMMERCE
burdens on, §§237-238

unqualified foreign corporations, §244

INVASION OF PRIVACY, §§409-416

JK

JUDGMENTS, FOREIGN
child custody, §§751-758

    Parental Kidnapping Prevention Act, §758

child support, §§746-750

class actions, §776

collateral estoppel, §§763, 768-782

consent, §764

default, §764

defenses, §§802-833. *See also* Defenses

    bootstrap doctrine, §§806-808

    contempt, §824

    Defense of Marriage Act, §816

    error or mistake, §825

    fraud, §§813-814

    international, §§827-833

    lack of due process, §830

    lack of jurisdiction, §§803-809

    law of the forum, §826

    not final or on the merits, §810

    not "last in time," §§811-812

    penal law, §§819, 821, 829

    procedural, §§822-825

    public policy, §§815-816, 829

    retaliation, §§827-828

    statute of limitations, §§817, 823

    tax judgment, §§820, 829

    Uniform Foreign Money-Judgments Recognition Act, §§831-833

direct estoppel, §§763, 768

enforcement, §§729-740

    federal court judgments, §§732-734

    federal implementing statute, §732

    foreign nation judgment, §§735-739

    full faith and credit, §§729-731

    procedure, §§731, 733-734

    state court judgments, §§729-731

enjoining foreign suit, §§788-796

enjoining testimony, §§798-801

federal courts, §§732-734

finality, §§742-758. *See also* Finality

foreign nations, §§735-740

    comity, §§737-739

    due process, §830

    reciprocity, §736

    res judicata, §740

    retaliation, §§827-828

    Uniform Foreign Money-Judgments Recognition Act, §§739, 831-833

forum non conveniens, §797

Full Faith and Credit Clause, §§729-732

judicial separation, §§894-897

local land, §§783-787

merger, §§566, 766, 777

on the merits, §§759-764

privies, §§772-774

res judicata, §§740, 765-771

spousal support, §§746-750

state courts, §§729-731, 734

successors in interest, §775

Uniform Child Custody Jurisdiction and Enforcement Act, §757

Uniform Interstate Family Support Act, §750

workers' compensation, §§778-782

JUDICIAL SEPARATION, §§892-897
See also Domestic relations; Marriage

JUDICIARY ACT OF 1789, §§707-710

JURISDICTION
See also Divorce; Minimum contacts

administration of estates, §§547-567. *See also* Administration of estates

annulment, §§888-891

child custody, §§899-905

choice of law, §46

competent court, §§197-204

constitutional basis, §§43, 48-49

continuance of, §§217-218, 905

debtors, §§185-189

defined, §41

divorce, §§76, 164-165, 837-885

domicile, §§3, 85-89

elements, §§42-45

foreign corporations, §§112-141, 243-245. *See also* Long arm statutes

general, §§120-124

implied consent, §§105-110

in personam

    bases for, §§69-170

      appearance, §§92-97

      domicile, §§85-89

      express consent, §§98-104

      implied consent, §§105-110

      long arm statutes, §§142-170. *See also* Long arm statutes

      minimum contacts, §§111-142. *See also* Minimum contacts

      nationality, §91

      personal service, §§70-84. *See also* Service of process

      residence, §90

substance vs. procedure, §§662-675

tolling statutes, §§672-674

tortious act, §§154-161

    physical presence theory, §§157, 159-160

    place of effect theory, §§158-160

transaction of any business, §§149-153

LONG-DISTANCE PURCHASES, §137

M

MARITIME ATTACHMENT, §175

MARRIAGE

See also Domestic relations

after divorce, §§596-605

annulment, §§886-891

capacity, §591

choice of law, §§587-609

common law, §592

custody of children. *See* Children; Divorce

formal requirements, §590

incestuous, §§593-595

interspousal immunity, §§429-432

place of, §§590, 849-851

polygamous, §§593-595

property rights, §§526-527, 543

remarriage after divorce, §§596-605

same sex, §609

separation, §§892-897

statutes governing recognition, §§606-609

    Defense of Marriage Act, §609

    Uniform Marriage Evasion Act, §607

validity, §§590-609

MINIMUM CONTACTS

See also Jurisdiction; Long arm statutes

contracts, §§166-167

divorce, §§76, 164-165, 844

for jurisdiction, §§46, 49, 76, 164-165

foreign corporations, §§112-141, 243-245

in rem jurisdiction, §§173-179

individuals, §§49, 118

insurance, §§130, 190-196

intangibles, §§180-184, 187-188

liability-producing act, §§125-141, 168

long-distance purchases, §137

modern rule, §§116-119, 173, 187

noncommercial actions, §138

partnerships, §118

presence, §§48, 72-84, 120-124

products liability, §§132-135

quasi in rem, §§173-179

single contact test, §§75-77

sister states, §119

trusts, §§136, 541

MONEY JUDGMENTS, §§54, 739, 831-833

MORTGAGES, §§520-522

MOST SIGNIFICANT RELATIONSHIP APPROACH

burden of proof, §647

capacity to contract, §472

charitable immunity, §433

contracts, §§466-468. *See also* Contracts

contribution, §444

corporations, §568

damages, §678

defenses. *See also* Defenses

    local public policy, §629

    penal law, §634

    privilege, §428

designation of applicable law, §450

guest statutes, §436

interspousal immunity, §432

legality of contract, §483

penal laws, §634

products liability, §427

property, §513. *See also* Property

    immovables, §516

    movables, §§534-535

public policy defenses, §629

Statute of Frauds, §§486, 662-663

statute of limitations, §675

theory of, §§313-318

torts, §§394-396. *See also* Torts

vicarious liability, §423

wrongful death, §403

N

NATIONALITY, §91

NEGOTIABLE INSTRUMENTS, §§181-183, 487-489

NO-FAULT INSURANCE, §442

NONCOMMERCIAL ACTIONS, MINIMUM CONTACTS, §138

NONRESIDENT DEFENDANTS, DUE PROCESS, §§208-213

NONRESIDENT MOTORIST STATUTES, §§106-108

NOTICE

See also Due process; Service of process

adoption, §§623-624

agents, §215

child custody, §904

due process requirements, §§211-213

quasi in rem actions, §61

statutory requirements, §212

waiver, §§214-216

O

OFFICERS' AND DIRECTORS' LIABILITY, §575

ON THE MERITS, §§759-764

See also Judgments, foreign

REMISSION, §258

RENVOI, §§257-266
definition, **§257**
divorce, **§310**
Federal Tort Claims Act, **§265**
partial, **§261**
property, **§515**
rejection of, **§§259-260**
remission, **§258**
situs of land, **§514**
title to land, **§310**
transmission, **§258**
vested rights, **§310**
whole, **§§260, 262-266**

RES IPSA LOQUITUR, §651

RES JUDICATA
See also Judgments, foreign
administration of estates, **§§560-567**
foreign judgments, **§§740, 765-771**

RESIDENCE
as basis for jurisdiction, **§90**
divorce, **§§846-848**
domicile compared, **§§11, 26**

RESTATEMENT (FIRST) APPROACH
See Vested rights approach

RESTATEMENT (SECOND) APPROACH
See Most significant relationship approach

RETALIATION, §§827-828

REVENUE LAW DEFENSE, §§635-637, 820-821

RULES OF CHOICE
See also Choice of law; Choice-of-law theories
formulated, **§359**
nonformulated, **§360**

RULES OF CIVIL PROCEDURE, FEDERAL
See Federal Rules of Civil Procedure

RULES OF EVIDENCE, §§646-658

S

SECOND RESTATEMENT
See Most significant relationship approach

SECURED TRANSACTIONS, §§539-540

SEPARATE MAINTENANCE
See Judicial separation

SERVICE OF PROCESS
agent to receive, **§215**
nonresident, **§§208-213**
notice, **§§211-213**
personal, **§§71-84**
resident, **§206**
types of, **§205**

waiver of, **§§214-216**

SINGLE CONTACT TEST, §75

SITUS OF ASSETS
See Administration of estates; Property

SPECIFIC CONTACTS, §316

SPOUSAL SUPPORT
finality of decree, **§§746-750**
jurisdiction, **§§873-878, 894**

STATE LAW, DETERMINATION OF, §§719-723
See also Federal and state law

"STATUS" OF LAWS, §344
See also Functional analyses

STATUTE OF FRAUDS, §§485-489, 659-663

STATUTE OF LIMITATIONS
choice of law and, **§693**
defense to judgment, **§817**
substance vs. procedure, **§§664-675**

STOCK CERTIFICATES, §§182, 546

SUBSTANCE VS. PROCEDURE
See also Federal and state law
applications, **§§645-679**
characterization, **§§286-287, 693, 711-725**
constitutional limitations, **§641**
damages, **§§676-678**
direct actions against insurer, **§679**
Erie doctrine, **§§710-725**
"federal law," **§704**
"procedure," **§644**
rules of evidence, **§§646-658**
state procedural rules, **§705**
Statute of Frauds, **§§659-663**
statute of limitations, **§§664-675**
  adverse possession, **§674**
  borrowing statutes, **§671**
  tolling statutes, **§§672-674**
"substance," **§643**
vested rights, **§308**

SUCCESSORS IN INTEREST, §775

SURVIVAL OF CAUSES OF ACTION, §§405-408

T

TAVERNKEEPERS' LIABILITY, §§422-423

TESTATE AND INTESTATE SUCCESSION, §518

THIRD-PARTY BENEFICIARIES, §§501-502

TITLE, QUASI IN REM JURISDICTION, §§59-62

TOLLING STATUTES, §§672-674

TORTS
charitable immunity, **§433**
choice of law, **§§384-444**
comparative negligence, **§441**

contribution among tortfeasors, **§444**

damages, **§§443, 676-678**

defamation, **§§161, 409-416**

dramshop statutes, **§§422-423**

Federal Tort Claims Act, **§§265, 293-294**

governmental interest analysis, **§§397-398**

guest statutes, **§§434-440**

immunities, **§§429-433**

invasion of privacy, **§§409-416**

long arm statutes, **§§154-161**

most significant relationship, **§§394-396**. *See also* Most
significant relationship approach

multistate injuries, **§§409-416**

no-fault insurance, **§442**

permissive use cases, **§§419-421**

place of wrong, **§§384-393**

principles of preference, **§§366-374**

privilege, **§428**

products liability, **§§132-135, 424-427**

survival of causes of action, **§§405-408**

tavernkeepers' liability, **§§328, 422-423**

vested rights, **§§384-393**

vicarious liability, **§§417-423**

Weintraub approach, **§§346-355**

workers' compensation, **§578**. *See also* Workers'
compensation

wrongful death, **§§400-404**

TRADITIONAL APPROACH TO CHOICE OF LAW

See Vested rights approach

TRANSACTING BUSINESS, §§150-153

TRANSFER, §§233-235

TRANSIENT PRESENCE, §§72-84

TRANSITORY ACTIONS, §§67-68

TRANSMISSION, §258

TRAUTMAN, DONALD

See Functional analyses

TREATIES, §252

TRESPASS TO LAND, §68

"TRUE RULES," §§358-360. *See also* Lex fori

TRUSTS

minimum contacts, **§136**

movable property, **§541**

testamentary or inter vivos, **§541**

U

UNIFORM ACTS

Child Custody Jurisdiction Act, **§§757, 900**

Child Custody Jurisdiction and Enforcement Act, **§§757-
758, 900**

Commercial Code

choice of law, **§§298-300, 466**

movable property, **§535**

secured transactions, **§§539-540**

Statute of Frauds, **§663**

stock certificates, **§546**

Conflict of Laws Limitations Act, **§675**

Divorce Recognition Act, **§§858, 870**

Foreign Money-Judgments Recognition Act, **§§739, 831-
833**

Interstate Family Support Act, **§§750, 883, 885**

Marriage and Divorce Act, **§847**

Marriage Evasion Act, **§607**

Probate Code, **§297**

Reciprocal Enforcement of Support Act, **§750**

Single Publication Act, **§413**

UNJUST ENRICHMENT, §509

UNKNOWN DEFENDANTS, §209

"UNPROVIDED FOR" CASE, §§334-335

USURY, §§478-480

V

VALIDITY PROBLEMS

See Contracts; Marriage

VENUE, §202

VESTED RIGHTS APPROACH

capacity to contract, **§§469-470**

charitable immunity, **§433**

contracts, **§§454-462**

corporations, **§568**

damages, **§§676-677**

defamation, **§§409-414**

designation of applicable law, **§447**

dramshop statutes, **§422**

guest statutes, **§435**

interspousal immunity, **§§430-431**

penal laws, **§§631-633**

permissive use cases, **§§419-421**

privacy, invasion of, **§§409-414**

privileged testimony, **§§654-656**

products liability, **§§425-426**

property

immovables, **§§514-515**

movables, **§§531-533**

inter vivos transactions, **§533**

testate and intestate transactions, **§532**

public policy, **§§626-628**

renvoi, **§§257-264, 310, 515**

revenue laws, **§§635-636**

Statute of Frauds, **§§485, 660**

statute of limitations, **§§664-674**

survival of causes of action, **§§406-407**

tavernkeepers' liability, **§422**

theory of, **§§302-312**

torts, **§§384-393**. *See also* Torts

vicarious liability, **§§418-422**

wrongful death, **§401**

VICARIOUS LIABILITY, §§417-423

VON MEHREN, ARTHUR
See Functional analyses

WXYZ

WEINTRAUB, RUSSELL
See Functional analysis

WIFE, DOMICILE OF, §§28-29

WILLS, FOREIGN EXECUTION OF, §297

WORKERS' COMPENSATION, §§578-585, 694, 778-782

WRONGFUL DEATH, §§400-404, 554

Notes

lex loci — old law ⇒ vested right syp.

↳ simple rigid

↳ Muster ~~based~~ bordhryan dilustr

Notes